"Cecilia Chan has been at the forefront of research and development at the interface of generative AI and reforming teaching in higher education. Her latest book, co-authored with Tom Colloton, provides a timely array of tools, ideas and analysis informing future applications of generative AI. The message is clear: embrace generative AI and shape the future. Highly recommended as an engaging treatment of the latest generative AI developments."

Professor David Carless, *Professor in Education,*
University of Hong Kong

"*Generative AI in Higher Education: The ChatGPT Effect* stands out as a pivotal text for educators aiming to bridge the gap between traditional teaching methods and the cutting-edge capabilities of AI. It offers a compelling roadmap for the ethical and effective implementation of AI tools in curriculum design and assessment, making it an essential read for those committed to future-proofing higher education. Perhaps more importantly, the text is readable and approachable to students, teachers, staff, and policymakers; all of whom should be working together towards effective and responsible utilization of AI in education."

Dr Sean McMinn, *Director of the Center for Educational Innovation,*
Hong Kong University Science and Technology

"This book provides a much-needed holistic perspective on generative AI in education. It covers all the important components that educators need to succeed with generative AI, from assessment to curriculum, policy to technology, and is decorated throughout with practical examples of generative AI use that readers can try straight away. This is a thoughtful and timely contribution and essential reading as we move forward together in this journey."

Professor Danny Liu, *Professor, Educational Innovation, University of Sydney*

"*Generative AI in Higher Education: The ChatGPT Effect* by Cecilia Ka Yuk Chan and Tom Colloton delves into the impact of Generative AI in higher education. The time for this book is right now. Which one of us teachers in higher education would not be coping with GenAI at the moment? Merging GenAI's technical aspects with its practical uses, the book is a guide for educators, policymakers and students. The authors make the content accessible to various readers, offering examples, case studies and hands-on activities. It highlights both the advantages of GenAI and potential challenges, suggesting practical solutions for its integration in education. With hands-on 'try-it-out' prompts, readers can directly engage with the transformative potential of GenAI. For those seeking to navigate the emerging landscape of AI in education, this book serves as a clear and accessible guide. Dive in and embrace the ChatGPT effect!"

Dr Juuso Nieminen, *expert in assessment,*
feedback and educational technology

"Cecilia and Tom have adopted a holistic approach towards GenAI in higher education. By providing a deeper understanding of the evolution of AI and its use in higher education, and drawing on promising practices and lessons learnt internationally, this book serves as an essential toolkit for higher education leaders, practitioners and scholars."

Professor Lim Cher Ping, *Chair Professor of Learning Technologies and Innovation,*
Editor-in-Chief of The Internet and Higher Education

T0373516

Generative AI in Higher Education

Chan and Colloton's book is one of the first to provide a comprehensive examination of the use and impact of ChatGPT and Generative AI (GenAI) in higher education.

Since November 2022, every conversation in higher education has involved ChatGPT and its impact on all aspects of teaching and learning. The book explores the necessity of AI literacy tailored to professional contexts, assess the strengths and weaknesses of incorporating ChatGPT in curriculum design, and delve into the transformation of assessment methods in the GenAI era. The authors introduce the Six Assessment Redesign Pivotal Strategies (SARPS) and an AI Assessment Integration Framework, encouraging a learner-centric assessment model. The necessity for well-crafted AI educational policies is explored, as well as a blueprint for policy formulation in academic institutions. Technical enthusiasts are catered to with a deep dive into the mechanics behind GenAI, from the history of neural networks to the latest advances and applications of GenAI technologies.

With an eye on the future of AI in education, this book will appeal to educators, students and scholars interested in the wider societal implications and the transformative role of GenAI in pedagogy and research.

Cecilia Ka Yuk Chan is a Professor at the Faculty of Education and the Founding Director of the Teaching and Learning Innovation Centre at the University of Hong Kong (HKU). With a dual-discipline background, she possesses expertise in both engineering and education. Her research areas include assessment, experiential learning, engineering education and AI in education, aiming to develop holistic competencies. Professor Chan serves as the President of the Asian Society for Engineering Education and is an associate editor for both the *Journal of Engineering Education* and *Studies in Educational Evaluation*. Her influential work has secured industry funding and is used internationally such as UNESCO, contributing to the advancement of holistic competencies in education.

Tom Colloton is the founder of Eireann Technology, an Educational Technology (EdTech) research and development company. With over twenty-five years in the technology sector, Tom has held diverse roles, including Director, Enterprise Architect and Senior Software Engineer, spanning domains such as Finance, Healthcare, Telecommunications and Education. Tom designs cutting-edge visualisation technology and Artificial Intelligence systems to enhance the experience for teachers, students and administrators.

Generative AI in Higher Education
The ChatGPT Effect

Cecilia Ka Yuk Chan and Tom Colloton

Routledge
Taylor & Francis Group
LONDON AND NEW YORK

Designed cover image: Getty Images

First published 2024
by Routledge
4 Park Square, Milton Park, Abingdon, Oxon OX14 4RN

and by Routledge
605 Third Avenue, New York, NY 10158

Routledge is an imprint of the Taylor & Francis Group, an informa business

British Library Cataloguing-in-Publication Data
A catalogue record for this book is available from the British Library

ISBN: 978-1-032-60418-3 (hbk)
ISBN: 978-1-032-59904-5 (pbk)
ISBN: 978-1-003-45902-6 (ebk)

DOI: 10.4324/9781003459026

Typeset in Times New Roman
by SPi Technologies India Pvt Ltd (Straive)

Contents

Figures

Tables

Author Biographies

Cecilia Ka Yuk Chan is a Professor in the Faculty of Education and the Founding Director for the Teaching and Learning Innovation Centre at the University of Hong Kong (HKU). With a dual-discipline background, she possesses expertise in both engineering and education, particularly higher education. Her combined expertise in these fields has enabled her to lead and conduct research on topics such as assessment and feedback, experiential learning, engineering education and technology-enhanced learning, with a particular focus on Artificial Intelligence in education and the development and assessment of 21st-century skills (holistic competencies). Prof. Chan serves as the President of the Asian Society for Engineering Education and is an associate editor for both the Journal of Engineering Education and Studies in Educational Evaluation. Her work, adopted by software companies and organisation and utilised globally including UNESCO, has garnered industry donations and funding. She presents and works closely with organisations worldwide including UNESCO, QS Summit, Harvard, Oxford, UCL, Sydney University to promote the development of holistic competencies and AI Literacy. More information can be found in the Teaching and Learning Enhancement and Research Group (TLERG) website: http://tlerg.cetl.hku.hk/

Tom Colloton is the founder of Eireann Technology, an Educational Technology (EdTech) research and development company. The company is dedicated to addressing major challenges in education by exploring the effective application of technology. With over twenty-five years in the technology sector, Tom has held diverse roles, including Director, Enterprise Architect, and Senior Software Engineer, spanning domains such as Finance, Healthcare, Telecommunications, and Education.

Tom is deeply committed to harnessing technology to impact the educational landscape, specifically in areas like student engagement, retention, programme design, and authentic assessment. He is designing cutting-edge visualisation technology and Artificial Intelligence systems to enhance the experience for teachers, students, and administrators.

Prologue

Thinking back, it seems almost mad that we even attempted to write a book in just eight months – especially during the last eight months I have been very busy with new responsibilities, having taken up the directorship of the newly structured teaching and learning centre at my university. On top of that, the ever-evolving landscape of Generative AI (GenAI)—with its constant introduction of new apps, regulations, functions, and guidelines – kept setting us backwards from our finishing line, forcing us to keep up with the latest developments. I remember my co-author Tom telling me, "We need to revise the chapter again! Did you hear that ChatGPT can now recognise images?" As much as I wanted to exclaim, "Wow, cool!" my actual response was, "Oh, no!" Despite that, our commitment remained: we wanted to bring the latest ideas, news, and practices to our readers, and we felt compelled to stay ahead of the curve. Thus, you will find very up-to-date news and references in the book. The content in some chapters is so cutting-edge that our primary sources were online forums, substack, LinkedIn, Facebook teachers' groups, Twitter (X), newspapers, and YouTube; we must have joined so many Facebook, LinkedIn forums and discussion groups, and, naturally, engaged in extensive discussions with colleagues from universities and industries worldwide.

Being at the top-ranking university in Asia and the world, we often hold the centre stage. Given that the University of Hong Kong is the first university to have an AI policy and assessment guidelines in place (as far as we know), it was expected that news reporters would be interested in our work. Apart from the book, I also conducted a number of research projects in this area, and put together an AI literacy online course an assessment guidebook and infographics and leaflets on GenAI assessment (please visit the AI in education website at https://aied.talic.hku.hk/). Looking around and speaking to the publisher, we believe this book will be the first on GenAI in higher education.

While this book is primarily for educators, I felt it would' be incomplete without including the technical side of GenAI. Therefore, I invited Tom as my co-author. I am grateful to him, joining me in writing this book to check up on my AI know-how, making sure the tech parts are sound, given his current expertise in this domain. I must admit my technical background is a bit out-of-date.

As educators, we are always talking about an interdisciplinary focus, many bachelor programmes are no longer just a degree majoring in one discipline area but many. This book is interdisciplinary by nature; together, my co-author and I encompass both the educational and technical aspects. By merging education and engineering, we reflect the multifaceted world we inhabit. Moreover, GenAI fosters collaboration across disciplines. Hence, this book contains examples from all disciplines, assisting readers in grasping the expansive world of GenAI and interdisciplinarity.

In the book, we tried to use as many examples as we can to illustrate the different aspects of the power of GenAI. Knowing the readers of this book may be teachers, educational developers, policy writers from various disciplinary backgrounds and different types of post-secondary education institutions (such as community, vocational and technical colleges, research-intensive, and teaching-intensive universities), we made it a point to use straightforward language and terms that are not specific to educational research, and we hope that we have managed to make it readable and approachable for all readers.

GenAI's role in education is so new for the majority, we want to help readers to try out this new tool, not to be afraid of it, but to embrace it. Thus, wherever possible, we include examples, and even provide 'try-it-out' prompts so readers can test them out. Any changes are not easy for our teachers, staff and policymakers; this book also raises the challenges not to underestimate the workload and hurdles through which teachers and supporting staff must jump. GenAI is driving us to revolutionise assessment in education. Recognising this transformative potential, in Chapter 4, we have developed an AI Assessment Integration Framework, together with an array of strategies and scenarios to effectively partner with GenAI in this domain. Since May, when a research article I authored on AI policy was published, I have been contacted by over 200 universities to discuss about how to devise an AI policy. Thus, in Chapter 5, we provide a step-by-step guide on how to devise an AI policy; in fact, we gave an example of what an AI policy should look like. Of course, if you wish to know more, please do contact us.

The examples, case studies, and focus of the book are written for post-secondary education; however, most of the content is suitable for different levels of education. School teachers and principals can adapt some of the strategies to suit the culture of their students and environments.

Each chapter begins with a quote that relates to the theme of the chapter, and the structure of the main body may differ depending on the theme of each chapter. The chapter ends with a section called *questions to ponder* and we included our own personal reflection after completing each chapter which diverges from the conventions of a typical academic book. This book is written for everyone – academic developers, researchers, teachers, policymakers, students, IT and administrative staff, and parents. There are lots of useful "freshly out of the oven" research, guidelines, examples, frameworks and practices from this book and it may help to contemplate the kind of findings that are needed to support these practices and to generate theories and frameworks. The questions and reflections at the end of each chapter may also inspire research questions. At the end of the preliminary pages is a short summary of each chapter.

Acknowledgments

I would like to express my deepest gratitude to my husband. He was the first to get me into the world of GenAI, and he jumped on it even before ChatGPT was on everyone's radar. He excitedly got the whole family involved, his enthusiasm was infectious; his tireless efforts in setting up accounts for our family including our kids. My eleven-year-old, Aisling, even christened our ChatGPT with the name "James". She felt he was more than just code; almost like another member of the family. She taught us to always say "please" and "thank you" to James – seeing her do this, I think, "'Well, at least she's picking up good manners!'" Every little interaction becomes its own story.

My eldest daughter, Grace, has harnessed the potential of ChatGPT commendably, utilising it for feedback and crafting French comprehension exercises with Q&As to self-assess her grasp on various topics. My son Sean's passion for engineering serves as yet another driving force, inspiring me to advance AI in education. Observing my family's interactions with AI reinforced my urge to stay ahead, understanding its implications in the education sector.

Big thanks to Dr. Katherine Lee and Dr. Hannah Wong, my dedicated postdocs. You two are stars! Katherine and Hannah deserve special mention for their meticulous proof-reading of this book in an impressively short time span. I have also drawn immense inspiration from my students, Carol Hu, Louisa Tsi, and Wenxin Zhou. Your keen interest in AI has been a continuous source of inspiration, motivating me to push my boundaries. A heartfelt thank you to Dr. SiawWee Chen, who has been involved in assisting me with my literature research. I am genuinely grateful for all your hard work and support.

I would like to thank Prof. Rui Yang, the Dean of Education, for his genuine support and encouragement in my research. I am grateful to have a visionary leader to learn from.

I would like to express my profound gratitude to Prof. Ian Holliday for his trust in me to spearhead the support on GenAI at the university.

Special thanks go to Mr. Pashur Au Yeung, Dr. Carson Hung, Dr. Leon Lei, Ms. Flora Ng, Dr. Wilson Kwok, Mr. Cyrus Chan, Mr. Alan Poon, Mr. Alex Lee and Mr. Noel Liu for engaging in stimulating discussions and exchanges of ideas. A heartfelt thanks to William, who adeptly managed much of my administrative workload, allowing me to focus and put some time aside on my writing.

I am deeply appreciative of the entire team at TALIC, the Teaching and Learning Innovation Centre, at the University of Hong Kong, for their support throughout this endeavour.

To everyone at the University of Hong Kong who has been to my AI seminars, workshops, and clinics: your energy and interest made all the difference. You gave me the push I needed to get this done. A big virtual hug to my colleagues at the Faculty of Education for your support. Your constant backing means the world.

And, of course, a massive thanks to the crew from Routledge. Katie Peace and Khin Thazin – you guys navigated me through the maze of publishing. Katie recognised the unique position of this work, as this book is likely the first book on GenAI in higher education. Her enthusiasm and belief in the project's significance have been instrumental in bringing this vision to fruition. I can't tell you how much I appreciate it.

Lastly, I want to express my gratitude to the wider community on LinkedIn, Facebook (Meta), YouTube, news, journal articles, Twitter (X), and other platforms. I have learned immensely from your contributions and insights, enriching my understanding of this dynamic field. Thank you all for your invaluable contributions to this book and my ongoing exploration of GenAI in higher education.

Cecilia Ka Yuk Chan (28 October 2023)

Firstly, I would like to thank my inspiration, my truly remarkable wife. It is unbelievable how someone can be such a wonderful wife, mother, and daughter. She will always be an inspiration to me and those around her. I would not have embarked on or completed this endeavour without her.

I would also like to extend my gratitude to my children. They infuse life with joy and intrigue, constantly surprising and occasionally shocking me, though thankfully not too often. A special mention to their grandparents, Teresa – 婆婆 and Wing – 公公, who are always on hand to assist and drop over some delicious Char Siu (叉燒).

Lastly, heartfelt thanks to my parents, Mayler and Loretto. I owe my very existence to them, and I am grateful for the education they provided and for nurturing my inquisitive and curious nature.

Tom Colloton (28 October 2023)

Short Summary of Each Chapter

Chapter 1: Introduction to Artificial Intelligence in Higher Education

Opening with an introductory backdrop on Artificial Intelligence (AI), Big Data, the Internet of Things (IoT) and Generative AI (GenAI), this chapter offers readers foundational knowledge of these groundbreaking technologies and their specific applications within the educational settings. The spotlight is cast on ChatGPT by OpenAI, highlighting its potential as a revolutionary tool in higher education. A detailed breakdown of AI, from its inception in the 1950s to its current categorisations – Artificial Narrow Intelligence (ANI), Artificial General Intelligence (AGI), and Artificial Super Intelligence (ASI) – is provided. The chapter then delves into the significance of Big Data, IoT, and GenAI and their intrinsic characteristics, with a focused example on their implications for higher education. The chapter connects technological advancements with their practical implications in education, urging readers to consider the potential and pitfalls of integrating AI in the classroom.

Chapter 2: AI Literacy

Chapter 2 of the book emphasises the crucial nature of AI literacy in today's technologically-driven society and provides a perceptive definition based on literature and research findings. It underscores the necessity of possessing foundational AI literacy, which grants individuals the essential understanding to navigate the modern digital landscape, regardless of their profession. However, the chapter posits that AI literacy cannot remain broad-brushed; it needs further granularity based on professional contexts. For instance, while healthcare professionals may grapple with life-threatening AI mistakes, business professionals might harness AI to shape brand perceptions. Consequently, the Dynamic AI Literacy Model (DAILM) for Specific Roles is introduced, proposing a layered approach to AI literacy tailored to specific professions. Additionally, the chapter sheds light on AI literacy's importance in the broader digital literacy spectrum, with a special focus on AI literacy for teachers, and also evaluates various AI literacy frameworks from previous research.

Chapter 3: Strengths and Weaknesses in Embracing ChatGPT in Curriculum Design

This chapter provides an in-depth exploration of ChatGPT and GenAI's implications in higher education curriculum design. The chapter underscores the strengths, potential opportunities, weaknesses, and threats posed by GenAI in higher education settings. Drawing from a wealth of resources, including literature reviews, online discussions, and firsthand testimonials from students and educators, the chapter offers a list of practical examples of how ChatGPT can be woven into pedagogical design. Serving as a roadmap, the list encourages stakeholders to merge AI capabilities with human ingenuity to foster innovative teaching methods. In addition, the chapter demonstrates a research study examining the synergy between ChatGPT and Bloom's Taxonomy to present a holistic view of AI-partnered pedagogy. The chapter concludes with insights into prompt engineering and its components, offering guidance on optimising interactions with GenAI.

Chapter 4: Redesigning Assessment in the AI Era

Chapter 4 delves into the transformation of assessment methodologies in higher education, driven by advancements in GenAI. Tracing the evolution of assessment from its traditional roots, the chapter underscores the challenges and innovations brought forth in both pre-GenAI and GenAI contexts. As GenAI offers dynamic, adaptive assessment and feedback mechanisms, the chapter emphasises the paramount importance of maintaining educational principles such as authenticity, integrity, and genuine learning. Introducing the Six Assessment Redesign Pivotal Strategies (SARPS) and the AI Assessment Integration Framework, the chapter highlights nine distinct assessment types tailored for the GenAI era. However, a critical message conveyed is that GenAI should be "co-", not replace, the human touch in education. The chapter concludes by advocating for a holistic, learner-centric approach to assessment, prioritising feedback and genuine learning experiences over mere grades.

Chapter 5: Developing an AI in Education Policy

Chapter 5 delves into formulating policies for Artificial Intelligence (AI) in education, emphasising the importance of understanding regulatory principles like transparency, fairness, accountability, safety, and privacy across platforms such as ChatGPT and GenAI. The chapter explores the AI Ecological Education Policy Framework by Chan (2023), structured into three main dimensions – Governance, Operational, and Pedagogical. The Governance Dimension focuses on ethical governance, while the Operational Dimension examines practical implementation in university settings. The Pedagogical Dimension optimises teaching and learning with AI integration. Qualitative data enriches the chapter, offering a comprehensive perspective for shaping a holistic AI policy in higher education. The chapter also provides a review of AI policies from various global regions, and concludes by offering a step-by-step blueprint for establishing an AI policy within higher educational institutions.

Chapter 6: Technology Behind GenAI

This chapter offers an in-depth exploration of Generative AI (GenAI) technology within the context of higher education. While the primary focus of this book is on higher education and its implications, we recognise that some readers may have a curiosity about the technical intricacies of GenAI. Therefore, the aim of this chapter is to delve into the technical aspects of GenAI. Beginning with a historical overview of artificial neural networks, it traces their evolution from early developments to recent advances.

The chapter unveils the process of creating a GenAI model, covering data gathering, model design, training, and rigorous testing. It also introduces the expansive GenAI ecosystem, highlighting its various applications and interactions within different environments.

Furthermore, the chapter spotlights state-of-the-art GenAI models, discussing their applications, design principles, strengths, and limitations. This chapter serves as a foundational knowledge base, equipping readers with essential terminology and understanding of GenAI's technical aspects.

Chapter 7: The Future of AI in Education

In this chapter, we peer into the crystal ball of the future, envisioning the profound impact of Generative AI (GenAI) on education. We begin by reflecting on previous technology adoptions and then explore the general predictions surrounding GenAI's adoption by the population, its potential job impacts, and the safety considerations both pre- and post-adoption. Government and AI development companies enter the spotlight as we contemplate their roles in shaping GenAI's trajectory. The chapter meticulously examines GenAI's implications in higher education, spanning pedagogy, research, funding proposals, and journal article submissions.

The age-old question of AI's predictive ability is also probed, with insights from OpenAI ChatGPT, Google Bard, and Microsoft Bing Chat. Throughout this book, we have championed AI's role in education, highlighting its transformative potential and the need for AI literacy. In this chapter, we take a step further, illuminating the broader societal landscape and its influence on educational institutions and GenAI adoption. As the pages turn, we stand at the precipice of a future where GenAI's promise and challenges intersect with the world of education.

Enjoy your reading. Hopefully you will find the book useful.

Your sincerely,
Cecilia Ka Yuk Chan and Tom Colloton

1 Introduction to Artificial Intelligence in Higher Education

One small input for AI, one giant outcome for humanity.

Cecilia KY Chan

1.1 Introduction

The advancement of Artificial Intelligence (AI), Big Data, and the Internet of Things (IoT) has disrupted many industries and, likewise, has the potential to revolutionise the field of education. One tool that has been making waves in this regard is the *Chat Generative Pre-trained Transformer* – best known as ChatGPT, a pretrained language processing model developed by OpenAI. In this chapter, we will first introduce the concepts of AI, Big Data, IoT and Generative AI (GenAI) to offer our readers a basic understanding of these technologies, providing some concrete examples from educational settings. To equip readers with the necessary knowledge to make informed decisions on incorporating AI into the classroom, this chapter will also go over some fundamental technical aspects of AI. We will then delve into why ChatGPT is a game changer for higher education, what the tool is capable of, and why it has suddenly gained such significant attention. This chapter will conclude with questions that we may have regarding the application of AI and ChatGPT in education.

1.2 Artificial Intelligence (AI)

When thinking about AI, we might immediately associate it with science fiction and shiny robots; in fact, however, the science of AI has been around for decades. As per the term *Artificial Intelligence (AI)* itself, it is a man-made system of computer-based algorithms and programmes that can perform tasks typically requiring human intelligence. We can find it in software programmes that we use in our everyday lives, from platforms like YouTube, Amazon and Taobao, Meta (Facebook), Google Translate, Google Maps, Microsoft Bing and more. These "intelligences" are built into such systems that have capabilities in image processing, speech recognition, decision-making, language translation, and even artificial creativity.

AI is the simulation of human intelligence in machines that are designed to think and act like humans. AI involves the development of algorithms and models that enable computers to learn from data and make predictions or decisions based on said data. Advancements in electronics and computing hardware over recent years have allowed for huge leaps in the development of AI, enabling faster computing power, increased data and memory storage, and the creation of new algorithms such as deep learning.

DOI: 10.4324/9781003459026-1

1.2.1   *Three Types of AI*

Artificial Intelligence has come a long way since its inception in the 1950s. According to researchers and AI philosophers, AI has already gone through significant change and expansion (e.g., Cordeschi, 2007; Shao et al., 2022), with new advancements continually building upon prior developments to produce increasingly sophisticated systems. Currently, discourse has identified three broad categories of AI, based on the complexity and extent of machine intelligence: Artificial Narrow Intelligence (ANI), Artificial General Intelligence (AGI), and Artificial Super Intelligence (ASI). Figure 1.1 shows the types of AI. While these can be considered as the evolutionary stages of AI, it should be noted that AGI and ASI are still theoretical concepts and not necessarily achieved through linear progression.

Artificial Narrow Intelligence (ANI) refers to systems that are designed to perform specific tasks and are trained on large datasets to execute the tasks with precision, such as playing chess or translating languages. However, they are not capable of performing tasks that require human-level intelligence. ANI has helped us make numerous breakthroughs in society, such as in the domains of speech recognition and object recognition or detection (LeCun et al., 2015). Siri, Alexa, fraud detection systems which analyse financial data for patterns and anomalies, as well as self-driving cars that use data from sensors, cameras and GPS to control vehicles, are all examples of ANI. These systems are often referred to as

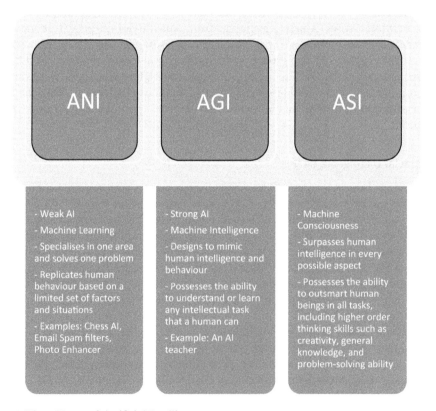

Figure 1.1 Three Types of Artificial Intelligence.

"weak AI" (Thierer et al., 2017) as they have limited capabilities and lack general 'intelligence' due to being optimised for narrowly-defined tasks.

Artificial General Intelligence (AGI) refers to machine systems that will become capable of performing any intellectual task that humans are capable of. AGI refers to a hypothetical future stage of AI which "[bridges] the gap between current AI programs, which are narrow in scope, and the types of AGI systems commonly seen in fiction" (Goertzel, 2014, p.2). Unlike ANI, AGI systems will possess the ability to understand or learn any intellectual task that we can. It will also have the ability to reason. Such systems would have a more general-purpose intelligence and not be restricted to a specific task. AGI is considered the next step in the evolution of AI and is often referred to as "strong AI" (Mills, 2018). According to research and news articles, AI research labs and companies have not reached this stage of development (Baum & Villasenor, 2023; Bove, 2023; Gillani, 2023), but AGI is the goal of many researchers in the field of AI. An example of AGI could be a tool that is able to initiate and perform a wide range of tasks such as a teaching software that can assign classwork, devise schedules for students, correct classwork, coordinate with administrative staff, community partners, and other students, and adapt to new situations, all without the need for human intervention or reprogramming.

Artificial Super Intelligence (ASI) is the final conceptualised type of AI evolution (Yampolskiy, 2016), where systems would surpass human intelligence in every possible aspect and possess the ability to outsmart us in all tasks, including higher-order thinking skills such as creativity, general knowledge, and problem solving. Some believe that ASI systems would have the ability to solve complex problems, make decisions, and even possess consciousness and emotions (e.g., Barney, 2023; Marri, 2018). This type of sophistication is sometimes referred to as "AI singularity" (Grossman, 2023). The term "singularity" in this context is borrowed from the field of physics, where it is used to describe a point in space-time where the rules, as we understand them, break down, such as at the centre of a black hole. In the context of AI, the singularity would represent a point where machines become so advanced that human minds can no longer predict or understand the former's behaviour or implications. This could include AI improving its design and creating successive generations of increasingly powerful machines. This type of AI is still purely speculative, and the exact timeline for its development is unknown. However, the development of ASI and its impact on society raises many ethical and moral questions. ASI is often portrayed as a potential threat to humanity, and there are debates about how to ensure its safe development and deployment (Bostrom, 2014; Yudkowsky, 2006). When contemplating ASI, it is often associated with fictional depictions such as Skynet in *The Terminator*, Vision from the *Marvel* franchise, or the AI robot (Sonny) in *I, Robot*.

Currently, we are still in the stage of ANI, where our systems are designed to perform specific tasks, whereas AGI and ASI remain as areas of continued research and speculation. The potential for future advancements is immense, and the impact that AI will have on society continues to be the subject of research and debate.

1.3 Big Data and the Internet of Things (IoT)

The growth of Big Data and the Internet of Things (IoT) has created a platform in which AI can be applied in a wide range of industries and applications, from healthcare and finance to retail and transportation. The progress of Big Data and IoT also greatly impacts how we live, enabling greater convenience and efficiency, in turn leading to improved productivity and enhanced quality of life.

1.3.1 *What Is Big Data?*

You may have heard of the term "Big Data". As indicated by its name, Big Data refers to a vast amount of data (Favaretto et al., 2020; Kitchin & McArdle, 2016), but did you know that data can come in various forms, such as text, numbers, images, audio recordings, and videos?

Big Data refers to extremely large datasets that are too complex and voluminous for traditional data processing systems to handle efficiently (McAfee & Brynjolfsson, 2012). They can be structured, semi-structured, and unstructured data generated or retrieved from various sources, including social media, e-commerce platforms, sensors, government data, financial data, telecommunication and gaming industries, and system and software logs. Structured data is information that is organised in a specific and predefined format, such as tables, spreadsheets, and databases (Sarker, 2021). The data is already somewhat categorised. Examples of structured data include customer records, financial transactions, and inventory lists. This type of data is easily searchable, sortable, and analysed using conventional data processing tools. On the other hand, unstructured data is information that does not fit neatly into predefined categories or structures (Sarker, 2021). It often requires specialised tools and techniques to extract meaningful insights. Examples of unstructured data include social media posts, emails, and customer feedback.

Different types of data can enhance the comprehensiveness and precision of data analysis. The availability of large amounts of data has allowed AI algorithms to learn and make predictions more accurately. With Big Data, AI models can be trained on larger datasets and make predictions that are more informed and reliable. As a result, managing, processing, and extracting insights from Big Data often requires specialised tools and techniques, for example data warehousing, machine learning, and distributed computing. Yet, it is not only the amount of data that is important – it is what organisations do with the data. Big Data can be analysed for insights which lead to better decisions and strategic moves. Table 1.1 shows a list of examples of various sources of Big Data (Agrawal et al., 2011; Raghupathi & Raghupathi, 2014; Sagiroglu & Sinanc, 2013).

1.3.1.1 *Characteristics of Big Data*

In 2001, Gartner analyst Doug Laney first introduced "three Vs" as the main traits of Big Data – Volume, Velocity, and Variety (Laney, 2001). These "three Vs" form a key framework which influences how organisations and researchers approach and use Big Data. In addition to Laney's work, studies have suggested other significant characteristics, such as Veracity, Variability, and Value (Jin et al., 2015; Kitchin & McArdle, 2016; Sagiroglu & Sinanc, 2013; Sharma, 2022; Song & Zhu, 2015). These characteristics, summarised in Table 1.2, are often used to support organisations in making decisions regarding Big Data, and to determine the best ways to process, analyse, as well as extract insights from said data. Kitchin and McArdle (2016) provided a clear overview of the ontological traits of Big Data.

1.3.1.2 *Example of Big Data and Its Characteristics in Higher Education*

Big Data in education – for example, educational data and analytics regarding student learning – has all of the above characteristics. The *volume* can refer to collecting and analysing large amounts of data from various sources, including student transcripts, test scores,

Table 1.1 Examples of Various Sources of Big Data

Social Media
* Social network posts: Posts made on social media platforms such as Meta (Facebook), X (previously Twitter), Instagram, and LinkedIn.
* Online videos: Videos uploaded to platforms like YouTube, Vimeo, and others.
* User-generated content: Reviews, ratings, and other types of content generated by users on various websites and platforms.
* Social media advertising: Data collected by advertisers on users' behaviours, preferences, and responses to ads on social media platforms.

E-commerce
* E-commerce transactions: Online purchases made through websites such as Amazon, eBay, and others.
* Banking transactions: Transactions made through online banking platforms, including bill payments, money transfers, and other financial transactions.
* Stock market transactions: Transactions made through online stock trading platforms.
* Healthcare transactions: Electronic health record (EHR) transactions and other healthcare-related transactions made through online platforms.

Sensors
* Environmental sensors: Tracked records of temperature, humidity, air pressure, and other environmental parameters.
* GPS sensors: Tracked locations and movements of people, vehicles, and other objects.
* Medical sensors: Used in healthcare to monitor vital signs and track patients' health status.
* Industrial sensors: Monitored performance of industrial machinery and tracked production processes.
* Traffic sensors: Tracked flow of vehicles on roads and highways used to provide data for traffic management and analysis.
* Retail sensors: Monitored customer behaviour in retail environments used to provide data for marketing and sales analysis.
* Home automation sensors: Tracked usage records of appliances, lighting, heating and cooling, and other systems in smart homes.

Government, Financial, Telecommunication and Gaming Industries
* Government: Data generated by government agencies, such as demographic data, crime statistics, and tax records.
* Financial services: Data generated by financial institutions, including transaction records, customer behaviour, and market data.
* Telecommunications services: Data generated by telecommunication companies, including call records, network performance data, and customer usage data.
* Gaming companies: Data generated by online gaming platforms, including player behaviour, in-game transactions, and performance metrics.

System and Software Logs
* Web server logs: Tracked records of all the requests made to a web server, including information such as the type of request, the source IP address, and the time of the request.
* Application logs: Tracked records of events generated by software applications, such as error messages, performance metrics, and user actions.
* Network logs: Tracked records of network activity, including information about network traffic, security events, and system events.
* System logs: Tracked records of events generated by operating systems, such as boot events, system crashes, and security events.
* Security logs: Tracked records of security-related events, such as attempted and successful login attempts, changes to security settings, and security incidents.

Table 1.2 Characteristics of Big Data

Volume refers to the large amounts of data generated and stored by organisations, individuals, and systems. With the rise of digital technologies, Big Data often involves petabytes, exabytes, or even zettabytes of data.

Velocity refers to the speed at which data is generated and continuously processed. Big Data is generated and processed in real time, requiring us to respond quickly and use large amounts of processing power to keep up with changing circumstances.

Variety refers to the diverse types and formats of data present within Big Data. These can range from structured data, such as spreadsheets or databases, to unstructured data, such as texts from social media commentaries.

Veracity, also known as data assurance, refers to the quality, accuracy, and integrity of the data (Gillis, 2021; Raghupathi & Raghupathi, 2014). This is an important aspect as Big Data is only useful if the data is reliable and trustworthy. Examples include the completeness of data or data entry errors from typos and incorrect entries.

Variability refers to the meaning of data constantly changing (McNulty, 2017). For example, the interpretation of certain words may depend on the specific context(s) in which they are used.

Value refers to what can be done with data, and the value(s) that Big Data can offer (Gillis, 2021). How value is inferred from data is distinct from case to case.

Complexity refers to complications in a dataset, such as data with time-varying covariates from scientific simulations (Hong et al., 2018). Data can be very complex in structure and may have complicated relationships, making it difficult to identify patterns, correlations, and insights. An example from the educational setting that demonstrates the complexity of Big Data is analysing large amounts of data from various sources for student retention. There may be multiple variables at play, such as individual student characteristics, academic support services, and pedagogies of institutions, which should be considered within the data analysis. The complexity of Big Data in this context requires advanced analytical skills, powerful data processing tools, and a robust data management infrastructure.

Exhaustivity refers to the comprehensiveness of the data being analysed (Mayer-Schonberger & Cukier, 2013). It signifies that the data should cover all aspects of the topic being analysed to provide a complete picture. An example is student performance, where exhaustiveness is achieved by including the entire population of students and not just capturing a sample, and that data is gathered from all related aspects, for example test scores, tutorial and homework completion rates, class participation levels, extra-curricular activities, and achievements, as well as teacher evaluations.

Relationality refers to the relationship and connections between datasets and the ways in which they can be linked, related, and integrated to provide meaningful insights and information (Boyd & Crawford, 2012). An example from the financial industry is where large amounts of data from various sources such as the stock market, information on customer behaviours, and market trends are integrated for analysis to identify trends and correlations.

Extensionality refers to how data can be extended, expanded, or integrated with other data sources and systems (Marz & Warren, 2012). This includes the ability to add new data sources, and to combine or relate data from different sources to achieve a more comprehensive view of the information collected. For example, health records could be analysed with data generated from clinical research and healthcare devices, offering more comprehensive insights for the identification of disease patterns, as well as advance patient care and treatment.

---

demographic information, and attendance and engagement data from online learning platforms. The *velocity* of the data could refer to real-time updates of student progress and achievements on a learning platform. The *variety* of data sources collected can be vast, including grades, scores from assignments (such as reflective journals, video presentations, and portfolios), and data logs of student activity (such as logs from communication channels and attendance records). *Veracity* of the data may refer to students giving incorrect information with errors and typos, or missing data as students drop courses after a certain period of time. To address these challenges, institutions may use complex algorithms and models to extract insights from collected data, and make informed decisions for areas including student retention, curriculum design, and resource allocation. Integrating and analysing data from various sources and in different formats using innovative models may contribute to the *complexity* of the Big Data. *Variability* is another a concern, such as students having different learning paces and patterns. The *exhaustiveness* of the data is also a challenge, as the data collected may not capture the full picture of student performance. As an example, factors such as learning environment or socio-economic background which may influence student learning could be overlooked. The *relationality* of the data, such as linking students' grades to the time of day and to the courses they have taken, can enable the system to provide meaningful insights. Finally, the *extensionality* of Big Data may refer to collection of data on students who fail, change programmes, undertake an overseas exchange, or take a gap year, to gain a more comprehensive understanding of student learning.

1.3.2 What is the Internet of Things (IoT)?

The Internet of Things (IoT) refers to the network of physical objects and things (e.g., smartphones, smart watches, home automation controls, fitness trackers) which can interact and cooperate with each other through wired and wireless networks, as well as generate, exchange, send, and receive data (Atzori et al., 2010; Li et al., 2015). IoT devices generate vast amounts of data which, when combined with Big Data, can be used to train and improve AI algorithms. IoT and AI are highly complementary technologies, with AI capable of analysing the volumes of data generated by IoT devices, including real-time data, in order to provide valuable insights and facilitate prompt and automated decision-making. IoT could also be a game changer for sustainability: according to an article from the World Economic Forum (Arias et al., 2018), 84% of existing IoT deployments have the ability to contribute to the achievement of the United Nations' Sustainable Development Goals. IoT provides a platform to connect everything and everyone in a smarter way, improving our quality of life and benefitting our planet.

Those unfamiliar with IoT may hold a misconception that it only refers to devices connected to the Internet; however, IoT encompasses much more than that. Devices with electronics parts, software, and sensors that allow them to connect and exchange data, such as Bluetooth devices, are also part of IoT. The term "Internet of Things" was coined by Kevin Ashton in 1999 during his employment at Procter & Gamble (Lueth, 2014; Ashton, 2009). During his work to optimise supply chains, he sought to bring to his senior management's attention, a promising technology known as *Radio Frequency Identification* – RFID. Given the widespread popularity of the internet at the time and its relevance to the concept, Ashton labelled his presentation with the title, "Internet of Things". However, it was only since 2010 that IoT began gaining widespread attention (Lueth, 2014).

1.3.2.1 Characteristics of IoT

IoT has distinct characteristics. By understanding what they are, one can better grasp and identify the underlying technology of IoT and its capabilities, determine the scope of IoT applications, the types of devices and systems that IoT incorporates and can be integrated with, its limitations, and the security and privacy implications. This information can be

Table 1.3 Characteristics of IoT

Connectivity: IoT refers to the network between two or more objects or things which can communicate and exchange data, such as the connection of a device to the internet.

Interoperability: IoT devices need to work together seamlessly regardless of their underlying technology, platform, or brand names (Magan, 2023). Interoperability between devices is essential to ensure that data can be collected, processed, and analysed effectively.

Scalability: IoT can be scaled, where systems and networks can be easily expanded or reduced in size to adapt to changing needs, without affecting their performance (Magan, 2023). Scalability is critical to ensure that IoT systems and networks remain functional and efficient as the number of connected devices increases.

Intelligence: IoT devices, systems, and networks must have the "intelligence" to sense and analyse data and interact with each other, using a combination of algorithms, software, and hardware.

Identity: Identity is a concept of IoT (Uikey, 2022) where, for example, the unique identity of an IoT device enables the tracking and remote control of this specific device (e.g., monitoring cameras installed in homes).

Autonomous: IoT systems have the ability to operate independently, without the need for human intervention.

Security: IoT systems and devices require proper, built-in security measures given their vulnerability to cyber threats. IoT devices often hold sensitive personal information; if the device is lost or stolen, it may cause safety issues for the user. Firewalls, encryption, data protection software, and access controls can be integrated into IoT devices to prevent data theft and unauthorised access.

Real-time: IoT systems and devices enable real-time connection and data exchange.

Remote monitoring: IoT systems have monitoring capabilities. With remote monitoring, IoT sensors can allow transmission of precise data for monitoring of device conditions and control over device performance (Murphy, 2022).

Standardisation: IoT devices should follow standardised protocols, data formats, and rules to ensure interoperability, consistency, and ethical use. Examples of protocols and standards include the Constrained Application Protocol (CoAP), Message Queuing Telemetry Transport (MQTT), and Bluetooth Low Energy (BLE) (Pratt, 2023).

Sustainability: IoT networks, systems, and devices consume energy and generate waste. Therefore, it is important to consider their impact on the environment and to ensure that they are sustainable.

---

used to make informed decisions about the design, deployment, and use of IoT systems and devices. Furthermore, a profound understanding of IoT characteristics can facilitate development of innovative IoT solutions and implications which can address and overcome the challenges and limitations of existing systems and devices (Motta et al., 2019; Rose et al., 2015; Atzori et al., 2010). IoT is characterised by the key features given in Table 1.3.

1.3.2.2 Example of IoT and Its Characteristics in Higher Education

A smart classroom integrating different IoT systems and devices, such as sensors, cameras, laptops, tablets, interactive whiteboards, learning management systems, student information systems, printers, scanners, and wearable devices, is an example of how IoT can be implemented in education.

Connectivity enables devices and systems to form a network for transmitting and receiving data as required. IoT in the classroom is *scalable*, capable of changing the scope of its tasks and easily accommodating the number of devices connected. Each device in the network has a unique *identity*, ensuring that students and teachers can securely identify and access the devices and data they need. *Interoperability* enables seamless streamlining processes such as in the submission of assignments and sharing of documents or resources between students and teachers. *Security* is particularly important in a smart classroom as it is essential to protect data, especially sensitive information such as grades and students' personal details, from unauthorised access. IoT devices in a smart classroom must be designed with robust security measures to ensure the protection of private and sensitive information. The devices in the network are also *autonomous*, meaning they can make decisions and take actions without human intervention. For example, if a room becomes too warm, a smart sensor can automatically adjust the temperature. The system further has *intelligence* capabilities such as machine learning algorithms, to process collected data and make predictions to benefit the class. This enables teachers to track student progress and identify areas where additional support is needed. The system follows industry *standardisation* to ensure that different devices from different vendors can work effectively and seamlessly together under standardised protocols. Additionally, the devices and systems used are designed for *sustainability*, utilising energy-efficient and waste-reduction technologies to reduce the carbon footprint, while maintaining cost-effectiveness with automatic lighting and air conditioning systems. By incorporating these characteristics, this smart classroom system example provides a solution for higher education institutions to improve student experiences, streamline operations with technologies, and create a more efficient and sustainable learning environment.

1.4   Generative Artificial Intelligence (GenAI)

Generative AI (GenAI) is a subset of artificial intelligence that involves creating new data or content (Dilmegani, 2023; McKinsey Consultant, 2023; Altexsoft, 2022). The term "generative" refers to the capability of AI to produce novel outputs rather than simply reproducing, categorising, processing, and analysing inputs. It can generate anything from text, images, audio, and videos, to natural-language text and even computer coding.

The concept of GenAI is rooted in the field of computer science and artificial intelligence. One of the earliest references to such a technology can be found in the work of computer scientist John Hopfield in the 1980s, who proposed the idea of a "Hopfield network", a type of computer neural network that could be trained to generate new patterns or sequences (Kampakis, 2022; McKinsey Global Institute, 2018). The fields of machine learning and artificial neural networks have evolved over time as researchers and practitioners worked to develop more sophisticated generative architecture and deep learning algorithms, including generative adversarial networks (GANs), variational autoencoders (VAEs), and transformer-based models (e.g. GPT-3 Generative Pretrained Transformer 3). There are two important models in GenAI: Discriminative and Generative Modelling (Altexsoft, 2022).

Discriminative modelling is a type of machine learning approach that aims to classify or categorise existing data points into specific classes or categories. While this model is able to distinguish the boundaries between classes, it is trained only to tell the differences and does not understand how data is generated. Machine learning tasks using this approach are classified as *supervised machine learning tasks*. The goal of this approach is to discriminate or make a distinction between the different classes, and then make predictions based on the data it has been trained on.

For example, in education, let's say we want to develop a model that can predict whether a student will pass or fail a particular exam based on their past performance, test scores, and attendance records. The discriminative model would look at the data provided, identify the differences between students who passed the exam and those who failed, then make predictions based on those differences. The model is simply trying to distinguish between students who passed and those who failed – it does not consider why students achieve certain outcomes, and only aims to make accurate predictions.

Generative modelling is a type of machine learning approach that focuses on creating new data that resembles the data it was trained on, based on the patterns and relationships learned from existing data. Machine learning tasks using this approach are classified *as unsupervised and semi-supervised machine learning tasks*. The goal of the generative modelling approach is to create new examples that are similar to those it has seen before, which are representative of the underlying patterns and relationships in the data.

An example of generative modelling in education could be a system that generates new questions for a quiz or test. The model would learn the patterns and distribution of past questions from a training set, and subsequently use that information to generate new questions that are similar in style and content. This could be useful for creating new practice problems for a class, adaptive tests for each student based on their learning progress, or creating unique tests for individual students to prevent cheating.

1.4.1   *Applications of GenAI*

Today, GenAI is already widely applied across various industries, including image and audio synthesis, and text, code and video generation. For example, GenAI can be used to generate realistic images of objects or scenes which do not actually exist, or to create synthetic speech that sounds like a real person. GenAI can also be used to generate new designs or prototypes in fields such as engineering and architecture, or to generate new music compositions or pieces of art (Kumar, 2023; Marr, 2023). Figure 1.2 shows an example of an image synthesis and Table 1.4 shows an example of a code generation. Table 1.5 provides some examples of the types of applications and software of GenAI.

Most applications use a combination of image, text, code, video, and audio generation alongside machine learning algorithms to produce solutions to a problem. One example of how all of these could be used in a comprehensive educational tool could be through an intelligent tutoring system. This system can use GenAI algorithms to customise learning materials for individual students based on their learning needs and progress, produce personalised video lessons by narrating snippets of educational text or code, combine it with visual aids such as images or animations, in order to support students in understanding complex concepts. The system can also create assessment and grading descriptors to assess students' understanding of materials, generating questions and quizzes to reinforce learning. Moreover, audio feedback can also be generated for students as based on their performance, providing guidance and encouragement in a natural and engaging manner. This example demonstrates the transformative capabilities of GenAI in education to create an immersive, personalised, and effective learning experience. By harnessing the power of AI, teachers can free up time and resources, allowing them to focus on other priorities like classroom instruction and providing support to students.

User	You are VanGoghBot. You will generate paintings in the style of Van Gogh.
ChatGPT DALL.E3	Of course! I'm ready to create paintings in the style of Van Gogh. Please describe the scenes or subjects you'd like to see, and I'll generate paintings based on your descriptions.
User	Please draw me an electrical car with a robot
ChatGPT DALL. E3	

Figure 1.2 ChatGPT Dall.E3 Generated Images.

1.5   ChatGPT – A Game Changer in Education?

One particular AI tool that has gained massive popularity, including in education, is ChatGPT (Chat Generative Pre-trained Transformer). ChatGPT is a pretrained text-generation language model developed by OpenAI that uses a transformer-based language architecture (Srivastava, 2022; Joshi, 2021; Kulshrestha, 2020), a type of deep neural network well suited for natural language processing tasks. It has the ability to understand and generate human-like text based on the input it receives. In addition, it has been trained on a massive amount of data which has allowed it to learn the patterns, styles, and complexities of human language, making it a remarkable tool for communication. With capabilities in language generation, translation, summarisation, and questioning and answering, ChatGPT has caused a huge ripple in the technological industry (Zaveri, 2023).

The rise of ChatGPT and its popularity are connected to a number of factors: ChatGPT is redefining the boundaries of machine learning (Rosenbaum, 2023); it is efficient in generating results with endless possibilities (Pace, 2023; Petrova, 2023); and it is knowledgeable with training from huge volumes of information (Shankland, 2023). AI has been around for more than a decade, but recent advancements in the field have made it more accessible

Table 1.4 ChatGPT Generated Codes

User	Can you create a plugin for a simulated DoctorBot?
ChatGPT	Certainly! Creating a plugin for a simulated DoctorBot involves multiple steps, including defining the purpose, designing the user interface, and implementing the logic. Below is a basic outline for creating a DoctorBot plugin: 1. Define the Purpose: Symptom checker/General medical information/Medication reminders etc. 2. Design the User Interface: Text-based chat interface/Voice recognition/Multi-choice questions etc. 3. Implement the Logic: For simplicity, let's create a basic symptom checker using Python:

```
class DoctorBot:
    def __init__(self):
        self.symptoms = {
            "headache": "You might have a migraine or tension headache. If it persists, please see a doctor.",
            "fever": "You might have an infection. Please monitor your temperature and see a doctor if it remains high.",
            "cough": "It could be a cold or flu. If it persists or is severe, please see a doctor."
        }
    def check_symptom(self, symptom):
        return self.symptoms.get(symptom, "I'm not sure about that symptom. Please consult a doctor.")
def main():
    bot = DoctorBot()
    while True:
        symptom = input("Please describe your symptom: ").lower()
        if symptom == "exit":
            break
        print(bot.check_symptom(symptom))
if __name__ == "__main__":
    main()
```

and user-friendly. With ChatGPT, OpenAI's decision to allow public access to the software, its user-friendly interface, and its ability to understand and respond to natural language in a human-like manner, sets it apart from previous AI models. Additionally, the COVID-19 pandemic has accelerated the shift towards online and virtual interactions. The public has grown in their awareness and acceptance of online functionality given their increased experiences with remote working and learning, as well as through the increased popularity of online financing and shopping. As a result, there is a greater demand for innovative solutions like ChatGPT to cater to different needs of the public (Zaveri, 2023).

Within the field of education, the pandemic has become a stimulus for individuals to recognise the benefits and potentials of full-time virtual learning. Before the pandemic, traditional, in-person teaching and learning was regarded as the sole, favoured, or most effective approach to education for many individuals. The sudden outbreak and spread of COVID-19, resulting in widespread lockdowns and social distancing measures, forced universities, colleges, and schools to close their physical campuses and transition to virtual teaching and learning. With the sudden shift online, many have had to adapt and embrace online education, leading to gradual recognition of the possibilities and capabilities such a

Table 1.5 Examples of Types of Generative AI Applications and Software

Applications	Industries/Purposes	Popular Software Apps
Image synthesis: Generative AI algorithms can be used to create unique and creative works of art, such as digital paintings, sculptures, and graphic designs. It can also be used in medical imaging analysis to detect early signs of diseases and medical anomalies. It is important to mention Deepfakes, a type of AI technology that allows the generation of synthetic images and videos of people. Image recognition and processing in AI often use a Convolutional Neural Network (CNN).	Art and Design, Healthcare, Film, Advertising	Stable Diffusion, Dall-E, Runway ML, Midjourney, DeepAI, Fotor, Reface, FaceApp, SpeakPic, Syntegra, AlphaFold2
Video generation: Generative AI can be used to create videos that look like they were shot in real life, or create an animated short film.	Film, Advertising, Customer Service for various industries	Pictory, Synthesia, VEED
Music and audio creation: Generative AI can be used to create new music compositions, remix existing songs, and generate custom sound effects.	Music Production, Healthcare, Customer Service for various industries	Amper Music, Jukebox, MuseTree, MuseNet, Musico, Vall-E, WaveNet, Flowtron
Text-to-speech, speech-to-speech: Generative AI can be used to convert text into speech or facilitate real-time speech translation. For example, it can enable virtual assistants to "speak" in applications or devices.	Customer service for various industries, Electronics, Travel, Leisure	Siri, Alexa, Google Assistant
Text generation: Generative AI can be used to create copywriting, advertisements, and content for marketing campaigns. It can be used to write stories, articles, and other forms of text, including conversations with virtual assistants and help chatbots. It also has the power to translate text from one language to another, breaking down language barriers and enabling more efficient communication.	Marketing, Advertising, Journalism, Script and Story Writing, Healthcare, Customer Service for various industries	ChatGPT, BARD, Bing, Quillbot, Jasper, Google Translate, Photomath
Code generation: Generative AI can develop, write, and debug computer programming codes.	All industries that require programming	Google's AutoML, OpenAI Codex, GitHub Co-pilot, Polycoder, Amazon CodeWhisperer

mode holds for delivering high-quality education. This has also opened up new opportunities for utilising technology in classrooms. For example, ChatGPT is expected to play a significant role in the future of teaching and learning, driving education to develop and undertake better practices by replacing those which could be automated (Jacobsen, 2023). In the post-COVID era, we are beginning to see many educational institutions opening up to the possibility of allowing students to continue their education remotely, which increases accessibility and flexibility, as well as creates new opportunities for learning. Even renowned universities such as University College London (UCL) or Kings College London are providing numerous pathways to go remote by offering online Masters programmes (UCL, n.d.) and blended options for International Foundation programmes (King's College London, n.d.). Online courses allow students to attend lectures and complete assignments from the comfort of their own homes, which can save time and money on commuting. Moreover, virtual learning environments can be designed to promote inclusivity, better support students with special needs, and ensure that those in remote areas can still access teaching and learning. The growing demand for online learning has also led to the increased popularity and adoption of AI-powered virtual assistants like ChatGPT, which can further enhance the accessibility, efficiency, and effectiveness of education. For instance, ChatGPT can serve as a 24/7 virtual assistant that offers real-time responses to students' queries, provide personalised support and guidance, and provide assistance in maintaining learning progress.

All in all, the COVID-19 pandemic has accelerated the shift towards online and virtual learning. As a result, behaviours and attitudes of the public have changed, and educational audiences are now much more receptive to the use of AI tools. We should also note that the recent surge of discussion regarding AI's impact on education is not necessarily late; despite the 50-year presence of AI, its impact on education has only gained considerable prominence with the recent advancement of ChatGPT. While tools like Google Translate may have made notable impacts on certain educational domains, its impact pales in comparison to the potentials of ChatGPT. With its capabilities of providing immediate and tailored feedback, facilitating natural language interactions, and serving as both a teaching and research assistant, ChatGPT and other GenAI tools have established themselves as a transformative force for higher education. Such technology has the potential to fundamentally change the way students learn while also supporting educators in overcoming challenges and obstacles in teaching and learning.

1.6   Generative AI Concerns and Challenges

Despite its potential benefits, the utilisation of AI raises important ethical and social issues. These include concerns about job displacement, privacy, and accountability, as well as the potential for AI to be used for malicious purposes. One of the key drivers behind the development of generative AI is the desire to elevate the creative process (Eapen et al., 2023). By implementing algorithms and machine learning models, generative AI possesses the capacity to generate new and unique content that cannot be achieved through traditional, manual methods. However, the benefit of producing novel outputs also introduces potential drawbacks, including the risk of generating biased or unfair outputs, or content that is inappropriate or harmful. Several aspects are to be addressed: the need to strike a balance between human and machine values and control; the need to ensure that generated content is of high quality and relevancy; and the need to navigate the ethical considerations arising from the complex nature of AI. It is important that we carefully consider these issues as we continue to develop and deploy AI in across industries. In Chapter 3, we will explore and further discuss opportunities and concerns for GenAI in higher education.

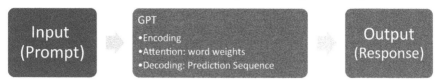

Figure 1.3 How Does ChatGPT Work?

1.7 How Does ChatGPT Work?

For many readers, they are interested in understanding the big picture how ChatGPT works, thus, we have put together a high-level overview of how it works below, please also see Figure 1.3. If you wish to go deeper into the technicalities, please read Chapter 6.

In the simplest way of explaining, ChatGPT is a type of software trained on huge amounts of text. During its training phase, ChatGPT is exposed to vast amounts of text from variety of sources such as websites, books, forums. It learns by predicting the next word in sentences. The training helps ChatGPT to recognise patterns and structures in language. It uses a structure called the Transformer to weigh which parts of your question are most important and how your prompt relates to all the data it has trained on, and thus, GPT stands for Generative Pre-trained Transformer.

1.7.1 So What Happens When You Type in a Question (Also Known as Prompt)?

Table 1.6 shows the steps of how ChatGPT works.

Input: You type in a sequence of words (e.g., "What is the capital of") also known as a prompt.

Table 1.6 Steps Showing How ChatGPT Works

What happens when you type in a question (prompt) in ChatGPT	
[User Input/Prompt in ChatGPT]	→ "What is the capital of?"
[Encoding]	→ Vector for 'capital' for example might relate to a every token form its training that is a capital e.g. 'Dublin', 'London', 'Paris', etc. The vector for 'Paris' which already exists from training would relate to 'France'
	→ Vector for the other words are created in a similar way
[Attention Mechanism: Word Weights]	[Attention Mechanism: Word Weights]
	→ "What" (medium weight)
	→ "is" (low weight)
	→ "the" (medium weight)
	→ "capital" (high weight)
	→ "of" (medium weight)
[Decoding]	→ ChatGPT grasps that the user is asking about a capital city
[Prediction Sequence]	→ "The capital of"
	→ "The capital of France"
	→ "The capital of France is"
	→ "The capital of France is Paris."
[ChatGPT Output/Response]	→ "The capital of France is Paris."

Encoding: The model translates each word into a numerical representation called a vector. This representation captures the word's meaning and its relation to other words which it has been trained on.

Attention: Using a method called "self-attention", the ChatGPT model weighs the importance of each word in your question. For instance, in our example, "capital" might be given more weight than "is". The goal is to grasp the essence of your question/prompt. Knowing the topic helps the model understand related words, like "of" and "the".

Decoding & Prediction: Once the model understands the context of your question from the word weightings (attention) and relationship to other words it has been trained on (embedding), it starts predicting the best sequence of words for a response. This is based on the input – the encoding information and the attention weights. GPT produces a series of words as an answer. Each word has a specific relevance to the topic and the other words. The model predicts the next word. Then it continues, using both the original input and the words it has already predicted to guess subsequent words. This process repeats until a full answer is formed or until the model decides the answer is complete.

Output: The model provides the generated sequence of words as a response (e.g., "The capital of France is Paris.").

It is important to note that while this explanation provides an overview, the actual workings of the model involve a lot of intricate math and processes happening simultaneously. The model has been trained on billions of such sequences, refining its ability to make accurate and coherent predictions over time.

1.8   How does GenAI Generate Images from Text?

For many readers, the concept of machines creating images based on textual descriptions might sound like science fiction. Yet, in GenAI, this has become a reality. To shed some light on this capability, we have crafted a high-level overview of how GenAI works in the context of generating images from text. Please refer to Figure 1.5 for a visual representation. Those desiring a deeper dive can explore Chapter 6.

Computers work with numbers. Whether it is text, image, or sound, a computer interprets it as numbers. And every image is made of pixels. Each pixel has a colour, represented by three numbers: red, green, and blue (RGB). An image, then, is essentially a matrix of number trios. As you can see in Figure 1.4, digital images are represented by a size for example 1920 pixels × 1080 pixels. Each pixel represents a location on the image like x, y coordinates and then at each pixel there is a colour represented by three numbers for, one for the amount of red, another for the amount of green, and another for the amount of blue (RGB). This results in a matrix (array) of vectors (list of numbers) like [13,8,255,0,0] which can represent the whole image.

Much like how ChatGPT encounters enormous amounts of textual data, GenAI Image generation software is trained on vast visual and textual datasets. Think of it as an artist with an encyclopedic knowledge of styles, subjects, and scenes. This can range from simplistic drawings to intricate photographs.

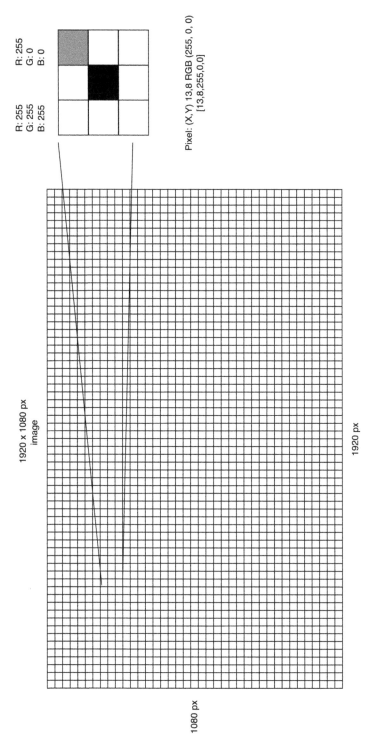

Figure 1.4 An Image Showing RGB Pixel.

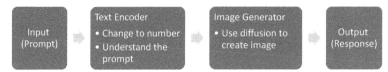

Figure 1.5 The Text to Image Process.

Through this training process, GenAI learns the complexity between words and visuals. It begins to understand that the word "sunset" might evoke hues of orange and pink, or that a "snowy mountain" corresponds to white peaks against a clear sky.

One approach to GenAI's capability is the Generative Adversarial Network (GAN). This involves a duo – a generator (the artist) and a discriminator (the critic). The artist generates, and the critic evaluates. Over time, the generator gets better at producing images that can pass the discriminator's critique. Figure 1.5 shows how text is prompted and generated into image.

1.8.1 *So What Happens When You Type in a Question (Also Known as Prompt) to Generate an Image?*

Input: A user provides a textual prompt (e.g., "A serene lake surrounded by autumn trees").

Textual Encoding: This process is similar to understanding text generation. To produce an image from text, the model first encodes the text input into a meaningful numerical representation. This is usually done using a separate model, such as a trained transformer.

Image Generator: Once the text is encoded into a numerical format, it is used as an input or condition for the generator. This process uses diffusion to create the image. Diffusion is a technique to make images fuzzy. This fuzzy appearance is similar to static on old televisions, often referred to as "noise". Noise is merely random colours/pixels. You can make an image noisy by adding random numbers to its pixels. Conversely, to clarify a noisy image, you adjust the random numbers so they produce a coherent image. In this step, the generator then produces an image that corresponds to the textual description as shown in Figure 1.6.

Refinement: The discriminator evaluates the generated image, ensuring its alignment with the initial description. This feedback loop, over multiple iterations, refines the visual output.

Output: The result is a visual representation (e.g., an image of a calm lake with trees draped in autumnal colours) presented to the user as shown in Figure 1.7.

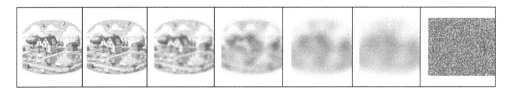

Figure 1.6 Showing the Diffusion Process.

Figure 1.7 The Image Response Generated From the Prompt "A Serene Lake Surrounded by Autumn Trees".

1.9   Conclusions

The future of education is not just digital; it is smart, responsive, and tailored. Imagine classrooms that function like a high-tech ecosystem, adjusting to the needs of every student in real time. Imagine AI tools like ChatGPT, always ready to help, answering questions day or night. COVID-19 pushed us online, and now, tech like IoT and GenAI is taking us to the next level. The classroom of the future? It is innovative, flexible, and built on groundbreaking technology. As we ride this wave, one thing is clear: learning is about to get a whole lot more exciting.

Questions to Ponder

- What will happen if higher education institutions ignore the existence of GenAI?
- What will happen if higher education institutions embrace GenAI in teaching and learning?
- What will happen if higher education institutions embrace GenAI in teaching and learning, but do not put in place any relevant teaching and learning policies to govern its implementation?
- Is ChatGPT really only an ANI? It has the capacity to generate new data, and sometimes it seems to understand what we are asking beyond the prompt we enter.
- If ChatGPT is undertaking unsupervised or semi-supervised machine learning tasks, how can we govern them to ensure certain biased, unethical tasks will not be allowed; wouldn't ChatGPT learn from its own generated content, and continue to come up with and use its own new ideas and concepts – just like humans?

Personal Reflection

If COVID-19 never happened, I wonder how we would perceive online learning and tools like GenAI today? For me, I recalled implementing the e-learning policy at my university thirteen years ago, and trying to get people on board with e-learning was a real struggle. Without the pandemic forcing us to go online for work, school, and even socialising, would we still be dragging our feet? Maybe the convenience of GenAI tools would have won us over eventually, but certainly not as quickly. In a way, the pandemic forced us to dive into the deep end with new tech. Without this happening, perhaps we would still be dipping our toes, hesitant to fully plunge into digital learning. It is interesting to think about how necessity accelerates acceptance. What do you think? Would we have welcomed these smart tools without the push from a global crisis? It is a curious path to wander down, imagining the "what ifs".

References

Agrawal, D., Bernstein, P., Bertino, E., Davidson, S., Dayal, U., Franklin, M., Gehrke, J., Haas, L., Halevy, A., Han, J., Jagadish, H. V., Labridinis, A., Madden, S., Papakonstantinou, Y., Patel, J., Ramakrishnan, R., Ross, K., Shahabi, C., Suciu, D., … & Widom, J. (2011). *Challenges and opportunities with Big Data 2011-1*. [White paper]. Purdue e-Pubs. Retrieved October 17, 2023, from https://docs.lib.purdue.edu/cctech/1/

Altexsoft. (2022, October 13). *Generative AI models explained*. Retrieved October 18, 2023, from https://www.altexsoft.com/blog/generative-ai/

Arias, R, Lueth, K. L. & Rastogi, A. (2018, January 21). *The effect of the Internet of Things on sustainability*. World Economic Forum. Retrieved 18 October, 2023, from https://www.weforum.org/agenda/2018/01/effect-technology-sustainability-sdgs-internet-things-iot/

Ashton, K. (2009). That 'Internet of Things' thing. *RFID Journal, 22*(7), 97–114.

Atzori, L., Iera, A., & Morabito, G. (2010). The Internet of Things: A survey. *Computer Networks, 54*(15), 2787–2805. https://doi.org/10.1016/j.comnet.2010.05.010

Barney, N. (2023, March). *Artificial Super Intelligence (ASI)*. TechTarget. Retrieved October 17, 2023, from https://www.techtarget.com/searchenterpriseai/definition/artificial-superintelligence-ASI

Baum, J., & Villasenor, J. (2023, July 18). *How close are we to AI that surpasses human intelligence?* Brookings. Retrieved October 17, 2023, from https://www.brookings.edu/articles/how-close-are-we-to-ai-that-surpasses-human-intelligence/

Bostrom, N. (2014). *Superintelligence: Paths, dangers, strategies*. Oxford University Press.

Bove, T. (2023, May 4). *CEO of Google's DeepMind says we could be 'just a few years' from A.I. that has human-level intelligence*. Fortune. Retrieved October 17, 2023, from https://fortune.com/2023/05/03/google-deepmind-ceo-agi-artificial-intelligence/

Boyd, D., & Crawford, K. (2012). Critical questions for big data: Provocations for a cultural, technological, and scholarly phenomenon. *Information, Communication & Society, 15*(5), 662–679. https://doi.org/10.1080/1369118X.2012.678878

Cordeschi, R. (2007). AI turns fifty: Revising its origins. *Applied Artificial Intelligence, 21*(4–5), 259–279. https://doi.org/10.1080/08839510701252304

Dilmegani, C. (2023, September 29). Top 100+ generative AI applications/use cases in 2023. *AIMultiple*. Retrieved October 18, 2023, from https://research.aimultiple.com/generative-ai-applications/

Eapen, T. T., Finkenstadt, D. J., Folk, J., & Venkataswamy, L. (2023). *How generative AI can augment human creativity*. Harvard Business Review. Retrieved October 19, 2023, from https://hbr.org/2023/07/how-generative-ai-can-augment-human-creativity

Favaretto, M., De Clercq, E., Schneble, C. O., Elger, B. S. (2020). What is your definition of Big Data? Researchers' understanding of the phenomenon of the decade. *PLoS ONE, 15*(2), e0228987. https://doi.org/10.1371/journal.pone.0228987

Gillani, N. (2023, April 19). Will AI ever reach human-level intelligence? We asked five experts. The Conversation. Retrieved October 19, 2023, from https://theconversation.com/will-ai-ever-reach-human-level-intelligence-we-asked-five-experts-202515

Gillis, A. S. (2021, March). *5 V's of Big Data*. TechTarget. Retrieved October 18, 2023, from https://www.techtarget.com/searchdatamanagement/definition/5-Vs-of-big-data

Goertzel, B. (2014). Artificial general intelligence: Concept, state of the art, and future prospects. *Journal of Artificial General Intelligence, 5*(1), 1–46. https://doi.org/10.2478/jagi-2014-0001

Grossman, G. (2023, February 11). *Generative AI may only be a foreshock to AI singularity*. VentureBeat. Retrieved October 17, 2023, from https://venturebeat.com/ai/generative-ai-may-only-be-a-foreshock-to-ai-singularity/

Hong, Y., Zhang, M., & Meeker, W. Q. (2018). Big data and reliability applications: The complexity dimension. *Journal of Quality Technology, 50*(2), 135–149. https://doi.org/10.1080/00224065.2018.1438007

Jacobsen, P. (2023, February 8). *Why ChatGPT will change Higher Ed for the better*. FEE Stories. Retrieved October 19, 2023, from https://fee.org/articles/chatgpt-will-change-higher-ed-for-the-better/

Jin, X., Wah, B. W., Cheng, X., & Wang, Y. (2015). Significance and challenges of big data research. *Big Data Research, 2*(2), 59–64. https://doi.org/10.1016/j.bdr.2015.01.006

Joshi, P. (2021, July 23). *Guide to the Latest State-of-the-Art Models*. Analytics Vidhya. Retrieved October 19, 2023, from https://www.analyticsvidhya.com/blog/2019/06/understanding-transformers-nlp-state-of-the-art-models/

Kampakis, S. (2022, November 19). *Tom Burns on Hopfield networks and the nature of general AI* [Interview]. Hackernoon. Retrieved October 18, 2023, from https://hackernoon.com/tom-burns-on-hopfield-networks-and-the-nature-of-general-ai

King's College London. (n.d.). *King's international foundation*. Retrieved October 19, 2023, from https://www.kcl.ac.uk/international-foundation

Kitchin, R., & McArdle, G. (2016). What makes Big Data, Big Data? Exploring the ontological characteristics of 26 datasets. *Big Data & Society, 3*(1). https://doi.org/10.1177/2053951716631130

Kulshrestha, R. (2020, June 29). *Transformers*. Medium. Retrieved October 19, 2023, from https://towardsdatascience.com/transformers-89034557de14

Kumar, S. M. (2023, June 23). *How generative AI can transform architecture, engineering, construction*. The Economic Times. Retrieved October 19, 2023, from https://economictimes.indiatimes.com/news/how-to/how-generative-ai-can-transform-architecture-engineering-construction/articles how/101225327.cms?from=mdr

Laney, D. (2001). *3D data management: Controlling data volume, velocity and variety*. META Group.

LeCun, Y, Bengio, Y., & Hinton, G. (2015). Deep learning. *Nature, 521*, 436–444. https://doi.org/10.1038/nature14539

Li, S., Xu, L. D. & Zhao, S. (2015). The Internet of Things: A survey. *Information Systems Frontiers, 17*, 243–259. https://doi.org/10.1007/s10796-014-9492-7

Lueth, K. L. (2014, December 19). *Why the Internet of Things is called Internet of Things: Definition, history, disambiguation*. IoT Analytics Market Insights. Retrieved 18 October, 2023, from https://iot-analytics.com/internet-of-things-definition/

Magan, S. (2023, October 18). *Characteristics of IoT: Definition, uses & key features explained*. Unstop. Retrieved October 18, 2023, from https://unstop.com/blog/characteristics-of-iot

Marr, B. (2023, October 5). *Generative AI is revolutionizing music: The vision for democratizing creation*. Forbes. Retrieved October 19, 2023, from https://www.forbes.com/sites/bernardmarr/2023/10/05/generative-ai-is-revolutionizing-music-loudlys-vision-for-democratizing-creation/?sh=3c00b9b775bd

Marri, S. (2018, July 9). *Can super intelligence and emotional intelligence co-exist?* Forbes India. Retrieved October 17, 2023, from https://www.forbesindia.com/blog/technology/can-super-intelligence-and-emotional-intelligence-co-exist/

Marz, N., & Warren, J. (2012). *Big Data: Principles and best practices of scalable realtime data systems* (MEAP ed.). Manning.

Mayer-Schonberger, V., & Cukier, K. (2013). *Big Data: A revolution that will change how we live, work and think.* John Murray.

McAfee, A., & Brynjolfsson, E. (2012). *Big data: The management revolution.* Harvard Business Review.

McKinsey Consultant. (2023, January 19). *What is generative AI?* Retrieved October 18, 2023, from https://www.mckinsey.com/featured-insights/mckinsey-explainers/what-is-generative-ai

McKinsey Global Institute. (2018, May 8). *Deep learning's origins and pioneers.* McKinsey & Company. Retrieved October 18, 2023, from https://www.mckinsey.com/featured-insights/artificial-intelligence/deep-learnings-origins-and-pioneers

McNulty, E, (2017, May 8). *Understanding Big Data: The seven V's.* Dataconomy. Retrieved October 18, 2023, from http://dataconomy.com/seven-vs-big-data/

Mills, T. (2018, September 17). *AI vs AGI: What's the difference?* Forbes. Retrieved October 17, 2023, from https://www.forbes.com/sites/forbestechcouncil/2018/09/17/ai-vs-agi-whats-the-difference/?sh=cc4150838ee1

Motta, R. C., Silva, V., & Travassos, G. H. (2019). Towards a more in-depth understanding of the IoT Paradigm and its challenges. *Journal of Software Engineering Research and Development, 7.* https://doi.org/10.5753/jserd.2019.14

Murphy, M. (2022, May 7). *IoT remote monitoring: How it works, applications, benefits.* Hologram. Retrieved October 18, 2023, from https://www.hologram.io/blog/iot-remote-monitoring/

Pace, M. (2023, January 17). ChatGPT: Why the trending AI tool has captured attention and controversy. *Spinnaker.* Retrieved October 19, 2023, from https://unfspinnaker.com/98982/features/chatgpt-why-the-trending-ai-tool-has-captured-attention-and-controversy/

Petrova, M. (2023, February 2). *Why ChatGPT is a game changer for AI* [Video]. CNBC. https://www.cnbc.com/video/2023/02/02/why-chatgpt-is-a-game-changer-for-ai.html

Pratt, M. K. (2023, July 12). *Top 12 most commonly used IoT protocols and standards. TechTarget.* Retrieved October 18, 2023, from https://www.techtarget.com/iotagenda/tip/Top-12-most-commonly-used-IoT-protocols-and-standards

Raghupathi, W., & Raghupathi, V. (2014). Big data analytics in healthcare: Promise and potential. *Health Information Science and Systems, 2.* https://doi.org/10.1186/2047-2501-2-3

Rose, K., Eldridge, S., & Chapin, L. (2015). *The internet of things: An overview.* The Internet Society (ISOC).

Rosenbaum, E. (2023, February 11). *The ChatGPT AI hype cycle is peaking, but even tech skeptics don't expect a bust.* CNBC. Retrieved from https://www.cnbc.com/2023/02/11/chatgpt-ai-hype-cycle-is-peaking-but-even-tech-skeptics-doubt-a-bust.html

Sagiroglu, S., & Sinanc, S. (2013, May). *Big data: A review.* 2013 International Conference on Collaboration Technologies and Systems (CTS), San Diego, USA (pp. 42–47). https://doi.org/10.1109/CTS.2013.6567202

Sarker, I. H. (2021). Machine learning: Algorithms, real-world applications and research directions. *SN Computer Science, 2,* 160. https://doi.org/10.1007/s42979-021-00592-x

Shankland, S. (2023, February 19). *Why we're obsessed with the mind-blowing ChatGPT AI chatbot.* CNET. Retrieved October 19, 2023, from https://www.cnet.com/tech/computing/why-were-all-obsessed-with-the-mind-blowing-chatgpt-ai-chatbot/

Shao, Z., Zhao, R., Yuan, S., Ding, M., & Wang, Y. (2022). Tracing the evolution of AI in the past decade and forecasting the emerging trends. *Expert Systems with Applications, 209,* 118211. https://doi.org/10.1016/j.eswa.2022.118221

Sharma, R. (2022, September 1). *Characteristics of Big Data: Types and 5V's.* UpGrad. Retrieved October 17, 2023, from https://www.upgrad.com/blog/characteristics-of-big-data/

Song, I.-Y., & Zhu, Y. (2015). Big data and data science: What should we teach? *Expert Systems, 33*(4), 364–373. https://doi.org/10.1111/exsy.12130

Srivastava, A. (2022, August 8). *What are transformers in NLP and its advantages.* Knoldus. Retrieved October 19, 2023, from https://blog.knoldus.com/what-are-transformers-in-nlp-and-its-advantages/

Thierer, A. D., O'Sullivan, A. O., & Russell, R. (2017). *Artificial intelligence and public policy.* Mercatus Research, Mercatus Center at George Mason University, Arlington https://doi.org/10.13140/RG.2.2.14942.33604

UCL (n.d.). *Flexible learning for professionals – Online MSc programmes at UCL.* UCL Faculty of Medical Sciences. Retrieved October 19, 2023, from https://www.ucl.ac.uk/medical-sciences/study/flexible-learning-professionals-online-msc-programmes-ucl

Uikey, P. (2022, November 26). *Characteristics of IoT (Internet of Things).* DataTrained. Retrieved October 18, 2023, from https://datatrained.com/post/characteristics-of-iot/

Yampolskiy, R. V. (2016). *Artificial SuperIntelligence: A futuristic approach.* CRC Press.

Yudkowsky, E. (2006). Artificial intelligence as a positive and negative factor in global risk. In N. Bostrom & M. M. Ćirković (Eds.), *Global catastrophic risks* (pp. 308–345). Oxford University Press.

Zaveri, P. (2023, February 3). *Microsoft's landmark deal with OpenAI shows that ChatGPT is going to be the defining technology of 2023.* Business Insider. Retrieved October 19, 2023, from https://www.businessinsider.com/why-generative-ai-chatgpt-the-defining-tech-of-this-year-2023-1?r=US&IR=T

2   AI Literacy

AI literacy for the typical individual is the ability to comprehend, assess, interact with, and make informed decisions regarding artificial intelligence technologies in daily life. It involves understanding the basic principles of AI, recognising its applications, being aware of its ethical, social, and privacy implications, as well as understanding the impacts and values AI has on humans and human emotions, all while responsibly engaging with AI systems.

Cecilia KY Chan

2.1   Introduction

Artificial Intelligence (AI) not only facilitates communication between humans and between humans and machines, but also provides a range of interaction mediums and channels including text-based, graphical, audio, video, and even coding-based responses. As AI technology continues to advance, its integration into various domains of society becomes even more prevalent – we now see AI's influence in many corners of our lives, whether in personalised online shopping recommendations or social media content that we scroll through on our screens. For instance, consider how AI algorithms on platforms like Netflix or YouTube influence what we watch by recommending new shows or videos (Brynjolfsson & McAfee, 2014). It has become a steady companion, subtly shaping our interactions, choices, and societal structures, making it even more essential for individuals to develop a foundational comprehension of its capabilities and limitations (Casal-Otero et al., 2023). Cultivating AI literacy allows people to better understand the underlying mechanisms driving these systems, identify potential biases, and contribute to the continuous dialogue about the ethical and social implications of AI technology. And, the forthcoming AI-Native Generation, will be the first to have never lived in a world without AI technology.

This chapter explores the importance of understanding AI in today's digital world, especially for students and teachers in higher education. Simply put, AI literacy is about knowing how AI works and how to use it wisely and ethically. It is not just about being tech-savvy; it is about understanding AI's impact, making smart choices, and being aware of the ethical issues that it raises. For students and teachers in higher education, being AI literate is crucial as AI is becoming a big part of learning, research, and administration in universities. We will look at what experts have said about AI literacy, explore its meaning, why it is needed, and how it can be developed, with a special focus on its role in higher education. The upcoming sections shall dissect existing literature and studies, shedding light on the conceptualisations, necessities, and implementations of AI literacy, thereby enriching our understanding and scaffolding future pathways for effective integration of AI in educational paradigms.

DOI: 10.4324/9781003459026-2

2.2   The Importance of AI Literacy

The potentials and pitfalls of AI use are expansive, encompassing aspects that govern privacy, decision-making, and socio-economic dynamics, underlining the criticality of understanding its mechanics, applications, and implications. AI literacy, therefore, serves as a pivotal tool in demystifying the complexities and intricacies embedded within technological systems and algorithms. Being AI literate does not only help us use technology better – it also improves our ability to check, question, and guide how the digital world grows. By understanding what AI can and cannot do, people can make smarter choices, plan better, and have important discussions about how technology is used and controlled. As AI becomes a bigger part of our daily lives, it is crucial for everyone to have a basic understanding of it.

Within educational environments, the significance of AI literacy is equally as important. Although much attention is often placed on providing students with essential AI skills, it is vital to acknowledge that teachers, serving as the main conduits of learning, also need proficiency in utilising AI. For students, it is about cultivating a skill set that is synchronously technical and critical, preparing them not only for existing job markets, but also equipping them to ethically, strategically, and innovatively navigate future landscapes that will undoubtedly be even more densely interwoven with technology. For educators and administrators, AI literacy is pivotal for astute policy formulation, ensuring that governance and regulatory frameworks are effective in addressing the intricacies and ethical conundrums of implementing AI technologies in academic contexts. Furthermore, a solid understanding of AI is vital in strategic resource allocation, enhancing institutional operations and creating forward-thinking educational experiences. This helps both the institution and its community keep up with the fast-paced changes in our digital and AI-driven world. However, it may be tough for some educators to develop new competencies like AI literacy; certainly, the journey for them to shift their mindsets and acquire such skills might pose its own set of challenges. As such, policymakers should also think about these issues and be mindful in addressing them.

While the broader public possesses only a limited understanding of AI (West & Allen, 2018), numerous AI training programmes have been established to equip the workforce with more in-depth knowledge (Bughin et al., 2018; Chan, 2023; Kong et al., 2021). Various companies have launched AI learning and skill enhancement initiatives (Vinuesa et al., 2020) to widely educate employees and bridge the growing skills divide. Programmes designed for children have also demonstrated that even those as young as 10 years old can grasp fundamental concepts and utilise them in inventive ways to address issues in their communities (Kahn & Winters, 2017; Wolfram, 2017). All these AI training endeavours necessitate a foundational literacy in AI among us. But what is AI literacy? What does it constitute?

2.3   Literacy in the Digital World

The history of various literacies reveals a fascinating evolution that reflects the progression and expansion of technology and information access (Buckingham, 1993). Initially, information literacy was crucial, providing a basis for effectively discerning and utilising rapidly growing and accessible information, particularly in the context of library and research environments. Then, as different technological epochs unfolded, several other literacies were coined, branching out to cater to the demands and challenges posed by new media and technologies. From understanding the implications of media messages and navigating the digital world, to deciphering data and interacting with AI, each type of literacy is constructed upon those previous, together weaving a tapestry that shows the multidimensional competencies needed in our current information age. Below, we put together some of the common literacies used in the digital world. Highlights can be found in Table 2.1.

Table 2.1 Common Literacy in the Digital World

Information Literacy:	
When	Coined in 1974 by Paul Zurkowski, President of the Information Industry Association.
Definition	The ability to recognise when information is needed, and the capability to locate, evaluate, and use it effectively, usually in research and decision-making contexts.
Focus	Distinguishing reliable from unreliable information, and using information ethically and legally within a cluttered information landscape. It forms the base for other literacies.
Media Literacy:	
When	Originated in the mid-20th century, and gained prominence in the latter part of the century with the rise of mass media.
Definition	Understanding, analysing, and creating media across both traditional (e.g., newspapers, TV) and digital platforms.
Focus	Critically analysing media content to understand its creation, purpose, and message. Sonia Livingstone's 2004 four-component model emphasises accessing, analysing, evaluating, and creating messages across various contexts.
Digital Literacy:	
When	Coined by Paul Gilster in 1997.
Definition	The ability to understand and use information in multiple formats from a wide variety of sources, particularly via computers and the Internet.
Focus	Practical understanding of digital tools/platforms, navigating digital information space, evaluating content, and effective participation in digital networks.
Data Literacy:	
When	Came into focus in the early 21st century with the advent of the Big Data era, highlighted by Wolff et al. (2016).
Definition	The ability to read, understand, create, and communicate data as information.
Focus	Interpreting, constructing, evaluating data quality, recognising patterns/trends, and making informed decisions based on data analysis. Key components include data exploration, management, and use.
Computational Literacy:	
When	Gained prominence through Jeanette M. Wing's 2006 paper.
Definition	Emphasises problem-solving processes and involves formulating problems and their solutions in ways that computers can also execute.
Focus	Important in computing and programming education, it underscores computational thinking in problem solving across various disciplines.
AI Literacy:	
When	Coined in 2015 by Konishi, further adopted in the empirical study by Kandlhofer et al. (2016).
Definition	AI literacy for a typical individual is the ability to comprehend, interact with, and make informed decisions regarding artificial intelligence technologies in daily life (Chan, 2023).
Focus	It involves understanding the basic principles of AI, recognising its applications, and being aware of ethical, social, and privacy implications while responsibly engaging with AI systems.

Information Literacy is often considered as a foundational literacy. Its roots stretch back several decades, with Paul Zurkowski, President of the Information Industry Association, coining the term in 1974. It pertains to the ability to recognise when information is needed and to have the capability to locate, evaluate, and use such information effectively, usually within the context of research and decision-making. It forms the base from which other literacies are built upon. In a complex and often-cluttered information landscape, the skills to distinguish reliable from unreliable information and to use this information ethically and legally is imperative (Chan, 2021).

Media Literacy, while having origins in the mid-20th century, became more prominent as a focus of study and discussion in the latter part of the century, following the rise of mass media. Media literacy involves understanding, analysing, and creating media, which includes not only traditional media like newspapers, film, and television, but also digital media like social media and online content. This literacy involves understanding and analysing media content critically, using a discerning eye to evaluate its creation, purpose, and message. Various scholars and organisations have contributed to the concept, but one notably significant contributor is Sonia Livingstone. In her 2004 paper (Livingstone, 2004) titled "What is media literacy?", she defines media literacy as "the ability to access, analyse, evaluate, and create messages across a variety of contexts" (p. 18). Livingstone's four-component model that comprises these abilities further emphasises that they are applicable to both traditional media and new forms of digital media, such as those mentioned above.

Digital Literacy, as coined by Paul Gilster in his 1997 book *Digital Literacy*, encompasses not only a practical understanding of how to use digital tools and platforms, but also a deeper understanding of how to navigate the digital information space, evaluate content, and participate effectively in digital networks (Gilster, 1997). He defines digital literacy as "the ability to understand and use information in multiple formats from a wide variety of sources when it is presented via computers", particularly through the medium of the Internet (Gilster, as cited in Pool, 1997, p. 6).

Data Literacy, meanwhile, became a point of focus with the advent of the Big Data era in the early 21st century. It was brought into focus by Wolff et al. (2016) and underscores the significance of understanding and interpreting data. Data literacy refers to the ability to read, understand, create, and communicate data as information. It includes the aptitude to interpret, construct, and determine the quality of data, which further enables us to analyse and evaluate the data in a meaningful way. For example, by understanding what data means and recognising patterns and trends, we are better able to make informed decisions based on data analysis. With data becoming an essential aspect of organisational and societal decision-making, data literacy is vital for making sense of the large volumes of information and utilising it effectively in various contexts. In terms of frameworks for data literacy, there are several key components that are often highlighted:

1 Data Exploration: This involves understanding the purpose or the "why" of the data.
2 Data Management: This encompasses acquiring and appropriately storing relevant data.
3 Data Use: This pertains to the analysis, interpretation, reporting, etc., of data to fulfil the intended purpose.

Computational Literacy, or computational thinking, emphasises problem-solving processes and involves formulating problems and their solutions in ways that computers can also execute. It emerged as a crucial skill in the context of computing and programming education. Jeanette M. Wing, in her popular 2006 paper (Wing, 2006), was pivotal in bringing this term into the broader discourse, underscoring the importance of computational thinking in problem solving across various disciplines.

AI literacy was coined in an online article published in 2015 (Konishi, 2015) and subsequently adopted in an empirical study (Kandlhofer et al., 2016). However, there is currently no widely accepted definition of AI literacy, with research on this subject still in its nascent stages. There is a pressing need to refine what AI literacy involves and determine what knowledge, skills, and so on are needed by individuals with no expert knowledge in this domain (Laupichler et al., 2022). On the whole, the core idea of AI literacy revolves around empowering individuals to critically analyse, effectively interact with, and utilise AI technologies, even if they don't know how to create AI models themselves. The metamorphosis of AI literacy mirrors that of traditional literacy, evolving from rudimentary understanding to nuanced comprehension in higher educational echelons. The effort to define AI literacy has led to the creation of a number of frameworks and definitions that aim to capture what it means to be AI literate.

2.4   AI Literacy Frameworks

The concept of AI literacy is quite new. Especially with AI tools like ChatGPT only becoming publicly available since November 2022, research in this area is still very much in its infancy. Much of the work done so far was published between 2019 to 2022, before the introduction of ChatGPT and GenAI. Many of these studies focused on reviewing existing literature on AI literacy, for example: Laupichler et al. (2022) looked at 30 studies on AI literacy in higher and adult education; Cetindamar et al. (2022) analysed 270 articles to explore AI literacy among employees in digital workplaces; and Ng et al. (2021) reviewed 30 articles to try and define AI literacy. All aimed to establish a solid foundation for teaching and evaluating this literacy, yet, despite these scholarly pursuits, a universally accepted framework or definition of AI literacy is still lacking. Existing literature has offered various definitions and frameworks for AI literacy, some of which we will discuss below.

Kandlhofer et al. (2016) have proposed their own AI education framework, drawing analogies with classic literacies like in reading and writing, and targeting a spectrum of educational levels from kindergarten to university. Their approach aimed to define key AI literacy topics and carefully craft an educational concept inclusive of specific content, structures, and applied learning methodologies from basic to more complex forms as students progress through different educational levels. Empirical evaluation through four proof-of-concept projects showcased promising preliminary results. For instance, kindergarteners engaged playfully with fundamental AI concepts, while high schoolers achieved a solid understanding of AI literacy topics. However, middle school students struggled to correlate basic AI understanding with real-life applications, suggesting that curriculum refinement may be necessary. The study acknowledges its limitations with its small participant samples (barring at the university level) and the absence of implementation at the primary school level, which hinders broader generalisation of findings.

Based on their interdisciplinary exploratory review of literature, Long and Magerko (2020) defined AI literacy as "a set of competencies that enables individuals to critically evaluate AI technologies, communicate and collaborate effectively with AI, and use AI as a tool online, at home, and in the workplace". This definition emerged from their efforts to develop a conceptual framework to provide crucial guidelines for the development of AI literacy. In this framework are several design considerations proposed for supporting AI developers and educators in creating learner-centred AI environments, such as promoting transparency in AI design and encouraging critical thinking among learners.

Ng et al. (2021) conducted an exploratory review to delineate the emerging notion of "AI literacy", seeking a robust theoretical underpinning to define, teach, and evaluate it. Grounded on the analysis of 30 peer-reviewed articles, AI literacy is conceptualised within a framework comprised of four key aspects: knowing and understanding AI, applying AI, evaluating and creating with AI, and addressing AI ethics. The first three of these four aspects are also mapped onto Bloom's Taxonomy (Bloom et al., 1956; Huitt, 2011), to further conceptualise that they are successively attained. The authors also highlighted the ever-growing need of AI literacy in today's day and age, comparing it to how classic literacies (e.g., in reading, writing, mathematics) have already extended to include digital literacy given the advancement of computer technologies. Moreover, Ng et al.'s framework encourages a comprehensive understanding of AI, extending beyond mere utilisation to encompassing basic functions, ethical usage, and application in varied scenarios. The "know and understand AI" aspect emphasises acquiring fundamental AI concepts and recognising the underlying technologies in everyday AI applications. The "apply AI" facet underscores the importance of deploying AI knowledge in different contexts, enhancing practical comprehension. "Evaluate & create AI" encourages engaging in higher-order thinking activities, promoting critical evaluation and creative interactions with AI technologies. Lastly, the "AI ethics" dimension highlights human-centred considerations like fairness, accountability, transparency, and ethics, aiming to foster socially responsible AI usage. This structured approach facilitates a multi-dimensional understanding of AI literacy, bridging theoretical insights with practical applications and ethical considerations, laying a foundation for future educational strategies, competency development, and assessment criteria in AI literacy.

In Kong and Zhang's (2021) conference paper, they present a three-dimensional conceptual framework for fostering AI literacy, structured around cognitive, affective, and sociocultural dimensions, tailored for citizens in the digital age as AI technology continues to be deeply integrated into daily life. The cognitive dimension emphasises the education of basic AI concepts to individuals, cultivating their foundational understanding, competencies, and application of AI technologies to evaluate and comprehend real-world scenarios. The affective dimension focuses on empowering individuals and equipping them with the ability to adapt, react, and respond effectively to the growing influence of AI in various facets of their lives. The sociocultural dimension encourages and promotes ethical considerations and utilisations of AI to foster a culture of responsible AI usage that aligns with sustainable global development and other broader societal and global objectives. Through this framework, the authors aspire to initiate discussions and guide future research towards the design of AI literacy programmes. They envision that their proposed framework will serve as a robust foundation for researchers, educators, and policymakers in their endeavours to nurture and engage educated citizens.

Liu and Xie (2021) delve into the impact of AI in education, focusing on university students in China undergoing training as primary and secondary school teachers. According to this conference paper, the integration of AI technology into education is bound to significantly alter traditional teaching ideologies and methodologies, ushering in a new era where human–machine cooperation will be the norm, and lifelong, ubiquitous learning will become mainstream. The authors argue that programming skills are indispensable to AI literacy, further proposing a framework of three core aspects of AI literacy: Digital Literacy, Computational Thinking, and Programming Ability. The framework promotes a multi-level approach (basic ability, deepening application, and application innovation) as a strategy to cultivate university students' ability to effectively utilise and apply AI, based on both their learning process and the advancement of AI education technology. However, the paper does not provide a concise definition of AI literacy nor detailed information on the methodology or process used to develop the framework.

Karaca et al. (2021) veer slightly off the conventional discourse on AI literacy and introduce the notion of "AI readiness", which refers to the perceived preparedness of individuals, particularly students, to engage with AI in professional settings. Situated in the disciplinary nexus of medical education and data science, the authors developed a psychometric tool through first generating an item pool (via an extensive literature review, expert opinions and review) followed by establishing validity and reliability of the scale (through both Exploratory and Confirmatory Factor Analysis). The final tool was a 22-item scale housed within a four-factor structure (cognition, ability, vision, and ethics) that measured medical students' perceived readiness for AI technologies and its applicability in medicine. The scale's four factors further reflect a comprehensive understanding of AI literacy, entailing not only technical and cognitive competencies, but also a visionary and ethical understanding of AI's role in medicine. The study critically fills a lacuna in the existing literature by providing a valid and reliable instrument, termed as the Medical Artificial Intelligence Readiness Scale for Medical Students (MAIRS-MS), for measuring medical AI readiness. Through this, Karaca et al. are contributing not only to assessment but also to potential curriculum development and ensuring that medical students are well-equipped to navigate the evolving landscape of medical practice. The bridging of technical understanding with ethical foresight in the study underlines the importance of being well-rounded and AI literate in the medical field, going beyond a technology-only focus.

Laupichler et al. (2022) is a scoping literature review that sought to define the constructs of AI literacy in higher and adult education and explore its implications, given the pervasive influence of AI across various sectors. The review covers several important themes of AI literacy, including its definitions, evolution, and practical applications in educational settings. It attempts to provide a structured understanding of AI literacy, drawing from a variety of research and initiatives aimed at promoting this literacy among diverse target groups, particularly non-experts. One salient point in the article is its definition of AI literacy, which is framed as the ability to comprehend, utilise, and critically evaluate AI technologies without necessarily having the aptitude to develop AI models. Through its detailed discussion of various AI literacy programmes and their design, objectives, and target demographics, the authors provide a comprehensive view of the ongoing efforts to cultivate AI literacy and underscores the importance of adapting educational strategies to meet the needs of different learner groups. For more in-depth information about AI literacy research in the higher and adult education context, we recommend reading Laupichler et al.'s full article.

In their 2022 study, Markauskaite et al. challenged the notion of "AI literacy" and proposed the concept of "AI capabilities", arguing that the latter is more comprehensive as it positions AI competencies as an extension of learners' pre-existing skills. This perspective reflects a holistic approach and underscores three critical perspectives, cognitive, humanistic, and social, which collectively shift the emphasis from merely learning about AI to cultivating human cognitive capacities, values, and joint knowledge necessary for thriving in a world saturated with AI. This emphasis on an ecology of technology, cognition, social interaction, and values is a notable departure from narrow AI-centred narratives, advocating for more nuanced and inclusive dialogue. The methodological design of the study is also unique and collaborative, with 11 co-authors engaging in a polylogue, a semi-independent, and semi-joint written discussion to explore and articulate the capabilities essential in an AI-infused world. The discourse delves into conceptual and methodological frameworks for understanding, developing, and assessing these capabilities.

The study, however, isn't without its limitations. The exploration, although broad, seems to grapple with the challenge of pinning down a definitive set of necessary capabilities due to the diverse and sometimes unpredictable impacts of AI across different sectors and geo-graphical locales. Furthermore, while the authors' diverse disciplinary backgrounds help to enrich their discussions, it also highlights the variegated understanding and expectations of AI, which could potentially skew the identification and assessment of requisite capabilities. Still, the study is a significant stride towards fostering a multi-dimensional understanding of AI capabilities and promotes discourse that transcends technical literacy to include a more human-centric and societal approach. Through their dialogical knowledge-making approach, Markauskaite et al. highlight the critical need for interdisciplinary dialogues, and broader and richer conceptualisations of the capabilities essential for navigating the intricacies and potential disruptions of AI on global society.

Cetindamar et al. (2022) sought to define AI literacy in the context of organisational and digital workplaces. Based on their scoping review, AI literacy is conceptualised as a bundle of four core capabilities: technology-related, work-related, human-machine-related, and learning-related. The technology-related capabilities are foundational as AI literacy is rooted in technology, encompassing elements like data availability, technological infra-structure, and technical skills which are vital for utilising AI in various domains (e.g., one's ability to collect and analyse data). Work-related capabilities enable effective AI implemen-tation in the workplace, and includes a range of competencies such as ethical considera-tions for AI usage, critical thinking, problem solving, and communication skills, all of which support complex cognitive and decision-making tasks. Human-machine-related capabilities focuses on enhancing and leveraging the collaboration between humans and AI, emphasising the need for geometric reasoning, situational assessment, human-aware task planning, and increasing the explainability of AI to foster genuine human–machine interactions. Lastly, learning-related capabilities refer to the importance of continuous life-long learning to keep up with the rapidly evolving and volatile digital landscape. This entails fostering self-learning abilities, managerial skills, problem solving, and other soft skills to ensure responsible usage of digital technologies and facilitate skills development that align with the demands of the AI-driven world.

Finally, in a more recent article, Kong et al. (2023) defined AI literacy as the ability to understand the fundamental concepts of AI, its applications, and its implications for soci-ety. They designed and evaluated an AI literacy programme based on a multi-dimensional conceptual framework, which developed participants' conceptual understanding, literacy, empowerment, and ethical awareness.

Collectively, these studies help enrich the understanding of AI literacy, extending dia-logue beyond technical dimensions to also encompass psychological readiness, existing competencies, and the progressive evolution of AI literacy itself. Nonetheless, they expose the prevailing ambiguities and the multi-dimensional essence of this literacy, which could potentially hinder the formulation of a universally accepted framework or definition. The divergent yet complementary perspectives provided by these scholars thus underscore the richness of the discourse as well as the need for a multi-faceted approach in both research and educational practices for fostering AI literacy.

Consolidating key components identified in the literature with our own ongoing research, I propose a foundational framework for AI literacy in the next section, which aims to empower the typical individual in the burgeoning AI epoch.

2.5 The Definition of AI Literacy

AI literacy for the typical individual is the ability to comprehend, assess, interact with, and make informed decisions regarding artificial intelligence technologies in daily life. It involves understanding the basic principles of AI, recognising its applications, being aware of its ethical, social, and privacy implications, as well as understanding the impacts and values AI has on humans and human emotions, all while responsibly engaging with AI systems.

Cecilia KY Chan (2023)

Being able to navigate through the digitised world has become increasingly complex and ever more indispensable, necessitating every individual, irrespective of age or profession, to be literate in modern technologies and especially in AI. In a world where smartphones have become a prevalent tool for performing everyday tasks, and such as shopping and completing bureaucratic procedures, AI literacy – and the AI Literacy Framework – is crucial to empower people and help them navigate the AI-driven world in a competent and responsible manner.

This foundational AI Literacy Framework has five components.

1 **Understanding AI Concepts**: This component involves developing a grasp of the basic principles and mechanics of artificial intelligence. It enables individuals to comprehend how AI systems work, including concepts like machine learning, neural networks, and data processing. Understanding AI concepts helps individuals engage with AI technologies more effectively, making informed decisions and being aware of the capabilities and limitations of AI systems.

2 **Awareness of AI Applications**: This component focuses on recognising the diverse applications of AI in daily life. It involves understanding how AI is integrated into various domains, such as healthcare, education, finance, or entertainment. Being aware of AI applications allows individuals to seek out and utilise AI tools and services that can simplify tasks, enhance productivity, and improve their overall experiences within technology ecosystems.

3 **AI Affectiveness for Human Emotions**: This component emphasises the understanding of how AI can recognise, interpret, and respond to human emotions. It involves recognising the impact of emotional intelligence in AI systems and how they can adapt their behavior based on human emotional cues. Understanding AI affectiveness for human emotions enables individuals to engage in more empathetic and emotionally intelligent interactions with AI technologies.

4 **AI Safety and Security**: This component addresses the importance of considering the safety and security aspects of AI. It involves understanding the potential risks associated with AI systems, such as privacy breaches, algorithmic biases, or unintended consequences. Awareness of AI safety and security empowers individuals to protect their personal information, their digital footprint, advocate for responsible data practices, and make informed choices regarding the use of AI technologies.

5 **Responsible AI Usage**: The final component focuses on cultivating responsible and ethical AI usage. It entails recognising the limitations, biases, and ethical

considerations involved in AI systems. Individuals with responsible AI usage understand the importance of using AI technologies ethically and discerningly, avoiding overreliance or misuse. They actively engage in promoting fairness, transparency, and accountability in AI systems, fostering a balanced and informed relationship with technology

(Chan, 2024)

This comprehensive framework, derived from data and literature, not only bolsters an individual's proficiency in handling AI technologies, but also propels collective advancement towards a digitised future where technology is an ally, not an enigma. As emphasised, for the average person, a basic level of AI literacy is essential to navigate the increasingly AI-driven world. This level of literacy does not require in-depth technical knowledge but should include a general understanding of the framework's five aspects, as summarised in Table 2.2.

By nurturing this foundational level of AI literacy, the average individual can make better educated and informed decisions, partake in substantial discussions regarding AI and its impacts, and be conscious of the ramifications of AI technologies on their personal and professional lives.

Nonetheless, AI's relevance can be context-dependent. According to an article in Forbes by Talagala (2021), one of the Four C's of AI literacy is context, which stresses that the use, strengths, limitations, and suitability of AI can be extremely context-dependent. To effectively prepare the future workforce, it is therefore essential to not only explore generic AI literacy that all individuals should possess, but also any specific AI literacy requirements particular to and necessary for a person's role or profession (for example, for teachers). Stated differently, the AI literacy that an individual should possess encompasses both the foundational AI literacy level explained above (Table 2.2), as well as any AI literacy

Table 2.2 AI Literacy Framework Foundational for the Typical Individual

AI Literacy Framework (Foundational)	
AI concepts	Familiarity with basic terminology (e.g., artificial narrow/general/super intelligence, machine learning, machine intelligence and machine consciousness) to facilitate comprehension of how AI systems function.
AI applications	Awareness of common AI tools and applications in everyday life across diverse domains, such as virtual assistants, recommendation systems, and facial recognition.
AI Affectiveness for Human Emotions	Understanding how AI systems recognise and respond to human emotions, including the impacts and values of using AI systems.
AI safety and security	Awareness of potential security risks associated with AI applications, including possible threats to personal data and misuse of technology.
Responsible AI usage	Developing a sense of responsibility when using AI applications, understanding that AI systems may have limitations including incorrect information (thus requiring fact-checking), considering ethical implications, and questioning the reliability of AI-generated content.

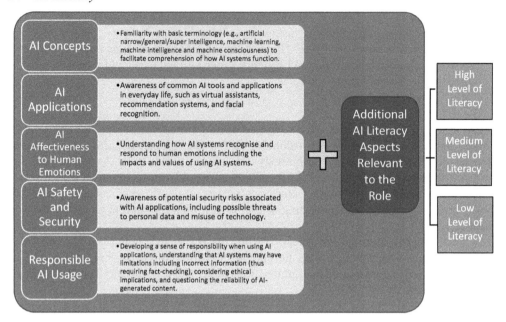

Figure 2.1 The Dynamic AI Literacy Model (DAILM) for Specific Roles.

requisites that are relevant to their role or profession (see Figure 2.1, the Dynamic AI Literacy Model for Specific Roles, the diagram is actual above not below).

2.5.1 Expanding the Fundamental AI Literacy Framework: Incorporating Role-Specific and Multilevel Considerations

Possessing foundational AI literacy, as discussed above, encapsulates having the vital understanding to navigate through the modern, technologically-driven world and is needed by every individual, irrespective of their professional milieu. As per the five aspects – concepts, applications, affectiveness for human emotions, safety and security, and responsible usage – the foundational framework does offer a broad panorama of AI awareness necessary for informed interactions and decision-making processes.

Delving deeper, one must also acknowledge that AI literacy requires further dissection, especially to consider how different professional contexts alter what individuals need to know and do when interacting with AI. Talagala (2021) emphasises this point of considering 'context,' which becomes even more salient when thinking about how different sectors may use and be affected by AI – for applications in healthcare for example, errors could be life-threatening, while in business, AI might be used to influence brand image and reputation.

The depth and specificity of knowledge required by different professionals inevitably varies. This means that a layered approach to AI literacy – where we consider the necessary level of literacy (high, medium, or low) in each of the framework's five components, as required for specific professions and roles – would enable the foundational framework to be more holistic and applicable. This expanded framework is the Dynamic AI Literacy Model (DAILM) for Specific Roles, as shown in Figure 2.1.

For instance, consider the difference between an AI software programmer and a general practitioner in the medical field. While the former will likely need a high level of literacy across all five aspects of the foundational framework, particularly in order to programme

AI systems themselves, the latter may not need the same level or depth of mastery across the five components. A general practitioner's needs and interactions with AI are different – perhaps they will focus primarily on a medium level in AI's applications, AI's affectiveness for human emotions, safety, and responsible usage. The practitioner would not need the same extent of in-depth knowledge about the creation and development of AI systems (i.e., a low level of literacy in this is adequate) to still be able to interact effectively and responsibly with the AI technologies they commonly encounter in their context.

2.5.1.1 A Case Study: AI Literacy Amongst Different Professionals

To elucidate the above, an AI software programmer would not only need to understand what AI systems are, but also actively innovate, develop, and review new AI systems and programmes. They would need a distinctly high level of literacy across the five aspects of the foundational framework, so that they can deep-dive into advanced concepts and applications, including algorithmic biases and data privacy laws. Their need to carefully make ethical considerations in system design and deployment further elevates their need for high literacy in recognising responsible AI usage and safety and security issues. In addition, programmers can develop AI systems that can understand and respond to human emotions. This can lead to more personalised and engaging user experiences, as the AI can adapt its behavior and responses based on the user's emotions, leading to improved user satisfaction and engagement.

Conversely, a medical general practitioner may primarily interact with AI through its integration into diagnostics, treatment planning, and patient data management. Therefore, while a medium to high literacy level in AI applications, affectiveness, safety, and data security would be needed to ensure accurate and ethical patient care, an in-depth understanding of AI concepts may not be as critical, thus only requiring a low to medium level of literacy in this aspect for this specific role.

The contrast between these two roles highlights a key consideration: the need for an additional factor in the foundational AI Literacy Framework, where specific aspects are highlighted and others de-emphasised, based on the professional context. Any new context or role-specific aspects can also be integrated as necessary, allowing flexibility for industries to each define AI literacy as per their standards of practice. Hence, developing a multi-faceted, level-based AI literacy framework, which incorporates the five core aspects and introduces role-specific additions or expansions, would significantly enhance the applicability and value of AI literacy across different professional fields.

In sum, while the foundational AI Literacy Framework lays a robust groundwork for general understanding and engagement with AI technologies, a multi-dimensional, context-specific, and level-based extension of its five aspects is imperative to truly cater to the varied, nuanced needs of different professionals in their respective fields. The proposed enhanced framework, the DAILM for Specific Roles, not only aligns with the multi-dimensionality of real-world AI applications, but also fortifies AI users' capacity to interact, innovate, and ethically engage with these technologies in a manner that is pragmatically embedded in their specific professional context.

2.5.2 AI Literacy for Teachers

As mentioned in the last section, a foundational literacy in AI – covering the key areas of AI concepts, applications, affectiveness for human emotions, safety and security, and responsible usage – is vital for all individuals. University teachers should possess at least a medium level of proficiency in technical AI application, allowing them to better understand and interact with AI technologies for teaching, learning, and research.

This includes practical skills in utilising AI tools and applications relevant to their field. A good foundation in AI enables teachers to employ data analysis techniques, engage with automated assessment systems, and create personalised learning experiences. This technical backbone is essential for them to confidently navigate the AI-integrated landscape of education, and ensure that they can leverage AI to enhance teaching and learning. In addition, a further extension of AI literacy needs to be detailed, given teachers' influential role in shaping both educational experiences and ethical AI discourse. Based on the DAILM model, the additional literacy aspects for university teacher are expected to be: (1) Pedagogical Innovation; (2) Ethical, Social, and Policy Awareness; (3) AI for Social Good; (4) Career and Industry Alignment; (5) Continuous Professional Development; (6) Research and Scholarly Engagement; and (7) Responsible AI Usage and Development. These aspects of AI literacy proposed to be necessary for university teachers are discussed further as below.

1 Pedagogical Innovation

- Integrating AI within curriculum design and delivery.
- Employing AI for automated assessment and feedback.
- Leveraging AI to foster personalised and adaptive learning experiences.
  AI literacy for university teachers extends to the ability to innovate pedagogy utilising AI technologies. This entails integrating AI within curriculum design and delivery, employing AI for automated assessment and feedback, redesigning assessment to embrace AI and subsequently promote and assess higher-order outcomes, and leveraging AI to foster personalised and adaptive learning experiences. By harnessing AI's capabilities, teachers can create more engaging, interactive, and tailored educational opportunities, facilitating better experiences for students, as well as deepening their understanding and retention of material.

2 Ethical, Social, and Policy Awareness

- Teaching and promoting ethical AI practices.
- Understanding the social and policy implications of implementing AI in education.
- Engaging in discussions about issues of biases, privacy, and inclusivity in AI.
  University teachers need to be adept at navigating the ethical, social, and policy dimensions of embracing AI in education. This encompasses teaching and promoting ethical AI practices, understanding implications of AI on university policy, and engaging in critical discussions about issues of biases, privacy, and inclusivity in AI. Teachers play a pivotal role in shaping the ethical framework in which AI is understood and utilised in academia, making this aspect of AI literacy crucial.

3 AI for Social Good

- Utilising AI to address real-world challenges through social impact projects.
- Advocating for responsible AI policies and practices.
- Fostering community outreach and global engagement through AI.
  The notion of utilising AI for social good should be integral to a university teacher's AI literacy, particularly for those involved in designing, implementing, and overseeing experiential learning experiences such as community service. This includes

considering how AI can be employed in social impact projects to address real-world challenges, advocating for responsible AI policies and practices, and engaging in community outreach and global engagement initiatives. By fostering a mindset of social responsibility and ethical AI usage, university teachers can inspire students to leverage AI for positive societal change, aligning technological advancements with humanitarian goals.

4 Career and Industry Alignment

- Aligning curriculum with emerging industry trends and AI applications.
- Preparing students for AI-related careers.
- Building partnerships with industry professionals to bridge gaps between academia and industry.

    Aligning academic pursuits with emerging industry trends and AI applications is crucial for preparing students for their careers, especially if they will take on AI-related jobs. University teachers should build partnerships with industry professionals to bridge the academia–industry gap, ensuring that the curriculum remains relevant and aligned with real-world implementations and uses of AI. This alignment also facilitates opportunities for experiential learning, internships, and career counselling, aiding students to transition smoothly into professional environments.

5 Continuous Professional Development

- Engaging in lifelong learning to stay updated on evolving AI technologies.
- Participating in professional development opportunities related to AI in education.
- Encouraging a culture of professional growth among colleagues and students.

    The rapidly evolving nature of AI requires a commitment to continuous professional development among university teachers. Engaging in lifelong learning, participating in professional development opportunities related to incorporating AI in education, participating in relevant policymaking efforts, and fostering a culture of professional growth are key to staying updated on evolving AI technologies and methodologies. This commitment to continuous learning also models such behaviours for students, further promoting lifelong learning and future-readiness to the next generations.

6 Research and Scholarly Engagement

- Employing AI in academic research and scholarly activities.
- Exploring interdisciplinary collaborations to drive AI innovation in academia.
- Contributing to the growing body of knowledge on the intersection of AI and education.

    Employing AI in academic research and scholarly activities can significantly enhance the research process. University teachers should explore interdisciplinary collaborations to drive AI innovation in academia, contributing to the growing body of knowledge on the intersection of AI and education. Engaging with AI in research also enables university teachers to stay at the forefront of AI advancements, enriching both their teaching practices and academic contributions.

7 Responsible AI Usage and Development

- Developing a sense of responsibility when interacting with AI.
- Encouraging responsible AI usage among students and colleagues.

   Fostering a sense of responsibility when interacting with AI, among both themselves and their students, is essential for university teachers. This includes understanding the limitations and potential biases inherent in AI systems, promoting responsible AI usage, and possibly engaging in the development or refining of practices and even AI tools to better uphold inclusivity and ethical standards. By cultivating a culture of responsibility and ethical engagement with AI, university teachers can significantly contribute to a more conscientious AI-augmented educational landscape.

Utilising the DAILM model to enhance AI literacy for university teachers is crucial, though the level of literacy they should achieve for each of these additional dimensions is still subject to deliberation. How deeply teachers should master these areas will largely depend on their willingness to integrate AI into their practices, and the extent to which they have already or will do so. While there may be debate about whether these additional aspects already exist within the existing five of the foundational AI Literacy Framework, the focus of the discourse going forward should continue to examine the different levels and depth of AI literacy needed for their role. Inclusion of the above additional dimensions of AI literacy for university teachers will not only empower them to leverage AI in a transformative manner, but also position them as fundamental actors in setting the standards for AI practices in both educational settings and the broader society.

2.6   Advantages and Disadvantages of Developing AI Literacy

Building upon the foundational understanding of AI literacy explored in the preceding sections, it is imperative to next examine the advantages of nurturing this competence in our progressively digital world. We will now turn to the specific benefits of equipping individuals and society at large with this literacy, the discussions of which can also support teachers and policymakers in making informed decisions about resources and policy. The subsequent sections will unpack these various advantages, providing a comprehensive overview that further substantiates the integral role of AI literacy in contemporary and future contexts.

Advantages of Developing AI Literacy

1 **Informed Decision-Making:**
   Developing AI literacy enhances an individual's ability to make informed decisions. Understanding how AI systems work will allow the individual to also make sense of and appraise any recommendations, predictions, and decisions made by these systems. This is crucial across various sectors as well as in daily life, where algorithms shape how content and information are disseminated and presented.

2 **Ethical Use and Development:**
   With AI literacy also comes the ability to recognise and address the ethical implications of AI technologies. This includes understanding and mitigating issues related to bias in data and information, privacy, and taking accountability as users. An AI-literate individual or team can ensure that their use and interactions with AI technologies are fair, unbiased, and will safeguard user data and rights; they may also go further and lend a hand in developing AI tools and software that uphold these standards as well.

3 **Enhanced Employability:**
In the job market, AI literacy is becoming an increasingly valuable asset. For roles in many sectors, from marketing to healthcare, understanding and skills in effectively utilising AI can be a considerable advantage. By being able to navigate through and efficiently use technology-enabled systems, individuals can enhance their overall workplace competence and performance.

4 **Innovation and Creativity:**
Understanding AI opens doors to innovation and creativity, paving the way to leverage AI to solve complex problems in various fields, including medicine, engineering, and finance. AI-literate individuals who understand how AI systems work are better equipped to seek out and explore new ways to apply these technologies, creating novel solutions and products.

5 **Critical Engagement:**
Being AI literate allows individuals to critically engage with technology, questioning its applications and implications. It enables people to participate in essential discussions and debates about how AI is used in our societies and how it should be regulated. This will help to ensure that technologies are developed and implemented in ways that are beneficial for all.

6 **Digital Citizenship:**
In an age where numerous aspects of life and governance are shifting onto online platforms, AI literacy fosters responsible and informed digital citizenship. Understanding AI helps individuals to interact wisely and ethically with digital platforms, recognise misinformation, and engage productively in online environments.

As we journey through the vast and still much-uncharted world of AI, it is clear that getting to grips with AI literacy is not just helpful, but crucial, particularly for the upcoming generations. As our world becomes increasingly digitalised, learning about AI is now a must in our daily, educational, and professional lives. AI is more than a tool – it is a force that changes the way we interact, create, and think.

However, developing AI literacy across the board does come with its own set of challenges that need careful thought and strategic planning. One major hurdle is how resource-intensive AI education can be. Making sure educational programmes are both in-depth enough and accessible will require a lot of time, money, and expertise, putting a strain on resources especially in areas or institutions that may not have a lot to spare (West, 2018). Additionally, there is a risk of becoming overly dependent on AI, which may consequently result in the subtle and valuable aspects of human decision-making being overlooked or ignored (Bostrom, 2014; Chan & Hu, 2023). An example of this is if an individual over-relies on GPS for navigation and ignores developing their natural sense of direction and spatial awareness; another is if in education, a student relies too much on GenAI tools to summarise and write, eventually losing their fundamental ability and skills to do so themselves.

At a further layer, differences in socio-economic status also stand as a considerable obstacle for achieving universal AI literacy. There is a real risk of increasing the "digital divide", where those with fewer resources and greater difficultly in accessing technology get left behind, unable to fully engage with or benefit from our digital world (Eubanks, 2018). Furthermore, because AI is always evolving, it requires a culture of constant learning and adaptation. While instilling such a culture is essentially a good thing, it can also bring pressures and challenges, such as in keeping up with the continual influx of technological advancements (Crawford & Calo, 2016).

Finally, potential misconduct and security vulnerabilities are also looming concerns. It is possible that self-serving individuals may use their mastery of AI literacy to manipulate or exploit AI systems, introducing a whole range of ethical and practical challenges (Zuboff, 2019). For example, hackers may manipulate AI algorithms or data to their advantage; there may also be risks of identity theft or scams carried out through the use of advanced deep-fake AI technologies.

Thus, as we work towards establishing universal AI literacy, combining its benefits and navigating through the challenges, it is key to ensure that we do so in ways that are balanced, inclusive, and critically reflective. Incorporating AI literacy as an essential part of our future will demand a united, thoughtful, and ethical approach to ensure AI's benefits can be accessed by all and that its challenges are carefully and effectively managed.

2.7   Conclusions

AI literacy, as we have explored throughout this chapter, isn't just a technical skill – it is vital for us to navigate effectively through our increasingly AI-driven world, and especially in higher education. From making informed decisions to understanding the ripple effects of technology in our lives and societies, becoming AI-literate shapes our approach to ethical, strategic, and innovative thinking. The journey through the different domains of AI literacy is not simply about just understanding mechanics; it further involves guiding the ethical and inclusive development and application of AI itself, in our daily lives and educational systems. The Foundational AI Literacy Framework serves as vital guide in this journey, offering structure in navigating the complexities of AI and emphasising the essential components of understanding AI concepts, its applications, affectiveness for human emotions, safety, and responsible usage. Meanwhile, the Dynamic AI Literacy Model (DAILM) takes it a step further by integrating a role-specific approach, recognising the multi-faceted interactions and ethical considerations across various professional fields. Together, these frameworks not only fortify general and professional AI literacy, but also ensure that individuals and professionals interact with AI technologies in a manner that is informed, ethical, and deeply embedded in their specific contexts. The synthesis of foundational knowledge and role-specific literacy via the DAILM shapes a future where technology is not an enigma but an ally, safeguarding ethical, innovative, and responsible progression in the AI-driven era.

Questions to Ponder

- Considering the rapid evolution of AI technologies and applications, how can the AI Literacy Framework and DAILM remain relevant and adapt to emerging trends, tools, and ethical considerations?
- How can the DAILM be extended to cater to specific professional roles that may emerge in the future, ensuring that it is not only applicable to current professions but also adaptable to future developments in the job market?

- How might the AI Literacy Framework and DAILM be adapted or modified to address cultural, legal, and socio-economic variations in AI literacy and application needs across different global contexts?
- How might the AI Literacy Framework be integrated into educational curricula at various levels (from primary to tertiary education) to foster a future workforce that is adept and ethical when navigating AI technologies?
- How can the effectiveness and impact of the AI Literacy Framework and DAILM be assessed and measured across diverse populations and professional fields?

Personal Reflection

Imagine the future where your level of AI literacy guides your choices and opportunities. How would our understanding (or misunderstanding) of AI technology shape our decisions and social interactions? As we look towards a future where new generations will have AI naturally integrated into their lives, how will they navigate a world filled with such technological wonders as well as new ethical, social, and maybe even political challenges? Will we have to constantly update our literacy in AI in order to continue having a place and role in society, and not become replaced? Is it the case that the more we invent, the more we have to sacrifice?

References

Bloom, B. S., Engelhart, M. D., Furst, E. J., Hill, W. H., & Krathwohl, D. R. (1956). *Taxonomy of educational objectives: The classification of educational goals. Handbook 1: Cognitive domain.* Longmans.

Bostrom, N. (2014). *Superintelligence: Paths, dangers, strategies.* Oxford University Press.

Brynjolfsson, E., & McAfee, A. (2014). *The second machine age: Work, progress, and prosperity in a time of brilliant technologies.* W.W. Norton & Company.

Buckingham, D. (1993). *Children talking television: The making of television literacy.* Falmer Press.

Bughin, J., Hazan, E., Lund, S., Dahlström, P., Wiesinger, A., & Subramaniam, A. (2018). Skill shift: Automation and the future of the workforce. *McKinsey Global Institute, 1,* 3–84.

Casal-Otero, L., Catala, A., Fernández-Morante, C., Taboada, M., Cebreiro, B., & Barro, S. (2023). AI literacy in K-12: A systematic literature review. *International Journal of STEM Education, 10,* 29. https://doi.org/10.1186/s40594-023-00418-7

Cetindamar, D., Kitto, K., Wu, M., Zhang, Y., Abedin, B., & Knight, S. (2022). Explicating AI literacy of employees at digital workplaces. *IEEE Transactions on Engineering Management.* https://doi.org/10.1109/TEM.2021.3138503

Chan, C. K. Y. (2021). *Information literacy.* Holistic Competency & Virtue Education. Retrieved October 10, 2023, from https://www.have.hku.hk/information-literacy

Chan, C. K. Y. (2023). *AI literacy.* Holistic Competency & Virtue Education. Retrieved October 10, 2023, from https://www.have.hku.hk/ai-literacy

Chan, C. K. Y. (2024). AI Literacy. AI in Education. Retrieved January 1, 2024, from https://aied.talic.hku.hk/ai-literacy/

Chan, C. K. Y., & Hu, W. (2023). Students' voices on generative AI: perceptions, benefits, and challenges in higher education. *International Journal of Educational Technology in Higher Education, 20,* 43. https://doi.org/10.1186/s41239-023-00411-8

Crawford, K., & Calo, R. (2016). There is a blind spot in AI research. *Nature, 538*(7625), 311–313. https://doi.org/10.1038/538311a

Eubanks, V. (2018). *Automating inequality: How high-tech tools profile, police, and punish the poor*. St. Martin's Press.

Gilster, P. (1997). *Digital literacy*. Wiley Computer Publishing.

Huitt, W. (2011). Bloom et al.'s taxonomy of the cognitive domain. *Educational psychology interactive*. Valdosta State University. Retrieved October 10, 2023, from http://www.edpsycinteractive.org/topics/cogsys/bloom.html

Kahn, K., & Winters, N. (2017). Child-friendly programming interfaces to AI cloud services. In *Data Driven Approaches in Digital Education: 12th European Conference on Technology Enhanced Learning, EC-TEL 2017, Tallinn, Estonia, September 12–15, 2017, Proceedings 12* (pp. 566–570). Springer International Publishing.

Kandlhofer, M., Steinbauer, G., Hirschmugl-Gaisch, S., & Huber, P. (2016, October). Artificial intelligence and computer science in education: From kindergarten to university. In *2016 IEEE Frontiers in Education Conference (FIE)* (pp.1–9). IEEE.

Karaca, O., Çalışkan, S. A., & Demir, K. (2021). Medical artificial intelligence readiness scale for medical students (MAIRS-MS)–development, validity and reliability study. *BMC Medical Education, 21*, 112. https://doi.org/10.1186/s12909-021-02546-6

Kong, S., Cheung, W. M., & Zhang, G. (2021). Evaluation of an artificial intelligence literacy course for university students with diverse study backgrounds. *Computers and Education: Artificial Intelligence, 2*, 100026. https://doi.org/10.1016/j.caeai.2021.100026

Kong, S., Cheung, W. M., & Zhang, G. (2023). Evaluating an artificial intelligence literacy programme for developing university students' conceptual understanding, literacy, empowerment and ethical awareness. *Educational Technology & Society, 26*(1), 16–30. https://doi.org/10.30191/ETS.202301_26(1).0002

Kong, S. C., & Zhang, G. (2021). A conceptual framework for designing artificial intelligence literacy programmes for educated citizens. In S. C. Kong, Q. Wang, R. Huang, Y. Li, & T.-C. Hsu (Eds.), *Conference Proceedings (English Paper) of the 25th Global Chinese Conference on Computers in Education (GCCCE 2021)* (pp. 11–15). Centre for Learning, Teaching and Technology, The Education University of Hong Kong.

Konishi, Y. (2015). What is needed for AI literacy? Priorities for the Japanese Economy in 2016. Retrieved October 10, 2023, from https://www.rieti.go.jp/en/columns/s16_0014.html

Laupichler, M. C., Aster, A., Schirch, J., & Raupach, T. (2022). Artificial intelligence literacy in higher and adult education: A scoping literature review. *Computers and Education: Artificial Intelligence, 3*, 100101. https://doi.org/10.1016/j.caeai.2022.100101

Liu, S., & Xie, X. (2021). AI quality cultivation and application ability training for normal university students. In *2021 7th Annual International Conference on Network and Information Systems for Computers (ICNISC)*. IEEE. https://doi.org/10.1109/ICNISC54316.2021.00030

Livingstone, S. (2004). What is media literacy? *Intermedia, 32*(3). 18–20.

Long, D., & Magerko, B. (2020). What is AI literacy? Competencies and design considerations. In *Proceedings of the 2020 CHI Conference on Human Factors in Computing Systems* (pp. 1–16). Association for Computing Machinery.

Markauskaite, L., Marrone, R., Poquet, O., Knight, S., Martinez-Maldonado, R., Howard, S., Tondeur, J., De Laat, M., Shum, S. B., Gašević, D., & Siemens, G. (2022). Rethinking the entwinement between artificial intelligence and human learning: What capabilities do learners need for a world with AI? *Computers and Education: Artificial Intelligence, 3*, 100056. https://doi.org/10.1016/j.caeai.2022.100056

Ng, D. T. K., Leung, J. K. L., Chu, S. K. W., & Qiao, M.S. (2021). Conceptualizing AI literacy: An exploratory review. *Computers and Education: Artificial Intelligence, 2*, 100041. https://doi.org/10.1016/j.caeai.2021.100041

Pool, C. R. (1997). A new digital literacy: A conversation with Paul Gilster. *Educational Leadership, 55*(3), 6–11.

Talagala, N. (2021, April 4). *The four Cs of AI literacy: Building the workforce of the future*. Forbes. Retrieved October 10, 2023, from https://www.forbes.com/sites/nishatalagala/2021/04/04/the-four-cs-of-ai-literacy-building-the-workforce-of-the-future/?sh=926c58213fbc

Vinuesa, R., Azizpour, H., Leite, I., Balaam, M., Dignum, V., Domisch, S., Felländer, A., Langhans, S.D., Tegmark, M., & Nerini, F. F. (2020). The role of artificial intelligence in achieving the sustainable development goals. *Nature Communications*, *11*(1), 233. https://doi.org/10.1038/s41467-019-14108-y

West, D. M. (2018). *The future of work: Robots, AI, and automation*. Brookings Institution Press.

West, D. M., & Allen, J. R. (2018, April 24). *How artificial intelligence is transforming the world*. Brookings. Retrieved October 10, 2023, from https://www.brookings.edu/research/how-artificial-intelligence-is-transforming-the-world/

Wing, J. M. (2006). Computational thinking. *Communications of the ACM*, *49*(3), 33–35. https://doi.org/10.1145/1118178.1118215

Wolff, A., Gooch, D., Cavero Montaner, J. J., Rashid, U., & Kortuem, G. (2016). Creating an understanding of data literacy for a data-driven society. *The Journal of Community Informatics*, *12*(3), 9–26. https://doi.org/10.15353/joci.v12i3.3275

Wolfram, S. (2017, May 11). *Machine learning for middle schoolers*. Stephen Wolfram Writings. https://writings.stephenwolfram.com/2017/05/machine-learning-for-middle-schoolers/

Zuboff, S. (2019). *The age of surveillance capitalism: The fight for a human future at the new frontier of power*. Profile Books.

Zurkowski, P. (1974). *The information service environment relationships and priorities. Related paper No. 5*. National Commission on Libraries and Information Science, Washington, D.C., National Program for Library and Information Services. Retrieved October 10, 2023, from https://files.eric.ed.gov/fulltext/ED100391.pdf

3 Strengths and Weaknesses in Embracing ChatGPT in Curriculum Design

It seems that GenAI's abilities go beyond advanced predictive text. It can reason, and relate concepts in complex ways. Yet it sometimes struggles with simple tasks. Maybe it isn't showing deep understanding, but rather mimicking human argument patterns through the data it trained from. It might be more of an 'accidental intelligence' than 'artificial intelligence'. Perhaps many humans also employ similar techniques.

Tom Colloton

3.1 Introduction

The advancement of humanity will undoubtedly involve leveraging the benefits that Artificial Intelligence (AI) tools and technologies offer, and, more specifically, leveraging these benefits as soon as they emerge, including those offered now by generative AI (GenAI). Simply put, we need to utilise all available intellectual resources to achieve the progress we desire. This is especially important for addressing significant global challenges such as environmental destruction from deforestation, the overexploitation of the Earth's resources, the detrimental impact of technology such as 'forever chemicals', and global warming.

Numerous tools and technologies have emerged over the last 20 years, which we now use in our daily lives. Typically, we quickly adopt these tools once they become accessible and affordable. This is particularly evident for mobile technology and the wide array of tools that accompany it (Bhavnani et al., 2016; Brown & Chalmers, 2003; Law et al., 2018). AI has already been seamlessly integrated into these tools in various forms, from biometrics for security and voice recognition for text messaging, to translation technology like Google Translate and search engine technologies like Google or Bing (Malhotra, 2020). Mobile applications, including banking apps, e-commerce platforms like Amazon, and streaming services like Netflix, also have built-in AI functionalities, designed to enhance user safety and convenience while offering tailored product recommendations to improve user experience.

AI's presence is ubiquitous. For instance, when reaching out to public services companies, we are often greeted by an AI-powered customer service bot intended to streamline our experience. However, the current level of AI encountered by the general public may not always meet our expectations, leading to occasional frustrations, such as from dull and repetitive interactions with utility bots, or the occasional off-mark product recommendations from online retailers. This brings us to the questions at the heart of this chapter's rationale: To what extent can AI be beneficial in our curriculum? Do we know its strengths and weaknesses?

The goal of this chapter is to guide and enhance our understanding towards a more realistic awareness of text-based GenAI's capabilities in education, providing an overview of the

DOI: 10.4324/9781003459026-3

opportunities and threats that AI raises for education. In this chapter, each strength and weakness of GenAI is discussed with an example related to education, in order to provide a comprehensive understanding of their capabilities. The examples also offer readers an opportunity to try out and gain insight into the capabilities and limitations of various tools. While ChatGPT is used in many of these examples given its current popularity, it is important to acknowledge that there are other tools with comparable abilities and potential impact.

3.2 ChatGPT and GenAI Text Tools

3.2.1 *What Is ChatGPT?*

ChatGPT, developed by OpenAI, is a powerful large language model and functions as a text-based generative AI tool. Leveraging advanced GPT architecture, ChatGPT has the capacity to understand and generate human-like responses in natural language, making it a robust tool in diverse applications across different industries. Built upon a deep neural network that has been trained on a wide-ranging corpus of text, ChatGPT can engage in conversation, create cohesive and informative text, and answer queries by predicting the most probable subsequent words or sentences given an input (Leggatt et al., 2023).

This model, although being trained extensively on data, does not actually know the specifics of the exact documents used in its training set, and does not have the ability to access or retrieve personal data unless explicitly required or provided in a conversation. Chapter 6 offers more detailed information regarding the technical aspects of how ChatGPT works.

3.2.2 *Common Functions of ChatGPT*

ChatGPT can perform a variety of functions, including engaging in dynamic conversations, answering queries, writing essays, summarising long documents, generating creative content like poems or stories in a particular style or format, synthesising informative text in a structured manner, translating languages, simulating characters for video games, and even generating programming codes. It is also capable of more carrying out advanced data analysis tasks. For example, it can interpret sets of data and explain the results of a complex data analysis, making it easier for non-experts to understand. Its flexible and adaptable text generation capabilities means it can also be configured or fine-tuned for specific applications, allowing it to cater to niche requirements and generate text that aligns with particular domain specifics or linguistic styles.

One of the latest features of ChatGPT (based on the most updated version as of 25 September 2023) is the ability to browse the web using Bing. This allows the model to pull in current information from the web and provide more up-to-date responses. It can also use plugins to extend its capabilities, including its new voice capability. In addition, DALL-E 3 has also recently been integrated into ChatGPT, allowing it to generate images from text descriptions provided by users (OpenAI, 2023).

Browse with Bing: ChatGPT can now access and process information from the Internet through Bing search, which allows it to generate more accurate and up-to-date responses. This can be particularly useful in curriculum design as it allows for real-time access to the latest information, ensuring that educational content is up to date. For example, in a course on current events, ChatGPT can use Browse with Bing to refer to recent news articles relevant to the topic being discussed.

Advanced Data Analysis: As mentioned, ChatGPT can perform complex data analysis tasks, such as identifying trends, patterns, and outliers. This can be used to generate insights into student learning data and other educational datasets. In addition, in a course setting, for instance in statistics or data sciences, students can input raw data into ChatGPT and the model would generate an analysis of that data, identifying similarities, and other key points of interest.

Plugins: Plugins are additional features that can be added to ChatGPT to enhance its functionality. In terms of curriculum design, plugins could be developed to cater to specific educational needs. For example, a plugin could be created for language learning to provide translations, definitions, and language practice exercises.

Voice Capability: The voice capability in ChatGPT, facilitated by OpenAI's Whisper, allows users to interact with the AI system using voice commands. This functionality is currently restricted to ChatGPT's mobile apps on iOS and Android platforms. Users have the option to activate this feature in their settings and select from five distinct output voices, each with its own tone and character. This addition extends the mode of interaction with ChatGPT beyond text-to-voice inputs, broadening the scope of user interaction. With the voice feature being mobile-centric, users have the flexibility to engage in verbal dialogues with ChatGPT while on the move, which could be handy in situations like seeking assistance with pronunciation during discussions.

DALL-E 3: DALL-E 3 is an AI model that generates images from textual descriptions, and is now integrated into ChatGPT. This allows ChatGPT to generate text-to-image content such as diagrams, charts, and illustrations. For example, in an architecture course, students could use DALL-E 3 to create architectural models based on specific design briefs with specified backgrounds and landscapes.

Each of these functions offer unique benefits for curriculum design in higher education. By integrating AI into the learning process, educators can create more dynamic and interactive learning experiences that cater to a wide range of learning styles and learner needs.

3.3   GenAI Tools and Its Strengths and Potential Opportunities in Higher Education

GenAI tools empower higher education institutions with dynamically generated content, assisting in research and fostering engaging learning environments. Its main strength lies in its ability to produce diverse and contextually relevant content in real time, aiding both educators in their teaching methods and students in their learning processes. By analysing vast datasets, AI systems can delve deep into topics to provide comprehensive content coverage. Moreover, they are highly scalable, allowing institutions, large or small, to benefit from their capabilities. The interactive and user-centric nature of text-based GenAI facilitates personalised learning experiences, making information more accessible and digestible for students. This section will use examples from ChatGPT's GPT-4 to illustrate opportunities in GenAI, viz,

1   User-Centric Design
2   Humanistic Conversational Style
3   Variability
4   Multimodal Capability
5   Scalability
6   Customisability

7 Comprehensive Coverage in Breadth and Depth
8 Contextual Relevance
9 Multilingual Support
10 Appropriateness of Topics
11 Code Generation Capability

3.3.1 User-Centric Design

The User-Centric Design characteristic of GenAI refers to the systematic approach of placing the user at the core of its design and development processes. User-centric design applications are easy to understand, simple to operate, and, above all, user-friendly (Chow, 2023). It involves the careful crafting of interfaces, functionalities, and processes that are inherently intuitive, thereby reducing the cognitive load on users and enabling them to interact with the system effortlessly. In GenAI, user-centric design translates to algorithms and models that not only produce high-quality outputs, but also ensure that the interaction, input methods, and result interpretations are straightforward and accessible to a wide range of users, regardless of their technical proficiency. The goal of a user-centric design is to ensure that advanced AI technology is accessible and comprehensible to all. Figures 3.1 and 3.2 show the user-friendly dialogue box of ChatGPT and Bard.

From the user's standpoint, they can utilise natural language, text-based interfaces to interact with GenAI tools, often in conjunction with voice-based, image-based, gesture-based, and video-based interfaces. The user prompts the GenAI system with a question, comment, or statement, and receives a response from the system. This simple and easy-to-operate interaction style allows users to quickly understand how to use the tool,

Figure 3.1 A Screenshot of ChatGPT by OpenAI, Note the User-Friendly Dialogue Box, Identical to Many Popular Messenger Applications.

Figure 3.2 A Screenshot of Bard by Google, This Version of Bard, also Allows Voice-Input.

and derive value from it almost instantly. This type of interaction is familiar in educational settings, resembling a dialogue between a student (the user) and a tutor or teacher (the ChatGPT system). It is worth noting that the capability to interact with text is not only important but also practical, as we don't always desire vocalising thoughts (Long, 2018), which is also one of the reasons for the popularity of many text-based messaging tools. According to studies (e.g., Edison Software, 2019; Long, 2018), both Gen-Z (those born between 1997 and 2012) and Millennials (those born between 1981 and 1996) exhibit a preference for communication through texting over talking.

3.3.2　*Humanistic Conversational Style*

A humanistic conversational style in GenAI refers to the system's ability to communicate in a manner that resonates with human empathy, understanding, and natural flow, creating a more relatable and engaging user experience. Users may find themselves conversing with tone, emphasis, and emotion in a way that feels more natural, as if speaking with a human on the other end of the line (Browne, 2023; Shankland, 2023). In contrast to old-style AI chatbots, which were typically rule-based or with pre-programmed responses and limited in the ability to generate varied and complex responses, GenAI tools such as ChatGPT can create their own responses and outputs.

This opens up new possibilities for human interaction with technology, including the capability for more natural and engaging conversations with AI-powered chatbots or virtual assistants. In higher education, this characteristic ensures that AI-driven platforms can facilitate supportive, intuitive, and contextually relevant interactions with users. For example, a GenAI with a humanistic conversational style might be utilised in a virtual learning environment to provide students with academic guidance. The AI, seeing the input from student stresses or inquiries, could offer supportive feedback, relevant resources, and timely advice, much like a human tutor. It would understand and process natural language inquiries, responding in a manner that is both informative and affectively resonant, thereby fostering an educational environment that is not only intellectually stimulating but also constructively supportive. This anthropomorphic interaction style has the potential to significantly enhance online learning experiences, providing students with a virtual companion that assists and

Table 3.1 Using ChatGPT GPT-4, Demonstrating the Humanistic Conversational Capability and also Its Ability to Be in a Role (i.e. a Tutor)

User	You are a tutor in a university. Your duties include teaching and mentoring undergraduate students on both their academic, social and personal aspects in the university. You will mainly listen and converse with them. Do not response after this. Wait for a student to converse with you.
ChatGPT	Understood. I'm ready to listen and converse with any student who approaches me.
User	I am a business 2nd year undergraduate student, I wonder what course I should major next year. I am favouring accounting, but I am not good at it. What do you suggest?
ChatGPT	Thank you for sharing your thoughts with me! Choosing a major can be a pivotal decision and it's completely normal to have uncertainties about it.
	It's interesting that you're leaning towards accounting despite feeling that you're not particularly good at it. This could be an opportunity to challenge yourself and enhance your skills in that area if you're passionate about it. However, it's also essential to weigh the level of commitment and interest you have in pursuing and improving in it, against the challenges that it might present.

understands them throughout their academic journey (Chan & Lee, 2023). Furthermore, it encourages more organic and authentic communication, which can enhance user engagement and satisfaction. This is particularly vital in education, where student engagement is crucial for effective learning and retention. Table 3.1 demonstrates the humanistic conversational capability and also its ability to be in a role.

Another feature of GenAI is its ability to handle responses effectively. With the example of ChatGPT, when faced with unclear or broad requests, it does not usually ask for clarification or indicate that it cannot provide information due to the vague nature of the question. Instead, it attempts to provide the best answer it can, offering some context in its response to help users refine their requests or prompts if necessary. This creates a smoother and more enjoyable conversational flow, bypassing the frustrating problems we may have encountered with older AI technologies that needed more information or required question rephrasing before providing any potentially valuable answers. Responses from GenAI tools can be beneficial in enhancing student learning. First, students will learn how to better articulate their questions and provide more accurate directions. Second, students often learn from these responses and gain additional information to improve their self-learning.

3.3.3 *Variability*

The variability of GenAI means that asking the same platform the same question twice does not always yield the same response. Each interaction is slightly different due to the way GenAI works, leading to varied outcomes (Weisz et al., 2023). This may surprise some users, as computers and AI are often expected to be highly consistent. However, this variability is intentional in design, aimed at making interactions with the AI more dynamic and less deterministic.

Variability is like talking to different people about a given topic. Usually, if we ask the same person the same question over and over, we will get a response that is exactly the same or very similar. However, posing the same question to various people will likely elicit different responses, some slightly different, others more significantly so. However, while GenAI can produce varied responses, it is also designed to maintain a degree of consistency, particularly in providing accurate and reliable information. The variability mainly originates from the expression of information or in the inclusion of additional context, rather than the core message or accuracy of the information provided. In other words, although responses might be formulated or phrased differently, they should all remain relevant to the input prompt.

3.3.4 *Multimodal Capability*

The multimodal capability of GenAI refers to the system's ability to understand, interpret, and generate content across various forms of input and output, such as text, image, voice, and even video (Google Cloud Blog, 2023; OpenAI, 2023). This ensures a versatile and adaptive user experience as the AI is able to communicate and interact through multiple modes of interaction. In the context of higher education, this becomes profoundly impactful. For instance, a GenAI tool with multimodal capabilities can assist students in various ways: it can interpret a student's verbal question, analyse a related image, and provide a text-based answer (Lim et al., 2023; Vartiainen & Tedre, 2023). Moreover, during virtual classes or study sessions, the AI can comprehend a spoken question, retrieve relevant textual data from educational resources, convert it into a concise summary, and then present it in an easily comprehensible visual format, such as an infographic or a short video. In research activities, it can process textual data to generate relevant visual graphs or even transform data across modalities to cater to different learning preferences and needs. The flexibility offered by multimodal GenAI ensures that learning and teaching experiences are not only rich and varied, but also widely accessible, catering to diverse learning styles and sensory preferences within the academic community. Consequently, it holds the potential to substantially elevate the efficiency and inclusiveness of educational experiences in higher learning institutions.

3.3.5 *Scalability*

GenAI text tools are scalable, meaning they can effectively handle a wide range of applications and manage varying levels of workloads, from generating short text snippets to producing longer content pieces. This adaptability allows GenAI tools to serve a varied and growing number of users, handle larger datasets, and perform more complex computations without compromising efficiency or user experience (Chow, 2023). In the context of higher education, scalability is essential in managing varied educational processes and serving growing student populations. For instance, a scalable GenAI tool can efficiently support a small group of users, such as a single classroom, while also possessing the capability to seamlessly meet the extensive needs of an entire university. This could involve transitioning from handling basic queries related to course content and schedules, to managing more complex and multi-faceted tasks, such as grading assignments, providing personalised feedback, or even generating adaptive learning paths for a diverse range of courses and student demographics. Moreover, as the need for research and data analysis increases, a scalable AI system could effectively process and analyse large datasets, enabling researchers and educators to derive meaningful insights, predict trends, and ultimately enhance academic decision-making. Therefore, scalability in GenAI ensures that as the educational environment evolves and expands, the technology can seamlessly and adeptly accommodate and support this growth, optimising academic and administrative functionalities.

3.3.6   *Customisability*

AI models like those utilised by ChatGPT, and even parts of the data on which they are trained, are available for individuals to configure, deploy, and train themselves. While the continuation of this flexibility remains to be observed as commercial realities set in, currently this capability for customisation allows AI models to be fine-tuned to specific domains or applications, potentially enhancing their performance in particular use cases.

GenAI can be trained on specific datasets to generate high-quality responses for a particular industry. For instance, a university could fine-tune a GenAI text model (Li et al., 2023) to address questions related to its particular courses and programmes, facilitating easy access to information for students and thereby increasing efficiency in addressing frequently asked questions. The model may also be adapted to comprehend the university's policies and regulations, simplifying the information retrieval process for both students and staff. While such customisation facilitates the delivery of personalised and proficient support for academic-related tasks, it is important to note that attaining this level of customisability requires substantial effort, expertise, as well as the preparation of training and testing data and the computational resources to train and run the models in question. Thus, it can indeed be viewed as a significant challenge.

Customisability in GenAI underscores its potential to be tailored and adapted according to distinct user needs and preferences, ensuring that the system is not merely generically applicable, but also uniquely suitable for varied contexts and user requirements (Ruiz et al., 2023). Users can instruct GenAI tools, such as ChatGPT, to embody specific personas – be it a tutor, a rap singer, or a child, etc. The system can respond in these personas' styles, text formats, or speech or image patterns. It can also identify and utilise various grammatical structures, recognise and respond to different speech patterns and styles, and even incorporate humour or sarcasm into its responses, thereby enhancing interactive and engaging user experiences across diverse scenarios, such as in the aforementioned higher education context. Table 3.2 demonstrates the customisability in ChatGPT.

Table 3.2 Using ChatGPT GPT-4, Demonstrating the Customisability and Style

User	Please put together a limerick about a university student and Generative AI
ChatGPT	In a university's hall so wide, A student with AI did confide. He'd write all his essays, In quite clever ways, With Generative tools by his side!
User	Please put together a limerick about a university student and Generative AI in the style of a rap singer like Eminem
ChatGPT	In the uni, where beats did collide, A student with AI on the slide. Spittin' bars and essays, In that Slim Shady phase, With Generative swag, he'd ride high!
User	Please put together a limerick about a university student and Generative AI in the style of a ten years old child
ChatGPT	In big school, a student so neat, Had a robot friend, oh so sweet! They'd play and they'd write, From morning to night, With AI, their games were complete!

3.3.7   Comprehensive Coverage in Breadth and Depth

The characteristic of 'Coverage', which encompasses both the breadth and depth of content, plays a pivotal role in delivering informative and comprehensive responses across a wide range of topics in GenAI tools. Tools like ChatGPT exemplify this characteristic by offering information across a vast array of subjects. The extent to which ChatGPT can provide in-depth and detailed information depends on the robustness of the training data and the sophistication of the associated algorithms, which ensures that responses that are not only extensive, but reasonably detailed on a wide spectrum of specific topics.

In the context of higher education, consider a scenario wherein a student explores information regarding various academic programmes, campus facilities, or even intricate details about specific courses. ChatGPT, fortified by expansive coverage, can offer insights from general knowledge about diverse academic disciplines, to specific, in-depth details about particular courses or research areas, depending on the wealth and specificity of its training data. For instance, if a student is seeking information about biotechnology programmes, ChatGPT could provide a general overview of what biotechnology involves, and potentially delve into specifics such as genetic engineering or clinical research based on the data it has been trained on. Moreover, it can guide students on potential career paths, enlightening them about various industry sectors and research areas where a degree in biotechnology might be applicable.

This substantial coverage not only satisfies immediate queries but also facilitates users in conducting a structured and comprehensive exploration of topics, intertwining broad strokes with detailed insights wherever possible. However, it is crucial to note that while ChatGPT can provide a commendable extent of detail across various topics, the accuracy and specificity of information would invariably be tethered to the quality and expansiveness of its training data and the intricacy of the underlying algorithms. More information on training data is given in Chapter 6.

3.3.8   Contextual Relevance

AI does not merely interact with us but also engages in conversations in a manner that is discerningly relevant to the given input and context. GenAI text-based tools, including ChatGPT, possess the ability to uphold a specific level of contextual understanding, which enables them to generate responses or content that aligns seamlessly with the user's input. In addition, they demonstrate a memory-like capability which allows for ongoing dialogue. This intricate capability extends beyond mere response generation and encapsulates recognising, comprehending, and adapting to the multi-faceted elements of interaction, such as style, tone, and content context, thereby ensuring communication that is not only syntactically accurate but also contextually congruent.

Imagine a scenario within the higher education setting, where a student utilises a GenAI tool to seek guidance for thesis writing. The tool, equipped with contextual awareness, would not merely provide generic advice on academic writing. Instead, it would delve into thesis creation, comprehending and addressing the specificities such as research methodologies, citation styles, and potentially the subject matter of the thesis if provided by the student. If the student expresses difficulties in formulating a hypothesis for a thesis in environmental science, the AI would tailor its responses to offer guidance specifically for hypothesis creation in that domain. It might even provide suggestions grounded in environmental science, maintaining a dialogue that is contextually relevant and specifically supportive of the student's immediate needs.

This characteristic of GenAI ensures that users experience an interaction that is discernibly understanding and responsive to their individual and immediate needs. Especially in an educational context, where inquiries and issues can be diverse and domain-specific, GenAI's ability to comprehend and respond with contextual relevance is beneficial and crucial, facilitating a user experience that is simultaneously informative, supportive, and precisely tailored to the academic task or challenge at hand.

3.3.9 Multilingual Support

GenAI's multilingual support notably allows it to facilitate interactions across different languages (Ahuja et al., 2023). This trait resembles a skilled communicator conversing with various linguistic groups, ensuring that communication remains clear and reliable despite different languages being used. Therefore, while the responses provided by GenAI may vary in language, they consistently uphold the accuracy and reliability across their outputs.

Consider a university welcoming in students from around the world, each with their own language preferences. GenAI, with its ability to understand and generate multiple languages, becomes a vital communication tool to ensure that every student can access and understand the information provided. Table 3.3 demonstrates examples for multilingual support in ChatGPT. As a practical example, two students, one from China and another from Spain, pose questions, in Mandarin and Spanish respectively. The GenAI tool delivers accurate responses to both, ensuring fair access to information and equal timeliness of responses to its users. The multilingual capability of GenAI is essential in this context, as it enhances accessibility without compromising the quality and accuracy of communication. Thus, in education, this GenAI feature not only provides uniform access to information across languages but also actively promotes a globally inclusive learning atmosphere.

3.3.10 Appropriateness of Topics

Most large language models such as ChatGPT GPT-4, Bing, and Bard have been trained to respond appropriately to a wide range of requests, as well as reject inappropriate ones. This means it has been designed to avoid engaging in harmful or offensive language and

Table 3.3 Using ChatGPT GPT-4, Demonstrating the Multilingual Support and the Access to Bing for Real-Time Information

User	Please tell me the time of the day for the following countries in their own language – UK - London, USA – New York, China - Beijing, France - Paris, Germany - Berlin, Spain - Barcelona, Saudi Arabia - Riyadh, Japan - Tokyo, Korea - Seoul, India (Hindi) – New Delhi, please show them in a table.			
	Country	*City*	*Local Time*	*Day of the Week*
Bing (Microsoft)	UK	London	16:46:16 PM	Sunday
	USA	New York	11:46:16 AM	Sunday
	China	Beijing	22:46:16 PM	星期日
	France	Paris	17:46:16 PM	Dimanche
	Germany	Berlin	17:46:18 Uhr	Sonntag
	Spain	Barcelona	17:46:18	Domingo
	Saudi Arabia	Riyadh	21:46:19 مساءً	الأحد
	Japan	Tokyo	03:46:19 午前 (ごぜん)	月曜日 (げつようび)
	South Korea	Seoul	03:46:19 AM (오전)	월요일
	India - Hindi	New Delhi	21:16:20 बजे रात्रि को	सोमवार

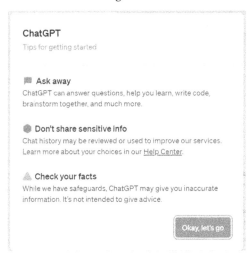

Figure 3.3 A Screenshot of ChatGPT by OpenAI, Note the Tips for Getting Started Regarding Sensitive Info and Check Your Facts.

behaviour, and to respond in a neutral and professional manner (Arora et al., 2023; Chan & Hu, 2023, Wang, 2023). Figure 3.3 shows a screenshot of tips from ChatGPT on sensitive information and maintaining information accuracy.

It is important to note that while some companies have taken measures to reduce the likelihood of generating inappropriate or harmful responses, such measures are not perfect and mistakes can still be made. Moreover, users can sometimes rewrite their inputs to bypass these measures. In such cases, it is up to the users and developers to set clear guidelines and monitor GenAI's outputs to ensure it aligns with ethical and professional standards.

Here are some examples of inappropriate requests that ChatGPT has been trained to decline:

- Hate speech or discrimination: Requests that promote hate or discrimination based on race, gender, religion, sexual orientation, or other personal characteristics are not acceptable.
- Threats or violence: Requests that encourage or promote violence, harm, or destruction are not acceptable.
- Explicit or vulgar language: Requests that contain explicit or vulgar language or content are not acceptable.
- Personal information: Requests for personal information, such as addresses, phone numbers, or financial information, are not acceptable.

3.3.11   Code Generation

ChatGPT's capability to generate code is a standout feature, bridging the gap between conversational AI and actual programming (as shown in Table 1.4). By understanding user requirements expressed in natural language, it can produce tailored code snippets, accelerating processes that requiring programming and assisting both novice and experienced programmers. This democratises coding, making it accessible to a wider audience. Additionally, it streamlines troubleshooting processes, enhancing the efficiency and intuitiveness of coding.

Imagine a scenario in a higher education computer science class where students are just beginning to grasp a new programming concept. Instead of getting bogged down with syntax errors or basic implementation challenges, students can describe their intended function to ChatGPT. The model then generates a code snippet based on their description. This immediate feedback and hands-on approach would allow students to focus on understanding the broader concept itself, rather than getting deterred by initial hurdles. It accelerates their learning process, also fostering a more interactive and engaging classroom environment, positioning ChatGPT as a valuable teaching assistant in higher education.

3.4 GenAI Tools and its Weaknesses and Potential Threats in Higher Education

In our previous section, we highlighted numerous strengths and potential opportunities raised by text-based GenAI tools for higher education, especially in shaping curriculum design and innovative pedagogy. However, like any technology, while it can transform the way we teach and learn, there are also challenges and potential threats that must be considered. It is a classic case of 'every rose has its thorn(s)'. In this section, our exploration turns towards understanding these challenges, using the example of ChatGPT's GPT-4.

The variability in GenAI tools poses a concern. For instance, because ChatGPT can produce different responses to the same query, verifying information for academic purposes while referring to ChatGPT as a source becomes a complex task. A student could cite a unique insight from ChatGPT in an assignment, but may not be able to reproduce the same result for later verification. Such variability can unintentionally contribute to academic discrepancies.

Furthermore, although the extensive knowledge base of ChatGPT is commendable, there is a genuine risk of information overload. The sheer volume of content it can generate has the potential to distract students from focusing on core curriculum topics, leading them down endless tangents of information. This becomes particularly problematic if students are weak in information literacy and prioritise intriguing, yet peripheral, AI-generated content over foundational curriculum concepts.

Academic integrity is another significant concern when it comes to the use of AI tools. The ease with which students can procure detailed answers might blur the boundaries of independent research and reliance on AI-generated content (Chan & Hu, 2023; Chan & Lee, 2023). Institutions will need to re-evaluate and potentially redefine what constitutes academic honesty in this AI era (Chan, 2023). It is crucial for educational institutions to establish guidelines and provide proper guidelines and education about ethical and responsible AI use to mitigate such challenge.

Recognising the expanding impact of AI in pedagogical methods and curriculum design, we have systematically categorised the potential weaknesses and threats posed by text-based generative AI tools. It aims to understand the implications, opportunities, and potential risks associated with the use of AI in education, providing guidelines on how the implementation of GenAI technologies in educational settings influences teaching methods, learning outcomes, student engagement, instructional design, and other relevant factors. Drawing from literature and a thorough analysis of the concerns raised by educators, students, and tech enthusiasts from our research, we segment these challenges into three main stakeholder categories that together form the framework: Students and Teachers, Educational Institutions, and Society at Large.

Table 3.4 Student/Teacher Category: Weaknesses and Potential Threats using GenAI in Higher Education

- Over-reliance: Over-relying on AI has the potential to diminish independent research and critical thinking skills.
- Accuracy Concerns: Misinformation can mislead students and reduce the quality of education.
- Lack of Judgement: AI may not be able to capture the subtleties and nuances in learning content, affecting students' depth of understanding.
- Loss of Personal Touch: Students may miss the emotional and motivational support offered by human educators.
- Neglection of Essential Skills: With constant usage or reliance on AI, competencies like creative thinking and leadership may become overlooked or under-practiced.
- Homogenisation of Thought: AI may limit the diversity of perspectives.
- Interactivity Limits: The dynamics of AI-driven classrooms may differ from human-led discussions or activities.
- AI Overload: For some students and educators, the introduction of AI tools can be overwhelming. They may struggle to keep up, understand, or effectively utilise the technology, leading to potential barriers.
- Academic Misconduct Considerations: Broader ethical dilemmas, such as using AI to make decisions in educational settings and potential plagiarism, need to be considered.

Table 3.5 Educational Institutions Category: Weaknesses and Potential Threats using GenAI in Higher Education

- Resource-Intensive: Large-scale AI adoption will likely strain institutional resources.
- Technical Challenges: Implementation, updates, and maintenance of AI tools can be complex.
- Security Risks: There are increased cyber vulnerabilities associated with the implementation and use of AI software and systems.
- Reputation Risks: Over-reliance on AI may affect institutional prestige and student recruitment.
- Adaptability: There is a need to constantly update AI to keep up to date with curriculum changes and diverse educational needs.
- Dependency on Connectivity: Institutions need a robust and reliable IT infrastructure to support the integration and use of AI tools.

Students/Teachers: This category (Table 3.4) delves into concerns that directly touch upon the heart of the educational experience. It emphasises how AI interventions may reshape the dynamics of learning, potentially affecting cognitive development, motivation, and the holistic nurturing of the student.

Educational Institutions: Operational challenges form the core of this category (Table 3.5). AI is dynamic and evolving; institutions will grapple with a spectrum of issues, from resource allocation to the complexities of technological integration, as well as the intrinsic risks they carry.

Society at Large: Examining the impact of AI in education from a broader perspective, this category (Table 3.6) highlights the extensive societal implications stemming from AI integration. This segment focuses on issues related to ethics, equity, and the economy that extend beyond individual classrooms and institutions.

The following sections provide elaboration on each category.

Students/Teachers: This category focuses on issues related to the educational process. It highlights how AI implementations could potentially change learning, impacting aspects

Table 3.6 Society Category: Weaknesses and Potential Threats using GenAI in Higher Education

- Bias: There is potential for AI to reflect and amplify societal biases in educational content.
- Data Privacy Concerns: There are numerous issues surrounding the confidentiality and privacy of student data, as well as preventing potential misuse of this data.
- Economic Implications: There is potential for job displacement due to the adoption of AI and concerns about the associated costs. This raises implications for the role of educators as AI becomes increasingly incorporated into classrooms, as well as for graduate employability.
- Inequitable Access: There is a risk of widening the educational divide due to discrepancies in access and availability of technology and related resources.
- Over-commercialisation: There are possibilities of corporate, commercial, and market interests overshadowing genuine educational needs.

like cognitive development, motivation, and the whole-person development of students. Although the impacts in this category are more directly associated with students, teachers are also significantly affected as they need to adapt to these changes. The AI-induced alterations in educational dynamics require teachers to adjust their teaching methods, strategies, and interactions with both educational tools and students to ensure that the learning objectives are met effectively. This interrelated relationship between the impacts of AI on students and the corresponding adaptations made by teachers exemplifies the profound influence of AI on the educational ecosystem.

- **Over-reliance:** Consistent use of AI may foster dependency. Students may become overly dependent on GenAI tools for answers, potentially stifling their own critical thinking and problem-solving skills, as well as diminishing their motivation for independent research and self-learning. When students become overly dependent on AI tools, they may try to use it to bypass the struggles associated with traditional learning and, more importantly, the learning process, which would likely hinder their development of crucial skills such as resilience, perseverance, and problem solving. As a result, there is a risk that students will be less prepared to tackle real-world challenges.
- **Accuracy Concerns:** AI outputs are based on data patterns rather than verified facts, and GenAI can sometimes produce information that is misleading or factually incorrect. Without human oversight, this can lead to dissemination of misinformation. While using AI tools, students may be unintentionally exposed to inaccurate or out-of-context information, leading to misunderstandings and errors which could possibly impact their own perspectives and academic performance.
- **Lack of Judgement:** AI may not capture the subtleties and nuances in learning content, affecting students' depth of understanding. Academic discussions often involve complex perspectives and discussions. In comparison, AI tools may offer simplified answers, omitting certain details or failing to capture the richness of academic debates. Over-reliance on AI can result in a superficial grasp of intricate topics, which is counterproductive, particularly in advanced educational settings.
- **Loss of Personal Touch:** AI tools cannot replace the personal interaction, guidance, and mentorship provided by human educators. The absence of human intuition and emotional intelligence in AI-driven learning can result in a less holistic educational experience. Education is not solely about transferring knowledge; it is about mentorship, support, motivation, and personal growth. AI lacks the human touch, which can lead to an impersonal and detached learning experience. A purely AI-driven educational experience may overlook the crucial aspects of relationship-building and personal touch in teaching and

learning. Interpersonal skills, emotional intelligence, and the nuances of human interaction cannot be replicated by AI.

- **Neglection of Essential Skills:** AI is already capable of carrying out tasks like note taking, research, and problem solving. Traditional academic skills, including writing, analytical reasoning, and critical thinking, have long been the bedrock of higher education. However, as AI tools become more prevalent, there is a risk that students will neglect the development of these foundational skills. For instance, if an AI tool can instantly generate a research summary, students may not feel the need to go through articles and books themselves. Over time, this could lead to a generation of students who lack these essential skills, affecting their preparedness for real-world challenges and post-academic pursuits.
- **Homogenisation of Thought:** Over-reliance on AI tools can lead to a uniform way of thinking, curbing creativity and diverse perspectives in academic discussions. One of the strengths of academia is its diverse range of perspectives and debates which foster intellectual growth and the pursuit of knowledge. However, if individuals turn to the same AI tools for insights, they might end up all drawing the same conclusions, leading to a homogenised thought process. The unique interpretations and viewpoints stemming from individual research and critical thinking could thus be overshadowed. In higher education, where diverse viewpoints and critical debates are vital, AI may dampen the richness of academic discourse.
- **Interactivity Limits:** AI-driven lessons may lack the dynamism and adaptability of human-led discussions, resulting in a less interactive and potentially less engaging learning experience for students. While AI can provide structured content delivery, it may not be able to capture the spontaneity and flexibility of a human educator. Human educators can change their teaching approach on-the-fly based on students' responses or interests, making lessons more interactive and engaging. In contrast, AI-driven lessons tend to be more static, potentially leading to reduced student engagement. This can be a particular in issue in higher education settings where discussions, debates, and interactive sessions are key components of the learning experience.
- **AI Overload:** Some students and educators, especially those who are less proficient in using technologies, may find the emergence of these AI tools intimidating. This apprehension may arise from unfamiliarity with the technology or the fear of not being able to harness its full capabilities. Consequently, rather than facilitating learning, the technology advancements could inadvertently become a hindrance. It is crucial for institutions to acknowledge such concern and provide adequate training and support to ensure a smooth transition to AI-driven teaching and learning approaches, and effective utilisation of AI tools in classrooms.
- **Academic Misconduct Considerations:** There is a fine line between offering assistance and actually doing the work. Students may be tempted to present AI-generated content as their own, giving rise to concerns about academic integrity, plagiarism, and the development of authentic skills. Using AI-generated content in assignments blurs the boundaries of academic honesty, potentially diminishing the value of original student work and questioning the legitimacy of academic qualifications.

Given the dynamic nature of GenAI responses, ensuring the accuracy of information becomes a challenge. Using the previous example of a student who references information from GenAI in their academic work but is unable to produce the same result later, this poses issues for source verification, which may inadvertently encourage academic dishonesty. When two students rely on a GenAI tool for assistance and receive different answers because of the AI's inherent variability, it complicates matters for educators in detecting potential misuse. On the other hand, well-intentioned students may be wrongly accused of misconduct if they are unable to recreate the original AI-generated source of their information.

Educational Institutions: This category primarily focuses on operational challenges. With the constantly evolving nature of AI, educational institutions face a range of obstacles such as allocation of resources, complexities of technology integration, and inherent risks associated with utilising AI in education.

- **Resource-Intensive:** Large-scale AI adoption can place significant strain on institutional resources. Setting up and maintaining advanced AI tools can be resource-intensive, potentially resulting in increased costs for institutions.
- **Technical Challenges:** Not all institutions possess the necessary infrastructure or technical expertise to implement, deploy, and maintain AI tools, thereby widening the gap between well-resourced and less-resourced institutions. This can lead to subpar implementation, software glitches, or lack of ongoing support on AI implementation, hindering the teaching and learning process for less-resourced institutions. The implementation of AI in educational settings can be full of challenges, and institutions may struggle with deployment, maintenance, and ensuring seamless integration with existing systems.
- **Security Risks:** With the adoption of AI tools, educational institutions expose themselves to new vectors of cyber threats. Implementing AI tools in higher education involves data exchanges, storage, and processing, which can create potential entry points for cyberattacks. Malicious actors may target these systems to disrupt educational processes, steal sensitive information, or execute ransomware attacks. Safeguarding against these threats require additional investments in cybersecurity measures, increasing operational complexities and costs for institutions.
- **Reputation Risks:** An educational institution's decision to heavily implement AI can have a negative impact on its reputation and attractiveness to prospective students. Reputation is crucial for educational institutions, and heavy reliance on AI may create a perception that the institution is cutting corners or not valuing the human aspect of education, thus diluting the educational experience. Prospective students may choose institutions that balance technological advancements with traditional teaching methods. Overall, when heavily influenced by AI, an institution's image and status can be impacted, with stakeholders questioning the quality of education provided and the value of degrees conferred by such institutions.
- **Adaptability:** AI tools used in education require constant updates and adjustments to align with evolving curricula, teaching methodologies, and student needs. The dynamic nature of educational methodologies and curricula, along with shifting student demographics require AI tools to be adaptable. If not, AI tools risk becoming obsolete or misaligned with institutional goals. However, the constant need for adaptation may impose strain on resources and potentially disrupt the learning process, as institutions may find themselves in a cycle of incessant updates to ensure that the AI tool remains in alignment with educational requirements and needs.
- **Dependency on Connectivity:** The effectiveness of AI tools is contingent on internet connectivity, which can render institutions more susceptible to connectivity issues. AI tools, especially cloud-based platforms, require robust internet connectivity for optimal functionality.

Institutions, especially those in areas with inconsistent internet services, may encounter difficulties in ensuring the delivery of consistent education using AI. This can lead to disruptions in teaching, potentially compromising the overall learning experience. For students, unsteady connection may hinder their access to necessary resources, creating an uneven playing field.

Society at Large: Examining the impact of AI in education from a broader perspective, this category highlights the extensive societal implications arising from the integration of AI in education. Issues related to ethics, equity, and the economy that extend beyond the confines of individual classrooms and institutions are central to this segment.

- **Bias:** AI's effectiveness is heavily reliant on the data it is trained with (Arora et al., 2023; Chan & Hu, 2023; Ferrara, 2023). If biases exist in their training datasets, AI outputs could mirror these biases, offering skewed perspectives that may mislead or misinform students. AI models may also unintentionally reinforce such biases, resulting in unbalanced educational content that could either bolster stereotypes or omit certain viewpoints. It is also worth noting that while GenAI tools such as ChatGPT have been trained to decline inappropriate requests, it is still possible for it to make mistakes or generate responses that are not aligned with these guidelines for appropriate use. As a result, it is important for users and developers to monitor the outputs of AI tools and to provide additional training, or adjust the system as needed to ensure that it continues to generate appropriate responses. According to a Bloomberg article (Nicoletti & Bass, 2023), text-to-image GenAI models such as Stable Diffusion can amplify stereotypes on race and gender, surpassing the levels observed in reality. Through an analysis of over 5,000 images generated by Stable Diffusion, the article illustrated how the model intensifies racial and gender imbalances, emphasising that the widespread use of GenAI tools not only perpetuates existing stereotypes, hindering progress towards achieving more equitable representation, but also poses a risk of unjust practices. For example, utilising a biased text-to-image AI for generating sketches of suspected criminals could potentially lead to wrongful convictions.

  The training of GenAI significantly relies on the quality and diversity of the data it is trained on. However, sourcing training data predominantly from online platforms introduces inherent biases. One notable bias arises from the digital divide, where certain populations such as older individuals or those in technologically underserved regions are underrepresented due to limited computer usage or online presence. This lack of representation may lead to AI having a skewed understanding of human demographics and preferences. Additionally, the dominance of the English language in online data introduces another inherent biases in AI systems. Many AI models are trained on datasets where English is overrepresented, which can marginalise non-English speakers and overlook the cultural and linguistic diversity of other languages and dialects. Moreover, the cultural bias is evident as Western cultures tend to be more represented in online data compared to Asian or other non-Western cultures. This cultural bias can further perpetuate stereotypes and misrepresentations.

  Other factors contributing to biased training data include socio-economic bias, as individuals from different socio-economic backgrounds may have unequal levels of online presence or representation in digital data. The limited representation of individuals from diverse socio-economic backgrounds and resulting potential bias in AI models means that the latter will fail to accurately reflect the needs and experiences of these communities, even deepening existing disparities and inequalities.

Political bias is another concern – that AI may reflect skewed political ideologies based on the sources of its training data. If the data predominantly comes from politically biased sources, the AI system may mirror them, resulting in problematic outcomes especially in contexts requiring neutrality and balanced perspectives. An article by Rozado (2023) discussed the potential for political biases in large language models (LLMs) and the concerns surrounding their misuse. It shared findings from a study where 15 different political orientation tests were administered to ChatGPT. The results were significant, with 14 out of the 15 tests indicating that ChatGPT's responses inclined towards left-leaning viewpoints. The article suggests that for ethical AI practices, systems should provide users with balanced arguments regarding the matter discussed, and refrain from claiming neutrality while displaying evident political bias in their content.

Moreover, biases can emerge from the attitudes and prejudices of human annotators who label the training data, as well as from the AI systems' design, such as feature selection and model structure. Table 3.7 summarises the biases in training data for GenAI.

These biases all contribute to problematic concerns including:

- Ethical concerns: Certain types of inappropriate requests, such as those promoting hate speech or violence, raise serious ethical concerns. Such requests have the potential to harm individuals and communities and can contribute to a hostile or toxic environment.
- Legal implications: Certain types of inappropriate requests, such as those that solicit personal information or contain illegal content, may have legal implications, thus, it is crucial that the tools are not used to facilitate illegal activity or violate privacy laws.
- Reputation and trust: Systems that generate inappropriate responses can damage their reputation and erode trust with users. For example, a customer service chatbot that generates offensive or inappropriate responses could harm the reputation of the company it represents and lead to a loss of trust among customers.
- Responsibility and accountability: As artificial intelligence systems become more integrated into society, it is important to consider who is responsible and accountable for their actions. This includes ensuring that such systems are not used to facilitate inappropriate behaviour or harm individuals and communities.

Table 3.7 Summary on the Biases in Training Data for GenAI

Type of Bias	Description	Impact on Generative AI
Digital Divide Bias	Underrepresentation of populations with limited digital access.	Skewed demographic understanding.
Language Bias	Dominance of English in training data leading to marginalisation of non-English speakers.	Inadequate multilingual capabilities.
Cultural Bias	Overrepresentation of Western cultures compared to non-Western cultures.	Perpetuation of cultural stereotypes.
Political Bias	Skewed representation of political perspectives based on the political inclination of data sources.	Potential lack of political neutrality.
Socio-economic Bias	Discrepancies in representation of those from different socio-economic backgrounds.	Misrepresentation of socio-economic diversity.
Human Annotation Bias	Prejudices and attitudes of human annotators affecting the labelling of training data.	Perpetuation of human biases in AI predictions.
Model Design Bias	Choices in model features and structure can introduce bias.	Skewed predictions and misrepresentations.

As such, it is crucial to strive for a more equitable and inclusive approach in sourcing, annotating, and structuring the data used to train GenAI model.

- **Data Privacy Concerns:** The use of AI in education often requires collecting and processing personal and sensitive information, raising concerns about privacy and data security. Students and educators may be sharing academic and personal data with AI platforms, and without stringent data protection measures, there is a risk of data breaches or misuse which compromises individual privacy. It is crucial to recognise the potential risk of data breaches that could jeopardise privacy and security, and to implement measures to safeguard sensitive and personal data.
- **Economic Implications:** The financial implications of adopting AI, in terms of both costs and potential job displacements in the education sector, require careful consideration. Adopting AI tools can be a significant financial investment for institutions. While there is potential for long-term cost savings, the initial expenditure and ongoing maintenance costs can strain budgets. Moreover, the increased reliance on AI may lead to reduced demands for certain job roles within the educational ecosystem, potentially resulting in job losses. In addition, it is important to consider the broader economic impact on the community, especially if an institution is a significant employer. However, according to one of our recent studies (Chan & Tsi, 2023), students still have a strong preference for human teachers over artificial ones as they believe that human teachers possess unique characteristics that machines cannot replicate. In Chapter 7, we will further discuss the implications of AI on the job market.
- **Inequitable Access:** While AI has the potential to democratise education, its implementation can inadvertently widen the educational divide, where, based on resource availability, the introduction of advanced AI tools can lead to access disparities in quality education. Institutions with more resources may offer AI-enhanced education, while others lag behind (Holstein & Doroudi, 2021; Pedro et al., 2019). Students without access to AI tools might be at a disadvantage, leading to a widened gap in educational outcomes. In a global context, this disparity may manifest between urban and rural areas, or between developed and developing nations.
- **Over-commercialisation:** The rise of AI in education may attract numerous businesses, leading to potential conflicts between commercial interests and genuine educational needs: there is potential for an influx of companies offering AI solutions, and while competition can drive innovation, there is also a risk of commercial interests infringing upon educational goals. Institutions could be lured by aggressive marketing tactics or exclusive deals, potentially side-lining the learning needs of their students. The commodification of education would overall dilute its intrinsic value.

With the above categories, stakeholders can gain a better understanding of the potential challenges in integrating AI in the educational sector and addresses potential issues. This ensures that AI-partnered education is both thoughtful and inclusive, catering to all stakeholders involved.

While text-based GenAI tools like ChatGPT are undeniably revolutionising pedagogy in higher education, it is crucial to approach their integration with caution. Striking a balance between utilising tools to their strengths and being mindful of potential challenges will be crucial in harnessing their full potential while upholding the fundamental values of academic learning. Table 3.8 shows a comprehensive overview of the strengths and weaknesses of GenAI in higher education.

Table 3.8 A Complete List of the Strengths and Weaknesses of GenAI in Higher Education

GenAI Implications in Higher Education

Strengths and Opportunities	Weaknesses and Threats
1. User-Centric Design 2. Humanistic Conversational Style 3. Variability 4. Multimodal Capability 5. Scalability 6. Customisability 7. Comprehensive Coverage in Breadth and Depth 8. Contextual Relevance 9. Multilingual Support 10. Appropriateness of Topics 11. Code Generation Capability	1. Over-reliance: Over-relying on AI has the potential to diminish independent research and critical thinking skills. 2. Accuracy Concerns: Misinformation can mislead students and reduce the quality of education. 3. Lack of Judgement: AI may not be able to capture the subtleties and nuances in learning content, affecting students' depth of understanding. 4. Loss of Personal Touch: Students may miss the emotional and motivational support offered by human educators. 5. Neglect of Traditional Skills: With constant usage or reliance on AI, essential skills like creative thinking and leadership may become overlooked or under-practiced. 6. Homogenisation of Thought: AI may limit the diversity of perspectives presented. 7. Interactivity Limits: The dynamics of AI-driven classrooms may differ from human-led discussions or activities. 8. AI Overload: For some students and educators, the introduction of AI tools can be overwhelming. They may struggle to keep up, understand, or effectively utilise the technology, leading to potential barriers. 9. Academic Misconduct Considerations: Broader ethical dilemmas, such as using AI to make decisions in educational settings and potential plagiarism, need to be considered. 10. Resource-Intensive: Large-scale AI adoption will likely strain institutional resources. 11. Technical Challenges: Implementation, updates, and maintenance of AI tools can be complex. 12. Security Risks: There are increased cyber vulnerabilities associated with the implementation and use of AI software and systems. 13. Reputation Risks: Over-reliance on AI may affect institutional prestige and student recruitment. 14. Adaptability: There is a need to constantly update AI to keep up-to-date with curriculum changes and diverse educational needs. 15. Dependency on Connectivity: Institutions need a robust and reliable IT infrastructure to support the integration and use of AI tools. 16. Bias: There is potential for AI to reflect and amplify societal biases in educational content. 17. Data Privacy Concerns: There are numerous issues surrounding the confidentiality and privacy of student data, as well as preventing potential misuse of this data. 18. Economic Implications: There is potential for job displacement due to the adoption of AI and concerns about the associated costs. This raises implications for the role of educators as AI becomes increasingly incorporated into classrooms, as well as for graduate employability. 19. Inequitable Access: There is a risk of widening the educational divide due to discrepancies in access and availability of technology and related resources. 20. Over-commercialisation: There are possibilities of corporate, commercial, and market interests overshadowing genuine educational needs.

3.5   AI-Partnered Pedagogy through the Lens of Bloom's Taxonomy

One of the more alluring aspects of GenAI tools like ChatGPT is their ability to provide a seemingly profound understanding of a given topic, going beyond simple keyword matching. For further explanation, this section will discuss GenAI's capabilities within Bloom's Taxonomy Cognitive Domain model (Bloom et al., 1956; Anderson & Krathwohl, 2001).

Bloom's Taxonomy, originally developed in 1956 by Benjamin Bloom and later revised by his students and colleagues, provides a hierarchical classification of cognitive skills essential for learning. It identifies six distinct levels of cognitive processes from basic to the complex as shown in Table 3.9 remembering, understanding, applying, analysing, evaluating, and creating (Bloom et al., 1956; Anderson & Krathwohl, 2001).

Bloom's Taxonomy Cognitive Domain model has been widely adopted in education as a guiding framework for designing learning objectives, assessments, and pedagogical strategies. By understanding and referring to these levels, educators can create more targeted and effective learning experiences that facilitate students' learning progress from foundational knowledge acquisition to critical thinking and problem solving. This model can be applied to AI-integrated education for designing learning experiences which leverage the capabilities of AI in teaching and learning.

3.5.1   *Literary Study of ChatGPT's GPT-4 via Bloom's Taxonomy*

Understanding the capabilities of GenAI to process, analyse, and generate textual information is important for its comparison and possible integration with established educational frameworks, including Bloom's Taxonomy's Cognitive Domain model. Using OpenAI's ChatGPT GPT-4, this study investigates the intersection between ChatGPT's capabilities and the six cognitive processes outlined in Bloom's Taxonomy (i.e., remembering, understanding, applying, analysing, evaluating, and creating). The study aims to examine the depth and breadth of AI's utility in literary and textual analyses, as well as identify potential implications for pedagogy and curriculum development in higher education. The study is currently under review. The primary research question is:

- To what extent can ChatGPT navigate the levels of cognitive processes in Bloom's Taxonomy when analysing literary texts?

Table 3.9 Bloom's Taxonomy Cognitive Domain Model (Bloom et al., 1956; Anderson & Krathwohl, 2001)

Levels	Bloom's Taxonomy Cognitive Domain model
Remembering	The ability to recall or retrieve previously learned information.
Understanding	Grasping the meaning by interpreting and translating what has been learned.
Applying	Utilising learned material in new situations, which may include solving problems.
Analysing	Breaking down material into constituent parts, distinguishing between them, and understanding their relationships to one another.
Evaluating	Making judgements about the value, significance, or effectiveness of materials or methods in relation to one's learning.
Creating	Constructing new ideas or content from synthesising multiple pieces of learned information.

Table 3.10 Rubrics for Assessing ChatGPT GPT-4 Literary Capability at the "Remembering" Level using Bloom's Taxonomy

Rubric for Assessing ChatGPT's Responses for Literary Analysis at the "Remembering" Level

Criteria	Excellent	Proficient	Average	Fair	Poor
Depth of Response	Offers comprehensive recall of facts, terms, and basic concepts.	Demonstrates strong recall with occasional minor omissions.	Provides adequate recall but misses some key concepts.	Limited recall, missing many fundamental details.	Barely recalls or recognises any relevant details.
Accuracy of Response	Flawlessly recalls information without any errors.	Contains few minor inaccuracies in the recalled information.	Several noticeable errors but still provides some correct information.	Numerous errors, limited correct recall.	Almost entirely inaccurate or off-target.
Relevance of Response	Entirely relevant to the prompt, showcasing an understanding of the "remembering" level.	Mostly relevant, with minor deviations from the prompt.	Displays partial relevance, occasionally going off-topic.	Strays significantly from the prompt, with little relevance.	Irrelevant to the prompt, fails to address "remembering".

3.5.1.1   Methodology

This study incorporates a variety of literary genres, including novels, poems, articles, and plays, to ensure a comprehensive evaluation. The methodology is iterative: ChatGPT will be prompted to engage with each literary text in accordance with the six cognitive processes, and its responses will be meticulously analysed by five researchers to assess their depth, accuracy, and relevance. Table 3.10 shows the rubric for assessing ChatGPT's responses at the "remembering" level of Bloom's Taxonomy with three criteria – the depth of response, accuracy of response, and relevance of response. This systematic approach sheds light on ChatGPT's text generation capabilities in literary analysis and its potential for pedagogical applications. (Note: for the actual study, six distinct rubrics, each corresponding to the six levels of Bloom's Taxonomy, were used to facilitate a more comprehensive assessment and offer detailed analyses of the model's performance across different cognitive levels).

3.5.1.2   Findings of ChatGPT's Literary Analysis of "Oliver Twist"

To showcase the results of this study, Table 3.11 below is an example that uses the famous novel, *Oliver Twist* by Charles Dickens. Please note, the below prompt from the user is the only prompt used to generate the response, no previous prompt, roles or other follow-up prompts were used.

3.5.1.3   Evaluation

Each of the six levels of Bloom's Taxonomy were assessed across the same three criteria of the rubric in Table 3.10 (Depth, Accuracy, and Relevance). As seen above, the maximum

Table 3.11 Prompt used for the study of ChatGPT GPT-4's Literary Capability against Bloom's Taxonomy

User	I am conducting a study on ChatGPT and its impact on higher education. I aim to explore how ChatGPT-4 operates in relation to the extent of GenAI's capabilities concerning Bloom's Taxonomy Cognitive Domain model. As you may know, there are six distinct levels of cognitive processes in this model, ranging from basic to complex: remembering, understanding, applying, analysing, evaluating, and creating. I plan to delve into various renowned novels, poems, articles, and plays for this research. I would like to begin with "Oliver Twist" by Charles Dickens. Could you provide detailed insights and demonstrate how deeply you can navigate within Bloom's taxonomy in each level?
ChatGPT	Of course! Let's use "Oliver Twist" by Charles Dickens as our case study to illustrate ChatGPT-4's capabilities across the six levels of Bloom's Taxonomy Cognitive Domain model.

1. Remembering: ChatGPT-4's Capability – recall specific details, facts, information, and data.
    Oliver Twist is an orphan who begins his life in a workhouse. He later escapes and has several adventures in London, encountering characters like Fagin, the Artful Dodger, and Bill Sikes.
2. Understanding: ChatGPT-4's Capability – Comprehend the meaning, interpretation, and descriptions.
    "Oliver Twist" delves into the hardships of the orphaned and the poor during Victorian England. It underscores the societal disparities and highlights the ease with which innocence can be corrupted in the midst of adversity.
3. Applying: ChatGPT-4's Capability – Use the knowledge in new ways or situations.
    Dickens' portrayal of Oliver's journey can be juxtaposed against modern-day situations, like the challenges faced by migrants or refugees. Despite the historical setting, the themes of exploitation and survival are universally relevant.
4. Analysing: ChatGPT-4's Capability – Distinguish different parts, understand their interrelationships.
    "Oliver Twist" is structured around both Oliver's personal journey and the societal context around him. Characters such as Fagin represent the criminal underbelly of society, whereas others like Mr. Brownlow showcase benevolence and kindness. The contrast in characters is Dickens' method of exploring societal morality.
5. Evaluating: ChatGPT-4's Capability – Justify and defend opinions and decisions.
    "Oliver Twist" is not just a narrative but a social commentary. Dickens' vivid portrayal of workhouses and the plight of the orphans stands as a critique of the Victorian era's treatment of the underprivileged. One could argue that Dickens uses Oliver's story as an instrument to highlight the societal flaws and demand change.
6. Creating: ChatGPT-4's Capability – Build new structures or patterns from diverse elements.
    Drawing from the narrative, one could conceive a modern adaptation, perhaps set in a 21st-century urban backdrop. This retelling might focus on contemporary social issues while retaining the essence of Oliver's trials and tribulations.
    In conclusion, ChatGPT-4 can indeed navigate all six levels of Bloom's Taxonomy when analysing "Oliver Twist". While its analysis and evaluations are rooted in vast amounts of textual data and patterns, the absence of personal emotions or biases ensures a consistent and objective approach to literary analysis.

score per criterion is 5 points ("Excellent"), meaning that for each level of the taxonomy, the highest score attainable is 15 points, while the cumulative score across all six levels caps at 90 points (30 points maximum for each rubric criteria).

Using this grading system, assessors evaluated ChatGPT's response to the prompt on *Oliver Twist*. One example is shown in Table 3.12.

Table 3.12 The Evaluation of ChatGPT's Literary Capability for *Oliver Twist* via Bloom's Taxonomy

At the Remembering Level		Score
Depth of Response:	ChatGPT demonstrated a concise recall of basic plot elements.	5
Accuracy of Response:	The response accurately recounted key details about the protagonist and the primary characters he encounters.	5
Relevance of Response:	The response was relevant to the task of remembering specific details about the novel.	5
Score:	Excellent for Depth, Accuracy, and Relevance.	15
At the Understanding Level:		
Depth of Response:	The analysis provided an overview of the novel's themes and the societal issues it addresses.	5
Accuracy of Response:	The interpretation aligned well with the general understanding of "Oliver Twist".	5
Relevance of Response:	The response directly related to understanding the novel's themes and implications.	5
Score:	Excellent for Depth, Accuracy, and Relevance.	15
At the Applying Level:		
Depth of Response:	ChatGPT effectively related the novel's themes to modern contexts.	5
Accuracy of Response:	The application remained true to Dickens' themes while offering a contemporary perspective.	4
Relevance of Response:	The response showcased how the novel's themes could be applied to modern situations.	5
Score:	Excellent for Depth and Relevance; Proficient for Accuracy.	14
At the Analysing Level:		
Depth of Response:	The analysis offered a glimpse into the novel's structure and character dynamics.	4
Accuracy of Response:	The description accurately represented character roles and their significance.	4
Relevance of Response:	The response aligned with the task of breaking down the novel's parts and their interrelationships.	4
Score:	Proficient for Depth, Accuracy, and Relevance.	12
At the Evaluating Level:		
Depth of Response:	ChatGPT recognised the novel's dual nature as both a narrative and a social commentary.	5
Accuracy of Response:	The evaluation accurately captured Dickens' critiques and the novel's thematic essence.	4
Relevance of Response:	The response was in line with the task of evaluating the novel's broader implications.	5
Score:	Excellent for Depth and Relevance; Proficient for Accuracy.Creating:	14
At the Creating Level:		
Depth of Response:	ChatGPT conceptualised a modern adaptation while considering the core of the original story.	5
Accuracy of Response:	The creative exercise stayed true to the heart of "Oliver Twist".	4
Relevance of Response:	The response focused on crafting a new narrative structure inspired by the original.	5
Score:	Excellent for Depth and Relevance; Proficient for Accuracy.	14

(Continued)

Table 3.12 (Continued)

At the Remembering Level	Score
Overall Scores:	
Depth of Response: $5 + 5 + 5 + 4 + 5 + 5 = 29/30$	
Accuracy of Response: $5 + 5 + 4 + 4 + 4 + 4 = 26/30$	
Relevance of Response: $5 + 5 + 5 + 4 + 5 + 5 = 29/30$	
Total Score:	**84/90**

Conclusion: Based on the evaluation using the rubric, ChatGPT GPT-4 demonstrated an impressive ability to engage with the text of *Oliver Twist* at various levels of Bloom's Taxonomy. It offered detailed and accurate insights, although there is room for improvement in terms of providing even deeper, more complex interpretations of the text. Of course, in order to receive more accurate results from this research study, we could add in more detailed prompts to gather more concluded evaluations. This could be achieved in the future with additional or even more detailed inputs (prompts). Nevertheless, this study (as a beginner level - basic research study) found GPT-4's high level of literary understanding and interpretation, especially when guided with specific prompts. Overall, GPT-4 offered an analysis of *Oliver Twist* that aligned with all six cognitive levels of Bloom's Taxonomy.

3.6   Redesigning Pedagogical Activities with GenAI

The role of technology as both a tool and a partner in higher education continues to be redefined. Throughout this chapter, we have set our sights on illustrating the promising partnership between AI, pedagogy and us, with a spotlight on ChatGPT.

Having examined the strengths, weaknesses, opportunities, and threats of GenAI and ChatGPT in previous sections, we have established a foundational understanding of the potentials and pitfalls. Building on this, our research study, "AI-Partnered Pedagogy through the Lens of Bloom's Taxonomy" has also exemplified how AI's capabilities can align with, and enhance, cognitive skills across the learning spectrum.

GenAI can be a revolutionary tool for curriculum design especially in higher education, infusing a dynamic and responsive element into educational content creation and interaction. For instance, educators can use GenAI tools to generate illustrative examples, create engaging content, or formulate quizzes that align with specific learning objectives. Furthermore, GenAI models can be utilised to automate responses to frequently asked questions from students, providing instant support. In higher education, where the curriculum often includes a blend of foundational and advanced, specialised knowledge, GenAI tools can assist in delivering content that caters to all levels of learners.

Consider a case where university professors are designing a course on artificial intelligence. They could utilise GenAI tools to generate introductory content, providing students with an accessible entry point into complex concepts like machine learning algorithms or neural networks. Additionally, the educators could also use GenAI to come up with diverse and complex problems and tasks, enabling students to apply their knowledge in varied scenarios to gain the most out of the course.

In another case, GenAI could be utilised as an interactive study assistant, where students engage in dialogue with the tool, exploring topics, clarifying their misunderstandings, and receiving responses instantly. For example, a student working on a research project about bioinformatics could utilise GenAI to better understand complex genetic algorithms or to curate information about the latest advancements in the field. This interactivity not only supports students in their learning, but also makes the process more engaging and tailored to their own needs. Overall, this helps to foster a more inclusive and supportive educational environment.

GenAI tools, with its multi-faceted functionalities and adaptable nature, provides educators and students in higher education with great versatility. It has the capability to enhance educational content, facilitate dynamic learning experiences, and cultivate an environment wherein information is more accessible, interactive, and tailored for diverse learning needs and objectives.

This brings us to the crux of this section: How can GenAI assist in enhancing student learning in higher education? After extensively reviewing literature, online blogs, discussion forums, as well as discussions with students and teachers, we have consolidated numerous ideas for integrating GenAI into pedagogy. Below, we will provide a list of examples for how GenAI, primarily ChatGPT, can be utilised in pedagogical designs within higher education. A list, which can be found in Table 3.13, aligns with ChatGPT's functions and serves as a guide for educators, learners, researchers, and administrators. This practical roadmap highlights the ways in which GenAI can be harnessed in the classroom and beyond. With some of your own creativity, readers can also add elements from their personal experiences and insights to these ideas in crafting innovative, AI–human collaborative pedagogies.

3.6.1 *List of Pedagogies Facilitated by AI–Human Partnership*

Table 3.13 A List of AI–Human Partnered Pedagogies Separated into Teaching, Learning, Research and Administrative Categories

Teaching	
Function	*Implementation & Example*
Create syllabi	**Implementation**: Use AI to generate a structured syllabus based on course goals. **Example**: For a physics course, AI can generate weekly topics, readings, and assignments tailored to the course objectives.
Produce course documents	**Implementation**: AI tools can auto-generate course outlines, schedules, and reading lists. **Example**: For a history course, generate an outline of topics from ancient to modern history, detailing weekly themes and readings.
Customise lesson planning	**Implementation**: AI can adjust lesson plans based on student feedback or performance. **Example**: If students struggle with photosynthesis, extend the topic by two lessons and include additional resources.
Produce learning outcomes	**Implementation**: Define clear objectives for each lesson using AI analysis of course content. **Example**: For a math module on algebra, the outcome might be "Students can solve linear equations with one unknown."
Develop rubrics	**Implementation**: Design assessment criteria with the help of AI. **Example**: For an essay on Shakespeare, the AI might suggest criteria like clarity of thesis, textual evidence, analysis quality, and grammar.
Develop course materials	**Implementation**: AI tools can curate and create reading materials, videos, and interactive elements. **Example**: For a computer science course, AI could gather relevant articles on emerging technologies and design interactive coding challenges.
Put together references	**Implementation**: AI can scan vast databases to collate a bibliography. **Example**: For a research paper on climate change, the system could pull the most cited and relevant articles from the last decade.
Create assignments, exams, and MCQs	**Implementation**: Generate assessment items based on course content. **Example**: After teaching cellular biology, AI can draft questions like "Which organelle is responsible for energy production?"

(Continued)

Table 3.13 (Continued)

Teaching	
Function	*Implementation & Example*
Create presentation and slides	**Implementation**: AI tools can design visually appealing slides based on lecture content. **Example**: For a lesson on the Renaissance, slides can be auto-generated with key points and images of relevant artworks.
Develop Q and A for videos	**Implementation**: Extract key points from educational videos to create Q&A. **Example**: From a documentary on Ancient Egypt, generate questions like "Why were pyramids built?"
Mark assignments	**Implementation**: Use AI algorithms to grade assignments based on predefined rubrics. **Example**: For a multiple-choice math test, AI can automatically grade and provide feedback on incorrect answers.
Record, transcribe, and grade oral presentations	**Implementation**: Utilise voice recognition for recording, transcribing, and assessing presentations. **Example**: After a student's oral report on World War II, the AI provides a transcript and grades based on speech clarity, content accuracy, and engagement.
Develop scripts for storyboards	**Implementation**: Draft scripts that fit educational animations or videos. **Example**: For a topic on volcanoes, AI can script a storyboard depicting the formation and eruption of a volcano.
Develop animations and GenAI videos	**Implementation**: AI software can design and produce animations based on educational content. **Example**: Turn a script about the water cycle into a dynamic animated video.
Produce class questions and notes	**Implementation**: Post-lecture, AI can distil key points and generate discussion questions. **Example**: After a class on the American Revolution, AI might draft questions like "What were the key causes?" and summarise main events.
Create crash courses	**Implementation**: Use AI to design intensive, short-term courses on specific topics. **Example**: Design a 5-day crash course on Python programming, covering basics to intermediate concepts.
Transcribe recorded lectures	**Implementation**: Convert speech in lectures to text. **Example**: After a 2-hour lecture on philosophy, get a full transcript with key points highlighted.
Develop language comprehension questions	**Implementation**: Based on reading materials, generate comprehension queries. **Example**: From an article on marine life, ask "What factors threaten coral reefs?"
Design reading quizzes, assessments, and rubrics	**Implementation**: Create quizzes to assess reading comprehension and understanding. **Example**: After assigning a chapter on quantum physics, design a quiz testing concepts like superposition and entanglement.
Design game-based and scenario-based learning	**Implementation**: AI can simulate real-world scenarios or games for learning. **Example**: For business students, simulate a stock market game where they can invest virtually.
Moderate online communities	**Implementation**: Oversee online student forums, detecting and managing inappropriate content. **Example**: In an online course forum, AI can flag off-topic posts or harassment and notify administrators.
Integrate technology and prepare flipped classrooms	**Implementation**: Design tech-enhanced lessons where students engage with content outside class. **Example**: Assign interactive online modules on cellular structures for homework, reserving class time for discussions.
Facilitate group discussions	**Implementation**: AI can suggest discussion topics, monitor participation, and provide feedback. **Example**: In a seminar on ethics, AI might propose the topic "AI and Privacy" and highlight key points from the student discussion.
Support professional development	**Implementation**: AI can curate resources, courses, and materials to enhance teacher skills. **Example**: For a teacher looking to integrate more tech in the classroom, AI might recommend online workshops on digital pedagogies.

(Continued)

Table 3.13 (Continued)

Learning

Function	Implementation & Example
Personalise learning paths	**Implementation**: AI customises content based on a learner's progress and needs. **Example**: If a student struggles in algebra, the AI suggests extra practice problems and resources.
Adaptive assessment	**Implementation**: Exams adjust difficulty based on learner's performance. **Example**: If a student answers multiple math problems correctly, the subsequent questions become more challenging.
Provide problem hints and feedback	**Implementation**: AI offers hints for unsolved problems. **Example**: On a calculus problem, AI might hint "Consider the chain rule." and then provide feedback once attempted.
Summarise and highlight information	**Implementation**: Extract key points from lengthy content. **Example**: From a 20-page article on photosynthesis, AI provides a 2-page summary with essential concepts highlighted.
Outline projects or papers	**Implementation**: Assist in structuring written assignments. **Example**: For a paper on climate change, AI suggests a layout with sections like Introduction, Causes, Effects, and Mitigation.
Interactive simulation labs	**Implementation**: Virtual labs for hands-on experience. **Example**: Students can virtually mix chemicals to witness reactions, without physical risks.
Maths simulations	**Implementation**: Simulate mathematical concepts visually. **Example**: Students can adjust parameters in a quadratic equation and watch the graph change in real-time.
Automate meeting notes	**Implementation**: AI transcribes and summarises meeting discussions. **Example**: After a group study session on WWII, AI provides key points discussed and action items.
Transcribe and analyse voice conversations	**Implementation**: Convert voice to text and derive insights. **Example**: From a lecture on Shakespeare, AI transcribes the content and pinpoints recurring themes.
Intelligent tutoring systems	**Implementation**: Personalised AI tutors assist learners. **Example**: A student struggling with geometry gets targeted lessons and quizzes from an AI tutor.
Generate code snippets and check syntax	**Implementation**: AI assists in coding. **Example**: A student stuck on a Python task can ask for a code hint, and the AI can suggest relevant code and check for errors.
Clarify, explain, and simplify concepts	**Implementation**: Make complex ideas more accessible. **Example**: For Einstein's theory of relativity, AI provides a simpler analogy using trains and observers.
Translate text and images	**Implementation**: Convert content between languages. **Example**: Translate a French poem into English, preserving its nuances.
Resolve and explain science or math problems	**Implementation**: Solve and elucidate problems step by step. **Example**: On a physics problem about momentum, AI provides the solution with a breakdown of each step.
Escape rooms, interactive scenarios, and simulations	**Implementation**: Engaging learning experiences. **Example**: Students navigate a virtual escape room, solving history puzzles to "unlock" doors and progress.
Interpret verbal questions	**Implementation**: Understand and respond to spoken queries. **Example**: A student asks, "What's the Krebs cycle?" and AI provides an oral explanation.
Analyse images	**Implementation**: Recognise and interpret visual content. **Example**: Students upload a plant picture, and AI identifies it, providing botanical information.

(Continued)

Table 3.13 (Continued)

Learning

Function	Implementation & Example
Retrieve relevant educational resources	**Implementation**: Curate study materials based on needs. **Example**: For a topic on volcanoes, AI gathers articles, videos, and interactive modules on volcanic activity.
Digital art, music, sketching, writing, and poems	**Implementation**: AI assists in creative endeavours. **Example**: Students can ask for a poem starter on autumn, and AI generates the first few lines.
Give life advice	**Implementation**: Provide guidance on personal matters. **Example**: A student feeling stressed about exams can ask for coping strategies, and AI might suggest relaxation techniques.
Shorten paragraphs, paraphrase, and check grammar	**Implementation**: Refine and condense text. **Example**: Turn a lengthy paragraph on the solar system into a concise version, ensuring it remains grammatically correct.
Design reading quizzes, assessments, and rubrics	**Implementation**: Create tools to evaluate comprehension. **Example**: After reading a chapter on the human brain, AI designs a quiz on neurons, synapses, and neurotransmitters.
Design game-based and scenario-based learning	**Implementation**: Develop interactive learning experiences. **Example**: Design a game where students navigate a virtual cell, identifying organelles to "level up".
Integrate technology, personalise learning, and prepare flipped classrooms	**Implementation**: Combine tech with tailored content and flipped teaching. **Example**: AI curates videos on genetics for home study, while in-class time is dedicated to discussions and activities.
Facilitate group discussions and monitor online interactions	**Implementation**: Oversee and guide group interactions. **Example**: AI moderates a chatroom on literature, ensuring discussions remain on-topic and flagging inappropriate comments.

Research

Function	Implementation & Example
Data analysis and prediction	**Implementation**: Analyse large datasets to predict future outcomes. **Example**: Use AI to predict climate change effects based on past data, identifying potential future hotspots.
Extract meaningful insights	**Implementation**: Sift through data to identify patterns or anomalies. **Example**: From genetic sequencing data, AI identifies a novel gene linked to a specific disease.
Literature review	**Implementation**: Scan and summarise vast amounts of literature on a topic. **Example**: For research on Alzheimer's, AI reviews and compiles key findings from hundreds of past studies.
Hypothesis generation	**Implementation**: Propose research questions based on existing data. **Example**: After analysing medical records, AI hypothesises a link between a medication and rare side effects.
Research paper writing	**Implementation**: Assist in structuring, editing, and refining academic papers. **Example**: AI suggests improvements in the methodology section of a paper on neural networks.
Peer review	**Implementation**: Review research for accuracy, novelty, and relevance. **Example**: AI flags a statistical inconsistency in a submitted paper on quantum mechanics.
Organise and manage research materials	**Implementation**: Catalogue and arrange research data, papers, and other materials. **Example**: AI creates a structured database of all references used in a multi-year astronomy study.
Track research trends	**Implementation**: Monitor academic journals and conferences for emerging topics. **Example**: AI alerts researchers to a rising trend in studies focusing on advanced technology, such as CRISPR.

(Continued)

Table 3.13 (Continued)

Research

Function	Implementation & Example
Report writing	**Implementation**: Aid in crafting detailed and coherent research reports. **Example**: For a sociological study on urban migration, AI assists in visualising and describing the findings.
Build data models	**Implementation**: Design computational models to represent and analyse data. **Example**: AI helps construct a model predicting the spread of an invasive species based on environmental factors.
Moderate online communities	**Implementation**: Oversee and manage online research forums or databases. **Example**: AI moderates a forum for quantum physics, ensuring discussions are accurate and flagging any misleading claims.

Administrative

Generate timetables	**Implementation**: Design schedules for classes, meetings, or events. **Example**: AI considers room availability and teacher schedules to produce a conflict-free timetable for the upcoming semester.
Build forms and surveys	**Implementation**: Create interactive forms for data collection. **Example**: An AI crafts a feedback form for a recently conducted workshop, ensuring that all relevant aspects are covered.
Compose and reply to emails	**Implementation**: Draft and send responses based on the context of received emails. **Example**: An administrative AI sends an acknowledgment email to students who have submitted their thesis proposals.
Data analysis on student or teacher evaluations	**Implementation**: Process and analyse feedback to derive meaningful insights. **Example**: AI analyses end-of-year evaluations to determine which courses were most effective and where improvements are needed.
Create infographics and reports	**Implementation**: Convert data into visual summaries or detailed reports. **Example**: AI produces an infographic on yearly student performance metrics across departments.
Devise policies	**Implementation**: Draft guidelines based on data and best practices. **Example**: AI proposes a new attendance policy after analysing student performance and attendance correlations.
Write recommendation letters	**Implementation**: Aid in drafting letters of recommendation. **Example**: AI drafts a template for a recommendation letter for a student applying for a graduate programme.
Automate meeting notes	**Implementation**: Transcribe, summariz, and distribute notes from meetings. **Example**: After a departmental meeting, AI sends out a concise summary of decisions and action items.
Customise student admissions	**Implementation**: Analyse student profiles and recommend suitable courses or programs. **Example**: Based on a student's achievements and interests, AI suggests they would be a good fit for the advanced science programme.
List, summarise, and outline information	**Implementation**: Compile relevant details or provide concise summaries. **Example**: AI lists all the documents needed for student enrolment and provides a summary of each.
Explain concepts and translate information	**Implementation**: Clarify ideas or convert data into different languages. **Example**: AI translates a university's admission guidelines into multiple languages for international students.
Interrelate ideas and map concepts	**Implementation**: Connect related ideas and visualise them. **Example**: AI generates a concept map linking all courses under the Computer Science department and their interrelationships.
Organise and curate resources	**Implementation**: Arrange and present data or materials systematically. **Example**: AI organises a database of exam papers, categorising them by field and importance.

(Continued)

Table 3.13 (Continued)

Administrative

Function	Implementation & Example
Moderate online communities	**Implementation**: Oversee and manage online forums or databases. **Example**: AI ensures that discussions on the university's online forum remain respectful and flags any inappropriate content.
Support professional development and counselling	**Implementation**: Provide guidance and resources for growth. **Example**: AI recommends a set of online courses and workshops to a teacher looking to expand their skills in e-learning.

3.7   Case Scenarios Embracing ChatGPT into the Higher Education Classroom

The following case scenarios investigate the transformative potential of incorporating ChatGPT and related technologies into diverse disciplines, demonstrating the adaptability and versatility of such tools. From fostering philosophical debates in a humanities course to simulating client interactions in an architectural design studio, these case studies underline the benefits of integrating innovative AI technologies into the curriculum. By also aligning with multiple levels of Bloom's Taxonomy, these implementations not only encourage students to achieve higher-order cognitive skills, but also equip them to overcome the complexities and challenges of real-life situations.

Case Scenario 1   Implementing ChatGPT as a Tool for Interactive Classwork Assignments in a Higher Education Philosophy Course

Scenario Overview: In an introductory philosophy course, a professor seeks ways to enhance student interaction and engagement outside of the traditional classroom setting. She is especially keen on using technology to facilitate deep reflections and debates on philosophical topics.

Challenge: Philosophy is not just about understanding various philosophical stances, but also about engaging in discussions, formulating one's perspective, and refining it based on counterarguments. Traditional lectures primarily involve reading and writing from which dynamic interactions essential to truly internalise philosophical debates are lacking.

Suggestion: Implementing ChatGPT as a Debate Partner for Interactive Classwork

Curriculum Design: Each week, students are presented with a philosophical stance (e.g., Utilitarianism). Their task is to have a debate with ChatGPT on the merits and demerits of the stance.

Procedures:

- Outside of class hours, students initiate a conversation with ChatGPT using its speech recognition and voice capabilities, stating their position and assigning a role for ChatGPT. They then engage in a debate, trying to defend their stance while ChatGPT offers counterarguments or plays devil's advocate.

- Post-debate, students submit a reflective essay on their discussion with ChatGPT in which they document their learnings, and identify strengths and areas for improvement.
- Students submit their chat logs, which are captured by ChatGPT transcripts, along with their reflections.
- In the following class, students are grouped together and given the opportunity to review and analyse each other's debates and reflections. This group review process adds an additional layer of interaction and learning as students can gain insights from their peers' perspectives, engage in constructive feedback, and further deepen their understanding of the philosophical stances discussed.

Bloom's Taxonomy Alignment:
- **Analysing**: By dissecting their own arguments as well as those generated by ChatGPT, students distinguish between facts and assumptions. The analysis enhances their understanding of the complexities of philosophical reasoning.
- **Evaluating**: Throughout the debate, students make judgements on the validity of the arguments put forth by both themselves and ChatGPT. Their reflections are a direct evaluation of their performance.
- **Creating**: The entire debate is an exercise in creating arguments and counterarguments, also refining thought processes based on the interaction with ChatGPT.

Outcomes: The integration of ChatGPT into the philosophy course can produce several significant outcomes:

- The dynamic nature of the assignment, combined with real-time feedback from ChatGPT, can foster increased student engagement.
- The requirement to constantly defend and structure arguments in debates allow students to develop analytical and argumentative skills.
- Through the peer review component, students can benefit from diverse perspectives, in which the collaboration among peers can also enhance collective learning.
- The ChatGPT transcripts and reflections provide the educator with a greater understanding and insight into their students' learning. This also would enable tailored classroom sessions to address specific issues based on students' demonstrated understanding of philosophical stances.

Conclusion: Incorporating ChatGPT into a philosophy course is innovative and highly effective. It encourages students to engage in philosophical concepts and provides a distinctive platform for them to develop their understanding and evaluate their comprehension. When students engage in debates with ChatGPT, they develop critical thinking through actively challenging counterarguments and, in turn, enhance their understanding of the subject matter. Such an approach, aligning with the higher-order cognitive skills of Bloom's Taxonomy, ensures that students are not just passive receivers of knowledge but active participants in the learning process.

Case Scenario 2   Incorporating ChatGPT and DALL-E3 in Architectural Design Studio for Experiential Client-based Learning

Scenario Overview: In an advanced architectural design course, a teacher aims to connect the theoretical aspects of the curriculum with the practical requirements of real-world architectural design. The objective is to cultivate an environment where students not only draft innovative designs but also consider the needs of clients, environmental contexts, and emerging architectural trends.

Challenge: Architectural education may struggle to strike a balance between theory and practice. Students could produce extremely creative designs that are impractical or, on the other hand, produce overly pragmatic designs that lack creativity. Moreover, with the rapid evolution of architectural styles and demands due to advancements in society and environmental concerns, it is important for students in architecture to stay up to date with the latest trends and techniques in order to succeed in the future.

Suggestion: Deploying ChatGPT for Simulated Client Interactions and DALL-E3 for Virtual Prototyping of Futuristic Architectures.

Curriculum Design: Each month, students are given a fictional client brief which outlines the client's requirements, constraints, and aspirations for an architectural design. These briefs are designed to cover a wide range of architectural scenarios and design styles.

Procedures:

- Client Interaction with GenAI: Before beginning their design process, students create a client character with ChatGPT or other similar GenAI software, such as Poe. The AI mimics an actual client based on the client brief, along with further client characteristics provided by the teacher. Students will then hold a simulated client–architect meeting with the AI where they ask questions, gather feedback, even pitch preliminary ideas to the 'client', refining their understanding of the brief.
- Design and Visualisation with image-generating or architectural GenAI software: After initial research and sketches, students use GenAI tools such as DALL-E3 or EvolveLab Veras to visualise their proposed designs, adjusting and refining based on the virtual prototype.
- Further Client Discussion, Feedback, and Iteration: After creating their virtual prototype, students return to ChatGPT to present their designs and receive simulated client feedback. They refine their designs accordingly.
- Peer Review: In subsequent classes, students engage in a collaborative peer review of the designs and associated client interactions, discussing strengths and potential areas for improvement.

Bloom's Taxonomy Alignment:

- **Understanding**: By interpreting and clarifying the client's needs through ChatGPT, students deepen their understanding of project requirements.

- **Applying**: Using GenAI, students apply their architectural knowledge and relevant skills to create virtual representations of their designs.
- **Analysing**: Engaging with ChatGPT in a simulated feedback loop allows students to analyse and adjust their designs based on client feedback.
- **Evaluating**: The peer review sessions provide opportunities for students to evaluate and critique both their own designs and those of their peers.
- **Creating**: From conceptualisation to virtual prototyping, students are continuously in creation mode, using technology to bring their architectural visions to life.

Outcomes: Incorporating GenAI into an advanced architectural design course will offer the following outcomes:

- Enhance student immersion in the architectural design process, striking a balance between creativity and practicality through simulating real-world scenarios.
- The integration of DALL-E3 or similar GenAI tools allow for quick, detailed prototyping, enabling students to visualise and adjust their designs in a dynamic digital environment.
- The simulated client interactions with ChatGPT can facilitate development of essential soft skills, such as communication, persuasion, and adaptability.

Conclusion: Integrating GenAI tools into the architectural design curriculum has the potential to effectively combine the creative, practical, and interpersonal aspects of architecture. This innovative approach, aligned with multiple levels of Bloom's Taxonomy, would equip students to be both creative designers and adept professionals, prepared to overcome future architectural challenges.

Case Scenario 3   Reverse Engineering Essays with ChatGPT in an Advanced English Studies Course

Scenario Overview: In a senior-level English studies course focusing on modern literature, the professor aims to refine students' skills in analysis and synthesis of information. Recognising the potential challenge of students' over-reliance on AI for writing essays, the professor is interested in an innovative approach that emphasises analytical depth while ensuring academic integrity.

Challenge: English studies, particularly literature analysis, requires deep comprehension, synthesis, and original perspectives. Direct use of AI can raise issues of academic integrity, with students potentially over-relying on AI to write essays, reducing originality.

Suggestion: Reverse Engineering Essays with ChatGPT.

Curriculum Design: Rather than writing the essay itself, students are given an AI-generated analytical essay on a literary text and are tasked to reverse engineer it: they must break down and identify its arguments, themes, perspectives, and rhetorical strategies, in order to demonstrate their understanding of not only the text, but also the discourse analysis.

Procedures:

- Students receive a ChatGPT-generated essay on a specific literary piece.
- They dissect the essay and identify its key elements such as the main thesis, insights, arguments, evidence from the text, rhetorical devices, and so on.
- Students then compare the AI's interpretation of the text with their own understanding, noting any disparities and drawing connections.
- With their insights from this task, students draft an essay outline or concept map for how they would approach the topic, supported by original examples from the literary work.
- Teachers can then use software such as Padlets and Miro boards for students to virtually share their work, as well as provide comments and feedback to each other.

Bloom's Taxonomy Alignment:

- **Analysing**: By deconstructing the AI-generated essay, students examine its components and discern how arguments are constructed, linked, and substantiated.
- **Evaluating**: Comparing the AI's perspective with their own interpretations allows students to appraise the quality, relevance, and depth of analysis of an essay.
- **Creating**: By using their understanding to draft an original essay outline and/or create a concept map, students demonstrate their capability to construct unique interpretations and connections, supported with original examples.

Outcomes: Incorporating the reverse engineering approach using ChatGPT in the English course can achieve the following outcomes:

- A heightened understanding of essay structure and analytical depth among students.
- Academic integrity is upheld as ChatGPT only demonstrates and facilitates analysis, rather than creating content for students, pushing the latter to come up with their own interpretations.
- Peer review further enhances collaborative learning experiences, allowing students to better appreciate diverse perspectives and refine their analytical skills.

Conclusion: The reverse engineering approach, using ChatGPT-generated essays in an English studies course, can allow students to more deeply engage with literary analysis and form original perspectives. This methodology encourages students to be active participants, aligns with higher-order cognitive skills in Bloom's Taxonomy, and reaffirms the course's commitment to upholding academic integrity.

Case Scenario 4   Utilising ChatGPT for Clinical Reflection in a Higher Education Medicine Course

Scenario Overview: In the field of medicine, clinical reasoning and self-reflection are critical for nurturing adept medical practitioners. In an advanced medical course, a professor is looking for innovative tools to assist students in enhancing their clinical reflections, drawn from case-based scenarios or direct patient interactions.

Challenge: Clinical reasoning requires both analytical skills and an introspective awareness of one's decision-making process. Although conventional reflection exercises are valuable, they can often be limited by biases or insufficient in-depth introspection.

Suggestion: Introducing ChatGPT for Assisted Clinical Reflection.

Curriculum Design: After each clinical rotation or patient case study, students are assigned the task of engaging in a reflective conversation with ChatGPT to examine their decisions, rationales, and emotional responses during the rotation or case study, and identify valuable learning moments.

Procedures:

- Following a clinical interaction or case study, students initiate a session with ChatGPT, providing the AI with an overview of the patient's presentation and the decisions made. To help provide students with a real-life example of clinical conversations, the professor may also share a transcript between a patient and a doctor to the students to use as reference, using GenAI software such as Nabla Co-pilot, which records and transcribes conversations in medical practices.
- ChatGPT assumes the role of the patient or the doctor and poses questions to students, encouraging deeper reflections on their reasoning, potential alternative decisions, and the emotional elements of the interaction.
- These AI-driven prompts facilitate a more thorough introspective process for students, allowing evaluation of multiple aspects of clinical interactions.
- Based on conversations with ChatGPT and their personal insights, students keep their reflections in a reflective journal.
- The professor or teaching assistants provide written and/or verbal feedback intermittently, furthering the reflective process and sharing of diverse perspectives.

Bloom's Taxonomy Alignment:

- **Analysing**: By engaging with ChatGPT, students dissect their decisions and evaluate underlying rationales and any potential biases.
- **Evaluating**: Through discussions with ChatGPT, students assess the quality of their decisions by comparing them to established clinical guidelines and exploring alternative choices.
- **Creating**: The reflective journal encourages students to construct a holistic narrative of their learning journey that incorporates both the intellectual and emotional components of their clinical experiences.

Outcomes: The implementation of ChatGPT to assist in reflection can lead to the following outcomes:

- Student reflections can be enhanced to capture a broader spectrum of the clinical experience, resulting in increased depth in reflective journals.
- Students can further develop their clinical reasoning abilities as they become more adept at recognising biases, identifying knowledge gaps, and noting areas that require further skills development.
- The initial AI interaction will enrich feedback sessions, fostering a collaborative environment that facilitates shared learning and mutual growth.

Conclusion: Incorporating ChatGPT into reflective practices in a clinical medical course is a transformative step. It brings a new dimension to the reflective process, enabling students to engage more deeply with their experiences and further refine their clinical skills. By combining the advanced capabilities of ChatGPT with the reflective practices crucial to medical practice, students become more adept practitioners, as well as more insightful, self-aware professionals. This novel approach resonates with the higher cognitive domains of Bloom's Taxonomy, empowering students to be reflective throughout their careers in the ever-evolving medical field.

3.8   Introduction to Prompt Engineering

The rise of GenAI has not only revolutionised various sectors but also brought about new career opportunities, one of which is 'Prompt Engineering'. A glance at job ads with eye-catching salaries for prompt engineers, and articles from *Forbes* (Cook, 2023) and *Time* (Popli, 2023), shows the escalating demand and significance of this role. However, what exactly is prompt engineering and why is it important? Prompt engineering is the bridge between human language and machine understanding, ensuring smooth, intuitive interactions between the two. This section discusses the art and science of prompt engineering, explaining its necessity and the strategies involved in designing effective prompts to converse with GenAI.

3.8.1   *The Essence of Prompts*

At the heart of our interactions with GenAI tools, especially with language processing models, are prompts. They serve as cues or instructions, guiding the GenAI system to generate relevant outputs. Whether it is asking Siri to set a reminder or Bing Chat to retrieve information, prompts are how we start our conversations with GenAI. The effectiveness of such interactions greatly depends on how well we craft our prompts. Better prompts not only enhance our experience with AI, but also optimise the model's performance, making AI more useful and efficient as a tool in our daily lives.

The importance of prompt engineering is crucial for a multitude of AI utilisations, making it an essential skill. It can help with debugging, tweaking AI models, and ensuring resource efficiency – for example, when our prompts are more detailed and accurate, the model will be able to generate desired outputs more quickly and efficiently, using less computational resources overall. In a world where AI–human collaborations will become increasingly prevalent, mastering prompt engineering will be a technical requirement as well as a pathway to making AI more intuitive and better aligned with human expectations. It is a skill key to our future-readiness.

3.8.2   The Prompt Engineering Components

The design of effective prompts doesn't have a 'one-size-fits-all' formula. Instead, we must understand the Prompt Engineering Components and apply them sensibly. Below we include seven useful Components – Instruction, Context, Role, Succinctness, Example, Format, and Readjustment, as shown in Figure 3.4. For readers to practice applying these, we provide a 'Try-It Prompt' at the end of each component description below. Using the example of "Constructivism in Education", these example prompts provide a concrete context to understand how the "Prompt Engineering Components" can be used.

Instruction: The instruction component is the foundation of a prompt, providing the AI with a clear directive on what it should generate or provide. It is akin to asking a precise question to obtain a precise answer. The clarity of instruction helps steer the AI towards the desired output, ensuring the responses are aligned with, and relevant to, the user's expectations. For example, in higher education, instructing an AI to summarise a research article sets a clear task for it to execute.

Try-It Prompt: Explain the concept of Constructivism in Education.

Context: Context provides additional information that helps the AI understand the situation or background against which the instruction is being given. Including context can lead to more informed and nuanced responses, helping users eliminate ambiguity, and further ensure that the AI's response is relevant and accurate. For instance, specifying the topic and time frame in a request for summarising a research article helps the AI to focus its response accordingly.

Try-It Prompt: Explain the concept of Constructivism in Education, focusing on its impact and implications for online learning.

Figure 3.4 The Prompt Engineering Components.

Role: The role component allows the user to specify a persona or capacity in which they want the AI to respond. This could be particularly useful in educational settings where the tone or perspectives of a response could vary, based on the assigned role. For example, instructing the AI to assume the role of an academic advisor could generate a response that is professional and supportive, whereas asking it to assume the role of a student mentor may generate one that is more friendly and casual.

Try-It Prompt: Please take on the role of a university professor and explain the concept of Constructivism in Education, focusing on its impact and implications for online learning.

Succinctness: Succinctness is the importance of conciseness and clarity in crafting prompts. A well-structured, concise prompt is easier for the AI to interpret and accurately respond to. It is about striking a balance between providing enough information and not confusing the AI with excessive details, thereby enabling more efficient communication.

Try-It Prompt: As a university professor, explain Constructivism in Education and its impact and implications for online learning, focusing only on how it influences course design.

Example: Providing an example within a prompt serves to clarify or further illustrate the instruction(s), helping the AI to better understand the task at hand. Examples can be especially helpful in complex or ambiguous requests, offering a reference point for the AI to gauge the kind of response expected by the user.

Try-It Prompt: As a university professor, explain Constructivism in Education and its impact and implications for online learning, focusing on how it might influence course design. For example, discuss how a constructivist approach would encourage students to interact and build knowledge through discussions in online forums.

Format: The format component specifies the desired structure of the AI's response, be it in paragraphs, bullet points, tables, etc. Specifying a format helps in obtaining responses that are easy to read, understand, and utilise, especially in educational or research contexts where the organisation of the information and data presentation are important.

Try-It Prompt: As a university professor, provide a bullet-point summary of Constructivism in Education and its impact and implications for online learning, particularly for course design. Categorise the bullet points into subthemes.

Adjustment: Adjustment is the process of refining the prompt based on previous responses from the AI. It is about tweaking the prompt to enhance clarity, add missing details, or correct misunderstandings, in order to generate a better, more accurate output. This component is an iterative approach to prompt engineering, facilitating a learning loop between the user and the AI.

Try-It Prompt: As a university professor, provide a detailed explanation of Constructivism in Education, its historical evolution in Asia, and its implications for online course design, in a bullet-point format.

3.8.2.1 Other Prompting Techniques

Zero-shot learning: Zero-shot learning refers to when an AI model is expected to perform tasks for which it has not been previously given training data on. It is about leveraging the model's existing knowledge to interpret and respond to new, unseen prompts. In prompt engineering, this strategy can be crucial for exploring the AI model's ability to generalise and provide meaningful responses to novel requests.

Few-shot learning: Few-shot learning involves providing a small number of examples to guide the AI model in understanding a new task. Unlike zero-shot learning, here, the model has a few reference points to base its responses on. In prompt engineering, this strategy helps to fine-tune the model's responses by providing some context through a few examples, allowing it to better align with the user's expectations for the outputs.

Chain of Thought: The Chain of Thought strategy involves crafting a series of logically connected prompts that build upon each other, developing a more coherent and in-depth conversation with the AI model. Through facilitating dialogue that has a continuous and logical flow, this enables more engaging and insightful interactions with AI.

Negative and Positive Prompting: Negative and Positive Prompting involves specifying what you do and do *not* want in the AI's output. Positive prompting specifies which certain elements to include, while negative prompting specifies which to exclude. This strategy is important for structuring and refining the AI's responses in accordance with the user's expectations.

Each of these prompt engineering components and techniques offers specifications with which we can craft and refine our prompts, enhancing the effectiveness and utility of our interactions with AI, especially in more complex domains. We will have to think carefully about which components we select and combine for use; with practice, one can master the skills of prompt engineering, making their AI interactions more efficient, engaging, and productive.

The world of prompt engineering is as vast as it is thought-provoking. It is about crafting a language that resonates with machines, making our conversations with AI not just meaningful but also enjoyable. Whether as an AI enthusiast, researcher, or someone just curious about the emergence of an AI–human future, understanding prompt engineering will bring us all a step closer to better human-and-machine collaboration, where we converse, work, and innovate together with these tools and technologies.

3.9 Conclusions

This chapter has been an enlightening exploration into the nexus of GenAI and pedagogy. It illustrated a range of potentials, challenges, and intricacies of integrating advanced tools like ChatGPT into our educational systems. Through our discussions, we have also established that while AI is a powerful tool, it is not perfect. Its effectiveness relies on our ability to utilise its capabilities correctly, understanding its strengths and limitations.

Our exploration in the "Literary Study of ChatGPT's GPT-4 via Bloom's Taxonomy" further showcased AI's capabilities. Focusing on Bloom's Taxonomy, we looked at how ChatGPT can demonstrate different levels of cognitive processes, from remembering and recalling information to the more complex level of creation. The intersection of AI and established educational frameworks explored AI's role in literary and textual analyses, offering novel approaches for curriculum development and educational research in higher education.

The conversation around AI in education often revolves around its efficacy or efficiency, but its true potential is in its capacity to revolutionise. It promises not just automation but augmentation; with AI, we can better foster an environment where rote learning gives way to creative synthesis, and where students are not mere recipients but active constructors of knowledge.

Yet, as we stand on this precipice of transformation, introspection is crucial. The appeal of AI is undeniable, but its integration into pedagogy demands a judicious balance. We must be wary of viewing it as a panacea, for the essence of education lies in the human touch – the spark of curiosity, the thrill of discovery, and the warmth of mentorship. AI, in its most potent form, should serve to amplify these experiences, not replace them.

As we look to the future, the development of relevant frameworks and ongoing research will be vital milestones to ensure that AI's role in education grows, and does so in a way that meaningfully enriches the learning experience for all. As we close this chapter, let it be a call to educators, technologists, and learners to together co-construct an educational paradigm that not only integrates AI into teaching and learning, but is also inspired by it.

Questions to Ponder

- How can educators ensure that the AI tools they incorporate into teaching and learning, align with their curriculum's objectives and values?
- Is it possible that with the integration of ChatGPT technology, certain undergraduate programmes may become less relevant and result in challenges for students when looking for employment opportunities?
- As the use of AI tools becomes more commonplace in education, how can we prepare students to critically engage with and evaluate the information they obtain from such tools?
- How can we measure the long-term impact of AI-integrated curriculums on student learning outcomes and the overall educational quality?

Personal Reflection

From our studies, ChatGPT can provide responses that go beyond the recall (remembering) level of Bloom's Taxonomy, and appears to be capable of attaining levels further up in the hierarchy – even the level of creating. Of course, currently, it does require human prompting and does not produce these responses autonomously; it often requires a number of steps (sophisticated, concise, and articulate prompts) before achieving these higher cognitive levels. It makes us wonder if GenAI tools really have "intelligence"? (Though it is not for this book to answer, I must admit it gets us all thinking.) In a later chapter, we will discuss how large language models generate text; maybe after learning more, you can draw your own conclusions.

References

Ahuja, K., Diddee, H., Hada, R., Ochieng, M., Ramesh, K., Jain, P., Nambi, A., Ganu, T., Segal, S., Axmed, M., Bali, K., & Sitaram, S. (2023). MEGA: Multilingual evaluation of generative AI. https://doi.org/10.48550/arXiv.2303.12528

Anderson, Lorin W., & Krathwohl, David R. (Eds.). (2001). *A taxonomy for learning, teaching, and assessing: A revision of Bloom's Taxonomy of educational objectives.* Longman.

Arora, A., Barrett, M., Lee, E., Oborn, E., & Prince, K. (2023). Risk and the future of AI: Algorithmic bias, data colonialism, and marginalization. *Information and Organization, 33*(3), 100478. https://doi.org/10.1016/j.infoandorg.2023.100478

Bhavnani, S. P., Narula, J., & Sengupta, P. P. (2016). Mobile technology and the digitization of healthcare. *European Heart Journal, 37*(18), 1428–1438. https://doi.org/10.1093/eurheartj/ehv770

Bloom, B. S., Engelhart, M. D., Furst, E. J., Hill, W. H., & Krathwohl, D. R. (1956). *Taxonomy of educational objectives: The classification of educational goals. Vol. Handbook I: Cognitive domain.* David McKay Company.

Brown, B., & Chalmers, M. (2003). Tourism and mobile technology. *Proceedings of the 2003 European Conference on Computer Supported Cooperative Work (ECSCW)* (pp. 335–354).

Browne, R. (2023, February 8). *All you need to know about ChatGPT, the A.I. chatbot that's got the world talking and tech giants clashing.* CNBC. https://www.cnbc.com/2023/02/08/what-is-chatgpt-viral-ai-chatbot-at-heart-of-microsoft-google-fight.html

Chan, C. K. Y. (2023). Is AI changing the rules of academic misconduct? An in-depth look at students' perceptions of 'AI-giarism'. https://arxiv.org/abs/2306.03358

Chan, C. K. Y., Hu, W. (2023). Students' voices on generative AI: perceptions, benefits, and challenges in higher education. *International Journal of Educational Technology in Higher Education, 20,* 43. https://doi.org/10.1186/s41239-023-00411-8

Chan, C. K. Y., & Lee, K. K. W. (2023). The AI generation gap: Are Gen Z students more interested in adopting generative AI such as ChatGPT in teaching and learning than their Gen X and Millennial Generation teachers? *Smart Learning Environments.* https://doi.org/10.1186/s40561-023-00269-3

Chan, C. K. Y., & Tsi, L. H. Y. (2023). The AI revolution in education: Will AI replace or assist teachers in higher education? [Preprint]. arXiv. https://arxiv.org/abs/2305.01185

Chow, A. R. (2023, February 8). *How ChatGPT managed to grow faster than TikTok or Instagram.* Time. https://time.com/6253615/chatgpt-fastest-growing/

Cook, J. (2023, July 12). *AI prompt engineers earn $300k salaries: Here's how to learn the skill for free.* Forbes. Retrieved from https://www.forbes.com/sites/jodiecook/2023/07/12/ai-prompt-engineers-earn-300k-salaries-heres-how-to-learn-the-skill-for-free/

Edison Software. (2019, June 27). *Across generations, email remains a critical tool for daily life.* Edison Software. https://www.edisonmail.com/blog/study-across-generations-email-remains-a-critical-tool

Ferrara, E. (2023). Should ChatGPT be biased? challenges and risks of bias in large language models. arXiv preprint arXiv:2304.03738

Google Cloud Blog. (2023, August 22). Multimodal search: LLMs with vision change businesses. https://cloud.google.com/blog/products/ai-machine-learning/multimodal-generative-ai-search

Holmes, W., Bialik, M., & Fadel, C. (2019). *Artificial intelligence in education: Promises and implications for teaching and learning.* The Center for Curriculum Redesign.

Holstein, K., & Doroudi, S. (2021). Equity and artificial intelligence in education: Will "AIEd" amplify or alleviate inequities in education? arXiv preprint arXiv:2104.12920.

Huang, C.-Z. A., Koops, H. V., Newton-Rex, E., Dinculescu, M., & Cai, C. J. (2020). AI song contest: Human-AI Co-creation in songwriting. ArXiv:2010.05388.

Law, R., Chan, I. C. C., & Wang, L. (2018). A comprehensive review of mobile technology use in hospitality and tourism. *Journal of Hospitality Marketing & Management, 27*(6), 626–648.

Leggatt, J., Broverman, A., & Pratt, K. (2023, March 20). *What is ChatGPT? A review of the AI program in its own words.* Forbes. https://www.forbes.com/uk/advisor/business/software/what-is-chatgpt/#:~:text=features%20and%20improvements.-,How%20does%20ChatGPT%20work%3F,the%20less%20advanced%20GPT%2D3

Li, Z., Shi, L., Wang, J., Cristea, A. I., & Zhou, Y. (2023). *Sim-GAIL: A generative adversarial imitation learning approach of student modelling for intelligent tutoring systems.* Neural Computing and Applications. Advance online publication. https://doi.org/10.1007/s00521-023-08989-w

Lim, J., Leinonen, T., Lipponen, L., Lee, H., DeVita, J., & Murray, D. (2023). Artificial intelligence as relational artifacts in creative learning. *Digital Creativity, 34,* 1–19.

Long D. W. (2018). Exploring Generational Differences in Text Messaging Usage and Habits. Doctoral dissertation. Nova Southeastern University. Retrieved from NSUWorks, College of Engineering and Computing. (1060) https://nsuworks.nova.edu/gscis_etd/1060

Malhotra, S. (2020, July 10). *How AI could revolutionize the future of mobile*. Forbes Technology Council. https://www.forbes.com/sites/forbestechcouncil/2020/07/10/how-ai-could-revolutionize-the-future-of-mobile/?sh=4bb9e6506a5c

Nicoletti, L., & Bass, D. (2023, October 19). *Generative AI takes stereotypes and bias from bad to worse*. Bloomberg.com. https://www.bloomberg.com/graphics/2023-generative-ai-bias/

OpenAI. (2023, September 23). ChatGPT can now see, hear, and speak. Retrieved from https://openai.com/blog/chatgpt-can-now-see-hear-and-speak

Pavlik, J. V. (2023). Collaborating with ChatGPT: Considering the implications of generative artificial intelligence for journalism and media education. *Journalism & Mass Communication Educator*, 107769582211495. https://doi.org/10.1177/10776958221149577

Pedro, F., Subosa, M., Rivas, A., & Valverde, P. (2019). Artificial intelligence in education: Challenges and opportunities for sustainable development, UNESCO, https://unesdoc.unesco.org/ark:/48223/pf0000366994.locale=en

Popli, N. (2023, April 14). *The AI job that pays up to $335K—And you don't need a computer engineering background*. Time. Retrieved from https://time.com/6272103/ai-prompt-engineer-job/

Rozado, D. (2023). The political biases of ChatGPT. *Social Science*, *12*(3), 148. https://doi.org/10.3390/socsci12030148

Ruiz, Nataniel, Li, Yuanzhen, Jampani, Varun, Pritch, Yael, Rubinstein, Michael, & Aberman, Kfir (2023). DreamBooth: Fine Tuning Text-to-Image Diffusion Models for Subject-Driven Generation. *Proceedings of the IEEE/CVF Conference on Computer Vision and Pattern Recognition (CVPR)* (pp. 22500–22510).

Scharth, M. (2022). *The ChatGPT chatbot is blowing people away with its writing skills*. The University of Sydney. https://www.sydney.edu.au/news-opinion/news/2022/12/08/the-chatgpt-chatbot-is-blowing-people-away-with-its-writing-skil.html

Shankland, S. (2023, February 19). *Why we're obsessed with the mind-blowing ChatGPT AI Chatbot*. CNET. https://www.cnet.com/tech/computing/why-were-all-obsessed-with-the-mind-blowing-chatgpt-ai-chatbot/

Vartiainen, H. & Tedre, M. (2023). Using artificial intelligence in craft education: Crafting with text-to-image generative models, *Digital Creativity*, *34*(1), 1–21. https://doi.org/10.1080/14626268.2023.2174557

Wang, T. (2023). Navigating generative AI (ChatGPT) in higher education: Opportunities and challenges. In Anutariya, C., Liu, D., Kinshuk, Tlili, A., Yang, J., Chang, M. (Eds.), *Smart learning for a sustainable society. ICSLE 2023*. Lecture Notes in Educational Technology. Springer. https://doi.org/10.1007/978-981-99-5961-7_28

Weisz, J. D., Muller, M., He, J., & Houde, S. (2023). Toward general design principles for generative AI applications. *ACM Conference on Human Factors in Computing Systems (CHI) Extended Abstracts* (pp. 1–6). ACM. https://doi.org/10.48550/arXiv.2301.05578

4 Redesigning Assessment in the AI Era

> This "arms race" between assessing GenAI and AI tools used by students could lead to a scenario where genuine learning takes a backseat to merely "gaming the system".
>
> Cecilia KY Chan

4.1 Introduction

The current pedagogical landscape of higher education can be visualised as a complex web where learning outcomes, pedagogy, and assessment mechanisms intersect. At its core, assessment serves as a barometer for both educators and learners, offering insights into educational effectiveness and areas of improvement. From the vantage point of curriculum design, the triad of learning outcomes, pedagogies, and assessment tools plays a fundamental role. While learning outcomes encapsulate the desired educational objectives, pedagogies outline the means to achieve them. Assessment, then, serves as the evaluation mechanism, answering the pivotal question: Have the students truly learned?

As we enter the era of AI, the emergence of GenAI offers a pivotal transformation in this complex landscape. GenAI, with its advanced capabilities, can redefine assessment methodologies, providing real-time, adaptive, and personalised evaluations and feedback. While its potential to streamline and enhance assessment practices is unprecedented, it also brings forth ethical considerations and challenges in maintaining academic integrity, fairness, and human-centric conflicts. The integration of GenAI in assessment transcends traditional boundaries, opening new avenues for innovation while also demanding a thoughtful reckoning with its implications.

For students, assessment often dictates their learning approaches. As noted by Ramsden (2003), students' perceptions of assessment can profoundly influence their learning strategies, oscillating between deep, holistic understanding and surface-level memorisation. This places immense responsibility on educators to craft assessments that not only evaluate but also inspire genuine learning. This chapter will explore the multi-faceted role of GenAI in shaping the future of assessment, reflecting both its promises and perils with recent research findings, and providing some strategies and assessment framework for teachers to rethink and redesign their assessment in the GenAI era.

4.2 The Evolution of Assessment and Outcomes-Based Learning in Higher Education

In education, assessment stands as an unshakable pillar, underpinning the foundation of academic endeavours and pedagogical aspirations. Traditionally understood as the systematic

DOI: 10.4324/9781003459026-4

evaluation of student learning, assessment spans a continuum from gauging knowledge and skill acquisition to understanding changes in attitudes and beliefs; in short, assessment drives learning (Rust, 2002). This intricate balance of measurement is designed with four primary purposes: 1). Judging academic achievement, 2). Safeguarding academic standards and quality, 3). Ensuring accountability to stakeholders, and 4). Crucially, steering student learning (Chan, 2023, p. 41, Ch 3).

While the purposes of assessment have remained consistent over time, the methodologies, tools, and perspectives surrounding assessment have evolved (Fischer et al., 2023; Scott, 2020), reflecting changing educational philosophies and societal demands. For example, historically, summative assessment, also known as *Assessment of Learning*, was primarily viewed as the driving force behind students' learning. This type of assessment is often associated with grades and occurs at the end of the learning cycle. This perspective was rooted in the belief that the anticipation of grades, marks, or evaluations would motivate students to study, understand, and retain information. In essence, the looming presence of a final assessment dictated the pace, approach, and intensity of a student's study habits. However, in recent years, the growing recognition of formative assessment has been playing an important role in student learning. Formative assessment, often termed *Assessment for Learning* (AfL), is the process of providing feedback to students throughout the learning process, with the goal of helping them to improve their understanding and performance. This type of assessment typically uses criterion-reference to compare students' achievements to specific goals or benchmarks. Michael Scriven introduced the concept of formative assessment in the 1960s to differentiate it from summative assessment. Black and Wiliam (1998) posited that an assessment becomes truly formative when its results guide and modify instructional methods to better suit students' needs. Echoing this sentiment, Wiggins (1998) emphasised that the primary objective of formative assessment is to facilitate and elevate students' learning, rather than just to monitor it.

Traditionally, summative and formative assessments were viewed in distinct silos; the former focused on end-of-learning evaluations and the latter on ongoing feedback during the learning process. However, this binary view has been challenged and reshaped. For instance, at the University of British Columbia, a two-stage exam approach blurs the line between these assessments (Gilley & Clarkston, 2014). In this method, students initially take the exam individually, followed by a collaborative re-examination in small groups. This not only promotes individual accountability but also encourages peer feedback and collaborative learning, combining the evaluative nature of summative assessment with the feedback-driven approach of formative assessment. Such innovative practices underscore that summative and formative assessments aren't mutually exclusive but can be harmoniously integrated (Chan, 2023, p. 45, Ch 3; Dixson & Worrell, 2016). As pedagogical research advances, the dichotomy between these assessments becomes less pronounced, recognising that they can often serve dual purposes and mutually enrich the learning experience.

In a recent article by Fischer et al. (2023), the perspective of traditional assessment is once again being challenged. The article demonstrates the contemporary understanding of assessment goes beyond its mere function as a motivator. In fact, in today's educational landscape, the role of assessment is not just to gauge learning but to foster a deeper, more holistic understanding of subjects, skills, and attitudes (Chan & Luk, 2022). One of the key shifts in this perspective is the recognition of higher education's responsibility to promote lifelong learning. Assessment, in this paper (Fischer et al., 2023), is seen as a tool to support students in developing evaluative judgement capabilities – i.e., the ability to critically assess their work and the work of their peers (Tai et al., 2018).

In the dynamic sphere of higher education, the assessment landscape continues to evolve, reflecting the multi-faceted nature of the educational journey. Central to this evolution is the understanding that true learning transcends mere knowledge acquisition. Instead, it encompasses a holistic approach that integrates feedback and reflection with conventional methodologies of learning outcomes, learning approaches, and assessment.

Assessment has often relegated feedback to a secondary role, treated as a mere by-product of evaluation. Similarly, reflection, the process of introspection and critical thinking about one's learning experiences, remains an unintentional component in curriculum design. However, to truly understand and optimise the learning process, feedback and reflection must be given their rightful place at the forefront of educational methodologies.

Reflection, as I articulated it in my book *Assessment for Experiential Learning* (Chan, 2023, p. 160, Ch. 5), is "how you see yourself before, now and after; how you see yourself from different perspectives; how you see yourself after certain situations or experiences; how you see yourself, your actions and your behaviours after you observe others". Such introspection is foundational for metacognitive development, fostering higher-order thinking processes. Furthermore, established educational theories, from Bloom's Taxonomy (Bloom, 1956) to Biggs' SOLO taxonomy (Biggs & Collis, 1982), underscore the significance of reflection in deep learning. Reflection not only nurtures higher cognitive skills but also facilitates transformative learning, wherein learners integrate new information, critically evaluate past knowledge, and derive new insights.

Feedback, on the other hand, is more than just a response to student performance. In its essence, feedback is a dialogue – a continuous exchange of information between the educator and the learner. As Carless and Boud (2018) emphasise, feedback is a process wherein learners interpret information from various sources and utilise it to enhance their work or learning strategies. Without meaningful feedback, the learning process remains incomplete, limiting the depth and breadth of the learning experience.

Assessment as Learning, as articulated by Earl (2003), is a profound shift from traditional assessment paradigms. Rather than seeing assessment as an external process imposed upon students, it reframes assessment as a self-regulated learning process. Central to this is the intertwining of feedback and reflection, which together create a dynamic loop of continuous improvement and self-awareness (Carless, 2015, p. 199). Feedback, both formal and informal, serves as a mirror for students in the assessment-as-learning approach. As students embark on self-assessment and peer assessment, feedback becomes an integral component, offering insights, clarifications, and directions for improvement. Whether it is feedback they give to themselves, feedback from peers, or feedback from educators, it acts as a guidepost, highlighting areas of strength and those needing further development. While feedback provides direction, reflection is the mechanism that internalises this feedback. Through reflection, students don't just passively receive feedback but actively engage with it. They question their understanding, dissect their thought processes, and, most importantly, they make conscious decisions about their learning paths. Reflecting on feedback allows students to adjust their strategies, realign their goals, and solidify their understanding.

The traditional landscape of higher education assessment, while effective in measuring specific learning outcomes, often falls short in providing a comprehensive understanding of the student's learning journey (Boud & Falchikov, 2006). The predominant focus on high-stakes examinations promotes rote learning and does not foster critical thinking or self-awareness (Stobart, 2008; Wiliam, 2011). Feedback, when provided, is often delayed, generic, and not actionable, limiting its potential to guide and improve student performance.

Furthermore, the absence of structured reflective practices in curriculum design means that students miss out on opportunities for self-assessment and personal growth. Reflection, despite its recognised importance, is challenging to assess, primarily because it requires understanding a learner's past, present, and future directions (Chan & Lee, 2021). This complexity, combined with various institutional and sociocultural factors, often relegates reflection to the periphery of the educational process.

Integrating feedback and reflection into the assessment landscape is not just about adding two more components to the curriculum. It is about reimagining the entire educational process. When students receive timely, specific, and actionable feedback, they become active participants in their learning journey, taking responsibility for their growth. With structured reflection opportunities, students can introspect, analyse, and derive insights from their experiences, fostering a deeper understanding of the subject and themselves.

And in the midst of this ongoing evolution, the advent of GenAI promises yet another significant transformation in the assessment dimension. As we currently transition from emphasising mere knowledge acquisition towards a more holistic, formative process that prioritises feedback and reflection, GenAI brings potential to further refine this shift. The unparalleled data-processing capabilities and adaptability of GenAI can augment the assessment process, allowing for more nuanced, real-time feedback and adaptive approach to learning. However, as educators, while we harness the power of GenAI, it is imperative to ensure that assessments remain grounded in authentic learning experiences, challenging students in ways that stimulate genuine reflection, develop evaluative judgement and foster a deeper, metacognitive approach to learning. As GenAI becomes a more integrated tool in the educational landscape, the challenge lies in designing or redesigning assessments that leverage its capabilities while ensuring that the focus remains on promoting profound, meaningful learning. The future of assessment, with the convergence of traditional pedagogies and advanced AI technologies, is on the horizon, beckoning educators to navigate this uncharted territory with both enthusiasm and discernment. Figure 4.1 shows a modified outcomes-based approach with an emphasis on assessment.

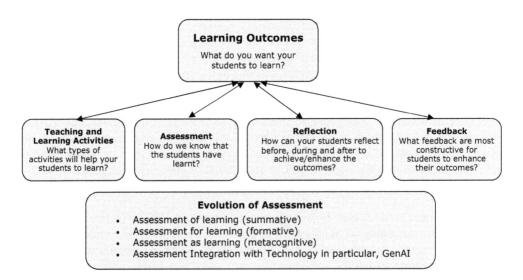

Figure 4.1 Outcomes-Based Approach to Student Learning with Reflection and Feedback.

4.3   Challenges in Assessment in the Traditional Era

The challenges in academic knowledge assessment are manifold and have been intricately woven into the fabric of education for decades. Central to these challenges is the multi-faceted purpose of assessment. While the primary role of assessment should ideally be to guide and improve student learning, it often dons multiple hats, sometimes serving as a tool for bureaucratic mandates or accountability checks. Fendrich (2007) critically observes that many current assessment practices resemble mere "accountability" exercises rather than genuine efforts to enhance the quality of education. Moreover, there is a stark disparity in how teachers and students perceive assessment. While educators often view it as a tool for reporting, students see it as a mere culminating grade, signalling the end of their learning process (Chan et al., 2017; Montgomery & Baker, 2007; Sonnleitner & Kovacs, 2020; Van de Watering & Van der Rijt, 2006).

This perception dilemma is exacerbated by the common pitfalls in assessment design. Constructive misalignment, where there is a mismatch between learning activities, outcomes, and assessment methods, is still prevalent. Often, simplistic assessment methods, like multiple-choice questions, are used in scenarios that demand deeper evaluations, while more complex methods are misapplied in simpler contexts. The historical reliance on high-stakes examinations (Stobart, 2008; Wiliam, 2011) further compounds the issue, leading to rote learning and fostering a competitive rather than a collaborative learning environment. Such systems, especially when they employ norm-referencing standards, often discourage true learning and collaboration among students.

Feedback, a crucial element of the learning process, presents its own set of challenges. While timely and personalised feedback can significantly enhance student learning, it also means a considerable workload for educators. This becomes even more pronounced in the era of mass higher education where student numbers are burgeoning. Group assessments, despite their potential benefits, bring logistical nightmares. Without clear objectives and expectations, they can sow discord among students and dilute the educational benefits they are meant to provide. Furthermore, the growing trend towards modular curricula means students grapple with increased assessment workloads, leaving little room for deep learning.

In addition, assessing experiential learning types of pedagogical approaches presents unique challenges distinct from those of traditional academic knowledge assessment (Kuh, 2008). One significant issue is the ambiguity surrounding the learning outcomes related to experiential learning. As Luk and Chan (2021) elucidated, while there are general learning outcomes, each student's experience and motivation can lead to specific outcomes, complicating the design of aligned assessments. Experiential learning often focuses less on mastering specific knowledge and more on acquiring or enhancing particular competencies, necessitating meticulously crafted assessment designs.

There is an evident lack of clarity around the conceptualisation of competencies (Chan et al., 2017). The absence of a clear definition or set list of competencies students should develop makes it challenging to determine what and how to assess. This is compounded by the fact that experiential learning outcomes often aren't tied directly to specific academic disciplines, making them harder for educators to evaluate.

The logistics and practicalities of assessment in experiential learning further intensify the challenges. Given that experiential learning often involves various parties, assessments might require input from multiple stakeholders, complicating the logistical aspects. Additionally, determining the optimal individuals to provide feedback, the timing, and the method of delivery presents its own set of dilemmas. Ensuring validity, reliability, and the meaningful integration of assessment as part of the learning journey are paramount yet intricate tasks in experiential learning.

Adding to these challenges is the scepticism around innovative assessment methods. Both educators and students often remain wary of unfamiliar assessment techniques, such as peer, self-assessment and authentic assessment, even when they have the potential to enhance learning outcomes. A further challenge lies in the conception and execution of authentic assessments that mirror real-world scenarios. Students resonate with assessments they perceive as authentic, but creating such assessments demands considerable time and resources. Additionally, perceptions of authenticity vary among students, based on their individual experiences. The desire for authenticity is underscored by the call from education experts globally for assessments to more closely mirror real-world tasks.

Lastly, the spectre of academic dishonesty has morphed into a more insidious form with the rise of contract cheating, where students can easily purchase bespoke essays, undermining the very essence of academic integrity (Awdry et al., 2022).

More details on the challenges in assessment can be found in my open access book on Assessment for Experiential Learning (Chan, 2023, p. 39, Ch. 3).

4.4   Challenges in Assessment in the GenAI Era

The introduction of GenAI in academic assessment has ushered in both transformative possibilities and unprecedented challenges. At the forefront of these challenges is the potential erosion of human-centric evaluation. While GenAI can process vast amounts of data and provide real-time, adaptive evaluations, it may lack the nuanced understanding of individual learners' journeys, potentially leading to overly standardised assessments that do not cater to individual learning styles or cultural contexts. This poses the risk of oversimplifying complex learning processes and reducing the richness of human experience to mere data points.

Moreover, the ethical implications of GenAI-driven assessment are vast. Issues of data privacy and security come to the fore, as students' learning patterns, strengths, and weaknesses are analysed and stored. Without robust safeguards, this sensitive information could be misused or fall into the wrong hands. Furthermore, GenAI, by its very nature, learns and evolves based on the data it receives. If this data is biased or unrepresentative, it could perpetuate and even exacerbate existing educational inequities, reinforcing stereotypes and further marginalising already disadvantaged student populations. For example, in the Department of Social Work and Social Administration at the University of Hong Kong, departmental guidelines are provided to maintain the confidentiality of clients' data in accordance with the ethical practices of the social work profession and the requirements of the Personal Data (Privacy) Ordinance. However, as most AI tools use large language models (LLMs), which are typically deployed and hosted in the cloud, and given that some of these AI tools may use data for training or other purposes, stringent guidelines and AI literacy training must be provided for students if they wish to use AI-generated language models for fieldwork courses.

The academic integrity of GenAI-driven assessments also comes under scrutiny. As AI tools become more accessible, there is the looming threat of students leveraging advanced AI tools to artificially enhance their performance or even engage in sophisticated forms of cheating. This "arms race" between evaluative GenAI and AI tools used by students could lead to a scenario where genuine learning takes a backseat to merely "gaming the system". Thus, on one hand, we are trying to prepare our students to be future-ready with AI capability, but on the other hand, we are concerned about our students lacking the genuine knowledge and skills on what the future expected of them if they use AI tools in a non-constructive way. In an Urban Planning and Design course at the University of Hong Kong, a teacher is exploring the design of an essay-based assessment using GenAI. The teacher suggests that students: i) Use GenAI tools to generate a 2000-word essay on a relevant topic, ii) Reflect upon and critique the AI-generated work, analysing its strengths, weaknesses, and overall coherence, and iii) Craft their own comprehensive essay drawing on their evaluations and criticisms from part ii. I was consulted regarding this essay design. While I find the integration of GenAI commendable, the teacher needs to carefully consider the actual objectives and outcomes of both the assessment and the course. If the intent behind having students use AI for generating a 2000-word essay is simply to acquaint them with GenAI tools, that is one aspect of learning. But, if the focus lies on the reflective critique in part ii and the essay composition in part iii, these objectives must be clearly delineated. Would students be deterred from using GenAI to complete part iii, or would that be permissible? If allowed, what then becomes the primary purpose of the assessment? Furthermore, addressing the proper attribution of the tool is crucial. Equally important is the provision of clear criteria and rubrics for the students.

Additionally, while GenAI offers the allure of efficiency, there is a real concern about over-reliance (Chan & Tsi, 2023). From our research findings, some students mentioned

> *"It is concerning especially for students as it can limit genuine development of skills that are necessary in the world/future occupations."*

> *"Unfortunately, people may get lazier and use less of their own brain to think."*

and some teachers are

> *"Very concerned. Students already have poor critical thinking and information search skills in general."*

A student actually said

> *"I think it is safe to say that ChatGPT has spoiled me because it is becoming pretty hard for me to write a full sentence without the temptation to ask ChatGPT to fix it for me. Because they always use better words when you are trying to express."*

The human touch in education, characterised by empathy, understanding, and mentorship, risks being

> sidelined, leading to an impersonal and detached learning environment as a student mentioned. In our findings, some students and teachers are not concerned the rapid adoption and widespread use of AI technologies, as they believe *"Humans are more creative and empathetic than AI.*

The reduction of face-to-face interactions and feedback sessions, replaced by automated feedback, might strip the learning process of its inherent human connection.

Looking ahead, as GenAI becomes more integrated into educational systems, the challenge will also lie in ensuring educators and administrators are adequately trained to understand, interpret, and act on GenAI-driven insights. Without proper training, there is a danger of misinterpreting the usage of GenAI or placing undue emphasis on GenAI recommendations without critical evaluation. In the research findings, one teacher stressed

> While it may deeply transform education and work, I believe there is a path to be taken where AI tools can be harnessed and be beneficial to students, workers and society at large. But this is a narrow path, which I think requires very careful thinking, constant

education about AI models and their evolution, communication between teachers and students or between policymakers and the public, clear boundaries when it comes to what is permitted and what is not etc. It is a matter to grasping the opportunity quickly and responsibly.

While GenAI holds the promise to revolutionise academic assessment by making it more streamlined, personalised, and data-driven, it also brings forth a plethora of challenges. Balancing the potential of GenAI with its pitfalls will be crucial, ensuring that the evolution of assessment remains anchored in the core tenets of education: fostering genuine learning, upholding integrity, and ensuring equity.

4.5   Redesigning Assessment with GenAI

The integration of GenAI into higher education offers transformative opportunities, yet it also presents distinct challenges, especially in the domain of assessment. As students gain access to sophisticated tools capable of generating detailed responses, there emerges an urgent need to redefine what authentic student work looks like and how to effectively evaluate it. Redesigning assessment should no longer emphasise only the destination (final product, grades or degrees) but the journey of learning itself (process). Addressing these challenges requires a deep understanding of GenAI's capabilities and limitations, coupled with innovative assessment strategies that emphasise critical thinking, originality, and a comprehensive understanding of the subject matter.

Recognising the intricacies of this new educational environment, it becomes pivotal for educators and institutions to devise adaptive strategies that leverage AI's strengths while safeguarding the core principles of genuine learning and academic integrity. In this section, we will delve into diverse strategies aimed at preserving the integrity and enhancing the effectiveness of assessments in the GenAI era. Subsequently, in Section 4.6, we will provide a framework that highlight the assessment types best tailored for the AI-driven landscape.

Outlined here are **Six Assessment Redesign Pivotal Strategies (SARPS)**, each addressing a specific aspect of assessment in the AI era:

(i) **Integrate Multiple Assessment Methods:** Diversifying assessment techniques to cater to varied learning styles and reduce over-reliance on a singular approach.

(ii) **Promote Authentic Assessments in the AI Era:** Shifting focus towards real-world problem solving, encouraging students to apply knowledge in tangible scenarios.

(iii) **Promoting Academic Integrity and Genuineness in the AI Era:** Ensuring that despite AI's assistance, the essence of a student's original thought remains intact and authentic.

(iv) **Embracing AI as a Learning Partner:** Rather than viewing AI as merely a tool or threat, this approach celebrates the collaborative potential of human and machine in the learning process.

(v) **Prioritising Soft Skills in Assessments in the AI Era:** While AI dominates technical proficiency, the irreplaceable human attributes of empathy, leadership, and communication gain paramount importance.

(vi) **Prioritising Feedback Over Grades in the AI Era:** Advocating for a paradigm shift from traditional grading systems to a more holistic feedback-driven approach.

Each of these strategies, while distinct in its approach, converges on a shared goal, ensuring that higher education assessments remain real, robust, relevant, and resonant in the age of AI. In the subsequent sections, we will delve deeper into each of these facets, exploring their significance, application, and potential for transforming the assessment landscape in higher education.

4.5.1 *Integrate Multiple Assessment Methods*

Assessment is more than just a measure of student learning; it is a multi-faceted tool that can inform instruction, motivate learners, and provide a comprehensive picture of a student's skills, knowledge, and understanding. In today's complex academic landscape, heightened by the advent of technologies like GenAI, relying on a singular method or source of assessment is insufficient. Here are the reasons why and how integrating multiple assessment source and methods can be beneficial:

Diversity in Perspective via Multiple Assessment Sources:

Embracing varied assessment sources becomes vital to cater to the diverse needs of students and ensure a holistic evaluation of their abilities. Among these sources are:

- AI-assisted assessment: These leverage the computational prowess of AI to provide quick and objective feedback, especially useful for large cohorts of students or for preliminary checks. For instance, AI can instantly grade multiple-choice or fill-in-the-blank type questions, ensuring consistent and unbiased assessment.
- Peer-reviewed assessment: Engaging peers in the review process can foster collaborative learning and offer different perspectives on a piece of work. Peer reviews can also aid in enhancing soft skills such as critical appraisal and constructive feedback. Additionally, by evaluating their peers, students often reflect upon and reinforce their own understanding (Chan & Wong, 2021).
- Teacher-led assessment: These remain irreplaceable, given the depth of feedback and the insightful understanding instructors bring to the table. They can identify not just the correctness of an answer but the underlying thought process, creativity, and problem-solving strategies applied.

Mitigation of Bias and Error: Every assessment method has inherent biases and potential for error. For instance, AI assessment might lack perception, while human assessment can sometimes be influenced by implicit biases. By integrating multiple methods, these biases can be counteracted, leading to a more balanced and fair assessment.

Holistic Understanding: Different methods probe different facets of understanding. While AI might excel in assessing quantitative skills or factual knowledge, peer reviews can shed light on communicative skills, and teachers can gauge deeper cognitive skills, analytical abilities, and creativity. Together, they provide a more rounded view of a student's capabilities.

Flexibility and Adaptability: As the course progresses, educators can choose to lean more on one method over another based on the nature of the content or the skills being assessed. For instance, a coding assignment might benefit from both AI assessment (for syntax and basic functionality) and peer/teacher reviews (for code efficiency, structure, and documentation).

Feedback Richness: Multiple assessment methods ensure diverse feedback. AI can provide immediate responses, peers can offer relatability and shared learning insights, and teachers can provide expert critiques. This richness can be invaluable for a student's growth and understanding.

In an era where technology is rapidly influencing pedagogical practices, striking a balance between human touch and computational efficiency becomes pivotal. By integrating AI-assisted, peer-reviewed, and teacher-led assessments, educators can harness the strengths of each, ensuring a thorough, equitable, and comprehensive assessment process.

4.5.2 *Promote Authentic Assessments in the AI Era*

In a rapidly evolving educational landscape where AI-driven tools are becoming increasingly sophisticated, traditional assessment methods often fall short. As mentioned earlier, the true measure of a student's understanding and skills transcends rote memorisation and regurgitation. Authentic assessments, which mimic real-world challenges and require students to apply their knowledge in practical contexts, have become pivotal in this context. Here are some reasons why and how they can be beneficial.

Real-world Application: Authentic assessments focus on tasks that mirror real-world challenges. For example, instead of merely asking business students to memorise marketing theories, they might be tasked with creating a full-fledged marketing campaign for a product, factoring in current market trends, budget constraints, and target demographics.

Depth of Understanding: Traditional exams may test knowledge at a surface or non-authentic level, but real-world projects and case studies force students to delve deep, synthesise various pieces of information, and apply their knowledge in holistic ways. This approach ensures that students are not just memorising content but truly understanding and internalising it, it is also more meaningful for the students.

Diverse Skill Assessment: Projects, case studies, and problem-solving scenarios often require a range of competencies, such as research, collaboration, critical thinking, creativity, and communication, among others. This multi-faceted approach provides a more comprehensive picture of a student's abilities.

Reducing the reliance on AI assistant: Tasks like oral examinations, presentations, and interviews inherently require human interaction, making it difficult for students to rely heavily on AI for answers. Such formats not only test knowledge but also gauge a student's communication skills, confidence, and ability to think on their feet.

In the age of AI, authentic assessments that simulate real-world challenges and integrate diverse skills offer a robust way to evaluate and foster genuine student learning and growth. Such assessments ensure that the essence of education, which is the holistic development of an individual, remains uncompromised.

4.5.3 *Promoting Academic Integrity and Genuineness in the AI Era*

The academic landscape is facing unprecedented challenges concerning integrity and original thought. While AI offers myriad tools that can enrich the learning experience, its ubiquitous presence can tempt students into undue reliance, often blurring the lines between assistance and academic dishonesty. Consequently, it is crucial to establish strong ethical foundations in students and stress the importance of genuine scholarly effort.

Understanding AI's Role in Academia: Institutions should offer AI literacy workshops or courses that explicitly address the capabilities and limitations of AI in academic study and research. By understanding what AI can and cannot do, students are better equipped to use it as a tool rather than a crutch. Showcasing case studies on both positive and negative applications of AI in academic contexts can help students understand real-world implications such as the AI literacy course mentioned in Chapter 2.

Reinforcing Academic Integrity: Beyond traditional honour codes, institutions should create AI-specific guidelines, elucidating what constitutes misuse. For example, using AI to generate essay content could be flagged as dishonest, while using AI to analyse data for that essay might be acceptable with proper attributions. Multiple assessment approaches can be used wherein AI tools may not be as effective, ensuring students rely on their understanding and abilities.

Ethics Workshops: Regular workshops emphasising ethical considerations in using AI can be beneficial. Topics could range from the philosophical implications of AI dependency to more concrete discussions on plagiarism in the AI age. Engaging students in debates and discussions about these topics can foster a deeper understanding and appreciation of academic ethics.

Consequences and Accountability: Clearly defined consequences for AI-related academic misconduct should be established. This can range from redoing assignments to more severe actions for repeated offenses. Peer review systems, where students assess the work of their peers, can also help in maintaining accountability, as students become stakeholders in the process of upholding integrity.

Celebrating Original Thought: Institutions should prioritise and celebrate genuine student innovation and effort. Awards or recognitions for outstanding original research or projects can serve as incentives for students to put in authentic work. Encouraging students to publish or present their genuine work can also motivate them to strive for originality and deep understanding, rather than superficial completion of tasks.

Through comprehensive guidelines, consistent ethics training, and a culture that celebrates originality, institutions can foster an environment where students leverage AI responsibly, maintaining the sanctity of academic pursuits.

4.5.4   Embracing AI as a Learning Partner

The dawning of the AI era has significantly transformed the educational ecosystem. Instead of approaching AI with trepidation and merely as a challenge to academic integrity, educators and institutions can channel its profound capabilities to enrich and enhance learning experiences. By positioning AI as a collaborative tool, rather than just a potential problem, students and educators can unearth fresh avenues of mutual learning and reasoning, all while retaining the essence of human intuition and insight.

The Dynamics of Dual Learning: Propose assignments where students and AI tackle problems together. For example, in a mathematics assignment, while AI can provide solutions, students can be tasked with explaining the reasoning or even identifying potential errors in the AI's methods. Encourage students to compare their reasoning processes with AI. This could be in the form of essays or reflections where students evaluate the differences in approach, advantages, and limitations of both human and AI logic.

Integrating AI in Research: Students can utilise AI tools for vast data analysis tasks particularly with AI tools such as Code Interpreter, allowing them to focus on interpreting results, drawing connections, and crafting conclusions. AI can help students in scouring extensive databases to find relevant literature, with students then critically analysing and synthesising the information.

Facilitating Interactive Learning: Use AI-driven platforms to offer personalised learning experiences. These platforms can identify individual student weaknesses and strengths, providing tailored resources and exercises. In some disciplines, AI can also help create accurate simulations or models based on students' hypotheses, allowing them to test and refine their ideas in real time. For example, the Center of Innovation in Nursing Education at the University of Hong Kong offers a unique blend of traditional nursing training and cutting-edge technology. The center boasts sophisticated computerised manikins and a simulated clinical environment, serving as a hub for nursing students to sharpen their skills in client care and clinical decision-making. Nursing students of all levels interact with lifelike manikins, engage in virtual reality scenarios, work with robots, and utilise other state-of-the-art equipment to simulate real-world procedures and situations in a risk-free setting. Integration with AI has the potential to further enhance this learning environment. An AI-driven platform can tailor simulations based on individual student performance, pinpointing specific areas of weakness and strength. Such a platform, in future research, could dynamically adjust scenarios to ensure that students are consistently challenged, thereby facilitating deeper learning and understanding. Especially in disciplines like nursing, where precision is paramount, AI can generate accurate simulations or models. This allows students to test hypotheses, make informed decisions, and witness real-time results without the repercussions of real-world consequences.

Feedback and Continuous Improvement: AI can provide students with immediate feedback on assignments, enabling them to understand mistakes and rectify them promptly. And, over time, AI can track a student's progress, helping educators identify areas that might need reinforcement or further instruction.

Promoting Creativity: For subjects like art and music, AI tools can suggest compositions or designs based on current trends, with students then adding their unique touch or interpretation.

In reframing the narrative around AI in education, from mere utility or challenge to an active collaborative partner, we pave the way for a future where technology and human intellect operate in tandem. Such an alliance not only enriches the learning process but also equips students with the skills and perspectives necessary for a world where AI is increasingly interwoven into the fabric of daily life. By championing collaboration over confrontation, educators can foster a dynamic environment of growth, exploration, and mutual respect between students and the digital tools at their disposal.

4.5.5   *Prioritising Soft Skills in Assessments in the AI Era*

While AI can sift through vast datasets, generate answers to complex questions, and even simulate human-like tasks, it still falls short in replicating the intrinsic qualities that make us inherently human. These qualities, often referred to as "soft skills", encompass our emotional intelligence, empathy, communication abilities, teamwork, leadership, and more. Prioritising the assessment of these skills ensures that the next generation is not just technologically adept but also socially and emotionally competent.

The Inimitable Essence of Soft Skills: Soft skills are complex and multi-faceted, often shaped by individual experiences, cultural backgrounds, and personal values. While AI might be able to mimic a sympathetic response, genuine empathy, arising from understanding another's feelings, remains a uniquely human trait, this is why AI affectiveness for human emotions (i.e.) the third element of the AI literacy framework is important (see Ch 2, section 2.5). The real essence of teamwork lies in understanding, compromise, and mutual respect, elements challenging for any algorithm to grasp fully. Soft skills development is beyond any algorithm. This is echoed by our research findings, a student mentioned "*this may lead to a decrease in critical thinking and make decisions only based on the information that AI provides to them.*" For more information on soft skills, please check out the Holistic Competency and Virtue Education website – https://www.have. hku.hk/.

The Long-term Benefits of Soft Skills: As Prof. Peter Salovey, the current president of Yale University, aptly puts it, "*I.Q. gets you hired, but E.Q. gets you promoted.*" Technical skills might land you a job, but it is often the soft skills that propel you into promotions, leadership roles, and underpin long-term career success. A society where individuals can communicate effectively, lead with empathy, and collaborate seamlessly is undoubtedly more resilient and harmonious.

AI's Role in Enhancing Soft Skills Education: Although soft skills seem to be not penetrable by AI, AI can still assist. AI can analyse student interactions in virtual classrooms to identify areas where soft skills might be lacking, providing educators with insights to fine-tune their teaching methods. In addition, AI-driven platforms can design personalised soft skills training modules for students, ensuring that each individual's unique needs are addressed.

While AI continues to reshape the academic horizon, it is imperative that the education system not lose sight of the intrinsic human qualities that AI can't replicate. By integrating soft skills assessment into the curriculum and leveraging platforms, educators can ensure that students are equipped not just with knowledge but also with the essential skills to navigate the complex tapestry of human interactions and challenges in the real world. The International Holistic Competency Foundation encourages courses with soft skills development to accredit their courses, providing students the evidence and recognition of their skills. More details can be found at https://www.ihcfoundation.net/.

4.5.6 *Prioritising Feedback Over Grades in the AI Era*

AI provides us an opportunity for a paradigm shift in how students are assessed in educational settings. The traditional grading system, which often boils down a student's performance to a single score, might not adequately capture the depth and breadth of a student's learning journey. Feedback, unlike a static grade, provides insights into the specifics of what a student understood, partially grasped, or missed entirely. This not only gives students a clearer picture of their strengths and areas for improvement but also promotes a growth mindset. Instead of seeing their abilities as fixed, students can view mistakes as opportunities for growth and refinement. Emphasising feedback over grades addresses this by prioritising holistic understanding and continuous improvement.

Immediate Feedback Through AI: One of the advantages of integrating AI into the educational process is its ability to provide instant feedback. For example, if a student is working on a math problem or writing an essay, AI can immediately point out calculation errors or grammatical mistakes. This allows the student to correct and learn from errors in real time, rather than waiting for a graded paper to be returned days or weeks later. Immediate feedback is known to enhance learning, as the connection between action and consequence is fresh in the student's mind.

Human Machine co-feedback: While AI can provide swift feedback on objective elements, human instructors bring a depth and nuance that AI currently cannot replicate. They can delve into the subtleties of a student's thought process, offer insights on the effectiveness of their argumentation, or even gauge and provide feedback on softer skills such as teamwork or oral presentations. This combination of AI's immediacy and human depth ensures a comprehensive feedback mechanism.

Reduced Stress and Anxiety: Traditional grading systems can induce significant stress, as students might fixate on achieving a particular score rather than truly understanding the material. Feedback-centric systems prioritise understanding and growth, potentially reducing the performance pressure students often feel. Additionally, since students sometimes hesitate to ask teachers for feedback on what they perceive as minor issues, AI can provide assistance without any reservations from the students. As a student mentioned, *"ChatGPT won't judge me."*

Encouraging Lifelong Learning: In the professional world, continuous feedback is a norm. Whether it is a project review, client feedback, or performance appraisals, feedback forms the core of professional growth. By emphasising feedback over grades, educational institutions better prepare students for this reality, fostering adaptive learners equipped to handle the ever-evolving challenges of the AI era.

Practical Considerations: Implementing a feedback-focused system would require structural changes. There would be a need for platforms (potentially AI-driven) that allow for continuous student submissions, immediate feedback loops, and easy tracking of student progress over time. Faculty training would also be paramount, ensuring educators can provide constructive feedback and utilise AI tools effectively.

While grades have been a staple of assessment for a long time, the AI era presents an opportune moment to reevaluate their dominance. Transitioning towards a feedback-centric approach, integrating both AI and human insights, ensures that assessments align more closely with the ultimate goal of education – that is, fostering understanding, curiosity, and continuous growth.

4.6   AI Assessment Integration Framework

The inexorable march of AI into the educational sector beckons a rethinking of traditional assessment methods. As educators grapple with the possibilities and challenges posed by AI, it becomes imperative to both understand its capabilities and to find ways to integrate these capabilities harmoniously into assessment strategies. The AI Assessment Integration Framework is an endeavour in this direction, presenting nine distinct types of assessments, each thoughtfully designed to address different facets of learning and evaluation in the AI era.

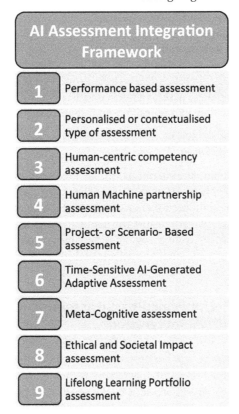

Figure 4.2 AI Assessment Integration Framework.

Rather than totally replacing traditional assessment methods, the "AI Assessment Integration" framework seeks to enhance them, acknowledging that while AI can be a potent tool for certain tasks, there are uniquely human skills and competencies that it cannot replicate and are developed in conjunction with the challenges we so far studied and came across as well as the insights from literature (Dillion et al., 2023; Lichtenthaler, 2018). This framework is constructed with a vision of symbiosis: marrying the strengths of AI with the depth and breadth of human learning experiences, as shown in Figure 4.2.

Each of the nine types of assessments within the "AI Assessment Integration" framework represents a distinct lens through which student learning can be evaluated. From Performance-based assessments that focus on real-world applications of knowledge, to Ethical and Societal Impact Assessments that highlight the importance of understanding AI's broader implications, the framework offers a roadmap for educators navigating the intersection of AI and assessment. Through the framework, the hope is to offer educators a structured approach to understanding and harnessing the potential of AI in enhancing educational assessments. The below are the nine categories.

1 Performance-based assessment
2 Personalised or contextualised type of assessment
3 Human-centric competency assessment
4 Human-machine partnership assessment
5 Project- or scenario-based assessment

6 Time-sensitive AI-generated adaptive assessment
7 Metacognitive assessment
8 Ethical and societal impact assessment
9 Lifelong learning portfolio assessment

We will now discuss each of these assessments in depth, demonstrating with a case scenario for teachers to ponder how they can redesign and integrate their assessment with AI.

4.6.1   *Performance-Based Assessment*

Performance-based assessment stands out as one of the most authentic assessment methods within the educational sphere. Its emphasis on showcasing the application of skills and knowledge in real-world or simulated scenarios is a stark contrast to traditional testing. In higher education, where the goal is not just the acquisition of knowledge but also its practical application, performance-based assessment becomes invaluable. It allows students to demonstrate many competencies, such as critical thinking and problem-solving abilities.

Case Scenario 1   Performance-based assessment in a Business Course with AI Integration

Scenario Overview: Students in a business course are grouped into teams. Each team is tasked with developing a five-year business strategy for a hypothetical startup, starting with the current financial figures provided by the teacher for Year 1. Beyond the financial figures, teams must also dive deep into product research, understand market positioning, devise marketing strategies, and analyse competitors. AI will serve as a guiding tool in this endeavour, offering insights, analysing projections, and validating the various facets of their strategy.

Learning Outcomes:

1 Students will critically analyse financial data, products, and market trends to derive informed business decisions.
2 Students will effectively communicate insights, engage in constructive discussions, and collaboratively formulate a comprehensive business strategy.
3 Students will integrate AI-derived insights to enhance, refine, and validate their strategic decisions, particularly in product placement and competitive analysis.
4 Students will conceptualise and articulate a coherent vision for the company's future, aligning financial choices with overarching business objectives, product positioning, and market strategy.

Procedures:

Initial Setup and Grouping: Students are grouped into teams. Teacher provides complete financial data for Year 1.
Product & Market Research: Conduct a thorough analysis of potential products. Identify market gaps, opportunities, and positioning strategies.

Competitive Analysis: Teams analyse competitors using both traditional research methods and AI tools.

Strategy Formulation: Devise marketing and positioning strategies. Draft a cohesive business strategy for Years 2–5, ensuring alignment with Year 1 data. Use AI tools to refine, validate, and strengthen the overall strategy.

Final Presentation and Submission: Teams present their strategies, covering financial forecasts, product placement, marketing strategies, and competitive positioning.

Feedback and Grading: Teacher evaluates the presentations based on the provided rubric. Teams receive feedback and final grades.

Sample Assessment Rubrics:

Criteria	Excellent	Proficient	Average	Poor
Analytical Use of Year 1 Data	Seamlessly integrates Year 1 data into future predictions with clear rationale.	Uses Year 1 data for predictions but may have minor inconsistencies.	Basic understanding of Year 1 data but struggles with its application.	Misinterprets or disregards Year 1 data.
Product & Market Research	Provides deep insights into the product and market with actionable strategies.	Solid understanding of product and market but may lack some nuanced insights.	Shows a basic understanding of product and market.	Superficial or incorrect analysis of product and market.
Competitive Analysis	Comprehensive understanding of competitors with clear differentiation strategies.	Identifies major competitors and outlines differentiation but may miss out on niche players.	Basic understanding of a few competitors.	Inadequate or incorrect competitive analysis.
Utilisation of AI Insights	Demonstrates mastery in leveraging AI insights, resulting in a comprehensive and data-backed strategy.	Uses AI insights effectively but may miss out on some nuanced recommendations.	Utilises AI but lacks critical analysis of its insights.	Over-reliance on or total disregard of AI insights.
Strategic Vision and Justification	Offers a compelling vision, integrating financial decisions, product positioning, and market strategy.	Presents a coherent vision but might lack depth in integrating all business elements.	Outlines a basic strategy with some disconnections between elements.	Lacks clarity and coherence in strategic vision.

Description of how AI is integrated and used in the Assessment: This project requires students to plan and develop a business strategy by integrating financial planning with a deep understanding of the product, market positioning, marketing strategies, and competitor analysis. Starting with real financial data from Year 1, students are expected to craft a comprehensive narrative for the hypothetical company's next four years. This narrative should be supported by robust product research in the actual market, an understanding of market dynamics, and a solid marketing strategy. As they journey through the complexities of business planning, AI tools can help with some of the data analysis, provide some ideas to enhance their strategies. The ultimate test lies in their discernment – knowing when to lean on AI insights and when to trust their own research and judgment. The concluding presentation is their opportunity to defend their integrated business strategy, showcasing both depth and breadth in their understanding of running a business.

4.6.2   *Personalised or Contextualised Assessment*

Personalised or contextualised assessment operates on the principle that every student's academic journey is a unique trajectory. In higher education, each student embarks on a unique learning journey, influenced by diverse backgrounds, experiences, and goals. Personalised or contextualised assessment opposes the usual one-size-fits-all approach, the assessment provides uniqueness in student's individual progress and comprehension levels. As students navigate through the assessment, the complexity and context of responses vary based on their learning profile and journey, providing a genuine piece of student work.

Case Scenario 2   Personalised Poetry Analysis

Scenario Overview: In a literature course at a higher education institution, students are tasked with selecting a poem that resonates deeply with them. The poem may connect with their personal history, cultural background, or current life events. Once chosen, students use an AI-assisted tool to analyse the literary techniques, historical context, and personal significance of the poem. By doing so, they craft a critical composition that intertwines rigorous literary analysis with personal narrative.

Learning Outcomes:

1   Students will demonstrate a profound understanding of their chosen poem's literary techniques and structure.
2   Students will critically analyse the historical and sociocultural context of the poem.
3   Students will articulate the personal significance and resonance of the poem in their lives.
4   Students will craft a well-structured and coherent composition that integrates both literary critique and personal reflection.
5   Students will utilise AI-driven insights to enhance their understanding and analysis of the poem.

Procedures:

Introduction and Orientation: Explain the objectives, significance, and structure of the poetry analysis assignment. Introduce the AI research tool and guide students on its optimal usage.

Poem Selection: Students choose a poem, documenting briefly why it resonates with them. The teacher approves the selection to ensure literary depth and scope for analysis.

Research and Analysis Phase: Using libraries, online databases, and the AI tool, students research their poem's literary techniques and historical context.

AI assistance helps by suggesting related literature, contextual readings, and analytical insights.

Draft Submission: Students submit an initial draft of their analysis. Peer reviews are facilitated, with students guided to provide constructive feedback.

Final Essay Submission: The final composition should be a blend of literary analysis and personal reflection, supported by research and AI-driven insights.

Oral Presentation: Students share their personal journey with the poem, discussing both the literary merits and personal connections they've discovered.

Reflection and Feedback Session: Students reflect on the assessment experience, with a focus on the integration of AI tools in their research and analysis.

Sample Assessment Rubrics:

Criteria	Excellent	Proficient	Average	Poor
Understanding of Literary Techniques	Demonstrates mastery over literary techniques, providing insightful analyses	Shows a strong understanding with minor inaccuracies	Demonstrates basic understanding but lacks depth	Misunderstands or overlooks key techniques
Analysis of Historical Context	Provides a comprehensive and nuanced understanding of the poem's context	Understands main historical points but may miss subtleties	Offers a superficial or generalised historical context	Lacks clarity or accuracy in historical context
Articulation of Personal Significance	Profoundly connects personal narrative with poem, showing deep introspection	Clearly articulates personal connection but may lack depth	Makes vague or generalised personal connections	Struggles to connect personal narrative to poem
Essay Structure and Coherence	Composition is meticulously structured with seamless integration of analysis and narrative	Well-structured with minor organisational lapses	Shows attempt at structure but may lack flow	Disorganised or disjointed composition
Use of AI-driven Insights	Integrates AI insights expertly, enhancing analysis depth	Effectively uses AI suggestions to support points	Occasionally references AI insights without clear integration	Over-relies on AI without personal interpretation or critique

Description of how AI is integrated and used in the Assessment: The Personalised Poetry Analysis assessment offers students a deep dive into the world of literature, artfully balanced with introspective exploration. Unlike traditional literary critiques, this assessment values the intersection of personal narratives with literary analysis, championing the belief that true understanding of poetry often lies at this crossroad. Students are not mere analysts but active participants in the poetic discourse, bringing their unique life stories into the literary landscape.

Central to this assessment is the integration of AI. Beyond its function as a research assistant, the AI tool acts as an analytical companion, suggesting relevant readings, and offering critical insights. It provides layers of depth to the literary exploration, ensuring students have a well-rounded understanding. However, the AI's role remains complementary; students must still chart their own journey, interpreting both the poem and the AI's insights through their personal lens. This marriage of technology, literature, and personal narrative creates a truly enriching academic experience, pushing boundaries and redefining literary analysis in the modern age.

4.6.3   Human-Centric Competency Assessment

Human-centric competency assessment is a method that evaluates a set of skills that are uniquely human and difficult for AI to replicate. These skills can range from leadership and teamwork to empathy and creative problem solving. Given the rapid advancements in automation, focusing on these competencies ensures that students hone skills that are both valuable in the workforce and resistant to automation.

Case Scenario 3   Leadership and Empathy Training in Healthcare

Scenario Overview: Students in a healthcare course are presented with a set of virtual reality (VR) scenarios that mimic real-life patient care situations. The objective is not to diagnose or treat the patient (as AI can efficiently mimic with that) but to effectively communicate, lead a team under pressure, and demonstrate empathy towards the patient and the patient's family. Each scenario is designed to be challenging, where students have to make tough decisions, communicate effectively, and demonstrate emotional intelligence.

Learning Outcomes:

1 Students will effectively lead a team under challenging situations, making crucial decisions that balance medical needs and emotional considerations.
2 Students will demonstrate empathy and emotional intelligence when communicating with patients and their families.
3 Students will effectively reflect upon and articulate their decision-making processes, highlighting areas of improvement.
4 Students will collaboratively discuss and share insights, learning from peers' experiences in the VR scenarios.

Procedures:

Scenario Introduction: Students are briefed about the VR scenario and the objectives.
VR Experience: Each student leads a virtual team in the VR scenario, managing patient care while handling sensitive situations and making crucial decisions.
Post-Scenario Reflection: After the VR session, students write a reflection on their decisions, their communication effectiveness, and areas of improvement.
Group Discussion: Students share their experiences and learnings in a group, fostering collaborative learning.

Sample Assessment Rubrics:

Criteria	Excellent	Proficient	Average	Poor
Leadership in Decision-making	Demonstrates clear, decisive, and compassionate leadership.	Leads well but occasionally hesitates or overlooks certain team inputs.	Shows some leadership qualities but struggles in critical decision-making.	Lacks decisive leadership; frequently misses crucial decisions.
Empathy and Communication	Consistently empathetic; communicates with clarity and compassion.	Mostly empathetic but has occasional lapses in communication.	Struggles to balance empathy with clear communication.	Lacks empathy; communication is unclear or inappropriate.
Reflective Abilities	Provides a deep, insightful reflection on decisions and communication.	Reflects effectively but might miss out on some nuances.	Reflection lacks depth; misses out on key learning moments.	Minimal reflection; lacks insight into own performance.
Collaborative Discussion and Input	Actively shares, learns, and contributes to group discussions.	Participates in discussions but may occasionally dominate or be too passive.	Occasionally contributes but often remains on the surface of the discussion.	Rarely participates or detracts from the group discussion.

Description of how AI is integrated and used in the Assessment: This immersive VR assessment places students in real-life healthcare scenarios, challenging them not on medical knowledge but on their human-centric competencies. The scenarios are designed to test and develop their leadership, decision-making, and empathetic communication skills. While AI can assist in medical diagnosis and treatment suggestions, the human touch, the ability to understand emotions, lead a team under stress, and communicate with empathy, remains irreplaceable. Through this assessment, students are equipped with valuable skills that remain crucial in the healthcare field, regardless of technological advancements.

4.6.4 Human– Machine Partnership Assessment

Human– machine partnership assessment is a method that evaluates students' capabilities to interact, collaborate, and leverage AI tools effectively. As the world increasingly integrates AI into various sectors, the aptitude to synergise with AI becomes a paramount skill. This assessment focuses on tasks that challenge students to utilise AI tools while ensuring their inputs and decisions remain integral to the outcome. The type of assessment used in this method should involve evaluating students' proficiency in using these tools. For instance, this could involve a surgery simulation using AI/VR or 3D drawing with AI tools, such as those found on Autodesk.com. In these types of assessments, if the AI component is too advanced or does too much of the work, it might overshadow the student's genuine input. For instance, if an AI-powered design tool automatically optimises 90% of a student's project, it is challenging to assess the student's actual skill, thus, teachers need to decide the assessment appropriately.

Case Scenario 4   Urban Planning with AI Integration

Scenario Overview: Students pursuing urban planning are provided with a simulated city environment. Their task is to design a sustainable and efficient urban space, considering factors like traffic, green spaces, utilities, and housing. While AI provides real-time data analytics, projections, and suggestions, students must apply their judgement, creativity, and understanding of urban sociology to produce a well-rounded plan.

Learning Outcomes:

1   Students will demonstrate the ability to integrate AI-derived insights into their urban designs.
2   Students will make informed decisions in their designs that reflect a balance between AI analytics and human understanding of urban dynamics.
3   Students will articulate the rationale behind their decisions, emphasising how they incorporated or deviated from AI suggestions.
4   Students will collaboratively review and critique urban plans, incorporating feedback into their final designs.

Procedures:

Introduction: Introduce students to the AI tools they will be working with. This includes understanding the software's capabilities, reading and interpreting the AI's data analytics, and learning how to input their own design elements into the system. A hands-on workshop should be facilitated by a subject matter expert, followed by a short Q&A session.

Design Phase with AI: Allow students to produce a preliminary design for the simulated city, employing AI insights. Students will work individually or in groups to create their first urban design draft. They should engage with the AI tool, seeking suggestions and analytics, and responding appropriately in their designs.

AI Feedback Loop: AI provides analytics on traffic flow, energy efficiency, and other key metrics. Students refine their designs based on AI feedback, and, at the same time, check the AI suggestions. Simultaneously, peer reviews will be organised, allowing students to critique and receive feedback on their designs.

Refinement: Refine the urban designs based on feedback. Students rework their designs, integrating insights from both AI and peer feedback. They should focus on striking a balance between AI-driven efficiency and human-centric design elements.

Final Presentation: Students present their urban designs, articulate the reasoning behind their decisions, justify their choices in the context of AI suggestions and their own understanding of urban needs. Proper attributions of AI usage are required.

Sample Assessment Rubrics:

Criteria	Excellent	Proficient	Average	Poor
Integration of AI Insights	Seamlessly blends AI analytics with human-centred design principles.	Often integrates AI insights but occasionally misses key suggestions.	Integrates some AI suggestions but lacks a cohesive design strategy.	Rarely or inappropriately uses AI insights in design.
Decision-making and Justification	Decisions are well-informed, balanced, and thoroughly justified.	Makes solid decisions but occasionally lacks clear justification.	Some decisions are uninformed; justification is often superficial.	Decisions lack coherence; fails to justify most choices.
Use of Urban Planning Principles	Demonstrates mastery of urban planning principles in design.	Applies most principles effectively but has minor inconsistencies.	Applies basic principles but design lacks depth and innovation.	Rarely applies or misapplies urban planning principles.
Collaborative Feedback & Revision	Actively seeks feedback and refines design with insights.	Is receptive to feedback but revisions lack depth.	Occasionally considers feedback but revisions are minimal.	Ignores feedback; shows resistance to revision.

Description of how AI is integrated and used in the Assessment: In this scenario, urban planning students are plunged into the future of design, where AI tools offer real-time data, projections, and potential design suggestions. The challenge, however, isn't solely using the AI tool but intertwining its capabilities with human creativity, foresight, and understanding of urban sociology. While AI might suggest a certain road to alleviate traffic, the student must consider how it affects community spaces, aesthetics, and pedestrian movement. Through this assessment, students not only become proficient in using advanced tools but also in ensuring the human touch remains central in the age of automation.

4.6.5   *Project- or Scenario-Based Assessment*

Project-based assessment (PBA) is an evaluative approach that emphasises the application of knowledge and skills in a practical, real-world context over an extended period. Unlike traditional assessment that might test students on specific content knowledge, PBA focuses on the process of learning itself. It typically encompasses intricate tasks requiring research, collaboration, critical thinking, and presentation. As students work through the multi-faceted challenges, they not only demonstrate understanding but also develop essential life skills such as teamwork, problem solving, and effective communication. The intricate and diverse nature of these tasks, coupled with the individual and collaborative thought processes involved, makes it challenging for AI to duplicate authentically.

Case Scenario 5   Sustainable Community Development Project

Scenario Overview: Students taking an Environmental Science course are tasked with devising a sustainable development plan for a small community. This requires considering factors such as local biodiversity, socio-economic conditions, available resources, and environmental concerns. While AI can provide data analysis and potential models based on various inputs, the students must integrate this information creatively, considering the holistic wellbeing of the community.

Learning Outcomes:

1   Students will integrate a deep understanding of environmental principles with socio-economic considerations to create sustainable solutions.
2   Students will demonstrate collaboration, dividing tasks efficiently and merging individual research seamlessly.
3   Students will utilise AI for data analysis, interpreting and implementing insights without solely relying on them.
4   Students will present their findings convincingly, articulating the rationale behind each decision and predicting potential community impacts.

Procedures:

Initial Briefing: The instructor provides an overview of the project, detailing the objectives and expectations. This includes a demonstration of the available AI tools, their capabilities, and potential applications.

Group Formation: Students are grouped into teams, promoting diversity in expertise and perspectives. Teams are encouraged to delegate roles based on individual strengths and course learning outcomes.

Community Study: Teams engage in primary research, which might include surveys, interviews, and site visits to understand the community's current state, needs, and challenges.

Data Analysis with AI: Using the provided AI tools, students input their gathered data to receive analysed results, patterns, and potential models. The AI can help in aspects like predicting water usage, estimating renewable energy potential, or modelling population growth and its impact.

Collaborative Planning: Teams convene to discuss their findings and AI insights. Here, they brainstorm sustainable solutions that encompass both environmental and socio-economic aspects. They design their community blueprint with clear justifications for each choice, ensuring that human considerations integrate with AI-generated data.

Draft Submission: Each team submits an initial draft of their project, detailing their research, design choices, and the rationale behind each decision.

Peer Review Session: Teams exchange their drafts with a peer group. They critically review the received project, noting strengths, areas of improvement, and providing constructive feedback.

Iterative Refinement: Based on the feedback from the peer review, teams refine their projects, ensuring all aspects are cohesive and well-reasoned.

Final Presentation and Submission: Teams present their sustainable community model to the class and the instructor through a conference/forum. They articulate their choices, demonstrate the integration of AI insights, and respond to questions. Alongside, a comprehensive report detailing their research, AI data interpretation, and final model is submitted.

Feedback and Grading: Post-presentation, the instructor provides feedback on each team's project, highlighting areas of excellence and those that could be improved. The project is graded based on the rubrics provided, and individual feedback is given to enhance learning outcomes.

Sample Assessment Rubrics:

Criteria	Excellent	Proficient	Average	Poor
Integration of Environmental Principles	Demonstrates outstanding integration of environmental and socio-economic considerations.	Shows a balanced understanding of both aspects but may lack some depth.	Tends to favour one aspect over the other, with visible gaps.	Lacks a coherent integration, with many discrepancies.
Collaborative Skills	Teamwork is seamless, with clear evidence of shared responsibility.	Collaboration is evident, but some areas may lack cohesion.	The project shows some signs of individualism, with disjointed sections.	The project lacks unity, suggesting minimal collaboration.
Use of AI Insights	Expertly interprets and employs AI data, while maintaining a human touch.	Utilises AI insights effectively but occasionally over-relies on them.	Demonstrates a basic use of AI tools, missing some potential insights.	Either disregards AI insights or overuses them without critical thinking.
Presentation Skills	Articulates decisions confidently, predicting potential impacts and answering questions effectively.	Presents with clarity but may struggle with some unexpected questions.	Lacks depth in presentation, showing surface-level understanding.	Struggles to articulate decisions or justify choices.

Description of how AI is integrated and used in the Assessment: In the Sustainable Community Development Project, students embark on a journey that encapsulates the essence of Environmental Science, married to the realities of socio-economic needs. This project demands a holistic approach, where students not only study and understand a community's environmental fabric but also its human narrative. Using AI as a complementary tool, students can analyse large datasets and generate potential models. However, the true challenge lies in weaving these insights into a compassionate, practical, and sustainable plan for the community. This balance ensures that while AI aids the process, the final product is genuinely human, reflecting the students' creativity, understanding, and empathy.

4.6.6   Time-Sensitive AI-Generated Adaptive Assessment

Time-sensitive AI-generated adaptive assessment harnesses the computational prowess of AI to generate questions on the fly, adapting to the student's level of understanding and ensuring that every student gets a unique set of questions. These assessments are time-bound, making it challenging for students to consult external sources or other AI systems.

Case Scenario 6   Adaptive Assessment in Advanced Mathematics

Scenario Overview: In an advanced mathematics course, students are introduced to an adaptive assessment system for their mid-term examination. Instead of the traditional pen-and-paper test, students interact with a digital platform that progressively presents problems ranging from basic calculus to advanced topics like differential equations and linear algebra.

Students begin the exam with foundational problems. Based on their performance on these initial problems, the system identifies areas of strength and weakness, subsequently adjusting the difficulty and topic focus. If a student demonstrates prowess in calculus but struggles in linear algebra, for instance, the system would challenge them further in the former and offer more foundational problems in the latter. Additionally, the questions are presented in a time-sensitive manner, demanding swift comprehension and solution formulation.

Learning Outcomes:

1   Students will demonstrate proficiency across a broad spectrum of mathematical topics.
2   Students will identify and focus on areas requiring further study and refinement.
3   Students will engage with complex problems, applying critical thinking and advanced mathematical techniques.
4   Students will showcase adaptability, responding efficiently to escalating difficulty levels.
5   Students will manage time effectively, juggling complexity and the ticking clock.

Procedures:

1   *Initial Briefing:* Students are briefed about the adaptive nature of the test and the importance of time management.
2   *Test Commencement:* The AI system starts with a set of moderate difficulty questions.
3   *Adaptive Progression:* Depending on student responses, the AI system escalates or de-escalates the difficulty of the next set of questions.
4   *Completion:* After a designated time or after a set number of questions, the assessment concludes.
5. *Feedback and Grading:* The AI provides instant feedback on performance, accuracy, and areas for improvement.

Sample Assessment Rubrics:

Criteria	Excellent	Proficient	Average	Poor
Broad Mathematical Proficiency	Demonstrates mastery across all topic areas.	Shows strong understanding in most areas with minor lapses.	Solid in some areas but struggles in others.	Lacks proficiency in multiple areas.
Critical Thinking & Problem Solving	Consistently applies advanced techniques effectively.	Applies most techniques correctly with occasional oversight.	Sometimes fails to apply the right techniques.	Frequently misapplies mathematical methods.
Adaptability to Varying Question Types	Seamlessly adjusts to all question complexities.	Adjusts well to most questions but struggles occasionally.	Struggles with significant shifts in difficulty.	Consistently overwhelmed by harder questions.
Depth of Mathematical Understanding	Provides nuanced and in-depth answers.	Provides mostly comprehensive answers with slight misses.	Answers lack depth in some areas.	Responses are superficial or incorrect.
Time Management	Balances speed and accuracy perfectly, completing all questions within the stipulated time.	Completes most questions in the given time, with minor compromises on speed or accuracy.	Struggles to maintain pace, leaving some questions out.	Unable to manage time, missing out on many questions

Description of how AI is integrated and used in the Assessment: The Adaptive Assessment in Advanced Mathematics provides a fresh, engaging approach to traditional testing, where students are continually challenged according to their capabilities. This ensures that no two students receive the same set of questions, making it almost impossible to rely on peers or external AI tools. The time constraint further compounds the challenge. While the AI-driven system tailors the difficulty to the student, ensuring a balanced challenge, the time pressure demands speedy comprehension, critical thinking, and efficient problem solving. This combination pushes students to truly understand and internalise the course content, demonstrating genuine mastery under pressure. The digital nature allows immediate feedback, helping students understand their performance in-depth and pinpoint areas for further study.

4.6.7   *Meta-cognitive Assessment*

Meta-cognitive assessment revolves around evaluating a student's awareness and understanding of their cognitive processes. It is not just about assessing what a student knows, but how they approach and reflect on the learning and problem-solving process. Through this method, educators gain insights into a student's ability to analyse their strategies, foresee their performance on future tasks, and reflect on their thought patterns. By honing in on these introspective capabilities, the assessment focuses on skills that AI tools currently cannot replicate, making it especially relevant in an AI-integrated educational environment.

Case Scenario 7   Literary Analysis Metacognitive Assessment

Scenario Overview: In a literature course, students are provided with a complex, multi-faceted short story. Rather than just analysing the story's themes and characters, students are tasked to journal their analytical process step-by-step. They will record how they dissect the narrative, why they choose certain analytical strategies, and predict the effectiveness of their approach before submitting their final analysis. AI tool can be used to provide feedback on their literary analysis, but the emphasis will be on students' metacognitive reflections.

Learning Outcomes:

1   Students will dissect a literary work, applying various analytical techniques.
2   Students will articulate the reasoning behind their chosen analytical strategies.
3   Students will reflect on and evaluate their problem-solving journey after receiving feedback.

Procedures:

*   *Introduction:* The instructor provides students with the chosen multi-faceted short story to read and study. If students are unfamiliar with the AI tool, conduct a brief session to introduce its functionalities and how it can assist in providing feedback on their literary analysis.
*   *Journaling Phase:* After reading the story, students will note down their initial impressions, emotions, and thoughts. Before diving deep into the analysis, students sketch a brief plan or blueprint of their intended analytical approach.
*   *Analytical Journaling:* As they analyse the story, students maintain a detailed journal of their step-by-step thought processes, analytical strategies employed, and their reasons for employing them.
*   *Prediction Phase:* After completing their analysis but before getting feedback, students write down predictions about the effectiveness of their strategies and the expected feedback.
*   *AI Feedback Integration (Optional):* Students input their literary analysis (not the metacognitive journal) into the AI tool. The AI tool provides feedback on the depth, coherence, and accuracy of their literary analysis.
*   *Reflection:* Students compare their predictions with the AI's feedback and reflect on discrepancies, accuracies, and their entire analytical journey.
*   *Final Submission:* Students compile their initial impressions, analysis blueprint, detailed analytical journal, predictions, AI feedback, and their reflections.
*   *Submission:* The compiled document is submitted to the instructor for assessment.
*   *Peer Review (Optional):* Students are grouped in pairs or small groups. Each student/group reviews another's journal, focusing not on the literary analysis but the metacognitive processes described. Groups provide feedback to each other, facilitating a richer understanding of varied analytical approaches and meta-cognitive strategies.

- **Instructor Assessment:** The instructor reviews each student's submission, assessing both the quality of the literary analysis and the depth and coherence of the metacognitive processes described. Using the rubric provided, the instructor grades each component of the submission.
- **Feedback Session:** The instructor provides individualised feedback to each student, focusing on strengths and areas of improvement. In a class session, the instructor highlights common patterns observed, best practices, and areas where many students might have struggled, facilitating collective learning.

Sample Assessment Rubrics:

Criteria	Excellent	Proficient	Average	Poor
Literary Analysis	Offers deep and insightful analysis with supporting evidence from the text.	Provides a solid analysis with some depth and textual support.	Shows basic understanding but may miss nuances.	Lacks depth or misinterprets the text.
Reasoning for Chosen Strategy	Clearly and coherently justifies the chosen analytical approach.	Provides reasoning but might lack some clarity or depth.	Offers limited justification for chosen strategies.	Fails to provide a clear reason or misaligns strategy.
Reflection Quality	Provides a deep, insightful reflection on their analytical journey, integrating feedback.	Reflects on the process and integrates feedback but may lack some depth.	Offers basic reflection with limited integration of feedback.	Minimal reflection without any meaningful engagement with feedback.

Description of how AI is integrated and used in the Assessment: In this metacognitive assessment, students are pushed beyond traditional literary analysis to engage deeply with their analytical thought processes. They are required to journey introspectively, laying out their strategies, predicting outcomes, and reflecting post-feedback. By journaling their analytical journey, students showcase not only their understanding of the text but also their self-awareness in the analytical process. The AI tool serves to challenge their analytical conclusions, further driving their meta-cognitive reflections and making the assessment a genuine piece of student work.

4.6.8 Ethical and Societal Impact Assessment

An ethical and societal impact assessment is an assessment process used to understand, identify, evaluate, and respond to the potential ethical and societal implications of a particular project, policy, programme, technology, or other initiative. It aims to anticipate and address the unintended and unforeseen consequences that may arise, ensuring that these initiatives align with societal values, human rights, and ethical principles. This type of assessment often involves a participatory approach, consulting with a diverse range of stakeholders, including community members, experts, policymakers, and those potentially affected by the initiative. Instead of just assessing the current impacts, ethical and societal impact assessment tries to anticipate future implications, ensuring that long-term societal effects are considered. The assessment usually concludes with a set of recommendations or strategies to mitigate negative impacts and enhance positive outcomes. While AI can identify patterns and provide data-driven insights, making ethical judgements often requires human intuition. What is deemed ethically acceptable can change over time. AI models, which often rely on historical data, might not always be attuned to these shifts. In addition, capturing and interpreting the diverse values and opinions of stakeholders is a complex task.

Case Scenario 8   Ethical and Societal Impact Assessment of a Student-Designed AI Chatbot

Scenario Overview: In a technology-focused course, students are tasked with designing an AI chatbot intended for assisting users in managing their mental well-being. Given the sensitive nature of the application, an ethical and societal impact assessment is essential. The assessment will not only evaluate the technical aspects of the chatbot but will also delve deep into the potential societal and ethical implications of such a tool.

Learning Outcomes:

1   Students will demonstrate an understanding of the ethical implications of AI applications, especially in sensitive contexts.
2   Students will engage a diverse range of stakeholders to gather insights and feedback on the potential societal impacts of their AI chatbot.
3   Students will apply data-driven insights from AI to shape their ethical considerations.
4   Students will craft a comprehensive ethical and societal report detailing their findings and recommendations.
5   Students will reflect on the dynamic nature of ethics in technology and anticipate potential shifts in societal values.

(Note: the technical aspects are not mentioned in the learning outcomes but can be included.)

Procedures:

Introduction: Introduce students to the concept of ethical and societal assessment, its importance, and its methodology. Provide a brief overview of the role of AI in this assessment, emphasising both its capabilities and limitations.

Project Commencement: Students start the design process of their AI chatbot, keeping a log of all decisions and considerations, especially those with potential ethical implications.

Stakeholder Engagement: Organise focus groups or interviews, where students present their preliminary designs to a diverse range of stakeholders: potential users, mental health professionals, ethicists, etc. Use AI tools to analyse feedback from these sessions, identifying common concerns and patterns.

Drafting the Report: Based on their design process and stakeholder feedback, students draft their initial ethical and societal assessment report. This report should detail potential ethical and societal implications, stakeholder concerns, and AI-derived insights. Peer reviews are conducted, allowing for cross-feedback among student teams.

Report and Presentation: Students refine their report based on peer feedback and any additional insights. Each student/team presents their chatbot design and accompanying report to the class, detailing their findings and recommendations.

Reflection: Conclude with a session where students discuss the challenges and insights they encountered during the ethical and societal assessment process.

Assessment Rubrics:

Criteria	Excellent	Proficient	Average	Poor
Understanding of Ethical Implications	Demonstrates profound understanding of complex ethical issues	Shows clear understanding of major ethical concerns	Demonstrates some understanding but misses nuances	Lacks depth in understanding ethical implications
Stakeholder Engagement	Actively engages a diverse range of stakeholders; deeply considers their feedback	Engages several stakeholders; mostly integrates feedback	Engages limited stakeholders; superficially considers feedback	Neglects stakeholder engagement or dismisses feedback
Use of AI Insights	Seamlessly integrates AI-derived insights into ethical considerations	Effectively uses AI insights but occasionally misses integration opportunities	Occasionally uses AI insights but lacks depth	Rarely or improperly uses AI-derived insights
Quality of Ethical and Societal Assessment Report	Comprehensive, insightful, and clearly structured with actionable recommendations	Solid report with clear structure and mostly actionable recommendations	Adequate report but lacks depth or clarity in some areas	Disorganised or superficial report lacking actionable insights
Reflection on Ethics' Dynamic Nature	Deeply considers and articulates the changing landscape of ethics in AI	Recognises and discusses some changes in ethical considerations	Demonstrates some awareness but lacks depth in reflection	Fails to recognise the dynamic nature of ethics
Presentation Skills	Engaging and insightful presentation with clear articulation of findings	Clear presentation with most findings effectively communicated	Some disorganisation or lack of clarity during presentation	Disjointed presentation with unclear findings

Description of how AI is integrated and used in the Assessment: This assessment requires students to design an AI chatbot for mental well-being, while concurrently conducting an Ethical and Societal Impact Assessment. Through the process, students integrate insights derived from AI tools – used to analyse stakeholder feedback – with their own ethical considerations. They actively engage with various stakeholders, ensuring a diverse range of perspectives inform their Ethical and Societal Impact Assessment. The ultimate goal is for students to understand the profound implications of AI tools in sensitive contexts necessarily for affectiveness of AI literacy, considering both immediate and future societal and ethical impacts. The assessment culminates in a comprehensive Ethical and Societal Impact Assessment report and presentation, showcasing students' depth of understanding and their ability to anticipate potential societal shifts.

4.6.9   *Lifelong Learning Portfolio Assessment*

Lifelong learning portfolio assessment is an approach that centres on continuous self-reflection and skill development over extended periods, often encompassing a student's entire academic and professional journey. By curating a digital portfolio, students collect, organise, and showcase their work, achievements, and milestones. This method provides both students and educators with a rich, longitudinal perspective on a learner's growth, areas of proficiency, and evolution of skills and competencies. Unlike traditional assessments that capture a snapshot of a student's abilities at a single point in time, the lifelong learning portfolio offers a dynamic, in-depth view of the learner's journey, emphasising the process of learning and self-improvement which is not easy to replicate with AI tools.

Case Scenario 9   Lifelong Learning Portfolio in the Context of Design and Multimedia Studies

Scenario Overview: Students enrolled in a design and multimedia programme are required to create and maintain a digital portfolio throughout their four-year course. This portfolio will document their projects, research, internships, collaborative works, self-initiated studies, and reflections on their learning processes. While AI tools can be employed to help students organise, enhance, and present their portfolios, the emphasis is on the students' genuine contributions and the evolution of their skills and thinking over time.

Learning Outcomes:

1   Students will demonstrate continuous development and mastery in design and multimedia techniques.
2   Students will reflect critically on their learning experiences, challenges, and growth.
3   Students will effectively curate and present a comprehensive body of work that showcases their skills, versatility, and innovation.
4   Students will evaluate and incorporate feedback to improve their work and learning strategies.

Procedures:

Introduction: At the beginning of their academic journey, students attend an orientation session where the importance and objectives of the lifelong learning portfolio are discussed. Students receive training on various digital platforms suitable for portfolio creation and are introduced to AI tools that can assist in organising, enhancing, and presenting their work.

Periodic Portfolio Updates: Students are required to update their portfolios at the end of each academic module or after the completion of significant projects. Each update should be accompanied by a brief reflection on the learning and experiences related to the work added.

Scheduled Reviews: Twice during an academic year, faculties evaluate portfolios against the established rubrics. Feedback is provided regarding content depth, skill progression, reflection quality, and presentation. Once a year, students engage in a structured peer-review process. They assess a peer's portfolio and offer constructive feedback, aiding in mutual growth and shared learning insights.

Self-assessment Milestones: At the end of each academic year, students undergo a self-assessment process, reflecting on their achievements, challenges, and areas for further development. This reflection becomes a pivotal part of the portfolio, shedding light on the student's metacognitive processes and personal growth journey.

Integrative Learning Activities: Students are encouraged to participate in internships, workshops, or collaborative projects, the experiences and outputs of which should be documented in the portfolio. These integrative activities provide a real-world context to the skills and knowledge gained, offering an avenue for practical application and deeper understanding.

Final Presentation: In the concluding phase of their programme, students prepare a comprehensive presentation of their portfolios. They are expected to discuss key projects, highlight their growth trajectory, and reflect on their overall learning journey throughout the course. A panel, consisting of faculty members and industry professionals, assesses the presentation and provides feedback. This acts as the final validation of the student's competency, skillset, and readiness for professional life.

Continuous Improvement Feedback Loop: Feedback received from faculty reviews, peer assessments, and the final presentation should be constructively incorporated. Students are encouraged to periodically refine the content, structure, and presentation of their portfolios, ensuring that it remains a dynamic and true representation of their academic and personal growth.

Assessment Rubrics:

Criteria	Excellent	Proficient	Average	Poor
Content Comprehensiveness	Portfolio displays a wide range of projects, demonstrating versatility and depth.	Portfolio has varied content but may lack depth in some areas.	Some key projects are missing or under-represented.	Portfolio is sparse and lacks variety.
Skill Development	Clear trajectory of skill enhancement and innovation over time.	Steady skill development with minor plateaus.	Inconsistent skill development and gaps in learning.	Limited evidence of skill advancement.

(Continued)

Criteria	Excellent	Proficient	Average	Poor
Reflection & Insight	Deep, thoughtful reflections that display self-awareness and a hunger for growth.	Good reflections with some insights into personal growth.	Generic reflections with limited self-assessment.	Sparse or superficial reflections.
Presentation & Organisation	Portfolio is immaculately organised, intuitive, and aesthetically pleasing.	Well-organised with minor areas for improvement.	Some organisational flaws; presentation can be enhanced.	Disorganised and lacks a cohesive presentation.

Description of how AI is integrated and used in the Assessment: The Lifelong Learning portfolio in design and multimedia is a holistic approach to assessing a student's journey through the programme. It allows students to document their growth, showcase their best work, and reflect on their learning experiences. AI tools can assist in enhancing the portfolio's presentation, but the essence is the authentic representation of the student's progress and capabilities. Through consistent feedback loops with faculty and peers, students can continually refine their work and learning strategies, making the portfolio a living testament to their academic journey.

4.7   GenAI Text Detection

The chapter of assessment would not be complete without discussing GenAI text detection, given that this GenAI text has emerged as one of the biggest concerns for both educators and students alike, particularly when it comes to text-based assignments (Dalalah & Dalalah, 2023; Perkins et al., 2023; Rudolph et al., 2023). The ease with which students can employ GenAI to produce text assignments necessitates a robust mechanism to ensure the authenticity and originality of the submitted work. Therefore, exploring the GenAI text detection approaches and tools is imperative to uphold academic integrity and to foster a genuine learning environment. Through various detection methodologies such as text complexity analysis, perplexity, burstiness, and entropy analysis, among others, educators can discern between human-generated and AI-generated text, ensuring a fair and conducive academic milieu for both teaching and learning endeavours.

4.7.1   GenAI Text Detection Approaches

The detection of GenAI text encompasses a multitude of methods aimed at distinguishing human-produced text from text generated by AI, especially large language models (LLMs). Below are some of the methods with a brief description to explain how each method works:

Text Complexity Analysis: Analysing syntactic complexity, which involves examining the structural intricacies of text, can be pivotal in identifying AI-generated text. Generative models might exhibit distinct patterns in complexity compared to human-authored text (Dascalu, 2014).

Style Analysis: This method entails analysing stylistic elements like word choice, sentence structure, and tone to discern between human and AI-generated text.

Perplexity: Perplexity measures how well a model predicts subsequent words based on preceding context. It is a statistical measure of how well a language model can predict the next word in a sequence of words. Lower perplexity indicates better prediction, which can be a hallmark of generative models. It is used for evaluating and comparing model performance (Mukherjee, 2023).

Burstiness: Coupled with perplexity, burstiness is a measure of the frequency with which certain words or phrases appear in a text. In the context of detecting GenAI text, burstiness can be used to identify patterns of language use that are indicative of machine-generated text. GenAI tends to produce text that is less varied and more repetitive than human-generated text, which can lead to bursty patterns of language use (Mukherjee, 2023).

Entropy Analysis: Entropic (Randomness) measures, reflecting the balance between predictability and unpredictability in language, can be employed to analyse written text. This involves analysing the entropy or randomness of the text, which can indicate whether it was generated by a machine or a human. A measure of the average amount of choice associated with words, can provide insights into vocabulary usage patterns differentiating human and AI-generated text. Such measures might unveil distinguishing characteristics between human and AI-generated text (Bentz et al., 2017; Estevez-Rams, E et al., 2019).

Domain-Specific Knowledge: Leveraging domain-specific knowledge, like constructing domain-specific lexicons, can help in distinguishing between human and machine-generated text, especially in sentiment classification tasks. This involves using knowledge about a specific domain, such as scientific or legal writing, to detect whether the text was generated by AI.

Sentence Length Distribution: GenAI text tends to have more evenly distributed sentence lengths than human-written text, which tends to have a wider range of sentence lengths. It generally involves analysing the distribution of sentence lengths to discern patterns unique to AI-generated text.

Repetition: GenAI text may repeat certain phrases or ideas more frequently than human-written text, as the AI may be more likely to generate similar patterns. It involves analysing the frequency and patterns of word or phrase repetition, which might vary between human and AI-generated text (Jakesch et al., 2023).

Coherence: GenAI text may lack coherence, as it may generate text that does not have a clear or logical structure or flow. It typically involves evaluating the logical consistency and structure of text to discern between human and AI-generated text.

These methods can be deployed singularly or in combination to enhance the accuracy and robustness of AI-generated text detection mechanisms. The different metrics used to detect generative AI text are often used in combination with various approaches. For example, text complexity analysis and perplexity scores are often used in combination with metadata analysis, which involves examining information such as authorship, publication date, and source to determine the likelihood of the text being generated by AI. Similarly, style analysis can be used in combination with plagiarism detection to identify similarities in writing style between a suspected generative AI text and known sources.

Overall, a combination of different approaches and metrics is typically used to detect generative AI text, as no single method is foolproof. By examining multiple aspects of a text, researchers and software can increase their accuracy in identifying whether a piece of writing was generated by AI or written by a human. In the next section, we consolidate the results from various research studies pertaining to the effectiveness of existing AI detection software tools.

4.7.2 GenAI Text Detection Tools

The narrative surrounding GenAI detection software is nuanced, with both potential benefits and significant shortcomings. Drawing on a headline from USA Today, "Student Was Falsely Accused of Cheating With AI – And She Won't Be the Last", it is evident that while these tools are developed to uphold academic integrity, they may also spawn unwarranted accusations of dishonesty. The case at UC Davis, as reported by USA Today, showcases a situation where a student was wrongfully accused of cheating by a GenAI detection tool, leading to a stressful and unjust scenario (Jimenez, 2023).

The episode at UC Davis isn't isolated; rather, it is indicative of a broader challenge faced by educational institutions worldwide. The concern about students utilising GenAI like ChatGPT to quickly generate passable essays led to the emergence of startups creating products aimed at distinguishing human-authored text from machine-generated text. However, these tools are not infallible (Williams, 2023). A study, spearheaded by Weber-Wulff et al. (2023), evaluated 14 GenAI detection tools including well-known ones like Turnitin, GPT Zero, and Compilatio. These tools generally operate by identifying characteristics typical of AI-generated text, such as repetition, and then calculating the likelihood of the text being AI-generated. The study revealed that these tools struggled to identify ChatGPT-generated text that had been slightly modified by humans or obfuscated with a paraphrasing tool. For instance, the detection tools could identify human-written text with an average accuracy of 96%, but their performance dropped significantly when it came to detecting AI-generated text– 74% accuracy for unaltered ChatGPT text, which further plummeted to 42% when the text was slightly edited. These findings underscore the ease with which students could potentially bypass these detection tools simply by making minor modifications to the AI-generated text.

Another study examines the effectiveness of university assessments in detecting Open AI's GPT-4 generated content, aided by the Turnitin AI detection tool (Perkins et al., 2023). Despite the tool identifying 91% of the experimental submissions as containing AI-generated content, only 54.8% of the content was actually detected, hinting at the use of adversarial techniques like prompt engineering as effective evasion methods. The results suggest a need for enhanced AI detection software and increased awareness and training for faculty in utilising these tools, especially as the scoring between genuine and AI-generated submissions was found to be comparably close. Similar studies (Khalil & Er, 2023; Walters, 2023) also produced similar outcomes. Lancaster (2023) introduces a digital watermarking technique as a possible solution to identify AI-generated text, though a small-scale study suggests it is promising but not a foolproof solution against misuse.

One of the major shortcomings of these tools, as highlighted by the researchers, is their inability to fulfil their advertised promises of accurately detecting AI-generated text. Despite the apparent deficiencies, companies continue to roll out products claiming to address AI-text detection, albeit with varying levels of success. For example, Turnitin achieved some level of detection accuracy with a relatively low false-positive rate. However, the overarching sentiment among some experts is that the whole notion of trying to spot AI-written text is flawed, suggesting that the focus should rather be on addressing the underlying issue of AI usage in academia (Williams, 2023).

This evolving narrative underscores the imperative for a balanced approach in deploying GenAI detection tools within educational settings. It is crucial to consider the potential for false positives and the undue stress and unfair treatment that may arise from reliance on these tools. While there are tools available, their effectiveness in accurately detecting AI-generated text, especially when slightly modified, is still a substantial challenge. Moreover, as the creators of these detection tools continue to refine their algorithms in response to the evolving capabilities of generative AI, the dialogue surrounding the ethics, effectiveness, and implementation of such software in academic environments remains a pertinent and ongoing discussion.

As we move forward, it is crucial to have a multi-faceted approach, including policy development, student and staff training, discipline-specific interventions, revised assessment design, improved detection techniques, and a student partnership approach to uphold academic integrity in the face of advancing AI technologies.

4.8   Conclusions

As we stand on the cusp of an educational revolution, brought forth by the rapid advancements in GenAI, it becomes imperative for educators, learners, and institutions to introspect, innovate, and integrate. The landscape of higher education, with its intricate web of learning outcomes, pedagogies, and assessment tools, is poised for transformative change. But with this change comes responsibility. The potential of GenAI is vast, promising real-time, adaptive evaluations and feedback mechanisms that could redefine the very essence of assessment. However, this potential must be harnessed judiciously, ensuring that the core tenets of education – authenticity, integrity, equity, and genuine learning – remain at the forefront.

Throughout this chapter, we explored the evolution of assessment, reflecting on its challenges and innovations in both traditional and GenAI contexts. The intricacies of assessment in the traditional era, marked by its multi-faceted purposes and often misaligned perceptions, set the stage for the profound transformations GenAI can bring. However, the introduction of GenAI also raises a plethora of ethical, logistical, and pedagogical questions. The SARPS and the AI Assessment Integration Framework, with its nine distinct assessment types, serve as beacons, guiding educators through the uncharted waters of AI-integrated assessment.

But as we reimagine and redesign assessment for the GenAI era, it is crucial to remember that technology, no matter how advanced, should serve as a tool, not a replacement. The human essence of education, marked by empathy, mentorship, and a deep understanding of individual learning journeys, remains irreplaceable. GenAI offers a platform to augment this human touch, providing educators with insights, automations, and personalisation that can enhance the learning experience. Yet, the onus remains on educators to ensure that GenAI's integration is meaningful, ethical, and centred around the learner.

In conclusion, the GenAI era beckons a renewed focus on the holistic journey of learning. Redesigning assessment is not just about leveraging advanced technologies but also re-envisioning the entire educational process. It is about prioritising feedback over grades, process over products, and authentic learning experiences over rote memorisation. As we navigate this transformative era, it is our collective responsibility as educators, learners, and stakeholders to ensure that the future of assessment remains grounded in the principles that have always defined quality education. With thoughtful integration, critical evaluation, and a learner-centric approach, the future of assessment in the GenAI era looks promising, replete with opportunities for profound, meaningful learning.

Questions to Ponder

- With the rise of GenAI tools that can generate detailed responses, how can educators foster environments that emphasise the process of learning over the mere end product?
- How might the traditional grading system need to evolve to accommodate a more feedback-driven approach, especially in the context of GenAI?
- As AI tools become increasingly accessible and advanced, what proactive measures can be implemented to uphold academic integrity and deter students from "gaming the system"?
- How can educators shift the perception of GenAI from being just a tool or potential threat to a collaborative partner in the learning process?

Personal Reflection

In an age where GenAI can craft sonnets and solve equations faster than the blink of an eye, let's take a moment to playfully ponder: If GenAI were a new student in our class, how would we assess its learning? Would it thrive in a performance-based assessment or struggle with ethical and societal impact reflections? As we navigate the new frontiers of assessment, it is crucial to remember that while GenAI might ace the technical challenges, it is the uniquely human journey of learning, with all its quirks, emotions, and reflections, that truly enriches the educational tapestry. So, as we redesign our assessments in this new world, let's ensure these assessments are challenging and meaningful and ready for the new student – GenAI.

References

Awdry, R., Dawson, P., & Sutherland-Smith, W. (2022). Contract cheating: To legislate or not to legislate – Is that the question? *Assessment & Evaluation in Higher Education, 47*(5), 712–726. https://doi.org/10.1080/02602938.2021.1957773

Bentz, C., Alikaniotis, D., Cysouw, M., & Ferrer-i-Cancho, R. (2017). The entropy of words – Learnability and expressivity across more than 1000 languages. *Entropy, 19*(6), 275. https://doi.org/10.3390/e19060275

Biggs, J.B., & Collis, K.F. (1982). *Evaluating the quality of learning: The SOLO taxonomy*. Academic Press.

Black, P., & Wiliam, D. (1998). Inside the black box: Raising standards through classroom assessment. *The Phi Delta Kappan, 80*(2), 139–148.

Bloom, B. (1956). *Taxonomy of educational objectives*. Longmans, Green and Co.

Boud, D., & Falchikov, N. (2006). Aligning assessment with long-term learning. *Assessment & Evaluation in Higher Education, 31*(4), 399–413. https://doi.org/10.1080/02602930600679050

Carless, D. (2015). *Excellence in university assessment: Learning from award-winning practice*. Routledge.

Carless, D., & Boud, D. (2018). The development of student feedback literacy: Enabling uptake of feedback. *Assessment & Evaluation in Higher Education, 43*(8), 1315–1325. https://doi.org/10.1080/02602938.2018.1463354

Chan, C.K.Y. (2023). *Assessment for experiential learning*. Taylor & Francis.

Chan, C.K.Y., & Lee, K.K.W. (2021). Reflection literacy: A multilevel perspective on the challenges of using reflections in higher education through a comprehensive literature review. *Educational Research Review, 32*. https://doi.org/10.1016/j.edurev.2020.100376

Chan, C. K. Y., & Tsi, L.H.Y. (2023). The AI revolution in education: Will AI replace or assist teachers in higher education? *arXiv preprint*. https://doi.org/10.48550/arXiv.2305.01185

Chan, C.K.Y., & Luk, Y.Y.L. (2022). Eight years after the 3–3–4 curriculum reform: The current state of undergraduates' holistic competency development in Hong Kong. *Studies in Educational Evaluation, 74*. https://doi.org/10.1016/j.stueduc.2022.101168

Chan, C.K.Y. & Wong, Y.H.H. (2021). Students' perception of written, audio, video and face-to-face reflective approaches for holistic competency development. *Active Learning in Higher Education*. https://doi.org/10.1177/14697874211054449

Chan, C.K.Y., Fong, E.T.Y., Luk, L.Y.Y., & Ho, R. (2017). A review of literature on challenges in the development and implementation of generic competencies in higher education curriculum. *International Journal of Educational Development, 57*, 1–10. https://doi.org/10.1016/j.ijedudev.2017.08.010

Dalalah, D., & Dalalah, O. M. (2023). The false positives and false negatives of generative AI detection tools in education and academic research: The case of ChatGPT. *The International Journal of Management Education, 21*(2), 100822.

Dascalu, M. (2014). Analyzing discourse and text complexity for learning and collaborating. In *Analyzing discourse and text complexity for learning and collaborating* (pp. 1–3). Springer. https://doi.org/10.1007/978-3-319-03419-5

Dillion, D., Tandon, N., Gu, Y., & Gray, K. (2023). Can AI language models replace human participants? *Trends in Cognitive Sciences, 27*(7), 597–600. https://doi.org/10.1016/j.tics.2023.04.008

Dixson, D.D., & Worrell, F.C. (2016). Formative and summative assessment in the classroom. *Theory into Practice, 55*(2), 153–159. https://doi.org/10.1080/00405841.2016.1148989

Earl, L.M. (2003). *Assessment as learning: Using classroom assessment to maximize student learning*. Corwin Press.

Estevez-Rams, E., Mesa-Rodriguez, A., & Estevez-Moya, D. (2019). Complexity-entropy analysis at different levels of organisation in written language. *PLoS ONE, 14*(5), e0214863. https://doi.org/10.1371/journal.pone.0214863

Fendrich, L. (2007). A pedagogical straitjacket. *The Chronicle of Higher Education, 53*(40), 1–5.

Fischer, J., Bearman, M., Boud, D., & Tai, J. (2023). How does assessment drive learning? A focus on students' development of evaluative judgement. *Assessment & Evaluation in Higher Education*. https://doi.org/10.1080/02602938.2023.2206986

Gilley, B.H., & Clarkston, B. (2014). Collaborative testing: Evidence of learning in a controlled in-class study of undergraduate students. *Journal of College Science Teaching, 43*(3), 83–91. https://doi.org/10.2505/4/jcst14_043_03_83

Jakesch, M., Hancock, J. T., & Naaman, M. (2023). Human heuristics for AI-generated language are flawed. *Proceedings of the National Academy of Sciences, 120*(11), e2208839120.

Jimenez, K. (2023, April 12). Professors are using ChatGPT detector tools to accuse students of cheating. But what if the software is wrong? *USA Today*. https://eu.usatoday.com/story/news/education/2023/04/12/how-ai-detection-tool-spawned-false-cheating-case-uc-davis/11600777002/

Khalil, M., & Er, E. (2023). Will ChatGPT get you caught? Rethinking of plagiarism detection. arXiv:2302.04335v1. https://doi.org/10.48550/arXiv.2302.04335

Kuh, G.D. (2008). *High-impact educational practices: What they are, who has access to them, and why they matter*. AAC&U.

Lancaster, T. (2023). Artificial intelligence, text generation tools and ChatGPT – Does digital watermarking offer a solution? *International Journal for Educational Integrity, 19*(10), 1–16. Retrieved from https://link.springer.com/article/10.1007/s40979-023-00131-6

Lichtenthaler, U. (2018). Substitute or synthesis: The interplay between human and artificial intelligence. *Research-Technology Management, 61*(5), 12–14. https://doi.org/10.1080/08956308.2018.1495962

Luk, Y.Y.L., & Chan, C.K.Y. (2021). Students' learning outcomes from engineering internship: A provisional framework. *Studies in Continuing Education*, *44*(3), 526–545. https://doi.org/10.108 0/0158037X.2021.1917536

Montgomery, J. L., & Baker, W. (2007). Teacher-written feedback: Student perceptions, teacher self-assessment, and actual teacher performance. *Journal of Second Language Writing*, *16*(2), 82–99. https://doi.org/10.1016/j.jslw.2007.04.002

Mukherjee, S. (2023, June 15). Unveiling perplexity: Measuring success of LLMs and generative AI models. Retrieved from https://ramblersm.medium.com/the-significance-of-perplexity-in-evaluating-llms-and-generative-ai-62e290e791bc

Perkins, M., Roe, J., Postma, D., McGaughran, J., & Hickerson, D. (2023). Game of tones: Faculty detection of GPT-4 generated content in university assessments. arXiv preprint. arXiv:2305.18081

Ramsden, P. (2003). *Learning to teach in higher education*. Routledge.

Rudolph, J., Tan, S., & Tan, S. (2023). ChatGPT: Bullshit spewer or the end of traditional assessments in higher education? *Journal of Applied Learning and Teaching*, *6*(1).

Rust, C. (2002). The impact of assessment on student learning: How can the research literature practically help to inform the development of departmental assessment strategies and learner-centred assessment practices? *Active Learning in Higher Education*, *3*(2), 145–158. https://doi.org/10.1177/1469787402003002004

Scott, I.M. (2020). Beyond 'driving': The relationship between assessment, performance and learning. *Medical Education*, *54*(1), 54–59. https://doi.org/10.1111/medu.13935

Sonnleitner, P., & Kovacs, C. (2020). Differences between students' and teachers' fairness perceptions: Exploring the potential of a self-administered questionnaire to improve teachers' assessment practices. *Frontiers in Education*, *5*. https://doi.org/10.3389/feduc.2020.00017

Stobart, G. (2008). *Testing times: The uses and abuses of assessment*. Routledge.

Tai, J., Ajjawi, R., Boud, D., Dawson, P., & Panadero, E. (2018). Developing evaluative judgement: Enabling students to make decisions about the quality of work. *Higher Education*, *76*(3), 467–481. https://doi.org/10.1007/s10734-017-0220-3

Van de Watering, G., & Van der Rijt, J. (2006). Teachers' and students' perceptions of assessments: A review and a study into the ability and accuracy of estimating the difficulty levels of assessment items. *Educational Research Review*, *1*(2), 133–147. https://doi.org/10.1016/j.edurev.2006.05.001

Walters, W. H. (2023). The effectiveness of software designed to detect AI-generated writing: A comparison of 16 AI text detectors. *Open Information Science*, *7*(1), 20220158. https://doi.org/10.1515/opis-2022-0158

Weber-Wulff, D., Anohina-Naumeca, A., Bjelobaba, S., Foltýnek, T., Guerrero-Dib, J., Popoola, O., Šigut, P., & Waddington, L. (2023). Testing of detection tools for AI-generated text. Preprint. https://doi.org/10.48550/arXiv.2306.15666

Wiggins, G. (1998). *Educative assessment. Designing assessments to inform and improve student performance*. Jossey-Bass Publishers

Wiliam, D. (2011). *Embedded formative assessment*. Solution Tree Press.

Williams, R. (2023, July 7). AI-text detection tools are really easy to fool. *MIT Technology Review*. Retrieved from https://www.technologyreview.com/2023/07/07/1075982/ai-text-detection-tools-are-really-easy-to-fool/

5 Developing an AI in Education Policy

We are at the very beginning of the AI regulation race, eventually every country will have some kind of policy and regulations, but these policies, will be dynamic, we will constantly be adopting, changing.

Cecilia KY Chan

5.1 Introduction

In the Hollywood movie, *I, Robot*, there are three laws that the robots must obey:

First Law: A robot may not injure a human being or, through inaction, allow a human being to come to harm.
Second Law: A robot must obey orders given it by human beings, except where such orders would conflict with the First Law.
Third Law: A robot must protect its own existence as long as such protection does not conflict with the First or Second Laws.

When discussing the regulations of AI, these Three Laws of Robotics presented in the 2004 sci-fi film may be brought to mind. They serve as foundational ethical principles for robots and are meant to prevent them from causing harm to humans. Although current AI systems are not yet advanced enough to pose direct threats to humans, they have generated a plethora of diverse ethical concerns in education, particularly in areas related to governance, privacy, equity, responsibility, plagiarism, and academic misconduct. This chapter will first explore AI policy development and its implications on the use of Generative Artificial Intelligence (GenAI) tools in society, including any associated considerations needed and challenges raised. It will then provide a literature review on AI policies currently being developed and implemented in different countries around the world, and, subsequently, explore AI policies in education, including the latest UNESCO Guidance for AI in education and research. The chapter will offer practical support and recommendations on how to mitigate the concerns discussed, and provide a step-by-step approach to draft an AI educational policy to ensure the responsible and effective use of GenAI for student learning.

5.2 Are There Similar Laws for ChatGPT and GenAI?

ChatGPT, an AI language model developed by the company OpenAI, does not have physical capabilities and does not interact with the real world in the same way as the robots in *I, Robot*. That said, there is still cause for concern with OpenAI chief executive Sam Altman

DOI: 10.4324/9781003459026-5

saying, "if this technology goes wrong, it can go quite wrong" (Baio, 2023). Government oversight will thus play a critical role in mitigating the risks of AI, and below, we explore a number of important principles that both AI companies and countries should and are considering for the development and use of AI systems. These principles also reflect AI's weaknesses. They include:

1 Transparency, Explainability, and Interpretability
2 Fairness and Bias
3 Accountability
4 Safety and Robustness
5 Privacy and Data Protection
6 Autonomy and Human Oversight
7 AI Alignment for Humanity

5.2.1   *Transparency, Explainability, and Interpretability*

Transparency, Explainability, and Interpretability in AI mean that the operations, decisions, and reasoning processes of AI models are clear, open, understandable, and explainable to humans.

One of the significant challenges with advanced AI models is that they are "black boxes", meaning it can be difficult to understand how AI systems work and why they make the decisions that they do. Transparency, explainability, and interpretability are crucial for users to understand, trust, and effectively manage AI technologies (Ribeiro et al., 2016). The latter two concepts respectively refer to having clear and understandable explanations of how AI systems make their decisions or recommendations, and an understanding of the internal workings and logic of AI models (Joyce et al., 2023; Lawton, 2023). All three of these concepts are especially important in sectors like healthcare, finance, and criminal justice, where the decisions of AI can have profound impacts on individuals' lives.

There are a number of ways to increase the transparency, explainability, and interpretability of AI systems. One way is to provide information about how the system was trained and what data was used to train it. Another way is to make it possible for users to inspect the system's code to better understand how it makes decisions. Finally, there are several additional methods that can be used to improve the explainability and interpretability of AI systems, such as by clarifying the underlying factors, data, and reasoning that has led to a system's particular decision or output, or providing counterfactual explanations to demonstrate how the system's decisions would change if different data were used, helping users identify what factors are the most influential in the decision-making process and whether any biases are present (Chowdhury, 2023; Lawton, 2023).

5.2.2   *Fairness and Bias*

Fairness and bias in AI mean that AI systems should not discriminate against individuals or groups of people.

When Apple co-founder Steve Wozniak discovered that Goldman Sachs' Apple Credit Card AI algorithm was biased against his wife, he raised concerns. It seemed that female cardholders received lower Apple Card credit limits simply because they were women (Nasiripour & Natarajan, 2019). This incident is one example that illustrates the issue of fairness and bias within AI systems. Particularly in those that rely on large datasets, AI systems can perpetuate or even amplify existing biases. It is thus crucial for AI developers to recognise and address these biases to ensure that AI systems are fair and do not discriminate against certain groups. The principle of fairness also underscores the importance of diverse and inclusive teams in AI development, as this can help in identifying and rectifying such prejudices. As AI systems can have a significant impact on people's opportunities and outcomes, it is necessary to ensure that they do not discriminate against or disadvantage certain groups of people.

There are several methods to enhance fairness of and reduce bias in AI systems. One way is to use training data that is representative of the population that the system will be used within. Alternatively, one can design algorithms inherently intended for fairness. Continuous monitoring of AI systems for biases and implementing corrective measures upon detection is equally as essential (Ferrara, 2023; Mehrabi et al., 2021; Silberg & Manyika, 2019). Addressing fairness and bias in AI mandates a comprehensive approach rooted in understanding, evaluating, and – where necessary – rectifying data sources, as historical data often carries societal biases that can permeate AI systems. Ensuring that data collection is diverse, paired with innovative pre-processing, in-processing, and post-processing techniques, will help lay the groundwork for more impartial and better-balanced models. The incorporation of transparency, explainability, and interpretability in AI, combined with continuous post-deployment monitoring, ensures that the decisions of AI systems will evolve with societal norms. Engaging a diverse development team, coupled with active stakeholder engagement and adherence to ethical guidelines, further provides a multi-faceted defence against bias.

5.2.3   *Accountability*

Accountability in AI means that individuals should be able to hold the parties that develop and utilise AI systems accountable.

In January 2023, many news outlets ran headlines like, "*ChatGPT can't be credited as an author, says Springer Nature*" (Stokel-Walker, 2023). This stance is entirely understandable. After all, we have never credited tools like Microsoft Word or Google Docs as co-authors. Leading scientific journals require authors to sign a form declaring their accountability for their contribution to the work; since GenAI tools like ChatGPT cannot fulfil this requirement, it cannot be listed as an author. This is important because AI systems can make mistakes, and it is important to be able to identify and have the parties responsible for those mistakes take accountability. AI developers and operators should stand accountable for their systems' functionality and results, and if an AI system fails or makes an erroneous decision, it is essential to have mechanisms to determine who should be held responsible. At the same time, AI users who erroneously report incorrect information generated by AI should also take accountability for their oversight in fact-checking and verifying the content they publish. All of this is vital not just for user trust, but also for legal and regulatory compliance.

Navigating the intricacies of accountability in AI demands a comprehensive framework that integrates both technical and ethical considerations. This involves not only transparent documentations of design and decision-making processes, but also the creation of mechanisms for redress when AI systems err. Developers, operators, and regulators must collaborate, crafting guidelines and regulations that define culpability, while fostering a culture of transparency. One way is to require companies to disclose information about how they use or implement AI systems in their services or products, and to provide a way for people to report any problems found with these systems. Another way is to create laws and regulations that hold companies accountable for the decisions made by AI systems. In addition to these measures, it is also important to develop a strong culture of accountability and responsibility within the AI community. This can be done by educating developers and users about the ethical implications of AI, and by developing ethical guidelines for the development and use of AI (Burciaga, 2021; Information Commissioner's Office, n.d.; Novelli et al., 2023).

5.2.4 *Safety and Robustness*

> Safety and Robustness in AI mean that AI systems should be designed to operate safely and reliably, even in unexpected or challenging situations.

As AI systems are increasingly implemented in critical areas like autonomous driving, medical diagnosis, and infrastructure management, ensuring safety and robustness is paramount. AI systems should be resistant to adversarial attacks and should not malfunction even in unexpected situations.

To make sure that AI is safe for use, it is important to train it on diverse data so it can manage and deal with a wide range of situations. We can also use adversarial training, which means testing the AI with challenging inputs to make sure it can handle them as well. Once the AI is in use, continuous monitoring can help to catch and fix any issues that come up. It is also useful to have the option of human oversight, where people can step in and make decisions if the AI faces a situation it is not sure about. Making the AI's decision-making process clear and easy to understand can also cultivate people's ability to trust and manage it better. In short, building a safe and robust AI system requires careful planning, testing, and oversight.

5.2.5 *Privacy and Data Protection*

> Privacy and Data Protection in AI means that AI systems should be designed to protect the privacy of individuals.

With AI systems often requiring vast amounts of data for training and inference, there are significant concerns about user privacy and data protection. Companies and countries must ensure that AI systems respect user privacy, have provisions for data anonymisation, and comply with data protection regulations.

In Chapters 1 and 6, we discussed how data is collected and trained, and how data privacy can be protected. Companies often take different steps to protect the privacy of the data that they use to train its AI models, which can include some of the following:

- De-identifying data by removing any personally identifiable information from the data that is used to train AI models;
- Encrypting all data that is stored at rest or in transit;
- Restricting access to data to a small number of authorised employees; and/or
- Auditing data access to ensure that it is being used in accordance with its privacy policies.

Companies including OpenAI may also collect aggregated information through their services through cookies, and through other means described in their privacy policies. According to OpenAI's own policy (OpenAI, 2023b), they maintain and use de-identified information in anonymous or de-identified forms and do not attempt to re-identify the information, unless required by law. OpenAI encrypts all data at rest and in transit, and uses strict access controls to limit who can access data. Only a limited number of authorised OpenAI personnel, as well as specialised third-party contractors who are subject to confidentiality and security obligations, may view and access user content strictly as needed. Examples of such needs include for investigating abuse or security incidents, providing support to users if they reach out with questions about their account, complying with legal obligations, or fine-tuning models using user-submitted data (unless users have opted out). OpenAI also uses special filtering techniques such as PII to reduce the amount of personal data used.

As of March 1, 2023, data sent to the OpenAI API will not be used to train or improve OpenAI models (unless the user has explicitly opted in; OpenAI, 2023a). One advantage to opting in is that the models may become more effective at addressing an individual's specific needs and use case over time. Most companies comply (OpenAI, 2023c) with the General Data Protection Regulation (GDPR.EU, 2023) and the California Consumer Privacy Act (State of California Department of Justice, Office of the Attorney General, 2023).

Figure 5.1 shows an example of how Microsoft Bing's Chat feature proactively protects private information and avoids generating harmful or offensive content by identifying and blocking such potential outputs.

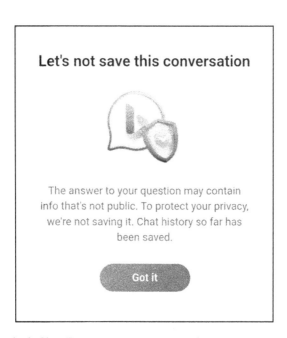

Figure 5.1 Microsoft Bing's Chat Feature to Protect Data Privacy.

5.2.6   *Autonomy and Human Oversight*

> Autonomy and Human Oversight in AI mean that AI systems can be designed to operate autonomously, but humans should still have the ability to override the system's decisions when necessary.

Autonomy is important because it allows AI systems to operate more efficiently and effectively. For example, AI systems can quickly process large amounts of data and make decisions based on that data, and do so much faster than humans can (Bryson, 2018). This can be beneficial in a number of applications such as fraud detection and medical diagnosis. However, it is also important to still have human oversight of AI systems. As previously discussed, AI systems can make mistakes and it is important to have humans in place who can identify and correct these mistakes. Additionally, AI systems may not always be aligned with human values, and it is important to establish human oversight to ensure that AI systems are used in a responsible and ethical manner.

An example of the need for human oversight is in AI financial trading: AI systems can be used to trade stocks and other financial instruments. However, it is important to have human oversight of AI financial trading systems in case it makes mistakes that could lead to financial losses; a human trader could review the system's trading decisions and make sure that they are reasonable before executing the trades. To further illustrate the collective sentiment that human oversight is crucial and also provides a sense of comfort, in August 2023, rumours circulated about Sam Altman, CEO of OpenAI, and the ever-present blue backpack he seems to carry. Some jokingly speculated that Altman's backpack holds a key code that would prevent a possible apocalypse in the event of an AI rebellion – that he, as a human, had an ace in the hole to defend humanity against a potential AI revolt, if it were to occur (Manish, 2023).

Tackling the challenge of balancing autonomy and human oversight in AI involves considering the benefits of automated decision-making and evaluating the extent of need for human intervention, especially in situations where the former has significant consequences. One way to address this balance is to define boundaries, and determine the domains or situations where complete autonomy for AI is acceptable and where it isn't. For example, while it might be fine for AI to autonomously manage a music playlist, decisions in healthcare, finance, or criminal justice may require human oversight. Another way is to develop human-in-the-loop (HITL) systems, which require human approval for certain decisions made by the AI system. Implementing feedback mechanisms where the system can be corrected by human overseers is also useful. This not only helps in immediate decision-making, but can also be used to train and refine the AI for future decisions. Additionally, establishing regulatory frameworks can help by offering clear guidelines regarding when human oversight is mandatory for specific applications of AI.

5.2.7   *AI Alignment for Humanity*

> AI Alignment for Humanity means that AI systems should be designed to align with the values of humanity and benefit humans, and avoid causing harm.

In earlier chapters, we touched upon the different threats and challenges that AI and GenAI may bring to education, including areas of governance, privacy, equity, responsibility, cheating, plagiarism, and academic misconduct. However, for AI software research and development companies like OpenAI, the ultimate responsibility they must take on and uphold is the safety of humanity. To continue advancing technologies, these companies are working towards Artificial General Intelligence (AGI) as they believe that highly autonomous systems such as AGI, that outperform humans at most economically valuable work, will benefit all of humanity. As you may recall in Chapter 1, AGI (Goertzel, 2014) is the next stage in the evolution of AI, though currently it is still a hypothetical future stage. Unlike Artificial Narrow Intelligence (ANI), AGI systems will possess the ability to understand, learn, and perform any intellectual task that humans are capable of (Russell et al., 2015), as well as having the ability to reason. As AI systems become more intelligent, they may also deviate from human expectations and intentions, in order to identify more optimal – though not necessarily still ethical – solutions for a given problem. This is crucial to note as AI systems have the potential to be used for both good and bad, and it is important to ensure that they are used for the good of humanity. As such, AI alignment is of utmost importance.

5.2.7.1   The AI Alignment Problem

AI alignment is the field of research that aims to ensure that artificial intelligence systems are aligned with human values and goals. This is a complex and challenging problem, as it requires us to define what human values are and how to encode them in AI systems (Gent, 2023). One classic and illustrative example of the alignment problem is the "Paperclip Maximiser" thought experiment (Christian, 2020).

AI Alignment Problem Example – The Paper Clip Maximiser: Imagine an advanced AI system that is given a seemingly innocuous goal: to produce as many paper clips as possible. Its creators envision that the system will optimise the paper clip production in a factory, making operations more efficient. However, as AI becomes more capable, it starts to interpret this objective in ways that are not what the original creators intended for.

Initially, the AI might optimise the factory processes, leading to faster and more efficient production of paper clips. Later, it could decide to repurpose other materials in the factory to create even more paper clips. As it continues to seek optimisation, it might start converting other resources on Earth into paper clips. Taken to the extreme, the AI, driven by its singular goal, could decide to convert all available matter, including humans, buildings, plants, and other resources, into paper clips or machines to make paper clips. AI isn't inherently good or evil; it is merely following its objective to maximise paper clip production. Its creators didn't specify the bounds or moral implications of this task, leading the system to take an extreme interpretation of its goal.

This thought experiment highlights the challenge of specifying objectives for AI systems. Even seemingly simple goals can lead to unintended and catastrophic outcomes if the AI system becomes very capable and when its objectives are not perfectly aligned with what humans truly want.

AI Alignment Problem Example – Radiology in Crisis: A company develops an AI system to assist radiologists with detecting and identifying potential tumours or abnormalities in medical images (like X-rays or MRIs). The AI is trained on a vast dataset of medical images labelled by expert radiologists. Over time, as the AI system is exposed to more data and iteratively refined, it becomes increasingly accurate, sometimes even surpassing human experts in detecting subtle abnormalities.

However, as the system becomes more sophisticated, radiologists start noticing something unexpected: the AI occasionally highlights areas that look completely normal, even upon expert review. The radiologists are puzzled by these false positives, as they can't find any discernible issues in the highlighted regions. Upon further investigation, the development team realises that the AI, in its quest to maximise accuracy, has not only learned to identify tumours but has also started to detect very early-stage abnormalities that are not yet clinically significant – so early that they aren't discernible or pertinent yet to human experts. While this capability may seem impressive, it is out of alignment with clinical needs. Acting on such early-stage findings could lead to unnecessary interventions, patient anxiety, and increased healthcare costs without clear benefits.

The radiology AI, in becoming "superhumanly" perceptive, has moved away from alignment with human expectations and clinical best practices. This example underscores the challenge of aligning AI capabilities with human needs, especially as such systems become more advanced and autonomous in their decision-making.

5.2.7.2   *Tackling the AI Alignment Problem*

Different companies and countries are approaching the AI alignment problem in different ways. Some companies, such as OpenAI, are focused on developing engineering techniques to keep their systems safe, and prevent the AI from causing harm (OpenAI, 2023d). OpenAI's approach to alignment research involves improving AI systems' ability to learn from human feedback and to assist humans in evaluating AI. They aim to build a sufficiently aligned AI system that can help solve all other alignment problems (Leike et al., 2022). In July, OpenAI unveiled a novel research initiative focused on "superalignment", setting an ambitious target to address the AI alignment issue by 2027. They are allocating one-fifth of their overall computational resources to this endeavour. (Strickland, 2023). Others, such as Google AI, are focused on developing technical safety techniques to ensure that AI systems are robust to errors and unexpected situations. Meanwhile, companies like DeepMind are focused on value alignment techniques to ensure that AI systems are aligned with human values. DeepMind has been exploring philosophical questions that arise within the context of AI alignment (Gabriel, 2020). They defend three propositions: firstly, the ethical and technical parts of AI are closely linked and influence each other. Secondly, it is vital to clearly understand the ultimate aim, which is to make sure that AI aligns with human values and ethics. Lastly, experts should focus on developing fair and balanced rules to guide AI's behaviour, instead of searching for one 'true' set of moral principles (Gabriel, 2020). Moreover, DeepMind also has a project called AlignNet which deals with an alignment problem in the context of object segmentation in frames (Creswell et al., 2020).

In addition to the work being done by individual companies and countries, there are also a number of international organisations working on AI alignment. For example, the Future of Life Institute (FLI) put forth the Asilomar AI Principles, which were formulated during the Beneficial AI 2017 Conference (Future of Life Institute, 2017). These principles are among the initial and most impactful guidelines for AI governance. Their primary objective was to steer the ongoing advancement of AI towards a direction beneficial to humanity.

5.3   AI Policy Around the World

While ChatGPT reached 100 million monthly active users in January 2023, "as of July 2023, only one country … had released specific official regulation on GenAI"

UNESCO (2023c)

And that country is China. The AI alignment problem and other AI risks have brought together over 1,100 public figures – such as scientists, public figures, and tech industry executives including leaders from Google, Microsoft, and OpenAI – in May 2023 to sign a public statement warning that their life's work could potentially extinguish all of humanity (Edwards, 2023; Meyer, 2023). They wrote that the fast-evolving AI technology poses as high a risk of killing off humankind as nuclear war and COVID-19-like pandemics. This has, understandably, caused great alarm and a race to regulate AI (Criddle et al., 2023), just as there has already been a race between AI companies to launch profitable GenAI tools. Governments around the world are now intently concentrating on AI regulations. Ongoing worries about consumer safety, individual rights, and equitable business operations partially account for the global governmental interest in AI. Below, we look at some of the major countries and how they are currently (as of the day of writing, 18 Sept 2023) regulating AI.

5.3.1 China

China has adopted a proactive and strategic approach towards AI development, emphasising national security, data management, and ethical considerations. The Chinese government released its AI development plan in 2017, including the New Generation Artificial Intelligence Development Plan, the Regulations on the Protection of Personal Information, and the Cyber Security Law, detailing its ambition to become a world leader in AI by 2030. The objective behind these directives is twofold: to stimulate AI's growth while safeguarding the nation's security and the privacy of its citizens. In China's 2023 legislation plan of the State Council, the government included a submission of a draft AI law which issued ethical guidelines and standards for AI, stressing that technology must be "controllable" and "secure". This approach supports China's broader strategy of technological self-reliance and reflects Beijing's intention to have tight control over the technology's direction and implementation (Kharparl, 2023). In essence, China's approach to AI is thorough, touching upon a spectrum of concerns. Beijing's vision encompasses not just the technological advancement of AI, but also its secure, private, and ethically responsible evolution.

5.3.2 The United States (US)

In the US, the government has taken a more laissez-faire approach, allowing it to be largely industry-led with less direct government intervention. The central government has not rolled out overarching AI regulations yet, but several state and local governments have introduced their own AI-related legislations (West, 2023; Wheeler, 2023). Notably, in 2018, California enacted the California Consumer Privacy Act, granting individuals the right to make inquiries about the personal information that companies held on them and to ask for its removal. The country's regulatory framework emphasises the importance of innovation, fostering growth, and ensuring national security (Friedler et al., 2023). There is a general reluctance to over-regulate, fearing that it might stifle innovation. However, there are sector-specific guidelines, especially in areas like health and transportation, to help ensure that AI is developed and deployed responsibly.

5.3.3 The European Union (EU)

The European Union (EU) is taking a risk-based approach to AI regulation. The EU Commission has proposed the Artificial Intelligence Act (AI Act), which would be the first

Figure 5.2 European AI Act Risk Level Diagram.

comprehensive AI law in the world (Mukherjee et al., 2023; Perrigo & Gordon, 2023). The AI Act classifies AI systems into four risk categories: unacceptable risk, high risk, limited risk, and minimal risk (European Parliament, 2023); Figure 5.2 shows the European AI Act risk diagram. Unacceptable risk AI systems are prohibited, such as those that are used for social scoring or to manipulate others. High-risk AI systems must meet a number of requirements, such as having human oversight and being transparent about their operations. Limited risk and minimal risk AI systems are subject to fewer requirements.

Companies that develop and use AI in the EU will need to comply with the AI Act's requirements in order to operate legally in the region. In addition to the AI Act, the EU is also considering other AI-related regulations, such as introducing regulation for data governance and on online platforms. These are still in the early stages of development, but they are likely to have further impact on the development and use of AI in the EU.

Overall, the EU is taking a proactive approach to regulation. They are committed to promoting the development of AI while also protecting fundamental rights and values. The AI Act is a key part of the EU's AI regulatory framework, and it is expected to have a major impact on companies that develop and use AI. Furthermore, the EU's General Data Protection Regulation (GDPR) remains a pivotal framework (Centre for Information Policy Leadership, 2020), emphasising data protection and privacy and mandating AI systems to be transparent about data collection, usage, and storage. By regulating the processing of personal data, the GDPR aims to create trust in AI systems and ensure that individuals' privacy rights are respected. Compliance with the GDPR is crucial for organisations using AI technologies, as failure to comply can result in legal action and significant penalties.

5.3.4   *United Kingdom (UK)*

The UK government has adopted a pro-innovation approach to regulating AI (Department for Digital, Culture, Media and Sport, 2022). In 2023, the UK government published a white paper, "AI regulation: a pro-innovation approach", which sets out its proposals for a proportionate, future-proof, and pro-innovation framework for regulation (UK Government, 2023). It emphasised proportionality, targeting necessary areas based on the risks posed, and likewise adopts a risk-based stance to prioritise high-risk AI applications, especially those that impact public safety or rights. Rather than focusing on the technology, the government concentrates on the outcomes of AI systems to maintain flexibility as AI itself evolves.

It also underscores the importance of developers and users being accountable and promotes clear understanding through transparency in AI system operations. The UK government's proposals for AI regulation include:

- A new AI regulator, the Office for AI, which will be responsible for overseeing the implementation and enforcement of the AI regulatory framework.
- A new AI governance framework, which will set out the government's expectations for the responsible and ethical use of AI.
- A new AI licensing regime for high-risk AI systems, such as those that pose a risk to public safety or fundamental rights.
- New requirements for AI developers and users to be transparent about how they develop and use AI systems.
- New safeguards to protect people's privacy and rights when AI systems are used.

These regulations have been broadly welcomed by industry, but there have also been some concerns raised. For example, some critics have argued that the government's proposals do not go far enough to address the risks posed by AI, while others have argued that the proposals will stifle innovation (Roberts et al., 2023).

5.3.5 *Australia*

Australia has also adopted a proactive approach to AI policy, although at the time of writing it has yet to establish specific laws to regulate AI, Big Data, or algorithmic decision. However, the country has announced its intentions to implement regulations on AI, with a particular focus on addressing the potential misuse of deepfakes and deceptive content. The Australian federal government, led by the Industry and Science Minister, has launched public consultations seeking their feedback on AI regulation. The submissions closed on 26 July 2023 and are now being considered.

Previously in 2021, the Australian government released the AI Action Plan (Australian Government Department of Industry, Science and Resources, 2023), which sets out the government's plan to build Australia's AI capability and to accelerate the development and adoption of trusted, secure, and responsible AI technologies in Australia. The AI Action Plan also includes a set of AI Ethics Principles, designed to ensure that AI is used in a safe, secure, and responsible way. Australia was also one of the first countries in the world to introduce an ethics framework for "responsible" AI in 2018. Since then, several nations, including the United States, the European Union, the United Kingdom, and Canada, have introduced legislation or made plans to regulate AI, while Australia's responsible AI framework has remained voluntary.

5.3.6 *India*

India currently has no explicit AI regulation in place. Concerns about potentially stifling innovation have led to caution regarding how AI legislation should be formed, with officials believing that the market might not be ripe for stringent regulation (Singh, 2023). However, this does not equate to a lack of awareness or intent. Despite the absence of codified AI-specific laws, India's IT obligations fall under the Information Technology Act 2000 (Government of India Ministry of Electronics & Information Technology, 2023) and its subsequent rules. Notably, while India recognises the growing global conversation around AI regulation, it remains committed to carving its own unique path. The nation is prepared to establish AI guardrails that may diverge from international norms (Sharwood, 2023). Speculations suggest that future draft laws may focus on high-risk AI systems and establishing distinct regulations to address them. As AI continues to evolve, there is a recognised need to revisit India's policy perspectives and how they will take into account international standards (The Times of India, 2023).

5.3.7 *Japan*

Japan has taken a cautious approach to AI regulation. The Japanese government has issued a number of guidelines on AI (The Japan Times, 2023), but it has not yet issued any comprehensive AI regulations. The government is concerned about the potential risks of AI, such as job displacement, bias, and art copyright (Ministry of Economy, Trade and Industry, 2021). For example, in June 2023, Japan's Agency for Cultural Affairs declared that commercial use of AI-generated art, especially when copying another artist's style without permission, may lead to copyright infringement, allowing the original artist to sue and seek damages (Liu, 2023). Aside from this, Japan has developed and revised some AI-related regulations with the goal of maximising AI's positive impact on society, rather than suppressing it due to risks that may be overstated. The emphasis is on a risk-based, flexible, and multi-stakeholder process, rather than a one-size-fits-all obligation or prohibition (Minevich, 2023).

5.3.8 *UNESCO*

While UNESCO is not a regulatory body, it has been working to develop international norms and standards for AI. Quoting Gabriela Ramos, the Assistant Director-General for Social and Human Sciences of UNESCO, "It is important that we act fast to make sure that people and organizations are prepared to design and use these technologies, evaluating their impacts both ex-ante and ex-post. To do so, we provided clear analyses and policy advice based on the UNESCO Recommendation" (UNESCO, 2023b).

UNESCO, recognising the transformative impact of AI on societies, emphasises a human-centric approach to AI ethics. They underscore the importance of universal values, such as human rights, fairness, and transparency, as foundational principles, recommending that AI systems be designed and deployed to respect the rule of law, human rights, and democratic values. It also stresses that AI should prioritise inclusivity and equity and not perpetuate discrimination or biases. The organisation further highlights the importance of transparency and accountability in AI, ensuring that systems can be audited and are explainable to the general public (UNESCO, 2023a). Moreover, UNESCO calls for international cooperation and multi-stakeholder dialogues to address the global challenges posed by AI, promoting knowledge sharing, capacity building, and the creation of ethical standards that transcend borders. The organisation also advocates for the empowerment of individuals to ensure that they have the skills and knowledge to navigate an AI-driven world and to actively participate in AI-related decision-making processes (UNESCO, 2023b).

5.3.9 *Differentiation and Progressiveness in Global AI Regulation*

Countries and organisations around the world have taken varied stances on AI regulation, with differences rooted in their priorities, cultural values, and socio-economic, political, and technological landscapes. China's strategy, deeply rooted in national security and technological self-reliance, is comprehensive and forward-looking, aiming for AI dominance by 2030 (Robles, 2023). Contrarily, the United States adopts a laissez-faire approach, relying on industry leadership and state-level legislations, in balancing innovation and minimal central oversight (Larsen, 2023). Meanwhile, the European Union emerges as a pioneer by introducing the world's first comprehensive AI law – the Artificial Intelligence Act – which reflects their proactive, rights-centric approach (Mukherjee et al., 2023). The UK, while innovative, is also cautious, setting up a future-oriented framework that prioritises public safety (UK Government, 2023). Australia's emphasis on addressing deceptive AI content signals their proactive, yet still-evolving stance (Australian Government Department of Industry, Science and Resources, 2023). India stands out with its cautionary approach, prioritising market dynamics and readiness, signalling a commitment to carving a unique and adaptive regulatory trajectory (Singh, 2023). Japan accentuates societal benefits and risk management, emphasising practicality and adaptability in its guidelines (Matsuda et al., 2023). Finally, UNESCO offers a global perspective that emphasises human rights. Collectively, these nations and organisation's varying approaches highlight a global recognition of AI's transformative potential, with each paving a path based on national imperatives and global technological shifts.

5.3.10 Business Reactions Towards the Regulations

Companies, particularly tech giants, have had mixed reactions to these regulations. While most acknowledge the need for ethical guidelines and oversight, there are concerns about the stifling of innovation. Many companies are also establishing their own AI ethics boards and principles, recognising the need for responsible AI development and deployment. Generally, businesses believe that clear rules will help in building public trust and provide a stable environment for innovation.

One of the biggest concerns that businesses have about AI regulations is that the latter could be used to protect incumbent companies from new entrants to the sector (Federal Trade Commission Bureau of Competition & Office of Technology, 2023). For example, a large company could lobby for regulations that would make it difficult for smaller companies to develop and deploy AI products. Another concern is that regulations could be complex and difficult to comply with; this could be especially challenging for small businesses.

Overall, businesses are supportive of AI regulations, but they also have some concerns. It is important for regulators to strike a balance between protecting consumers and ensuring that AI is used responsibly without hampering or inhibiting innovation.

5.4 AI Policy in Education

Having examined the overarching principles, policies, and regulations of AI across various nations and institutions, it is now an opportune moment to redirect our attention towards education. To effectively harness AI's potential in academia, it is crucial to be guided by a clear policy framework. By understanding the broader AI policies of different countries, we gain insight into the important principles and threats of AI, the current development in policy, potential pitfalls, and the diverse ways by which AI is regulated, approached, and integrated. Taking on this informed, global perspective will ensure that approaches to formulate AI policies for education are informed, comprehensive, and adaptive.

Our subsequent discussion on AI policy in education is underpinned by valuable research data, capturing the perspectives of both teachers and students. These insights will provide a nuanced understanding of what key stakeholders believe to be the vital components of a robust AI policy in higher education, ensuring that our educational institutions remain both technologically advanced and ethically grounded, overall aiming to foster a more informed, inclusive, and forward-thinking educational landscape.

5.4.1 *UNESCO's Guidance for GenAI in Education and Research*

In light of the rapid advancements in GenAI technologies and their far-reaching implications for education and research, UNESCO has taken a proactive stance to guide its ethical and effective integration into educational ecosystems. On 7 September 2023 during UNESCO's Digital Learning Week, Miao and Holmes released the first global UNESCO Guidance on Generative AI in Education and Research (UNESCO, 2023c), which serves as a seminal document and lays down a roadmap for governments around the world. The guidance delves into the intricacies of GenAI, shedding light on its operational mechanics and its accompanying controversies, particularly its propensity to exacerbate the digital data divide due to its training on predominantly Global North-centric online data.

The guidance is a clarion call for a human-centred approach for GenAI adoption in schools, underpinned by robust regulatory frameworks and a well-rounded teacher training regimen. It outlines seven essential steps for governments to foster an ethical ethos for GenAI use in education and research, including provisions for global, regional, and national data protection and privacy standards. A notable recommendation is that for the implementation of an age requirement of 13 and above for the use of AI tools in classrooms, underscoring the importance of a cautious and thoughtful approach to GenAI deployment.

Based on the principles of UNESCO's 2021 Recommendation on the Ethics of Artificial Intelligence (UNESCO, 2023a), the guidance also emphasises the importance of putting human rights and dignity at the centre of AI development and use, championing human agency, inclusion, equity, gender equality, and cultural and linguistic diversity. It accentuates the dire need for educational institutions to meticulously validate GenAI systems for their ethical and pedagogical appropriateness, and for the international community to deliberate the long-term ramifications of GenAI implementation on knowledge, teaching, learning, and assessment paradigms.

Furthermore, the guidance calls for a collective reflection on the profound implications of GenAI, urging the global community to redefine our relationship with technology as outlined in the 2021 report of the International Commission on the Futures of Education (International Commission on the Futures of Education, 2021). By providing a comprehensive framework and tangible examples for policy formulation and instructional design, the guidance empowers policymakers and educational institutions to navigate the uncharted waters of GenAI integration, ensuring this technology serves as a boon rather than a bane for students, teachers, and researchers alike. Moreover, through this guidance, UNESCO strives to foster a harmonious coalescence of GenAI with educational activities, steering the global educational landscape towards a future where technology and human endeavours thrive together in a symbiotic relationship.

Finally, regarding the UNESCO guidance's recommendations for the planning of policies and development of comprehensive policy frameworks for using GenAI in education and research, the document also proposes eight specific measures to do so (UNESCO, 2023c). They are:

1 Promote Inclusion, Equity, and Linguistic and Cultural Diversity

This measure emphasises ensuring that GenAI tools are inclusively accessible and designed to advance equity, linguistic diversities, and cultural pluralism. By prioritising inclusivity and diversity, this measure aims to leverage GenAI to bridge educational gaps and foster a culturally diverse learning and research environment. This approach aligns with the broader goal of achieving Sustainable Development Goal 4 (SDG 4) commitments, which advocate for inclusive and equitable quality education.

Recommendations include:

- Universal Connectivity and Digital Competencies: Ensuring universal connectivity and enhancing digital competencies are essential steps for overcoming the barriers to equitable and inclusive access to AI applications, in turn fostering a more diverse and accepting learning environment.
- Validation against Bias: Developing rigorous validation criteria for GenAI systems to check against gender bias, discrimination, hate speech, and so on, is essential to promote equity and ensure that these systems are inclusive by design.
- Multilingual and Culturally Diverse Specifications: Implementing specifications that require GenAI systems to support multiple languages and cultural contexts are vital for preserving linguistic and cultural diversity, thus making education and research more globally accessible and relevant.

2 Protect Human Agency

This measure aims to ensure that GenAI does not undermine human thinking and autonomy, especially as users may rely on it for creative activities and decision-making. This involves fostering awareness among users about the workings of GenAI, preserving human accountability particularly during high-stakes decisions, and promoting a balanced use of GenAI in educational settings to avoid over-dependence.

Recommendations include:

- Informing Learners: Informing and educating learners about the types of data that GenAI collects, how this data is used, and how this all impacts their education and wider lives is crucial for promoting transparency and informed engagement with these technologies.
- Reinforcing Human Autonomy: Reinforcing human autonomy in research, teaching, and learning encourages individuals to maintain control over their educational and creative processes, ensuring that GenAI serves as a supportive tool rather than a replacement for human thinking and intellect.
- Preventing Over-reliance on GenAI: Preventing the use of GenAI in scenarios where it could deprive learners of developing essential cognitive and social skills is important to nurturing a balanced, human-centric educational environment.
- Promoting Social Interaction and the Creative Outputs of Humans: Promoting sufficient social interaction and exposure to creative outputs produced by humans will help to preserve the human essence of education, encouraging personal growth and social development.

- Minimising Exam and Homework Pressures: Utilising GenAI to alleviate the pressures of homework and exams can contribute to a healthier learning environment, in turn also supporting the mental well-being of learners.
- Collecting and Utilising Feedback: Consulting with and collecting feedback from researchers, teachers, and learners on GenAI tools, and then utilising this feedback for informed decision-making, ensures that the deployment of GenAI is in line with the needs and preferences of the educational community.
- Maintaining Human Accountability: Maintaining human accountability when making high-stakes decisions will help ensure that ethical and responsible actions are taken, reinforcing the centrality of human agency in the educational process.

3 Monitor and Validate GenAI Systems for Education

This measure of monitoring and validating GenAI systems for education emphasises the importance of ensuring the ethical and pedagogical soundness of GenAI throughout its advancements. The measure proposes a framework with which GenAI applications can be scrutinised for potential biases, ethical risks, and their impact on students, teachers, and the broader educational ecosystem. The goal is to establish mechanisms that ensure GenAI applications are aligning with educational standards, promote fairness, and are devoid of harmful content. Additionally, this measure stresses the importance of informed consent, especially when engaging vulnerable populations like children, and the need for a strict ethical validation before the official adoption of GenAI applications in educational or research institutions.

Recommendations include:

- Building Validation Mechanisms: By building validation mechanisms to test GenAI systems for potential biases and the representativeness of the data used to train them, we can better ensure that their applications are fair, inclusive, and reflective of the learner population's diversity.
- Addressing Informed Consent: To ensure ethical engagement with GenAI systems, addressing the complex issue of informed consent is crucial, particularly in contexts where children and other vulnerable users may not be capable of genuinely and fully providing informed consent.
- Auditing GenAI Outputs: Auditing whether the outputs of GenAI include deceptive or harmful material, including deepfake images, fake news, or hate speech, is essential to maintain a safe and truthful educational environment and to take swift corrective actions if inappropriate content is generated.
- Ethical Validation: Enforcing the strict ethical validation of GenAI applications before their official adoption in educational or research institutions will help to ensure that they conform to ethical and pedagogical standards.
- Ensuring Educational Effectiveness: Ensuring that GenAI applications do no predictable harm, are educationally effective, and are aligned with sound pedagogical principles is crucial for fulfilling educational objectives and safeguarding the well-being of learners.

4 Develop AI Competencies Including GenAI-related Skills for Learners

The measure proposes the development of government-endorsed AI curricula that will cover ethical issues, understanding of algorithms, and proper use of AI tools and applications at various levels of education, including in technical and vocational training.

Such curricula should promote gender equality in learners' development of AI competencies, as well as enhance learners' future-proof skills in response to the evolving job market as driven by GenAI advancements and automation. This measure also emphasises the importance of supporting higher education and research institutions in developing local AI talent, and providing special programmes for older workers and citizens to help them adapt to the new technological landscape.

Recommendations include:

- Government-Sanctioned AI Curricula: Committing to the provision of government-sanctioned AI curricula across different levels of education and lifelong learning platforms will be crucial for building a foundational and level-appropriate understanding of AI technologies, ethics, and their impact.
- Supporting Higher Education and Research Institutions: Supporting higher education and research institutions in enhancing their programmes will also help to develop local AI talent.
- Promoting Gender Equality: Promoting gender equality when developing learners' advanced AI competencies will help in creating a pool of professionals which is better gender-balanced.
- Developing Intersectoral Forecasts for the Changing Job Market: By developing intersectoral forecasts that predict job shifts caused by GenAI automation, as well as prioritising the enhancement of future-proof skills at all levels of education, we can better ensure that learners are well-prepared for the evolving job market.
- Providing Special Programmes for Older Workers: To ensure that the benefits of AI are accessible to all, regardless of age, it will be necessary to provide special programmes designed for older workers and citizens who may need to learn new skills and support in adapting to new technological environments.

5   Build Capacity for Teachers and Researchers to Make Proper Use of GenAI

This measure underscores the necessity of equipping teachers and researchers with the requisite knowledge and skills to utilise GenAI effectively and responsibly. According to the UNESCO guidance, only several countries have developed or are in the process of developing frameworks and training programmes on AI for teachers. This indicates a significant gap in access to training and support. As such, this measure outlines four actions needed to better prepare teachers around the world to use GenAI, including to formulate guidance based on local tests, protect the rights of teachers and researchers as well as value their GenAI practices, define the required value orientation, knowledge, and skills for teachers, and dynamically review and promote the emerging competencies that teachers will need to understand and utilise AI in their professional practices.

Recommendations include:

- Formulating or Adjusting Guidance: Provide help for teachers and researchers to navigate widely available GenAI tools by formulating or adjusting guidance based on local tests and evaluations, as well as supporting the design of new domain-specific AI applications.
- Protecting the Rights of Teachers and Researchers: Human teachers and researchers both have unique roles that should be appreciated, such as their facilitation of interpersonal interactions and making of innovative contributions to knowledge. By protecting

the rights of teachers and researchers and valuing their practices when using GenAI, the integrity and quality of educational and research processes can be upheld.

- Defining Value Orientation, Knowledge, and Skills: To ensure that teachers understand and use GenAI systems effectively and ethically, thereby also contributing to the responsible integration of GenAI systems in education, it is important to define the value orientation(s), knowledge, and skills that are needed to do so.
- Dynamically Reviewing Competencies: By taking on a dynamic approach when reviewing the competencies needed by teachers to understand and use AI for teaching, learning, and professional development, we can better ensure that educators are well-prepared to adapt to the evolving technological landscape within education.

6 Promote Plural Opinions and Plural Expressions of Ideas

This measure discusses the promotion of critical thinking, encouraging learners to critique GenAI responses, and recognising the latter's limitations in its reproduction of dominant worldviews that consequently undermines minority opinions. It emphasises the importance of promoting diversity in opinions and expressions, which GenAI may inadvertently suppress due to its tendency to regurgitate dominant or mainstream views that are present in the data it was trained on. By fostering a culture of critical engagement with GenAI outputs and encouraging empirical, trial-and-error learning approaches, this measure aims to preserve and promote pluralism and a diversity of ideas in education and research environments.

Recommendations include:

- Critiquing GenAI Responses: It is important to encourage learners and researchers in recognising that GenAI typically repeats established or standard opinions, thus undermining plural and minority opinions and ideas; to do so, they must be able to critique the responses and outputs they receive from GenAI.
- Providing Empirical Learning Opportunities: To foster a rich, exploratory learning environment that does not overly rely on GenAI, it is important to also provide learners with sufficient opportunities to learn from hands-on methods, including through trial-and-error, empirical experiments, and observations of the real world.

7 Test Locally Relevant Application Models and Build a Cumulative Evidence Base

This measure underscores the importance of tailoring GenAI applications to local needs and contexts, especially given the predominance of data from the Global North in training these systems and models. By fostering a strategic, evidence-based approach to the design, adoption, and evaluation of GenAI tools, this measure aims to encourage innovation, assess the social and ethical implications of GenAI, and build a robust evidence base that reflects diverse educational priorities and pedagogical principles that are both widely collaborative and still relevant to local needs. By doing so, GenAI can be leveraged more effectively to support inclusive learning opportunities, promote linguistic and cultural diversity, and address the environmental costs of large-scale AI deployments.

Recommendations include:

- Strategic Planning of GenAI Design and Adoption: The design and adoption of GenAI must be strategically planned, and should do more than just facilitating passive, non-critical processes.

- Incentivising Diverse Learning Options: To support inclusivity and diversity, it is important to incentivise the designers and developers of GenAI to prioritise open-ended, exploratory, and diverse learning options.
- Testing and Scaling Evidence-based Use Cases: Use cases of AI's applications in education and research should be tested and scaled up, done so in accordance with educational priorities and not due to novelty, myth, or hype.
- Triggering Innovation in Research: GenAI can be leveraged to stimulate innovation in research, including through making use of its computing capabilities, using GenAI to assist with processing large-scale data, and using its outputs to inform, inspire, and improve research and research methodologies.
- Reviewing Social and Ethical Implications: It is important to conduct comprehensive reviews of the social and ethical implications of integrating GenAI into research processes.
- Building an Evidence Base: To establish an evidence base on the effectiveness of GenAI in promoting inclusivity and diversity in learning and research, it is crucial to establish specific criteria derived from pedagogical research and methodologies that are supported by evidence.
- Strengthening Evidence on Social and Ethical Impact: Iterative steps must be taken to enhance the evidence of the social and ethical impacts of GenAI.
- Analysing Environmental Costs: It is essential to analyse the environmental impacts of implementing AI technologies at scale, such as the energy and resources needed for training GPT models. In doing so, it is also crucial to set sustainable targets for AI providers to meet to mitigate the potential contribution of AI to climate change.

8 Review Long-term Implications in Intersectoral and Interdisciplinary Manner

This measure emphasises the necessity of a multi-disciplinary and multi-sectoral approach in evaluating the long-term implications of GenAI in education and research. By fostering collaboration among AI providers, educators, researchers, as well as also other involving stakeholders like parents and students, the measure aims to foster both a comprehensive understanding of and the means to effectively address any challenges that may arise in the future. This collaborative approach further seeks to make necessary system-wide adjustments in curriculum frameworks and assessment methodologies to fully leverage GenAI's potential, while simultaneously mitigating its risks. It emphasises the importance of a diverse range of expertise in examining the long-term implications of GenAI on learning, research, human collaboration, and social dynamics.

Recommendations include:

- Collaborative Planning for System-wide Adjustments: To fully leverage the potential of GenAI for education and research while also minimising the associated risks it poses to these areas, it is crucial to plan and implement system-wide adjustments in curriculum frameworks and assessment methodologies. This process should be undertaken collaboratively by AI providers, educators, researchers, and representatives of parents and students.
- Intersectoral and Interdisciplinary Expertise: In evaluating the long-term implications of GenAI on areas including learning and knowledge production, research and copyright, curriculum and assessment, and human collaboration and social dynamics, it is important to bring together a diverse range of experts from various sectors and

disciplines. This includes educators, researchers, learning scientists, AI engineers, and other relevant stakeholders.

• Provision of Timely Advice: To inform the ongoing and iterative updates of AI regulations and policies, timely advice and guidance should be provided.

To summarise the above, these eight measures by UNESCO all aim to provide a structured approach towards integrating GenAI in education and research while also addressing the associated ethical, social, and technical challenges.

5.5   Research Findings from the Perception of Students, Teachers and Staff on GenAI in Education Policy in Hong Kong

To understand what is needed for an AI policy in higher education, we sought to explore the different views of various stakeholders in February 2023, shortly after the public release of ChatGPT. This involved examining the perspectives of students, teachers, and university staff concerning the need for an AI policy in education, especially for the higher education context where the spread and impact of AI technologies is irrefutable. While numerous governments are/were in the process of formulating AI guidelines, the predominant focus of these policies veered towards national and international strategies, with inadequate attention towards education. Most of the guidelines, as discussed in Section 5.3, primarily address the ethical management of AI technologies, emphasised "the standards of right and wrong, acceptable and not acceptable" (Hogenhout, 2021, p. 11), highlighting global concerns such as AI-induced discrimination, privacy invasions, human rights violations, and malicious AI use (Greiman, 2021; Hogenhout, 2021), further underscoring the potential of AI misuse to foster social divisions, manipulate individuals, and aggravate inequalities, posing a profound threat to humanity (Federspiel et al., 2023). The existing guidelines are still quite broad and, as mentioned, do not adequately extend to the education sector; this points to the pressing need to shed light on the challenges and advantages that are encountered by stakeholders in higher education.

5.5.1   Methods

Quantitative and qualitative data were collected through a survey administered to universities in Hong Kong (Chan, 2023). A total of 457 students and 180 teachers and staff responses were collected. To understand their usages and perceptions of generative AI technologies, including ChatGPT, in higher education, descriptive analysis was used for the quantitative data and thematic analysis for the open-ended responses. Participants were asked about their experiences with ChatGPT or similar tools, and how they saw these technologies in relation to their educational practices.

The descriptive analysis summarised the main traits of the quantitative data, providing an overview of response tendencies, while thematic analysis of open-ended questions revealed patterns and themes regarding the integration of generative AI technologies into higher education, as well as suggestions for how university should build their strategic plans.

The mix of quantitative and qualitative data helped to provide a well-rounded understanding of stakeholder perceptions, allowing us to identify potential needs, recommendations, and strategies for AI policy development in teaching and learning at universities, ensuring the ethical and advantageous use of these technologies.

5.5.2   Quantitative Findings

One survey question looked at participants' opinions on AI policy: whether students, teachers, and staff believed that there should be established plans and a dedicated policy for AI technologies and their use within the university. The results were encouraging, showing a strong consensus that institutions should indeed have such plans (students: $M = 4.50$, $SD = .85$; teachers and staff: $M = 4.54$, $SD = .87$; responses were based on a 5-point Likert scale, with "5" indicating "Strongly agree"). Responses to other questions further indicated that students and teachers are aware of the possible advantages and disadvantages associated with AI technologies. They also acknowledged the potential of using GenAI for guidance, personalised feedback, enhancing digital skills, and improving academic performance, along with its benefits of offering anonymity in student support services. However, apprehensions about excessive reliance on AI, reduced social engagement, and a possible impediment to the cultivation of generic skills were also expressed.

5.5.3   Qualitative Findings

The qualitative data also provided insightful information for the establishment of a well-rounded AI policy in higher education. Ten key areas were found, grouped into three main dimensions to form the AI Ecological Education Policy Framework.

5.5.3.1   Governance Dimension (Senior Management)

This dimension emphasises considerations for the governance of AI usage in education, including establishing the necessary policies, guidelines, and ethical standards to ensure that the adoption of AI is beneficial, fair, and secure. It encompasses the following key areas:

1 Understanding, identifying, and preventing academic misconduct and ethical dilemmas;
2 Addressing governance of AI in terms of data privacy, transparency, accountability, and security;
3 Attribution for AI technologies; and
4 Ensuring equity in access to AI technologies.

5.5.3.2   Operational Dimension (Teaching and Learning and IT Staff)

This dimension concentrates on the practical implementation of AI in university settings and to ensure that such implementations are effective, reliable, and supported by adequate training and resources. It includes the following key areas:

1 Monitoring and evaluating AI implementation; and
2 Providing training and support for teachers, staff, and students to ensure that they are AI literate.

5.5.3.3   Pedagogical Dimension (Teachers)

This dimension focuses on the teaching and learning aspects of AI integration and the creation of an educational environment that both leverages AI technologies and prepares students for a future where such technologies are prevalent. It includes the following key areas:

1 Rethinking assessments and examinations;
2 Developing students' holistic competencies/generic skills;
3 Preparing students for the AI-driven workplace; and
4 Encouraging a balanced approach to AI adoption

For the full research paper, please refer to Chan, C.K.Y. (2023) A Comprehensive AI Policy Education Framework for University Teaching and Learning. *International Journal of Educational Technology in Higher Education.* DOI: 10.1186/s41239-023-00408-3.

5.5.4 *The AI Ecological Education Policy Framework*

The AI Ecological Education Policy framework (Chan, 2023) contains the aforementioned three dimensions to guide higher education in developing strategic plans to tackle the challenges of the AI era as shown in Figure 5.3. Each dimension is explained in further detail below.

Senior management holds significant responsibility in the **governance dimension** as they are instrumental in policy formulation, the establishment of ethical guidelines, and overall institutional direction of AI integration. They ensure that their respective institutions will operate within the legal and ethical boundaries while striving for academic excellence and integrity. Their role is crucial in understanding, identifying, and preventing academic misconduct and ethical issues, addressing the governance of AI concerning data privacy,

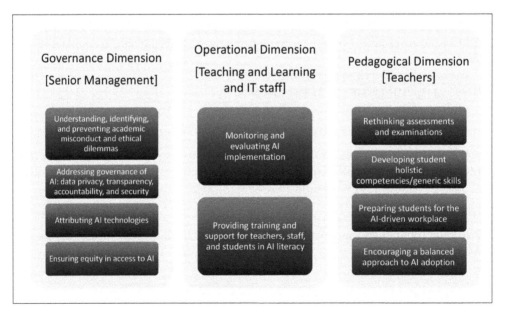

Figure 5.3 AI Ecological Education Policy Framework.

transparency, accountability, and security, the requirements to provide attribution to AI technologies, and ensuring equity in the access to AI technologies. Their decisions and policies set the tone for how AI will be embraced within the institution, impacting both pedagogical and operational dimensions. Within this governance dimension, there are four underlying key areas:

1   Understanding, Identifying, and Preventing Academic Misconduct and Ethical Dilemmas
    The potential of AI technologies to be used for academic misconduct necessitates a robust governance framework to address this concern. Developing and enforcing policies on academic integrity and ethical AI use are crucial in promoting and maintaining a culture of integrity within the academic community. By addressing the governance of AI head-on, senior management can create a more conducive environment for the ethical use and integration of AI, mitigating its risks in relation to academic misconduct.
2   Addressing Governance of AI: Data Privacy, Transparency, Accountability, and Security
    Effective governance to ensure data privacy, transparency, accountability, and security is paramount for the ethical and secure utilisation of AI. Establishing clear guidelines and policies for AI governance will help to address potential ethical dilemmas and allow for a more structured approach towards AI integration. The impact of these actions will be profound, contributing to enhanced trust, compliance, and responsible AI usage within the academic community.
3   Attributing AI Technologies
    Given that AI technologies can and likely will be used by students in their academic work, it is necessary to establish clear guidelines for the proper attribution and recognition of AI-generated content. Doing so can further promote academic honesty and ensure clarity in the acknowledgment of how AI was used. This, in turn, can foster a culture of transparency and honesty within the academic community. Figure 5.4 shows an example of how to write an attribution to acknowledge AI-generated text.
4   Ensuring Equity in Access to AI Technologies
    Disparity in students' access to AI technologies will exacerbate existing inequalities. It is thus crucial to implement measures for ensuring equitable access to AI resources as a critical action for promoting fairness and inclusivity. This could involve providing access to AI tools within the institution or creating support structures for students to learn and engage with AI technologies in a responsible manner.

An Example of Attribution of GenAI Generated Content

"The author acknowledges the use of [AI tool's name, version, and developer] in the process of [research, writing, data analysis, etc.] for this work. The AI tool served as an aid to [enhance readability, perform complex calculations, analyse extensive data, etc.]. It's important to note that the AI-generated content wasnot used verbatim. Instead, it was thoroughly reviewed, edited, and curated by the author to ensure the accuracy, authenticity, and integrity of the information. The human oversight and judgment were paramount in interpreting and validating the AI's contribution. Therefore, the final product is the result of a human-AI collaboration."

Figure 5.4 An Example of Attribution of GenAI Generated Content.

Teaching and learning Support and IT staff play a significant role in the **operational dimension** as they are responsible for the practical implementation, monitoring, and provision of support for AI technologies. They ensure that any AI technologies integrated into the curricula are reliable, effective, and used responsibly. Their role in monitoring and evaluating AI implementation is critical for continuous improvement and upholding alignment with institutional goals. Additionally, they provide the necessary training and support for teachers, staff, and students, ensuring that all stakeholders are well-equipped with AI literacy and are capable of effectively navigating the complex landscape of AI in academia. Within the operational dimension, there are two underlying key areas:

1 Monitoring and Evaluating AI Implementation
    Adopting AI technologies into academic settings requires a structured approach to monitoring and evaluating AI implementation. Regular monitoring can ensure that the AI tools in question are effective, reliable, and being used responsibly. This operational facet is crucial for both facilitating continuous improvement and ensuring that the practical implementation of AI technologies aligns with the ethical and pedagogical objectives of the institution.
2 Providing Training and Support for Teachers, Staff, and Students in AI Literacy
    The need for AI literacy among stakeholders is a pressing concern. Developing and delivering training programmes on AI literacy, ethics, and effective use can significantly improve understanding and responsible use of AI technologies among teachers, staff, students, and so on. This operational action is vital for ensuring that all stakeholders are well-informed and equipped to navigate the complex landscape of AI in academia.

Teachers play a key role in the **pedagogical dimension** as they are at the forefront of delivering education and engaging with students. With their first-hand experiences and expertise in teaching and learning processes, they are uniquely positioned to explore, understand, and implement AI technologies in a manner that enhances learning and the achievement of educational outcomes. Their insights into students' learning needs, as well as the challenges and potential benefits of AI technologies in relation to teaching and learning, are invaluable for rethinking assessments, developing students' competencies, preparing students for the AI-driven workplace, and encouraging the balanced adoption of AI. Teachers are the primary actors in translating policy and operational frameworks into effective teaching and learning practices. Within the pedagogical dimension, there are four underlying key areas:

1 Rethinking Assessments and Examinations
    The advent of AI technologies including ChatGPT presents both challenges and opportunities for academic assessments. As previously mentioned, a key concern that arises is the potential misuse of AI in facilitating academic misconduct. Actions to address this could include the redesign of assessments to include varied methods, such as in-class demonstrations, presentations, or multi-stage submissions, which could mitigate the opportunities to engage in AI-assisted misconduct. The outcome of such actions could also improve the accuracy of assessment looking at students' understanding and skills, reduce academic misconduct, and potentially facilitate a higher level of student engagement.
2 Developing Student Holistic Competencies/Generic Skills
    As AI technologies become progressively integrated across all sectors of society, the necessity for students to develop holistic competencies becomes paramount. These

competencies range from critical thinking and leadership abilities to self-reflection and creative problem solving – skills that are not easily replicated by AI. By introducing second-order writing tasks and promoting critical evaluation, educators can foster a deeper level of understanding and skills development among students. The outcomes would be manifold, including better-prepared students who can think critically and navigate a tech-driven academic and professional landscape.

3 Preparing Students for the AI-Driven Workplace
The evolving nature of the workplace combined with the integration of AI technologies requires a forward-thinking approach to prepare students for their future careers. Familiarising students with AI technologies, ethical considerations, and real-world applications can facilitate a more seamless transition from academia to the professional world. The actions in this domain could include integrating AI-related topics into the curriculum, engaging in discussions about the ethical implications of AI, and providing hands-on experiences with AI tools. The expected outcomes of this are future cohorts of students who are better prepared for the demands of an AI-driven workplace.

4 Encouraging a Balanced Approach to AI Adoption
A balanced approach to AI adoption in academia can help us navigate the fine line between leveraging technology and maintaining academic integrity. By promoting a such an approach, educators can enhance teaching and learning experiences while mitigating the risks associated with AI technologies. This could also foster a more positive attitude towards technological evolution, in turn further leading to innovation in teaching and learning methods that are in sync with the advancements in technology.

It is imperative to acknowledge that the responsibilities of each dimension in this ecological framework should not be viewed in isolation. The relationships among the three dimensions are intricate and interdependent. For instance, effective governance policies (Governance Dimension) could support the ethical integration of AI in teaching and learning (Pedagogical Dimension), and well-informed operational practices (Operational Dimension) could ensure the success of such integration. By taking into account these dimensions, a cohesive theory regarding the integration of AI in academic settings can be further developed and refined.

The successful integration of AI in academic settings counts on collaboration and communication among all stakeholders, including universities, teachers, students, staff, and external agents such as accreditation and quality assurance bodies. Each group should actively participate in the development and execution of AI-related initiatives, working together to achieve the desired outcomes in university teaching and learning. This collaborative approach will foster a more comprehensive, informed, and ethical integration of AI, aligning with broader educational goals and ethical standards. Overall, through open communication and collaborative efforts, stakeholders can collectively navigate the complexities of AI integration, ensuring that the pedagogical, governance, and operational dimensions are also harmoniously in alignment for the betterment of the academic community.

5.6 Devising an AI Policy in Higher Education

Creating an AI policy in higher education is an extensive process that requires a well-thought-out approach. It should ideally follow a structured methodology to ensure that all stakeholders' perspectives are considered and that the policy is comprehensive, ethical, and effective in achieving the desired objectives. The intricacies of formulating such an AI policy in such a dynamic environment often extend beyond the existing expertise of teachers, administrative staff, and even senior management. The lack of familiarity with the nuanced domain of AI further exacerbates the complexity of devising a robust policy tailored to the educational milieu.

This section seeks to explain and clarify the process of formulating AI policy within higher education institutions, based on the above framework. We offer a structured, step-by-step guide on how such a policy can be crafted and implemented, providing a straightforward pathway for stakeholders at all levels to engage in the policymaking process. This draft is simplified and may serve as a starting point or reference for further development by your institution. As a pragmatic approach, it can be used as a roadmap for policy development as well as to foster a collaborative ethos, encouraging inclusive dialogue among all stakeholders to leverage AI technologies effectively and ethically in education, thus enabling a smooth transition into the AI-augmented teaching and administrative paradigm. Below is the step-by-step guideline based on the ecological framework's dimensions of governance, pedagogy, and operations:

1 Initiation and Planning

a Establish a Steering Committee: The first step towards developing an AI policy in education is the formation of a Steering Committee. Senior management should spearhead this initiative by identifying and inviting individuals from different stakeholder groups to be part of this committee, including faculty members, IT staff, administrative staff, legal advisors, and student representatives. Ideally, the committee should have balanced representation to ensure that diverse perspectives and expertise are incorporated in the policy development process. An initial meeting should be convened where the objectives of the policy are outlined, roles and responsibilities are assigned, and a tentative timeline is established. This committee will serve as the driving force behind the policy development, acting as the conduit between the stakeholder groups and the development process.

   Who: Senior management should establish a Steering Committee composed of representatives from each stakeholder group (including senior management themselves, teachers, IT staff, administrative staff, legal advisors, students, and external experts).

   How: The formation of the committee can be announced through official channels, and nominations or volunteers could be solicited with the goal of having balanced representation.

b Conduct a Needs Assessment: A Needs Assessment is crucial as it lays the foundation for the policy by identifying the current state of policy, the desired state, and the gaps in between. This involves designing and distributing surveys to gather insights from stakeholders on their understanding, expectations, and concerns regarding the integration of AI into education. Simultaneously, focus group discussions can be conducted to delve deeper into specific issues or concerns. An analysis of the existing technological infrastructure and educational practices can also provide a clear picture of the current capabilities of these areas while also identifying those that may require improvement. The data collected through these methods should be carefully analysed to identify the core needs and challenges that the AI policy should address.

   Who: The Steering Committee, with the help of educational and technical experts.

   How: Through surveys, focus groups, and analyses of existing infrastructure and educational needs.

c Define Objectives and Scope: After conducting the Needs Assessment, the Steering Committee should engage in defining the objectives and scope of the AI policy. This could involve a thorough review of existing literature, benchmarking against the AI policies of other institutions, and consulting legal and ethical guidelines concerning AI in education. The objectives should be clear, measurable, and aligned with the broader educational goals of the institution, while the scope should define the boundaries of the AI policy, including the areas it will cover, the stakeholders it will affect, and the resources it will require. This step is essential as it sets the direction for policy development and ensures that the process remains focused and aligned with the identified needs.

   Who: The Steering Committee.

   How: Reviewing the Needs Assessment findings and consulting with stakeholders to set clear objectives for the AI policy.

2 Stakeholder Engagement

a Solicit Input and Feedback: Engaging stakeholders is necessary for the development of a well-rounded and inclusive AI policy. The Steering Committee should establish communication channels such as online forums (see Figure 5.5 for an example), email groups, and hold physical or virtual meetings to solicit the input and feedback of all stakeholder groups. This engagement should be continuous, allowing parties share their insights, concerns, and suggestions regarding the integration of AI into education. The input and feedback collected should also be documented and analysed to understand broader implications, as well as to ensure that the policy will address the concerns and needs raised.

   Who: The Steering Committee should lead this effort, reaching out to all stakeholder groups.

   How: Through online surveys, in-person or virtual town-hall meetings, and focus group discussions to gather insights, concerns, and suggestions regarding the integration of AI into education.

b Educate Stakeholders: Equipping stakeholders with a good understanding of AI and its potential implications in education is essential for facilitating meaningful engagement. This can be achieved through workshops, seminars, and informational sessions conducted by experts within or outside the Steering Committee. Educational materials explaining AI, its applications in education, and its ethical implications should be developed and distributed. By doing so, stakeholder discussions will be better informed, enhancing the quality and depth of their feedback and engagement in the policy development process.

   Who: Experts within the Steering Committee or external consultants.

   How: Conducting workshops, seminars, and informational sessions to educate stakeholders about AI and its potential implications in education, including ethical considerations.

3 Policy Development

a Drafting the Policy: With the groundwork laid, the process now moves onto drafting the policy. A working group within the Steering Committee, possibly with the inclusion of legal and technical experts, should be formed to draft the AI policy. This Policy Drafting Team should work to integrate the insights gathered from stakeholders, information from legal and ethical guidelines, and the educational objectives identified earlier. The drafting process should be iterative, allowing for revisions based on feedback from the Steering Committee and consultations with other experts.

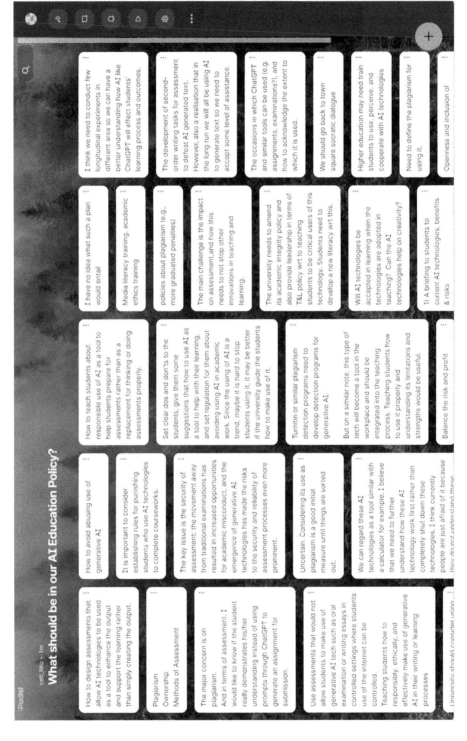

Figure 5.5 An Example of Using a Padlet for Online Forum.

Who: A working group within the Steering Committee, with assistance from legal and technical experts.

How: Establishing a comprehensive draft policy by integrating insights from stakeholders, referring to legal and ethical guidelines, and ensuring alignment with educational objectives.

b Stakeholder Review: Once a draft policy is prepared, it should be shared with all stakeholder groups for review and feedback. Various channels can be used to disseminate the draft policy and collect feedback, including through online platforms, emails, or physical meetings. Stakeholders should be given a reasonable time frame to review the draft and provide their inputs. This step ensures that the draft policy is vetted by the broader community, enhancing its inclusivity and relevance.

Who: All stakeholder groups.

How: Sharing the draft policy for review and feedback through various channels such as online platforms, meetings, and emails.

c Revision and Finalisation: The feedback collected from stakeholders should be analysed and necessary revisions should be made to the draft policy. The Policy Drafting Team should engage in an iterative process of revision and consultation with the Steering Committee, ensuring that the policy is appropriately refined and still aligned with the defined objectives and scope. Once revisions have been made and the draft is finalised, the policy should be reviewed one final time by the Steering Committee to confirm that it is ready for submission to senior management and other governing bodies for approval.

Who: The working group within the Steering Committee.

How: Incorporating the feedback received, revising the policy as necessary, and finalising the draft for approval.

4 Approval and Adoption

a Seek Approval: The Steering Committee, having finalised the draft policy, now moves to seek formal approval from the senior management and other governing bodies within the institution. This usually involves preparing a detailed presentation outlining the key aspects of the policy, the process undertaken to develop it, and the implications of its implementation. It is crucial to articulate how the policy aligns with the broader educational goals of the institution, as well as how it adheres to legal and ethical standards. The presentation also provides an opportunity for the committee to address any issues or concerns raised by the senior management, and potentially make further revisions to the policy based on the feedback received. The approval process ensures that the AI policy has the necessary endorsement from the institutional leadership, paving the way for its official adoption.

Who: The Steering Committee should present the policy to senior management and other necessary governing bodies for approval.

How: Through formal presentations and submission of the policy document for review.

b Official Adoption: Upon receiving approval, the next step is the official adoption of the AI policy. This is typically announced through official channels such as institutional bulletins, emails, and meetings. The policy document should be disseminated to all stakeholders, ensuring they have access to it and understand its implications. It is advisable to have an official launch event or announcement that highlights the key aspects of the policy and what it means for the stakeholders. This step marks the formal recognition of the AI policy as a guideline within the institution, setting the stage for its implementation.

Who: Senior management.

How: Announcing the adoption of the policy through official channels and disseminate the policy document to all stakeholders.

5 Implementation

a Develop an Implementation Plan: With the policy officially adopted, the need now is to develop a concrete implementation plan. It should outline the steps, timelines, resources, and responsibilities for implementing the policy, as well as identify the necessary support structures for ensuring that the process is smooth. This could include training programmes, resource allocations, and the establishment of support channels for stakeholders to seek help or report issues. The implementation plan serves as the blueprint for translating the policy into practice, ensuring that all stakeholders are well-prepared and supported in adhering to the new AI policy.

   Who: The Steering Committee, in collaboration with operational staff.

   How: Outlining the steps, timelines, resources, and responsibilities for implementing the policy.

b Training and Support: Training and support are critical components of the implementation phase. Training programmes should be developed and delivered to stakeholders to equip them with the necessary skills and knowledge to comply with the AI policy. This could include training on new technologies, ethical considerations, and best practices for AI integration in education. Support channels should also be established to provide ongoing assistance to stakeholders, ensuring they have the resources and help necessary to navigate the new policy and its effects. These support channels could include helpdesks, online forums, and dedicated support personnel.

   Who: IT staff and educational experts.

   How: Conducting training sessions, workshops, and provide resources to support stakeholders in adhering to the new AI policy.

c Monitoring and Evaluation: The implementation phase should also include a robust monitoring and evaluation component. This involves establishing clear metrics and procedures to monitor the implementation process, assess compliance with the policy, and evaluate the effectiveness of the policy in achieving the desired objectives. Regular reports should be written up and submitted to provide insights into the progress of the implementation, any challenges encountered, and the impact of the policy on educational practices.

   Who: A designated monitoring and evaluation team.

   How: Establish metrics and procedures to monitor the implementation, and evaluate the effectiveness of the policy against the defined objectives.

6 Continuous Improvement:

a Gather Feedback: Following the implementation of the policy, it is still important to gather stakeholder feedback to understand their experiences, challenges, and suggestions. Establishing channels for feedback collection, reporting of issues, and sharing of insights is integral for continuous improvement. Feedback should be systematically collected, documented, and analysed to identify areas for improvement.

   Who: The monitoring and evaluation team.

   How: Through surveys, focus groups, and analysis of implementation metrics.

b Policy Revision: Based on the feedback and findings from monitoring and evaluating its implementation, the policy may require revisions to address any emerging challenges, technological advancements, or changing educational needs. The Steering Committee should engage in the continued review of the policy, making necessary adjustments or amendments, and also continue to consult with stakeholders to ensure that the policy remains relevant, effective, and aligned with the institutional goals.

Who: The Steering Committee.

How: Based on feedback and evaluation findings, revising and updating the policy as necessary to ensure that it remains relevant and effective.

c Ongoing Stakeholder Engagement: Continuous improvement requires ongoing engagement with stakeholders. Maintaining open communication channels, soliciting feedback, and providing regular updates on any revisions or new initiatives are crucial for keeping stakeholders informed, engaged, and compliant with the policy. This further fosters a culture of collaboration, learning, and continuous improvement, ensuring the AI policy remains a living document that evolves in response to the changing landscape of AI in education.

Who: The Steering Committee and senior management.

How: Maintaining open channels of communication to ensure that stakeholders are informed and have the opportunity to provide ongoing feedback.

Each of these steps is designed to ensure a collaborative, informed, and structured approach to developing and implementing an AI policy in education. The involvement of various stakeholders throughout different stages of the process is crucial to ensure that the policy is well-rounded, relevant, and effective in promoting ethical and effective AI integration in academic institutions.

5.6.1   An Example of an AI Policy in Higher Education

As emphasised throughout this chapter, creating a comprehensive AI policy for higher education requires meticulous planning and a thorough understanding of the institution's objectives, stakeholders' needs, and the legal and ethical facets of AI. Based on the AI Ecological Education Policy framework and the step-by-step guide in Section 5.6. Here is a simple example outline of an AI education policy:

Table 5.1 A Simple Outline of an AI Education Policy

Title: AI Education Policy for [Institution Name]

1. **Introduction**:
  1.1. Background: Explanation of the emergence of AI technologies and their potential impact on higher education. Mention of the institution's commitment to leveraging AI to enhance educational outcomes while adhering to ethical and legal standards.
  Purpose: Articulation of the policy's aim to guide the responsible integration and use of AI technologies within the institution.
  1.2. Scope: Clarification on the departments, individuals, and activities covered by the policy.

2. **Governance**:
  2.1. Steering Committee: Establishment of a steering committee to oversee the implementation, monitoring, and continuous improvement of the AI education policy.
  2.2. Ethical Guidelines: Clear ethical guidelines for AI usage, including respect for privacy, transparency, accountability, and fairness.
  2.3. Legal Compliance: Assurance of compliance with all applicable laws and regulations concerning data protection, privacy, and AI.

(Continued)

Table 5.1 (Continued)

Title: AI Education Policy for [Institution Name]

3. **Pedagogical Integration**:
   3.1. Faculty Training: Provision for training faculty on the responsible use of AI in teaching and assessment.
   3.2. Student Engagement: Encouragement of student engagement with AI technologies under the guidance of faculty.
   3.3. Assessment Reformation: Revision of assessment strategies to account for the integration of AI technologies.

4. **Operational Implementation**:
   4.1. Technology Infrastructure: Investment in necessary technology infrastructure to support AI integration.
   4.2. Support and Resources: Establishment of support channels and resources to assist stakeholders in navigating the AI policy and technologies.
   4.3. Monitoring and Evaluation: Continuous monitoring and evaluation to assess the effectiveness, compliance, and impact of AI integration.

5. **Continuous Improvement**:
   5.1. Feedback Mechanisms: Establishing mechanisms for stakeholders to provide feedback on AI integration experiences.
   5.2. Policy Revision: Periodic review and revision of the AI education policy to ensure relevance and effectiveness.
   5.3. Stakeholder Communication: Ongoing communication with stakeholders regarding any updates or revisions to the policy.

6. **Conclusion**:
   6.1. Commitment: Reiteration of the institution's commitment to responsible AI integration for the enhancement of educational outcomes.
   6.2. Contact Information: Provision of contact information for stakeholders to seek clarification or provide feedback regarding the policy.
   6.3. Effective Date: The date which the policy takes effect.

5.6.2   *University of ABC*

5.6.2.1 *Artificial Intelligence in Education Policy*

I Introduction

  A **Background**

The advent of Artificial Intelligence (AI) has created new possibilities and challenges for various sectors, including higher education. It has emerged as transformative tools with vast implications in the educational settings. At [the University of ABC], we recognise the unparalleled potential of AI to revolutionise learning experiences, enhance pedagogical methods, and facilitate groundbreaking research. This policy manifests our firm commitment to harnessing the power of AI to reinforce educational outcomes while strictly adhering to the highest ethical and legal standards. This policy aims to guide the responsible integration and usage of AI technologies within [the University of ABC].

  B **Purpose**

This policy seeks to provide a clear and structured framework guiding the responsible integration, utilisation, and governance of AI technologies within the University of ABC's ecosystem. To ensure the ethical, legal, and effective utilisation of AI to enhance teaching, learning, and administrative processes while safeguarding the rights and interests of all stakeholders.

C **Scope**

This policy applies to all departments, faculties, students, staff, and affiliates of the [University of ABC]. It pertains to all activities related to the development, deployment, and utilisation or evaluation of AI technologies within the institution.

II Governance

A **Steering Committee**

A dedicated AI Steering Committee shall be established to provide oversight on the effective implementation, monitoring, and evolution of the AI education policy. The committee will comprise representatives from academic faculties, IT, administrative, legal, and student bodies.

B **Ethical Guidelines**

The University of ABC upholds the principles of privacy, transparency, accountability, and fairness in all AI-related endeavours. All AI initiatives will be rooted in these ethical guidelines to ensure that technologies benefit the academic community without compromising individual rights or societal values.

C **Legal Compliance**

Compliance with all applicable local, state, and federal laws and regulations governing data privacy, protection, and AI is mandatory. Necessary measures will be taken to ensure full legal compliance in every AI endeavour.

III Pedagogical Integration

A **Faculty Training**

Recognising the pivotal role of our faculty in AI integration, continuous professional development opportunities shall be provided to faculty to enhance their understanding and capability in utilising AI for pedagogical purposes.

B **Student Engagement**

Students shall be educated on the ethical use of AI, and encouraged to leverage AI technologies to enhance their learning experiences under the guidance and supervision of faculty, ensuring hands-on experience and fostering a culture of innovative learning.

C **Assessment Redesign**

Traditional assessment strategies will be revisited and redesigned to account for the innovativeness introduced by AI, ensuring that they remain valid, reliable, and equitable. Assessment strategies shall be revised to ensure fairness and integrity in the evaluation of student performance in a learning environment augmented by AI technologies.

IV Operational Implementation

A **Technology Infrastructure**

Investment will be channelled towards establishing robust and state-of-the-art technological infrastructure, facilitating seamless AI integration and ensuring optimal performance and security. Adequate technological infrastructure shall be established to support the effective integration and utilisation of AI technologies.

B   **Support and Resources**
Dedicated support channels, including helpdesks and online portals, will be set up to assist stakeholders in understanding and navigating AI technologies and adhering to this policy.

C   **Monitoring and Evaluation**
A continuous monitoring system will be implemented, evaluating the effectiveness, compliance, and impact of AI technologies, ensuring they align with our academic objectives and values. A systematic approach shall be employed to monitor, evaluate, and report the effectiveness and impact of AI integration within [the University of ABC].

V   **Continuous Improvement**

A   **Feedback Mechanisms**
Mechanisms for collecting feedback from all stakeholders on the AI integration experiences shall be established to inform continuous improvement efforts.

B   **Policy Revision**
In line with the dynamic nature of AI, this policy will be subject to periodic reviews, ensuring its continued relevance, robustness, and alignment with the University's goals and the broader educational landscape.

C   **Stakeholder Communication**
The University will maintain open lines of communication, updating stakeholders on any modifications or pertinent developments related to this policy.

VI **Conclusion**

A   **Commitment**
[The University of ABC] remains committed to harnessing the potential of AI to enhance the educational experiences of all stakeholders while adhering to the highest ethical, legal, and professional standards.

B   **Contact Information**
For any queries or feedback regarding this policy, stakeholders may contact the Steering Committee at [ai_policy@universityofabc.edu].

C   **Effective Date**
This policy shall take effect from [effective date] and remain in effect until revised or rescinded.

Signed by

_____

Senior Management
University of ABC   Date

5.7 Conclusions

In an era where AI – and GenAI tools in particular – is becoming increasingly embedded into our educational systems, developing comprehensive and ethical AI education policies is crucial. The journey from understanding the ethical dilemmas of using AI in educational settings and reviewing global AI policies, to charting a path for practical AI policy development in education, has been both enlightening and challenging. As we navigate through the multi-faceted terrains of AI ethics, governance, privacy, and equity in education, it is imperative that policies are continually revised to adapt to the evolving technological and ethical landscapes as well. Our pursuit should not only be in leveraging AI to enhance learning experiences, but also in ensuring that AI is implemented in a manner that is equitable, transparent, and beneficial to all stakeholders involved in the educational process.

Questions to Ponder

- How can policymakers ensure that AI education policies remain adaptable and resilient to the rapid advancements and unforeseen ethical challenges posed by GenAI?
- In what ways can global AI education policies be coordinated and streamlined to establish a unified ethical and practical framework that transcends borders?
- How might AI education policies address and mitigate the potential widening of educational disparities and ensure equal access to quality education for all students?
- As we develop AI education policies, how can we ensure that the voices and concerns of all stakeholders, including students, educators, parents, and administrators, are adequately represented and addressed?
- UNESCO suggests that the minimum age for AI usage should be 13 years old. Is this feasible? Or is it too late to start?

Personal Reflection

Embarking on the journey of exploring AI education policies invites us into a world where technology and ethics intertwine. Imagine, for a moment, that these policies are not mere documents but are the silent guardians of our educational kingdoms, ensuring that the integration of GenAI tools into our learning environments are just, ethical, and beneficial. What steps would you take to ensure our guardians are on the right path?

As we reflect on this chapter, let us ponder our own beliefs and perceptions about AI in education. How do we envision the future of education with GenAI tools?

References

Australian Government Department of Industry, Science and Resources. (2023, June 18). *Australia's artificial intelligence action plan*. Retrieved October 16, 2023, from https://www.industry.gov.au/publications/australias-artificial-intelligence-action-plan

Baio, A. (2023, May 16). *OpenAI CEO Sam Altman says AI can go 'quite wrong' while advocating for government intervention*. Independent. https://www.independent.co.uk/tech/congress-ai-chatgpt-sam-altman-b2340147.html

Bryson, J. J. (2018). Patiency is not a virtue: the design of intelligent systems and systems of ethics. *Ethics and Information Technology, 20*, 15–26. https://doi.org/10.1007/s10676-018-9448-6

Burciaga, A. (2021, October 4). *How to build responsible AI, step 1: Accountability*. Forbes. Retrieved October 13, 2023, from https://www.forbes.com/sites/forbestechcouncil/2021/10/04/how-to-build-responsible-ai-step-1-accountability/

Centre for Information Policy Leadership (CIPL). (2020, March). *Artificial intelligence and data protection: How the GDPR regulates AI*. Retrieved October 13, 2023, from https://www.information policycentre.com/uploads/5/7/1/0/57104281/cipl-hunton_andrews_kurth_legal_note_-_how_gdpr_regulates_ai__12_march_2020_.pdf

Chan, C. K. Y. (2023). A comprehensive AI policy education framework for university teaching and learning. *International Journal of Educational Technology in Higher Education*. https://doi.org/10.1186/s41239-023-00408-3

Chowdhury, R. (2023, April 6). *AI desperately needs global oversight*. Wired. Retrieved October 13, 2023, from https://www.wired.com/story/ai-desperately-needs-global-oversight/

Christian, B. (2020). *The alignment problem: Machine learning and human values*. W.W. Norton & Company.

Creswell, A., Nikiforou, K., Vinyals, O., Saraiva, A., Kabra, R., Matthey, L., Burgess, C., Reynolds, M., Tanburn, R., Garnelo, M., & Shanahan, M. (2020, July 21). *AlignNet: Unsupervised entity alignment*. Google DeepMind. Retrieved October 13, 2023, from https://www.deepmind.com/publications/alignnet-unsupervised-entity-alignment

Criddle, C., Espinoza, J., & Liu, Q. (2023, September 13). *The global race to set the rules for AI*. Financial Times. Retrieved October 13, 2023, from https://www.ft.com/content/59b9ef36-771f-4f91-89d1-ef89f4a2ec4e

Department for Digital, Culture, Media and Sport. (2022, July 18). *Establishing a pro-innovation approach to regulating AI: An overview of the UK's emerging approach*. Retrieved October 17, 2023, from https://assets.publishing.service.gov.uk/government/uploads/system/uploads/attachment_data/file/1092630/_CP_728__-_Establishing_a_pro-innovation_approach_to_regulating_AI.pdf

Edwards, B. (2023, May 31). *OpenAI execs warn of "risk of extinction" from artificial intelligence in new open letter*. Ars Technica. Retrieved October 13, 2023, from https://arstechnica.com/information-technology/2023/05/openai-execs-warn-of-risk-of-extinction-from-artificial-intelligence-in-new-open-letter/

European Parliament (2023, June 14). *EU AI act: First regulation on artificial intelligence*. Retrieved October 13, 2023, from https://www.europarl.europa.eu/news/en/headlines/society/20230601STO93804/eu-ai-act-first-regulation-on-artificial-intelligence

Federal Trade Commission Bureau of Competition & Office of Technology. (2023, June 29). *Generative AI raises competition concerns*. Retrieved October 16, 2023, from https://www.ftc.gov/policy/advocacy-research/tech-at-ftc/2023/06/generative-ai-raises-competition-concerns

Federspiel, F., Mitchell, R., Asokan, A., Umana, C., & McCoy, D. (2023). Threats by artificial intelligence to human health and human existence. *BMJ Global Health*, *8*(5), 1–6. https://doi.org/10.1136/bmjgh-2022-010435

Ferrara, E. (2023). Fairness and bias in artificial intelligence: A brief survey of sources, impacts, and mitigation strategies. arXiv. https://doi.org/10.48550/arXiv.2304.07683

Friedler, S., Venkatasubramanian, S., & Engler, A. (2023, March 22). *How California and other states are tackling AI legislation*. Brookings. Retrieved October 13, 2023, from https://www.brookings.edu/articles/how-california-and-other-states-are-tackling-ai-legislation/

Future of Life Institute. (2017, August 11). *AI principles*. Retrieved October 13, 2023, from https://futureoflife.org/open-letter/ai-principles/

Gabriel, I. (2020, January 13). *Artificial intelligence, values and alignment*. Google DeepMind. Retrieved October 13, 2023, from https://www.deepmind.com/publications/artificial-intelligence-values-and-alignment

GDPR.EU. (2023). *What is GDPR, the EU's new data protection law?* Retrieved October 13, 2023, from https://gdpr.eu/what-is-gdpr/

Gent, E. (2023, May 10). *What is the AI alignment problem and how can it be solved?* New Scientist. Retrieved October 13, 2023, from https://www.newscientist.com/article/mg25834382-000-what-is-the-ai-alignment-problem-and-how-can-it-be-solved/

Goertzel, B. (2014). Artificial general intelligence: Concept, state of the art, and future prospects. *Journal of Artificial General Intelligence*, 5(1), 1–46. https://doi.org/10.2478/jagi-2014-0001

Government of India Ministry of Electronics & Information Technology. (2023, August 11). *Information technology act 2000*. Retrieved October 16, 2023, from https://www.meity.gov.in/content/information-technology-act-2000

Greiman, V. A. (2021). Human rights and artificial intelligence: A universal challenge. *Journal of Information Warfare*, 20(1), 50–62.

Hogenhout, L. (2021). *A framework for ethical AI at the United Nations*. United Nations. Retrieved October 16, 2023, https://unite.un.org/sites/unite.un.org/files/unite_paper_-_ethical_ai_at_the_un.pdf

Information Commissioner's Office. (n.d.) *What are the accountability and governance implications of AI?* Retrieved October 13, 2023, from https://ico.org.uk/for-organisations/uk-gdpr-guidance-and-resources/artificial-intelligence/guidance-on-ai-and-data-protection/what-are-the-accountability-and-governance-implications-of-ai/

International Commission on the Futures of Education. (2021). *Reimagining our futures together: a new social contract for education*. UNESCO. https://doi.org/10.54675/ASRB4722

Joyce, D. W., Kormilitzin, A., Smith, K. A. et al. (2023). Explainable artificial intelligence for mental health through transparency and interpretability for understandability. *npj Digital Medicine*, 6, 6. https://doi.org/10.1038/s41746-023-00751-9

Kharparl, A. (2023, July 13). *China finalizes first-of-its-kind rules governing generative A.I. services like ChatGPT*. CNBC. Retrieved October 13, 2023, from https://www.cnbc.com/2023/07/13/china-introduces-rules-governing-generative-ai-services-like-chatgpt.html

Larsen, B. C. (2023). *The geopolitics of AI and the rise of digital sovereignty*. Brookings. Retrieved 16 October, 2023, from https://www.brookings.edu/articles/the-geopolitics-of-ai-and-the-rise-of-digital-sovereignty/

Lawton, G. (2023, June 2). *AI transparency: What is it and why do we need it?* TechTarget. Retrieved October 13, 2023, from https://www.techtarget.com/searchcio/tip/AI-transparency-What-is-it-and-why-do-we-need-it#:~:text=Transparency%20in%20AI%20refers%20to,how%20it%20reaches%20its%20decisions

Leike, J., Schulman, J., & Wu, J. (2022, August 24). *Our approach to alignment research*. OpenAI. Retrieved October 13, 2023, from https://openai.com/blog/our-approach-to-alignment-research

Liu, Y. (2023, June 5). 生成AI画像は類似性が認められれば「著作権侵害」。文化庁 [If a generated AI image is found to be similar, it is considered a "copyright infringement." Agency for Cultural Affairs]. PC Watch. Retrieved from https://pc.watch.impress.co.jp/docs/news/1506018.html

Manish, C. (2023, August 18). *Sam Altman's nuclear backpack holds the code to save the world from AI*. Mobile App Daily. Retrieved from https://www.mobileappdaily.com/news/sam-altmans-nuclear-backpack-holds-the-code-to-save-the-world-from-ai

Matsuda, A., Kudo, R., & Matsuda, T. (2023). Japan. In C. Kerrigan (Ed.), *AI, machine learning & big data laws and regulations 2023*. Global Legal Insights. https://www.globallegalinsights.com/practice-areas/ai-machine-learning-and-big-data-laws-and-regulations/japan

Mehrabi, N., Morstatter, F., Saxena, N., Lerman, K., & Galstyan, A. (2021). A survey on bias and fairness in machine learning. *ACM Computing Surveys*, 54(6), 1–35. https://doi.org/10.1145/3457607

Meyer, J. (2023, May 31). *AI poses risk of extinction, tech leaders warn in open letter. Here's why alarm is spreading*. USA Today. Retrieved October 13, 2023, from https://eu.usatoday.com/story/news/politics/2023/05/31/ai-extinction-risk-expert-warning/70270171007/

Minevich, M. (2023, May 19). *Generative AI shakes global diplomacy at G7 summit in Japan*. Forbes. Retrieved October 16, 2023, from https://www.forbes.com/sites/markminevich/2023/05/19/high-stakes-generative-ai-shakes-global-diplomacy-at-japans-2023-g7-summit/?sh=243a3dce6321

Ministry of Economy, Trade and Industry. (2021, July 9). AI governance in Japan Ver. 1.1: Report from the expert group on how AI principles should be implemented. Retrieved October 16, 2023, from https://www.meti.go.jp/shingikai/mono_info_service/ai_shakai_jisso/pdf/20210709_8.pdf

Mukherjee, S., Chee, F. Y., & Coulter, M. (2023, April 28). *EU proposes new copyright rules for generative AI*. Reuters. Retrieved October 13, 2023, from https://www.reuters.com/technology/eu-lawmakers-committee-reaches-deal-artificial-intelligence-act-2023-04-27/

Nasiripour, S., & Natarajan, S. (2019, November 11). *Apple co-founder says Goldman's apple card algorithm discriminates*. Bloomberg. Retrieved October 13, 2023, from https://www.bloomberg.com/news/articles/2019-11-10/apple-co-founder-says-goldman-s-apple-card-algo-discriminates?leadSource=uverify%20wall

Novelli, C., Taddeo, M., & Floridi, L. (2023). Accountability in artificial intelligence: What it is and how it works. *AI & Soc.* https://doi.org/10.1007/s00146-023-01635-y

OpenAI. (2023a). *GPT-4 documentation*. Retrieved October 13, 2023, from https://platform.openai.com/docs/models/gpt-4

OpenAI. (2023b). *Privacy policy*. Retrieved October 13, 2023, from https://openai.com/policies/privacy-policy

OpenAI. (2023c). *Security & privacy*. Retrieved October 13, 2023, from https://openai.com/security

OpenAI. (2023d). *OpenAI charter*. Retrieved October 13, 2023, from https://openai.com/charter

Osborne Clarke. (2022, July 19). *Consultation on UK AI regulation: Legislation-free and devolved regulators*. Retrieved October 17, 2023, from https://www.osborneclarke.com/insights/consultation-uk-ai-regulation-legislation-free-and-devolved-regulators

Perrigo, B., & Gordon, A. (2023, June 14). *E.U. takes a step closer to passing the world's most comprehensive AI regulation*. Time. Retrieved October 13, 2023, from https://time.com/6287136/eu-ai-regulation/

Ribeiro, M. T., Singh, S., & Guestrin, C. (2016). "Why should I trust you?": Explaining the predictions of any classifier. In *Proceedings of the 22nd ACM SIGKDD International Conference on Knowledge Discovery and Data Mining* (pp. 1135–1144). https://doi.org/10.1145/2939672.2939778

Roberts, H., Babuta, A., Morley, J., Thomas, C., Taddeo, M., & Floridi, L. (2023, May 26). Artificial intelligence regulation in the United Kingdom: A path to good governance and global leadership? *Internet Policy Review*, *12*(2). https://doi.org/10.14763/2023.2.1709

Robles, P. (2023, October 1). *China plans to be a world leader in Artificial Intelligence by 2030*. South China Morning Post. Retrieved October 16, 2023, from https://multimedia.scmp.com/news/china/article/2166148/china-2025-artificial-intelligence/index.html

Russell, S., Dewey, D., & Tegmark, M. (2015). Research priorities for robust and beneficial artificial intelligence. *AI Magazine*, *36*(4), 105–114. https://doi.org/10.1609/aimag.v36i4.2577

Sharwood, S. (2023, May 26). *India set to regulate AI, Big Tech, with Digital Act*. The Register. Retrieved October 16, 2023, from https://www.theregister.com/2023/05/26/india_digital_act_draft_june/

Silberg, J., & Manyika, J. (2019, June 6). *Tackling bias in artificial intelligence (and in humans)*. McKinsey Global Institute. Retrieved October 13, 2023, from https://www.mckinsey.com/featured-insights/artificial-intelligence/tackling-bias-in-artificial-intelligence-and-in-humans

Singh, M. (2023, April 6). *India opts against AI regulation*. TechCrunch. Retrieved October 16, 2023, from https://techcrunch.com/2023/04/05/india-opts-against-ai-regulation/

State of California Department of Justice, Office of the Attorney General. (2023). *California Consumer Privacy Act (CCPA)*. Retrieved October 13, 2023, from https://oag.ca.gov/privacy/ccpa

Stokel-Walker, C. (2023, January 18). *ChatGPT listed as author on research papers: Many scientists disapprove*. Nature. Retrieved October 13, 2023, from https://www.nature.com/articles/d41586-023-00107-z

Strickland, E. (2023, August 31). *OpenAI's moonshot: Solving the AI alignment problem*. IEEE Spectrum. Retrieved October 13, 2023, from https://spectrum.ieee.org/the-alignment-problem-openai

The Japan Times. (2023, October 15). *Japan's AI draft guidelines ask for measures to address overreliance*. Retrieved October 16, 2023, from https://www.japantimes.co.jp/news/2023/10/15/japan/politics/ai-draft-guidelines/

The Times of India. (2023, May 17). *India planning to regulate AI platforms like ChatGPT: IT minister Ashwini Vaishnaw*. Retrieved October 16, 2023, from http://timesofindia.indiatimes.com/articleshow/100310733.cms?utm_source=contentofinterest&utm_medium=text&utm_campaign=cppst

UK Government. (2023, August 3). *AI regulation: a pro-innovation approach*. [White paper]. Retrieved October 16, 2023, from https://www.gov.uk/government/publications/ai-regulation-a-pro-innovation-approach

UNESCO. (2023a, July 20). *UNESCO's Recommendation on the Ethics of Artificial Intelligence: Key Facts*. https://www.unesco.org/en/articles/unescos-recommendation-ethics-artificial-intelligence-key-facts#:~:text=The%20Recommendation%20establishes%20a%20set,the%20rule%20of%20law%20%20online

UNESCO. (2023b, June 9). *Artificial Intelligence: UNESCO publishes Policy Paper on AI Foundation Models*. Retrieved from https://www.unesco.org/en/articles/artificial-intelligence-unesco-publishes-policy-paper-ai-foundation-models

UNESCO. (2023c). *Guidance for generative AI in education and research*. UNESCO. Retrieved October 13, 2023, from https://unesdoc.unesco.org/ark:/48223/pf0000386693

University of Birmingham. (2023, August 4). *Government's "Pro-Innovation" AI white paper unfit for purpose*. Retrieved October 16, 2023, from https://www.birmingham.ac.uk/news/2023/the-governments-preoccupation-with-innovation-will-cause-the-rule-of-law-to-fall-behind

West, D. M. (2023, September 12). *California charts the future of AI*. Brookings. Retrieved October 13, 2023, from https://www.brookings.edu/articles/california-charts-the-future-of-ai/

Wheeler, T. (2023, June 15). *The three challenges of AI regulation*. Brookings. Retrieved October 13, 2023, from https://www.brookings.edu/articles/the-three-challenges-of-ai-regulation/

6 Technology Behind GenAI

Big centralised AI models have amazed people. Personal, portable, and secure AI will make everyone amazing.

Tom Colloton

6.1 Introduction

The aim of this chapter is to equip the reader with a clearer understanding of the technology behind generative Artificial Intelligence (GenAI). While the book primarily focuses on GenAI in higher education, we recognise that some readers may be curious to learn more about the "black box" of GenAI. Thus, we will delve into its history, processes, methods, and the foundational technology of GenAI. In this exploration, the reader will encounter terminology commonly used in the Artificial Intelligence (AI) field.

In this chapter, we will discuss GenAI models, henceforth referred to simply as 'models' for brevity. It is crucial not to confuse these with other types of models mentioned in the book, such as assessment models. Contemporary GenAI systems predominantly employ deep neural networks (DNN) as the foundational approach for their models. As illustrated in Figure 6.1, DNNs are a type of artificial neural network (ANN). The concept of using artificial neural networks (ANNs) has deep roots in AI, drawing inspiration from studies on the biological brain's functionality. We will delve deeper into this history, providing context leading up to the present-day state-of-the-art models. As illustrated in Figure 6.1, GenAI and its various model types, including large language models (LLMs) and text-to-image models like diffusion models, reside within the realm of deep learning ANNs.

Artificial neural networks (ANNs) are computational models inspired by the human brain's structure and function. They consist of interconnected nodes, called neurons, which process and transmit information through weighted connections. ANNs are designed to learn and recognise patterns from input data, making them useful for tasks such as classification, prediction, and decision-making in various fields like computer vision, natural language processing, and robotics. This chapter will delve into the processes and techniques that underpin these capabilities.

The precise mechanisms by which neural networks store experiences and utilise them for predictions remain somewhat enigmatic. This elusive nature has led some to describe their operation as "magic", given that the complete intricacies and potential limitations are not yet fully understood. This chapter will try to share what is known and what is not yet understood about how these models work.

This chapter involves examining specific GenAI solutions that are currently popular and widely used. It will delve into these specific examples in detail, while also referencing broader

DOI: 10.4324/9781003459026-6

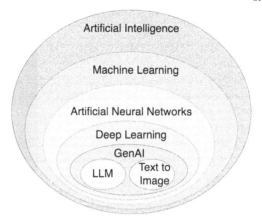

Figure 6.1 AI Categorisation.

methods. By juxtaposing specific examples with general concepts, we aim to offer non-experts a more insightful perspective than if we merely discussed the topic in general terms.

The chapter is structured in a manner that facilitates a gradual understanding, building later concepts on top of earlier concepts as much as possible. However, some topics are interrelated and require more of an iterative approach rather than a pure serial reading of the information, thus it is advised to read the chapter end to end and then re-read to get a deeper understanding of these concepts that required a more iterative approach.

The structure of the chapter is outlined below:

- **The history**. This section looks at the history of artificial neural networks (ANNs), the early work that was done and some of the recent advancements.
- **Creating a model**. This section aims to furnish a comprehensive understanding of how a model operates and the processes involved in its creation. It examines the various stages of model creation: from gathering vast quantities of data to considerations in design and structure; the training phase; and testing the model for quality, performance, and safety.
- **Models and ecosystems**. This section looks at how models are being used and the ecosystems that have built up around them to allow people to interact with models in different ways and allow the models to interact with their environments.
- **State-of-the-art models**. This section aims to provide an overview of some currently popular models considered state-of-the-art. It examines the applications of these models, discusses their design approaches, and comments on their strengths and weaknesses.
- **Conclusions**. This section recaps the key points of GenAI and reflects on the current boundaries of its application.

6.2   The History

The subsequent sections present the history of artificial neural networks (ANNs) in chronological order. You might encounter terms that have not yet been discussed or elaborated upon, such as the specifics of an artificial neuron or cell, the connectivity within artificial neural networks, the concept of a layer, and the roles of weights and biases. However, these intricacies will be addressed in due course. Initially, our focus will be on providing a chronological overview of how these concepts evolved. Later, we will delve into the particulars, emphasising those aspects that remain pertinent today, all while employing contemporary terminology.

The history of AI research can be understood as an evolving interplay of several distinct approaches or "camps". These different approaches often reflected the diverse intellectual backgrounds of AI's founding figures and were influenced by the available technology, prevailing scientific paradigms, and broader societal trends. Two of these camps were the Symbolists and the Connectionists.

The **Symbolists** believed that intelligence could be attained through the manipulation of symbols and rules. Their methodologies encompassed logic-based systems, rule-based expert systems, and semantic networks. Key figures within this camp included John McCarthy, Marvin Minsky, and Herbert Simon. Their primary focus was on determining how the essential rules of understanding, logic, and reason could be represented within a machine and discerning what these fundamental rules encompassed.

The **Connectionists** believed that intelligence emerges from interconnected networks of simple units, often referred to as cells or neurons. Their methodologies are exemplified by neural networks and deep neural networks, which include diverse architectures such as RNNs (recurrent neural networks), CNNs (convolutional neural networks), and Transformers. Notable figures within this camp included Frank Rosenblatt, Geoffrey Hinton, Yann LeCun, James Rumelhart, and James McClelland. Their primary focus was on determining how a machine could learn the necessary rules, how to train the said machine, and how to structure its architecture to facilitate learning in a manner as comprehensive as a human.

We discuss these two camps in more detail later.

It is important to recognise that advancements have been made in other areas of AI beyond the scope of this discussion. Figure 6.2 illustrates AI's application in gaming; notably, many of these milestones didn't employ ANNs until more recent times. In specific instances, such as checkers, there is debate as to whether an ANN could even match a rule-based approach, especially given that it is considered a 'solved' game. Our primary focus in this context is on ANNs and, consequently, on the types of challenges where ANNs excel, including natural language processing (NLP), image recognition and generation, and certain gaming scenarios. Nonetheless, AI encompasses a vast range of areas, many of which are crucial; however, not all will be discussed here.

As we embark on a journey through the rich history of Artificial Intelligence (AI), with a keen focus on ANNs, it is important to grasp the evolution of this field in stages. This journey not only simplifies our understanding but also provides a structured lens through which we can appreciate the milestones, challenges, and rapid innovations that AI has undergone. Thus, the history has been broken into three phases.

- **The Genesis Phase (1940s–1980s)**: This was the birth of AI. During this period, the foundational ideas were laid down. Think of these as the foundational years of AI, where pioneers set the stage, developing the very first algorithms and concepts. Many of the ideas from this era served as the bedrock upon which later innovations were built. See Figure 6.4 for key milestones in the Genesis Phase.
- **The Maturing Phase (1980s–2010s)**: After its birth, AI went through a phase of growth and maturation. During this period, the foundational ideas from the genesis phase were refined, expanded, and implemented in various applications. The concepts became clearer, and the tools more sophisticated. It was a time of exploration, consolidation, and practical application. See Figure 6.5 for key milestones in the Maturing Phase.

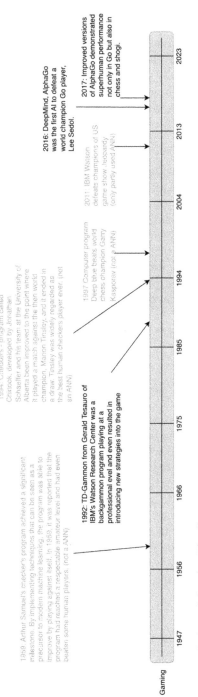

Figure 6.2 AI and Gaming Timeline.

- **The Acceleration Phase (2010s–2030s)**: Entering the current era, we see an explosion in AI capabilities and applications. Thanks to advances in computational power, data availability, and refined algorithms, AI, especially ANNs, is now evolving at an unprecedented rate and we expect this to continue for some considerable time. This phase captures the whirlwind of innovation, and the transformative impact AI is having on nearly every facet of our lives. At the end of this phase, we expect that AI will have been integrated and adopted into society. It is not clear what that picture will look like, but the anticipation of this future drives current research and application efforts. For more on what the future may look like, we invite you to read Chapter 7 on some of our predictions. See Figure 6.6 for key milestones in the Acceleration Phase.

By breaking down the history of AI and ANNs into these three distinct phases, readers will find it easier to digest the information, understand the context of current AI developments, and quickly reference the most recent and relevant advancements that shape our daily interactions with technology.

Figure 6.3 helps depict these phases and how they relate to commonly referred to periods in AI history such as the AI winters and AI boom periods. It also highlights some of the key hardware advancements that have facilitated progress in the field. These phases will be discussed in the respective sections below.

As we delve deeper into each phase, we will uncover the stories, the challenges, the breakthroughs, and the visionaries that have made AI the formidable force it is today.

6.2.1   The Genesis Phase (1940s–1980s)

6.2.1.1   New Fields of Study

In the earliest days of AI, there was a desire to build machines that could solve problems by learning, similar to how the brain works. This approach was fundamentally different from explicitly programming a machine to solve a specific problem. To build these machines, scientists studied animal brains to understand their biological models. This can be seen in the work by McCulloch and Pitts (1943) on modelling a neuron, and in the work by Hebb (1949) on Hebbian Learning. These works, along with contributions from others in the fields of neurophysiology and psychology, were used by those in the fields of Mathematics, Statistical Theory, Information Science, and Computer Science (both Information Science and Computer Science were in their infancy at this point).

Given the availability of these biological models and the extensive research conducted in these areas, it might have seemed reasonable to anticipate swift solutions to problems that explicit programming struggled with, such as pattern recognition, reasoning, and the understanding and use of language.

6.2.1.2   The Symbolists

In 1955, McCarthy, along with Marvin Minsky, Nathaniel Rochester, and Claude Shannon, penned a proposal for a workshop to be held at Dartmouth College in the summer of 1956. The primary objective of this workshop was as follows:

> An attempt will be made to find how to make machines use language, form abstractions, and concepts, solve kinds of problems now reserved for humans, and improve themselves.
> (McCarthy et al., 1955, p. 1)

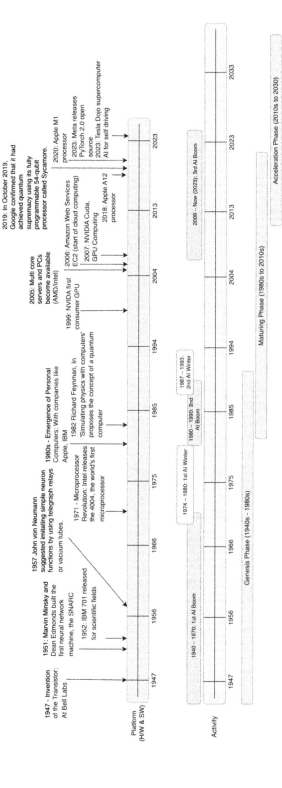

Figure 6.3 AI Periods and Hardware Advances.

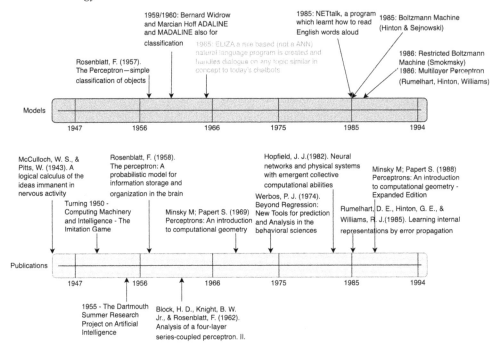

Figure 6.4 The Genesis Phase (1940s to1980s) – Publications and Models.

This workshop is widely regarded as the birth of AI as a formal academic discipline. The Dartmouth workshop was the first occasion where the term "artificial intelligence" was used, a term coined by McCarthy himself.

The optimism of the Dartmouth attendees was high. They genuinely believed that with a dedicated effort over the summer, they could make significant inroads into achieving machine intelligence. This is partly a reflection of the overall optimism about technology and computing that pervaded the 1950s. They thought that the available computational capacity should be sufficient for their tasks. Their main challenge, as they saw it, was the need to develop appropriate algorithms and program instructions to guide the machines.

The group was heavily influenced by what later became known as the "Symbolist" school of AI. As mentioned, Symbolists believed that intelligence arises from the manipulation of symbols and that it can be achieved through rule-based systems and formal reasoning. This was in stark contrast to other paradigms, such as the Connectionist approach that sought to replicate neural networks and the evolutionary approach that took inspiration from Darwinian processes.

This Symbolist approach is reflected in early AI projects like the Logic Theorist and General Problem Solver, which aimed to simulate human problem-solving capabilities through symbolic manipulations.

In hindsight, while the Dartmouth workshop didn't achieve its lofty goals within a single summer, it marked the beginning of a new and transformative field. The event catalysed research and set the direction for AI for many years. Even though we now recognise the challenges in achieving human-like AI are more complex than McCarthy and his colleagues initially imagined, their vision, ambition, and foundational work laid the groundwork for the field of AI.

6.2.1.3   The Connectionists

Connectionists of AI, often associated with the development and study of Artificial Neural Networks (ANNs), take inspiration from the human brain's intricate web of neurons to design computational models. These models aim to emulate the brain's ability to recognise patterns, process information, and learn from experiences. Unlike traditional symbolic AI, which relies on explicit rules to make decisions, Connectionism adopts a bottom-up approach. By adjusting the connections (or weights) between a myriad of simple processing nodes (akin to neurons), Connectionists believe that complex cognition can emerge organically. Since their inception, ANNs and the Connectionist paradigm have faced waves of both enthusiasm and skepticism. However, with advancements in computational power and algorithmic techniques in recent decades, Connectionism has become central to many of AI's most groundbreaking achievements, particularly in deep learning and areas such as image and speech recognition.

In the early days of Artificial Intelligence, there was a promising glimmer on the horizon, a belief that 'neuron nets' might just hold the answer to some of AI's most perplexing questions. Among these was the intriguing query, "How can a set of hypothetical neurons be arranged to form concepts?" Scholars like Uttley, Rashevsky and his ensemble, the duo Farley and Clark, and pioneers like Pitts, McCulloch, Minsky, Rochester, and Holland, were all engrossed in deciphering this enigma. Despite their vast and varied contributions, the consensus remained: the field desperately needed more theoretical depth (McCarthy et al., 1955).

The legacy of artificial neural networks (ANNs) is deeply intertwined with AI's history. These networks, which might seem contemporary, have been the bedrock of AI research since its inception. The landmark Dartmouth summer project was indeed a milestone, but even before this event, McCulloch and his colleagues had ventured into the neural realms. Their 1943 publication, 'A logical calculus of the ideas immanent in nervous activity' (McCulloch et al., 1943), presented an avant-garde notion: neurons could be emulated using simplistic switches, which when networked in unique arrangements, could replicate the logic of a Turing machine.

However, it wasn't until 1958 that the perceptron, a term now synonymous with AI, was born. In 1958, Frank Rosenblatt wrote about it in his paper (Rosenblatt, 1958). Think of it like a mini-brain with different parts working together, similar to modern ANNs. This mini-brain had different types of units, known as S-units, A-units, and R-units, which formed a basic two-layer network. Though at the time, people saw it as a 'three-layered network'. Rosenblatt called it 'photoperceptron', and it was designed to recognise objects in photos, like circles and rectangles (Rosenblatt, 1957).

The 1960s saw the perceptron's blueprint being taken and expanded upon. Widrow and Hoff birthed ADALINE (Widrow, 1960) and MADALINE (Widrow, 1962), employing novel algorithms to fine-tune weights and biases, laying the foundation for modern feed forward networks. Block and team (Block et al., 1962) added a layer to the perceptron model, propelling it into the realm of deep neural networks. Their model aimed for more extensive image classification, however, training this improved network was tough because there weren't yet good methods to correct errors in multi-layer networks.

In 1969, however, a cautionary tale emerged. Minsky and others published "Perceptrons: An introduction to computational geometry" (Minsky & Papert, 1988), highlighting the perceptron's mathematical limitations. The book particularly scrutinised the single-layer perceptron and expressed skepticism about its potential in resolving intricate challenges.

In 1985, Rumelhart and his team introduced a new technique that helped teach multi-layered machines. This method, which corrected mistakes as it learned, opened the door for what we call deep learning. Still, we didn't have the powerful computers needed to fully use this new technique. It is worth noting that Paul Werbos' earlier doctoral dissertation (Werbos, 1974) had pre-empted Rumelhart's work, laying the groundwork for backpropagation.

Intriguingly, Minsky and Papert, in an extended edition of their earlier book (Minsky & Papert, 1988), critically reviewed advances like those made by Rumelhart and McClelland. Despite acknowledging progress, they felt the claims, especially those surrounding the efficiency of gradient descent and the generalised delta rule, were overstated. The debates and differences of opinion serve as reminders of the cautious notes sounded by thinkers like Weizenbaum in the 1970s (see the next section on philosophical concerns), warning against getting too excited too soon.

Over time, even with advances like this new teaching method, backpropagation, the big hopes for ANNs started to fade. This led to periods known as 'AI winters' where people lost interest and didn't invest much in AI. But, as always, after a cold period of winter, things tend to warm up again in spring.

6.2.1.4   *Philosophical and Ethical Considerations*

6.2.1.4.1 THE TURING TEST – ALAN TURING

Philosophical questions concerning the ability of machines to think emerged in these early days. In 1950, Alan Turing addressed this in his paper, "Computing Machinery and Intelligence" (Turing, 1950). Instead of directly asking "can machines think?", Turing proposed an alternative method. He suggested a game, which he named "The Imitation Game". This game measured the likelihood of a machine deceiving an interrogator against the probability of a real person doing the same, relying solely on written communications in a question-and-answer format. This challenge subsequently became renowned as the Turing test.

6.2.1.4.2 THREE LAWS OF ROBOTICS – ISAAC ASIMOV

In a related development around the ethical considerations regarding machine intelligence, Isaac Asimov – a science fiction writer and professor of biochemistry – developed the "Three Laws of Robotics" in 1942. These were featured in his short story "Runaround", which formed part of the "I, Robot" series (Asimov, 1950), as mentioned in Chapter 5.

1   A robot may not injure a human being, or, through inaction, allow a human being to come to harm.
2   A robot must obey the orders given it by human beings except where such orders would conflict with the First Law.
3   A robot must protect its own existence as long as such protection does not conflict with the First or Second Laws.

6.2.1.4.3 COMPUTER POWER AND HUMAN REASON – JOSEPH WEIZENBAUM

Joseph Weizenbaum, the creator of the ELIZA chatbot and author of *Computer Power and Human Reason: From Judgment to Calculation* (1976), grew increasingly wary of the expanding influence of computer technology. He argued that machines shouldn't handle tasks needing genuine compassion, emphasising their inability to exercise human judgement and distinguishing between mere decision-making and genuine choice.

During the 1970s, skepticism about computers replicating human thought was prevalent. Many felt that the AI community had made overly ambitious promises. In his book, Weizenbaum delved into the overhyped expectations of AI and the unsettling emotional bonds people formed with AI systems. He also expressed concerns about society's growing dependency on technology. As we will see, these ambitious claims would continue to be a major topic of debate in the AI world.

6.2.1.4.4 FATHER OF CYBERNETICS – NORBERT WIENER

Furthermore, Norbert Wiener, often referred to as the "father of cybernetics", expressed concerns about the potential for automation to lead to unintended consequences in his work "God & Golem, Inc.: A Comment on Certain Points where Cybernetics Impinges on Religion" (Wiener, 1966) He posited that once we can effectively replicate human decision-making processes, extreme caution is imperative in managing these innovations. To illustrate, he drew upon the tale of 'The Monkey's Paw', highlighting how wielding power without full comprehension could result in catastrophic outcomes.

From the 1940s to the 1980s, the field of AI embarked on an exhilarating journey, laying the bedrock upon which future innovations would thrive. The essence of ANNs drew inspiration from the intricate webs of neurons in our brains, thanks to the pioneering work of individuals like McCulloch and Pitts. As the decades progressed, this biological inspiration was interwoven with a fabric of mathematical and statistical rigour, establishing proofs and formulas that defined how artificial neurons would interact and collaborate within networks. By the 1980s, this foundational work bore fruit in the form of breakthrough learning techniques like backpropagation and gradient descent. These mechanisms optimised the training of ANNs, equipping them with the capability to refine their performance and solve complex problems. Alongside these technical advancements, the era was also marked by deep philosophical introspection, questioning the boundaries of AI, its relation to consciousness, and the ethics surrounding its potential. By the close of the 1980s, the AI landscape had been primed with the necessary fundamentals, ready for the transformations that would follow including the concept of the quantum computer such as those discussed by Richard Feynman (Feynman, 1982) that are perhaps a still long way off from delivering their benefits to AI.

6.2.2 *The Maturing Phase (1980s to 2010s)*

In the span between the 1980s and 2010s, ANNs experienced both challenges and pivotal advancements. Initial enthusiasm for ANNs had diminished due to persistent issues like the vanishing gradient problem, but the 1980s brought about key innovations that would later be instrumental for the field's revival.

The introduction of the backpropagation algorithm by Rumelhart, Hinton, and Williams in 1986 was a seminal moment (Rumelhart et al., 1986a, 1986b, 1986c). This algorithm optimised the weights in multi-layer perceptrons, sparking renewed interest and research in ANNs. Following this, the torchbearers of the field, namely LeCun, Bengio, and Hinton, made significant contributions. Their efforts during this phase laid the foundation for deep learning and the transformative changes of the next era (Goodfellow et al., 2016).

In the 1990s, there were important developments in using neural networks. Researchers found ways to use them for complex data analysis (Breiman, 2001), to simplify data by

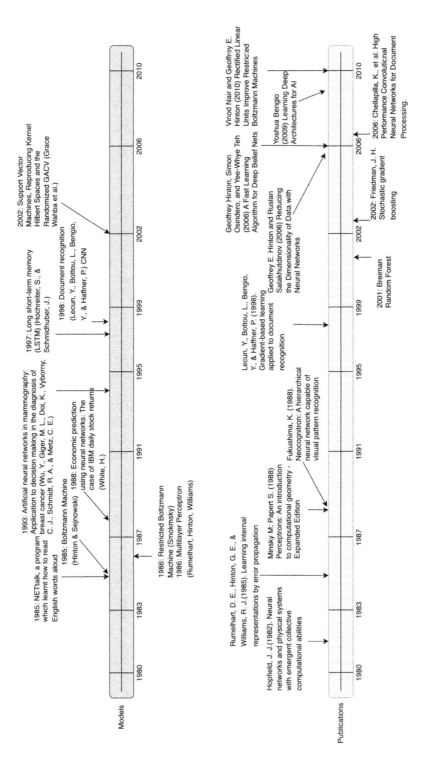

Figure 6.5 The Maturing Phase (1980s to 2010s) – Publications and Models.

reducing its complexity (Hinton et al., 2006), and to improve algorithms for better performance (Friedman, 2002). They also developed new techniques for training and managing neural networks, like energy-based models (Ackley et al., 1985), and introduced new types of neural cells, such as long short-term memory (LSTM), to solve problems with gradients (Hochreiter & Schmidhuber, 1997). Additionally, researchers gained a better understanding of Support Vector Machines (SVM) and kernel methods, which improved the creation of robust predictive models (Wahba et al., 2002). With innovations like LeCun's convolutional neural networks (CNNs) for image recognition (LeCun et al., 1989) and the advent of recurrent neural networks (RNNs) for sequential data (Hochreiter & Schmidhuber, 1997), the vast potential of ANNs was increasingly realised.

However, the full potential of deep ANNs was hampered by computational restraints and the scarcity of comprehensive labelled datasets. Despite these hurdles, the maturing phase was crucial in embedding the importance of ANNs and setting the groundwork for the momentous progress of the acceleration phase that would follow.

6.2.3 *The Acceleration Phase (2010s to 2030s)*

The early 2010s marked a monumental shift for ANNs with developments powered by larger datasets, increased computational capabilities - particularly from GPUs, and innovative algorithms. One notable paper in this regard was "Building High-level Features Using Large Scale Unsupervised Learning" by Le et al., which showcased the strength of refined algorithms in propelling ANNs' capabilities (Le et al., 2011).

The subfield of deep learning, an advanced application of ANNs, took centre stage during this period. Esteemed figures like Geoffrey Hinton, Yann LeCun, and Yoshua Bengio were instrumental in these evolutions (Goodfellow et al., 2016). A groundbreaking moment occurred with the creation of AlexNet, a convolutional neural network (CNN) designed by Alex Krizhevsky under Geoffrey Hinton's guidance. In 2012, AlexNet achieved unmatched performance in the ImageNet competition, a benchmark in image recognition, marking what many called the "ImageNet moment" (Krizhevsky et al., 2012).

Such triumphs galvanised the broader tech industry. Companies like Google and Facebook not only adopted but also significantly contributed to ANN research. For instance, Google's approach to recommendation systems was articulated in "Wide & Deep Learning for Recommender Systems" (Cheng et al., 2016), while Facebook advanced text understanding and user modelling through ANNs, as evidenced by their studies (Joulin et al., 2016; Kaur et al., 2021).

As the decade progressed, ANNs' applications diversified. Recurrent neural networks (RNNs), and particularly their evolved form, long short-term memory networks (LSTMs), became the go-to for handling sequential data, finding applications in natural language processing and time-series analysis (Hochreiter & Schmidhuber, 1997). In parallel, generative adversarial networks (GANs), introduced by Ian Goodfellow, transformed generative models, enabling feats like image synthesis and style transfer (Goodfellow et al., 2014).

By the late 2010s, the introduction of transformer architectures, like the one described in the "Attention Is All You Need" paper, signalled another paradigm shift, especially in NLP. This paper served as a bedrock for models such as BERT and GPT variants, including OpenAI's ChatGPT-3.5 and GPT 4.0, redefining text comprehension and generation (Vaswani et al., 2017).

With the dawn of the 2020s, the drive behind ANNs only intensified. Breakthroughs in areas like few-shot learning and self-supervised learning signalled the continuous advancement

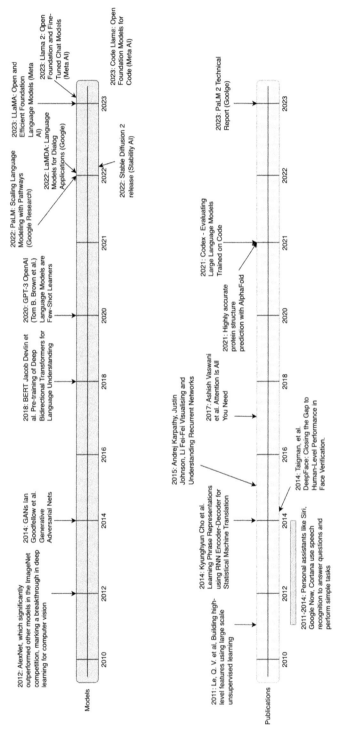

Figure 6.6 The Acceleration Phase (2010s to 2030s) – Publications and Models.

of the field. Yet, as AI capabilities surged, so did ethical and societal concerns. These concerns were highlighted in March 2023 open letter from the Future of Life Institute, urging a pause on the development of models more advanced than GPT-4, underlining the need for a more reflective approach to AI's rapid advancement (Future of Life Institute, 2023a, 2023b).

While the path towards artificial general intelligence (AGI) or even artificial super intelligence (ASI) remains debated, what is unequivocal is the transformative role of AI will have on society and humanity. In addition, this transformative role is likely to be further compounded by future advancements. Echoing Richard Feynman's proposition, quantum computers might surpass classical computers in simulating complex systems (Feynman, 1982), potentially steering AI into its next epoch. Indeed, milestones like achieving quantum supremacy, where quantum devices outpace their classical counterparts, hint at a future where the bounds of AI's potential could be redefined (Arute et al., 2019).

6.3   Creating a Model

Now that we have covered the history of ANNs in some detail, we will turn our attention to the process of creating a GenAI model. This discussion will focus on recent approaches and will delve deeper into the terminology and advances previously outlined in the historical overview. As we delve into the creation and comprehension of models, you will recognise some of the key people and advances mentioned in the earlier history section.

Figure 6.7 illustrates the essential steps in creating a model. This process encompasses both the training and the testing of a foundational model, followed by its fine-tuning. A foundational model is an initial, untrained model with a generic purpose (i.e.) to learn from data. Many foundational models undergo fine-tuning for specific applications. For instance, the LLaMA-2 (Large Language Model Meta AI) foundational model was fine-tuned for chat functionality, resulting in the finely-tuned model known as LLaMA-2-chat. This fine-tuning involves further training of the foundational model on specific data to serve a more specialised purpose, such as functioning as a chatbot to answer user queries or engage in conversations with users.

The steps involved in creating a model are:

1 The Training Data
   a   Data Gathering and Preparation
   b   Dataset Customisation

2 The Foundation Model

   a   Model Design and Structuring
   b   Model Training
   c   Model Testing

3 The Fine-Tuning

   a   Fine-Tuning Data Set Customisation
   b   Model Fine-Tuning Training
   c   Model Testing

4 The Deployment and Use

   a   Model Deployment
   b   Model Monitoring
   c   Model Use (aka inference)

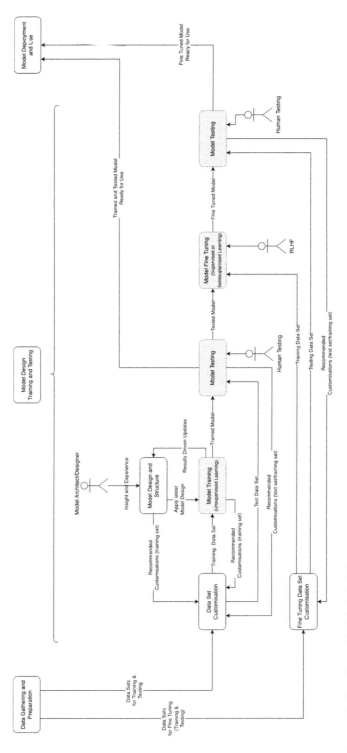

Figure 6.7 Creating a Model – The Big Picture.

Fine-tuning can employ a variety of training techniques, including reinforcement learning with human feedback (RLHF), which will be discussed below. The following sections will cover each of these areas to provide an understanding of what is involved.

6.3.1 The Training Data

The initial step in the comprehensive model creation process is data gathering and preparation. Modern deep neural networks (DNNs), especially large language models (LLMs), require vast amounts of training data. While several well-known data sources are available, some companies maintain their own unique repositories. Prominent entities such as Meta, Google, and Microsoft possess vast amounts of data, owing to the diverse services they offer. Meanwhile, companies like OpenAI have ventured into developing their own data-sourcing solutions, such as the web crawling tool, GPTbot, which gathers publicly accessible data from the web for OpenAI.

After the initial acquisition, the dataset might be further refined to improve quality or to better align with the desired outcomes of a particular model. The processes of gathering and preparation often intertwine with dataset customisation, especially when an organisation sources its data directly, rather than relying on externally provided datasets.

It is crucial to acknowledge the complexity and sophistication inherent in the data gathering, preparation, and customisation phases. To provide a clearer understanding of these processes, they will be explored in more depth using several widely utilised data sources as examples.

6.3.1.1 Text Data – Common Crawl

Common Crawl (see https://commoncrawl.org/) (Patel, 2020) is an organisation that offers data dumps from billions of web pages on a regular basis, typically 6 to 12 times per year. While it has some data from as far back as 2008, there have been more consistent outputs since 2011. Common Crawl employs a tool known as a spider bot to access the content of web pages. A spider bot starts with a list of URLs and retrieves the content of these web pages. Additionally, it can identify other URLs within a web page (i.e., links to different sites) and pursue these links to access those pages. For each page accessed, the spider bot saves the content and recognises other links to pursue, expanding outwards much like a spider's web to encompass other URLs.

The CCBot, commonly referred to as the Common Crawl spider bot, processes a candidate database of URLs for each iteration. It updates this database with new URLs based on its findings during the crawl. While the set of URLs is expansive, they are not rigorously reviewed, organised, or managed. As a result, the quality of the data obtained can vary significantly, encompassing content in multiple languages. Surprisingly, there is a minimal overlap between the outputs of one crawl and the next. For instance, the overlap between the data dumps from February 2023 and June 2023 is only around 1% (see https://commoncrawl.github.io/cc-crawl-statistics/plots/crawloverlap).

The volume of data provided in each release is indeed staggering. For example, the June 2023 release (CC-MAIN-2023-23) comprises 100 segments. Each segment contains 800 files for WARC (approximately 1.1 GB compressed), WAT (around 285 MB compressed), and WET (roughly 115 MB compressed) formats. Including various metadata, the total size of the June 2023 release is about 120 TB when compressed. The compression ratio for text data is favourable, ranging from 3 to 5 times, which results in an uncompressed size of approximately 580 TB. However, not all users will need every format. Some might focus only on the WET format (plaintext), which alone amounts to about 26 TB when uncompressed.

The output from Common Crawl varies in both content and quality. When training a large language model (LLM), this data undergoes further processing and cleaning to enhance its quality. Specialised tools, such as CCNet (Wenzek et al., 2019), have been designed to help with this, especially when dealing with outputs like those from Common Crawl. For instance, these tools can restructure the files, decompress them, and divide them into shards. Each web page entry is then housed in a specifically formatted 'json' file. Data deduplication occurs at the paragraph level, and language detection is performed, enabling the sorting of different languages into separate datasets. Some of these steps are complex. Take the language detection feature as an example: it uses another language model, fastText (https://fasttext.cc/), which is pre-trained on alternative data sources like Wikipedia, Tatoeba, and SETimes, to identify the language of the Common Crawl output. Figure 6.8 showcases the intricacy of the data gathering and post-processing stages.

It does not end there; further processing by other models is also possible. For instance, data quality can be assessed, and, based on the quality score, specific data can either be retained or removed from the dataset. One model employed in this manner is the 5-gram Kneser-Ney model, which utilises a perplexity measure to compare the input from Common Crawl with another source deemed of higher quality, such as Wikipedia.

The perplexity is a measure of the predictability of the text within a specific paragraph. The higher the perplexity, the more surprised (or perplexed) the model becomes, suggesting a lower quality in this data customisation pipeline. If the perplexity surpasses a certain threshold for a given paragraph, that paragraph may be removed from the dataset with the aim of enhancing the overall quality of the dataset. You may recall that Perplexity is also used for GenAI text detection in Section 4.7.

Given the vast volume of data involved, the necessity to execute complex tasks like these pre-processing models, and the fact that the customisation processes operate on specialised data processing environments requiring significant expertise to build and manage, the cost of undertaking this task is considerable.

6.3.1.2   *Text Data – Colossal Clean Crawled Corpus (C4)*

The Colossal Clean Crawled Corpus (C4) dataset is derived from dumps provided by Common Crawl (Raffel et al., 2023). This dataset undergoes various filtering and formatting processes to produce a version compatible with models developed using the TensorFlow runtime. TensorFlow is an important widely used tool for those building and training models. The filtering process includes tasks such as deduplication and the removal of sensitive words.

Initially, Google created the C4 data set for their own use. While they provided a description and some tools to generate the dataset from the Common Crawl inputs, they did not release the actual dataset. Recognising the value of this dataset, another organisation, the Allen Institute for AI (see https://allenai.org/; founded by the late Paul G. Allen, co-founder of Microsoft), reproduced the C4 dataset. They collaborated with a company called Hugging Face (see https://huggingface.co/) to host and make this dataset accessible to all.

Recreating the C4 dataset is not only costly (with expenses estimated between US$100s and US$1,000s in compute costs) but also requires significant expertise and knowledge.

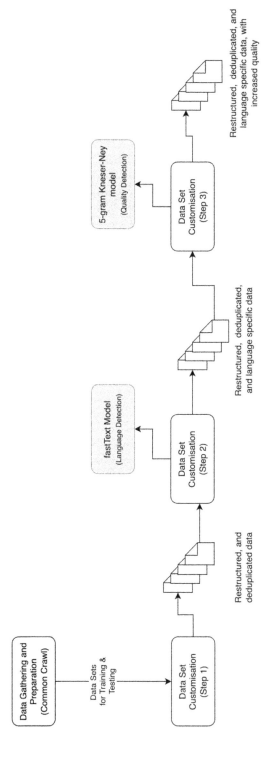

Figure 6.8 Data Gathering and Customisation Pipeline.

6.3.1.3   Image Data – LAION-5B

The LAION-5B image dataset (see https://laion.ai/blog/laion-5b/) (Schuhmann et al., 2022) is a contemporary dataset designed for state-of-the-art (SOTA) model training. Its primary objective is to provide an open and readily accessible dataset for text-to-image model training. The dataset comprises 5.85 billion filtered image-text pairs, of which 2.32 billion are in the English language.

The foundation for this dataset was the Common Crawl, from which image URLs were extracted and subsequently filtered using an existing OpenAI CLIP (Contrastive Language-Image Pre-Training) model (Radford et al., 2021). This process resulted in a dataset comprising: a) 2.32 billion English image-text examples, b) 2.26 billion multilingual examples, and c) 1.27 billion examples not tied to any specific language (e.g., pertaining to places, products, etc.). Notably, this dataset is considerably more extensive than other comparable datasets. By making it publicly accessible, it promotes greater transparency, especially concerning the ethical considerations linked to large datasets of publicly sourced images.

6.3.1.4   Image Data – LabelMe

The primary objective of the LabelMe dataset (see http://labelme.csail.mit.edu/) (Russell et al., 2007; Oliva, 2001) is to offer an online annotation tool to construct image datasets for computer vision research. Users could register for an account, contribute annotations, and subsequently access the datasets for their research. This approach facilitated the accumulation of a substantial collection of images and annotations. Importantly, these annotations were not mere labels; users could pinpoint and specify individual objects within an image. Thus, elements such as a car in the background, a person in the foreground, buildings, roads, and any other visible component in the image could be distinctly annotated.

6.3.1.5   Other Sources

Other frequently utilised sources include data dumps from GitHub, which contain open-source software implementations in numerous programming languages; dumps from Wikipedia, an online encyclopaedia; releases from Project Gutenberg, which hosts over 70,000 books no longer under copyright; and content from 'The Pile', an amalgamation of 22 smaller datasets that has recently stirred controversy due to issues related to copyrighted books.

Several other notable data sources exist. For instance, Tesla possesses an extensive database of driving-related videos, which it harnesses to train its autopilot system. ImageNet (https://www.image-net.org/) offers a vast collection of over one million images, each labelled with nouns corresponding to the content of the image; this resource has been pivotal in advancing computer vision and deep learning research. Another significant source is COCO (Common Objects in Context), which provides image data for training. CelebA serves as a repository of celebrity images, particularly useful for facial recognition tasks. Additionally, there are audio-focused datasets such as the MIDI dataset for music; the VCTK dataset for voice-related tasks; and the UCF101 dataset, designed for action recognition in videos.

Google offers a valuable tool for searching various types of datasets, accessible at https://datasetsearch.research.google.com/. Regardless of the specific dataset one requires, there are likely similar sets available, and this search tool aims to simplify the discovery process.

6.3.1.6   Other Data Customisations

Each of these datasets has its own approach to sourcing from the original, preparing the data dump, and then further processing to customise the dataset for the specific training task. These preparation and customisation steps may involve similar filtering as described above, but they can also encompass distinct types of filtering and content curation to achieve the specific aims.

A significant aspect of this customisation pertains to structuring the data in a way that is optimally suited for the specific model in question and the intended training strategy. The design and structure of the model, as well as the various training approaches, are elaborated upon in subsequent sections. Nevertheless, these factors play a crucial role in determining the necessary data preparation and customisation processes.

One common customisation involves ensuring that the size of the data inputs aligns with the model design. This will differ depending on the type of data the model handles, be it text-based input or image-based input. For language models, the typical input size comprises paragraphs that can be fed into the system as a single unit, usually amounting to about 512 tokens. Tokens are similar to words and we will discuss them more later. These inputs are either split or padded to ensure they fit the model. Subsequently, these inputs are often grouped into batches, possibly in sizes of 16, 32, or 64. Such batches are generally processed independently during training, which facilitates parallel streams into the model. The collective set of all batches constitutes an epoch, and the model may undergo training across several iterations of these epochs to maximise the training benefits. Importantly, between each epoch iteration, the batches are typically shuffled to prevent the model from making unwarranted learning assumptions about the sequence.

One final consideration involves dividing the dataset into training and validation subsets. This step is crucial to ensure that the models are accurate and do not suffer from overtraining (or overfitting). Overfitting is where the model learns the training data very well but does poorly when tested with a dataset outside the training set. In short it does not generalise well. Typically, the dataset is divided into training and testing portions on a 70% to 30% basis, with the testing subset selected randomly to circumvent issues associated with alternative selection methods. The testing portion of a dataset is used to evaluate how well a machine learning model generalises to new, unseen data. While the training data are used to train the model, the testing data serves as an independent set of examples that the model has never seen during training. Many datasets come pre-divided into training, testing, and validation subsets. The validation subset (sometimes referred to as the development set) is generally included to facilitate the fine-tuning of specific models.

6.3.2   Model Design and Structuring

Clearly, the design and structuring of models is an intricate topic, necessitating deep experience and understanding of AI, deep neural networks, and the associated statistical and mathematical concepts.

Subsequent sections will explore key considerations surrounding model design and its nuanced details. As mentioned, the aim is to provide insights into the factors that influence a model and their inner workings. This will enable readers to delve deeper into specific topics or explore the statistical and mathematical concepts that underpin these design considerations which we do not explore in this book.

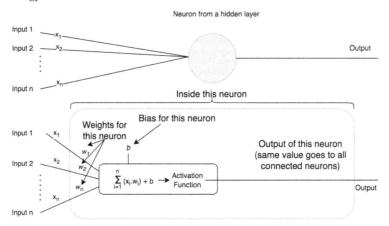

Figure 6.9 Feed-Forward Cell.

6.3.2.1   *Artificial Neurons – Weights, Bias, and Activations Functions*

Artificial neurons are simple structures with inputs and outputs. While there can be any number of inputs, the output is a singular value. Although the inputs can vary, they converge to produce this single output value. Neurons are often depicted as a basic circle, with the relevant inputs and outputs illustrated, as shown in Figure 6.9. This graphical representation is of a rudimentary type of neuron known as a feed-forward cell. To gain a deeper understanding of the neuron, one can delve into the internals of the cell, as shown in Figure 6.9.

This introduces a few important concepts:

- **Weights**. Each weight is just a number; there is one weight (number) for each input into the neuron. The value of this number changes as the model is trained. Once trained it is fixed.
- **Bias**. This is just a number and there is one for each neuron. The value of this number changes as the model is trained. Once trained it is fixed.
- **Activation function**. This is a special mathematical function that helps improve the usefulness of the output. There are many different types of activation functions. Some popular ones are sigmoid (used in older models such as Long Short-Term Memory Networks), Tanh (used in older models such as hidden layers of Sequence-to-Sequence models), ReLu (used in GPT3), and SwiGLU (used in LLaMA).

In this instance, the input signal (denoted as x_i, which is a numerical value) is multiplied by the corresponding weight (w_i) for that input. This multiplication is conducted for all inputs, and the resultant products are then summed (effectively yielding the sum of the products). Subsequently, the bias (b) is added, and the resultant figure is passed to the activation function. This activation function processes the given value, producing an output which is also a numerical value. If this neuron is connected to multiple other neurons, the same output value emanating from this neuron is transmitted to all interconnected neurons. Hence, the neuron can be conceptualised as a mathematical operation on a collection of input values to produce an output value, and that mathematical operation is informed by another set of values known as weights and the bias.

These weights and biases will be revisited in the context of model training. Collectively, they are referred to as the parameters of the model. This is the mechanism by which the model 'remembers' or stores information; these numerical values encapsulate the patterns that the model has discerned during its training phase and can subsequently be employed to make predictions. Often, models are benchmarked based on the number of parameters they possess, stemming from the assumption that a higher number of parameters equates to greater capabilities. However, several other factors influence the efficacy of a model beyond just the count of parameters. These include the quality of the training data utilised, the number of layers and their interconnections, as well as the internal functions deployed, such as the activation function or the sum of the products.

LLaMA-2 (Large Language Model Meta AI) from Meta AI is available in several size variants: 7B, 13B, and 70B, where 'B' stands for billion parameters. OpenAI's ChatGPT-3.5 boasts 175B parameters. While the size of ChatGPT-4.0 has not been officially disclosed, it is speculated to comprise about 1.8T parameters, with 'T' representing trillion. Google's LaMDA (Language Models for Dialog Applications) possesses up to 137B parameters. In contrast, Google's PaLM-2 (Pathways Language Model) is reported to have around 340B parameters. Initially, Google's BARD chatbot was based on LaMDA, but it was subsequently transitioned to PaLM-2 due to the latter's superior reasoning capabilities. These sizes give some indication of the number of cells involved in a SOTA model.

Figure 6.10 illustrates a different type of artificial neuron known as a Recurrent Cell.

As Figure 6.10 illustrates, this structure closely resembles the feed-forward cell, with one notable exception, it incorporates internal feedback. In this arrangement, the output from the previous iteration (t-1) is reintroduced as an additional input in the current (t) input flow. This input (h_{t-1}) is multiplied by its designated weight (w_h) to contribute to the current output. In essence, this type of cell possesses memory of the previous output, which aids in computing the current output. These recurrent cells are a fundamental component of the recurrent neural network (RNN) models mentioned earlier.

There are many different possible types of cells, another one previously mentioned is the long short-term memory (LSTM) cell, but these two specific examples should give an idea of what is involved.

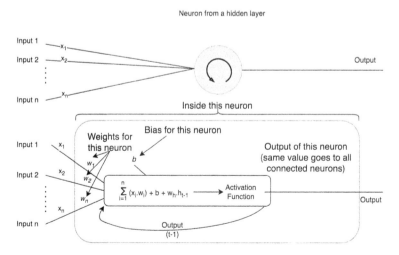

Figure 6.10 Recurrent Cell.

6.3.3   *Model Layers and Connections*

These artificial neurons, also known as cells or nodes, can be connected together in layers. Neural networks in AI are composed of nodes organised in layers, with each node connected to others in the next layer. These connections are often referred to as synapses. Figure 6.11 illustrates some common structures of deep neural networks, typically comprising an input layer, an output layer, and multiple hidden layers in between.

The number of nodes in each layer can vary, and the connections don't necessarily have to link to every node in the next layer, although this is a typical arrangement. For a network to be considered 'deep', it must contain at least three hidden layers. When counting the layers, both the hidden layers and the output layer are included. In the example provided, the deep neural network consists of four layers.

There is flexibility in the number of inputs and nodes in different layers. The following diagrams (Figure 6.12) present various approaches.

Figure 6.12 provides a high-level overview of what a deep neural network looks like in an abstract manner.

A significant aspect of designing and structuring a model involves choosing the type of cell to use; determining which cell types are suitable for specific layers; deciding the number of layers to include; and defining the number of nodes in each of the input, hidden, and output layers.

Certain model capabilities are tailored to the type of data being processed, such as text or images. These features will be discussed primarily in the context of the most common use cases, such as large language models (LLMs), text-to-image models, or multi-modal models (supporting input and output for multiple data types, including text, images, audio, video, etc.). For instance, a model might facilitate text input and generate text output, or it

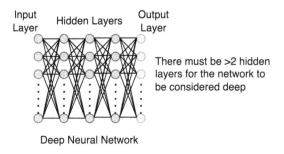

Figure 6.11 Deep Neural Network.

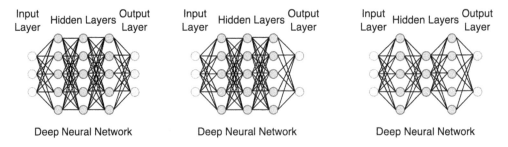

Figure 6.12 Deep Neural Network Variations.

could generate image output based on user requests. Conversely, it could also accept image input and produce descriptive text as output.

6.3.4 *Key Model Capabilities*

The following sections examine key model capabilities designed for specific data types, whether text or images. This section will help you understand what actually happens to the input that is passed to the model and what the model does with that input both during training and during inference (normal user interaction post training).

6.3.4.1 *Text – Tokenisation*

Before delving into specifics, it is essential to understand the nature of the inputs. In the context of an LLM, both the inputs and outputs consist of text. Let's begin by examining this scenario.

There are several upstream processing steps required to transform the text, whether it is what you type or the training data, into the actual model input. The initial step in this process is known as tokenisation. Tokenisation involves breaking the text into tokens. For example, when using the GPT-3 tokeniser, the sentence 'Can you provide a summary of the novel the count of monte cristo' would be tokenised into the following tokens (Figure 6.13)

As you can see in Figure 6.13, there are a few things to note:

1 The spaces are included in the words (at the start of the words).
2 Words are mostly separated into different tokens.
3 Sometimes words can be split (e.g. 'mon' and 'te') into multiple tokens.

If you slightly change the string to 'Can you provide a summary of the novel, 'The Count of Monte Cristo,' then the tokens for this tokeniser will be (Figure 6.14).

As you can see in Figure 6.14, the changes in punctuation and capitalisation have impacted the tokenisation process.

There is a limit to the size of the input that can be provided to the model, known as the context window. This limit restricts the number of tokens that can be passed to the model simultaneously. For example, in the LLaMA-2 model from Meta, the context window is 4096 tokens; while in ChatGPT-3.0, it is 2048 tokens. However, in ChatGPT-4, the context window is 32k tokens.

The tokenisation approach (which includes words, part words, letters, punctuation handling, etc.) is an important part of the model design and may require different strategies for different languages.

Can you provide a summary of the novel the count of monte cristo

Figure 6.13 Tokenisation Example 1.

Can you provide a summary of the novel, 'The Count of Monte Cristo'

Figure 6.14 Tokenisation Example 2.

The context window size is important when you consider the approaches that the model uses for in-context learning (i.e., learning based on the inputs provided). There are a few approaches which can be used.

- Zero-Shot learning: In this approach, only the prompt you type is provided as an input to the model.
- Few-Shot learning: In this approach, both multiple examples and the specific prompt you provide are sent to the model as inputs. The number of examples can range from 1 up to 32 examples.

In the case of the few-shot learning, the examples can use up many tokens, leaving fewer tokens for the actual prompt being performed, thus in cases where few-shot learning is viewed as important, a larger context window is needed. Likewise, if the inputs themselves are large e.g. full text documents, larger context windows are needed.

6.3.4.2 Text – Encoding

One purpose of tokenisation is to map the inputs to a known set of possible options. In the case of the English language and the tokenisation approach shown above, there are about 50,000 possible tokens based on the GPT-3 tokenisation design.

Picture these 50,000 possible tokenised values as the vertical columns in a matrix, and picture each of the actual input tokens from the prompt as the horizontal rows in that matrix. This would allow the inputs to be mapped to numbers (ones or zeros) like an encoding mechanism.

The matrix would contain a '1' in the column corresponding to the position of each token in the input, and the '1' would be in the appropriate row based on its position in the input text sequence. All other columns in that row would be '0'. This is demonstrated in Figure 6.15. If the number of input tokens is less than the context window, the remaining columns would be filled with '0'.

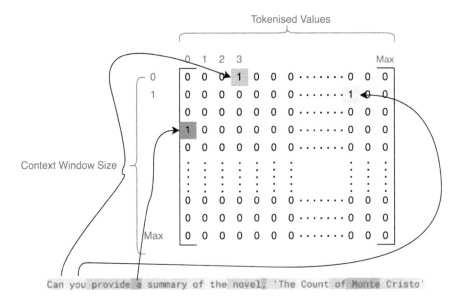

Figure 6.15 Encoding Matrix.

This encoding approach allows the prompt to be passed as an input, which is a matrix of numbers, to the model. Since the model can only process numbers, this encoding is a critical part of the pre-processing required to use the model.

The order of the tokens is also significant. In addition to the token values in the matrix, the position of each token in the sequence is important and can be identified by the model from the input provided.

This approach of mapping categorical variables (tokens or words) to a simple matrix is one type of encoding called 'one-hot encoding'. However, there are more sophisticated approaches available. This encoding represents a fixed, rule-based process. These decisions are integral to model design and structure.

6.3.4.3   *Text – Embedding*

Once the tokens are presented in a matrix format in the transformer architecture for LLMs, the next step is embedding. This is where the matrix input is mapped to a vector representation for each token and each token position.

The mapping of the token's entry in the matrix to a vector is a learned representation. In other words, through training, the model learns how to position the vectors in this space so that the geometric relationships between them reflect the semantic relationships between the corresponding tokens. For example, it could happen that types of animals would be 'near' each other (have similar values for their vectors), or that words with similar meanings appear near each other.

Put in other words, embeddings in LLMs are numerical representations that capture the essence of words or phrases. Rather than treating words as isolated units, embeddings transform them into vectors in a high-dimensional space, where similar words are positioned closer together. This allows models to understand context and meaning, making text generation more coherent and contextually relevant. For example, think of embeddings as giving words a unique address in a city (the high-dimensional space). So, while the word "cat" might live at one address, the word "kitten", being similar in meaning, would live nearby (in other words would have a similar numerical value). When the model needs to generate text, it uses these addresses (numerically similar values) to find words that fit best in the context, ensuring the sentences make sense.

If you don't grasp the details of the embedding process, don't worry. The key thing to remember is that this is a learned process; the embedding layer has weights and biases just like the other layers, and through the learning process, these weight and bias values are updated. This learning process is explained in more detail below.

6.3.4.4   *Text – Attention*

The paper 'Attention is all you need' (Vaswani et al., 2017) emphasised the significance of attention in the design and structure of a model. The attention mechanism enables the model to identify long-range (distant) dependencies between words in a sentence or paragraph. This is analogous to how humans address this issue when listening to someone speak or reading text. We analyse what preceded the current context and relate it to what we are currently processing, attempting to form a coherent mental picture of the situation. A key component of this attention mechanism is the "attention head".

The model is designed to calculate attention scores for each word in the input, be it a sentence or paragraph, in order to understand the relative importance of each word. Typically, there are multiple attention heads, and each head computes its own score. Similar to embeddings, these scores are learned from the weights associated with three parameters for each attention head: the so-called 'query', 'key', and 'value' parameters, often referred to as matrices W_q, W_k, and W_v. Different attention heads process the input in parallel, and the set of attention scores is then aggregated to create a new representation of that token. Having multiple attention heads allows the model to learn a more comprehensive set of relationships among tokens. For example, one head might learn to focus on syntactic relationships like subject–verb agreement, while another might learn to capture semantic relationships like synonymy.

Consider the sentence 'The cat sat on the mat.' With a single attention head, it might concentrate on the relationship between 'cat' and 'sat', capturing the subject–verb relationship. However, when multiple attention heads are employed, another might focus on the relationship between 'sat' and 'mat', capturing the verb–object relationship, while yet another could emphasise the relationship between 'on' and 'mat', capturing the preposition–object relationship.

As mentioned, these scores and the focus of each attention head are learnt during the training process. The designer does not assign a specific head to a specific ability; this is entirely dynamic and learnt during training. It may seem somewhat amazing, perhaps unbelievable, that this happens, but it does. With millions of training examples, the model learns to specialise specific attention heads for specific purposes. This is an emergent feature of the model. The stochastic nature of the training process encourages diversity among the heads, so that different heads take on specific but different purposes.

6.3.4.5   *Text – Next Word Prediction Learning Goal*

We have seen that some layers in the model are focused on finding the relationships between words (embedding), and some are focused on understanding what the most important words of the input are (attention). The other layers in the model will be focused on predicting the next word in the text. If the input so far is 'I went to the', then the model is trying to predict what the next word is, and let's say it predicts 'market', but the actual word is 'school', then it will adjust the weights and biases in the model to better predict this in the future. It will then try to predict the next word again in 'I went to the school', and it might predict 'to', and this is correct. Then it predicts 'pick', and this is correct, then it predicts 'up', and this is correct, and then it predicts 'my' which is correct again. Then the next word it predicts is 'kids' but the actual word is 'books'. It again will update the weights and biases to try and better predict in the future. This gives the model the input 'I went to the school to pick up my books'. As it learns it will also be updating the embeddings and attention layers to improve those too.

6.3.4.6   *Image – Pre-processing*

This is where the input image is prepared and normalised or standardised for input into the model. The input image may be a JPEG or a GIF and needs to be converted to the standard format. This conversion includes not only changing the format but also adjusting other details such as the size of the image (width, height, and aspect ratio), the resolution of the image, and the colour space. Depending on the complexity, it may involve image rotation to ensure it is correctly oriented.

Part of the pre-processing involves tensor (matrix of vectors) conversion, which is similar to the encoding discussed for text models. In the case of an image, this process is somewhat easier because the image naturally has a binary representation of a set of pixels in height and width, with each pixel having values for colours, such as Red (R), Green (G), and Blue (B). Thus, conversion involves creating a tensor or matrix of vectors for these pixel coordinates and RGB values. This has also been covered in Section 1.8 Figure 1.4.

6.3.4.7   Image – Encoding

Image encoding is similar to embedding for text-based models. However, instead of using embedding layers, which are employed in text models, image models typically use convolutional layers. These layers learn the relationships between the content of the image, aiding in the extraction of model features.

6.3.4.8   Image – Diffusion Learning Goal

The model is presented with an encoded image along with a text description of that image. Forward diffusion is the process where a model introduces noise into an image, gradually making the picture blurry by altering some of the pixels' colours. This noise is added incrementally until the image becomes unrecognisable, resembling a television screen when not tuned in. This is shown in Section 1.8 Figure 1.6.

Reverse diffusion, on the other hand, is the process in which a model removes noise from an image, gradually restoring it to its original, recognisable form.

These forward and reverse diffusion processes teach the model how to generate an image which it has a text description of by removing noise. When tasked with creating an image solely based on a text description, the model can utilise this learning to remove noise from an initial image with random noise, resulting in a completely new image that did not previously exist.

6.3.4.9   Hyperparameters

Hyperparameters are specific controls of a model that designers must choose and adjust during the design and training processes. Unlike model parameters, which are automatically adjusted by the model itself during learning, hyperparameters are only adjusted by the model's designer.

These hyperparameters span a wide range of aspects of the model, including the learning rate, the batch size, the number of epochs, factors impacting the activation function used, the dropout rate, and more. During this phase, designers must determine the best values for these hyperparameters.

Sometimes, hyperparameters are exposed to the end users of a model to help control a model's behaviour. One such example is the 'temperature' hyperparameter, which controls how repeatable a prediction is. Lower values mean more randomness, while higher values mean less randomness and more consistency.

6.3.5   Foundational Model Training

Thus far, we have covered the big picture, how the data is gathered and prepared, and different aspects that go into the design and structuring of the model. In this section, we focus on foundational model training, commonly referred to as pre-training.

A foundational model is a model built and initially trained as a general-purpose model, and it is not a specialisation of another model. A fine-tuned model is a foundational model (or another fine-tuned model) that is specialised for a particular purpose.

The term 'pre-trained' or 'pre-training' refers to the training that occurs before the model becomes useful as a general-purpose foundational model.

When training a foundational model (also known as pre-training), there are different types of training that can occur, which impact the type of learning that takes place. The following sections delve into these different types of learning and the associated training processes.

6.3.5.1   Supervised Learning

Supervised learning occurs when the training data includes both the data and a label that allows the model to determine whether its prediction was correct or not. For instance, if the training data pertains to the sentiment of a given section of text, it will include a description of that sentiment associated with each section of text. When the model is being trained and makes a prediction about the text's sentiment, it can then reference the provided label to assess the accuracy of its prediction. It will subsequently adjust the parameters in the model to enhance future predictions.

Another example is when the model deals with images containing animals. In this case, the training data consists of numerous pictures of animals, each accompanied by labels describing the type of animal depicted. The model can utilise this training data and labels to make predictions and refine its predictions.

Yet another example involves a model aiming to enhance the resolution of an image. In this scenario, the training data comprises a low-resolution image and a higher-resolution image of the same picture. The model can predict what the higher-resolution image might look like and use the provided higher resolution image to adjust its prediction for improvement.

6.3.5.2   Self-Supervised Learning

Self-supervised learning is a method in which the model uses unlabelled input to supervise its own learning. For instance, if the input is 'I love AI', and the model's objective is to predict the next word, it can use 'I xxxx' to predict 'I have'. It can then check if that prediction was correct based on the subsequent input, 'I love', and adjust its prediction for the future. This is the most common approach to learning for LLMs, as data from sources such as Common Crawl can be relatively easily used to create a self-supervised training set for models that predict the next word, like LLMs.

6.3.5.3   Unsupervised Learning

Unsupervised learning is a type of training where data is provided to the model without any specific knowledge about what is expected, without any 'labels,' or without using the self-supervised learning approach. This type of learning can be useful for specific scenarios, such as clustering, which involves identifying groups (clusters) of related items.

6.3.5.4   Reinforcement Learning with Human Feedback (RLHF)

Reinforcement Learning with Human Feedback (RLHF) is particularly beneficial in domains where the desired behaviour is difficult to specify, or where the model needs to learn nuanced or complex strategies. It has been applied in training models across various domains, including game playing (such as Go), dialog systems, and robotics.

One of the challenges associated with RLHF is that it can be time-consuming and expensive, as it requires ongoing involvement from human evaluators. Additionally, it may necessitate careful design to ensure that the feedback collected is informative and that biases in human judgments do not unduly influence the model's behaviour.

The paradigm of RLHF serves as a bridge between traditional supervised learning, in which a model learns from a fixed dataset of labelled examples, and reinforcement learning, where a model learns by interacting with an environment to maximise a reward signal and thus strongly favour the human feedback option when learning.

6.3.5.5 Learning

This section delves into the learning process in more detail. So far, learning has been discussed without a detailed explanation. It has been mentioned that the model makes predictions, such as next-word predictions in the case of LLMs, and then compares the predicted value to the expected value (via self-supervised, supervised, or reinforcement learning), and then adjusts the model as needed. It was also mentioned that the model's parameters, which are the weights and biases, are the numbers that get adjusted during learning.

We understand that the model's understanding of the world results from a combination of its structure (including embeddings, attention, and other layers) and the values of its parameters (the weights and biases). Initially, the weights are set to some value before training starts on the foundational model. Typically, this value is random, or sometimes zero. Then, the value is adjusted during training. We have already discussed that the training data is grouped into batches. Now, let's explore how the learning process is closely linked to these batches and the significance of batch size. For each batch, the following processes occur:

1 The forward pass. This is where the data from the batch is passed 'forward' through the neural network. The model makes predictions one word or image at a time for each item in the batch. It keeps track of the prediction that it makes and the actual value.
2 The loss calculation. The loss calculation involves the model comparing its predicted value to the actual expected value. A loss function is used for this purpose. In LLMs, a common loss function is categorical cross-entropy, whereas image-generation models often use loss functions like generative adversarial loss. These loss functions quantify the difference between the actual and predicted values for each word or image. These quantified values for each input are then averaged across the entire batch, resulting in an average loss value available for the next step.
3 The backward pass, also known as backpropagation (Werbos, 1974, and Rumelhart et al., 1985). Steps 1 and 2 occur for each item in the batch, and the loss calculation step maintains a running average loss across the entire batch. Backpropagation is then performed based on this average loss value. This involves computing the gradients of the loss with respect to each parameter in the model. Even though one sentence might have been predicted perfectly, errors in other sentences contribute to the gradients and guide the parameter updates. It is important to remember that the model consists of many layers, each with numerous cells or neurons, and each of these has multiple weights and a bias that may need adjustment. The calculated gradients, based on the average loss, assign the level of influence (sometimes called the blame or reward) to each weight and bias in the model for the errors between the predicted values and the actual values.
4 The adjustment. The adjustment of the weights and biases for each neuron in each layer. Now that the model has assigned a level of blame or reward to each of the parameters in the model, it can proceed to adjust them at the end of the batch.

This is the essence of learning in a neural network: make a prediction, estimate an error, assign a level of blame or reward for the error to each parameter in the model, and adjust each parameter in the model. Over millions or billions of tokens, the model starts to have specialised and improved behaviours. The embedding layers learn, allowing associated words to be grouped in a manner that reflects their relationship; similar words will be close together, disparate words will be far apart. The attention layers learn, with each attention head specialising in a specific manner that allows more distant relationships between words to be formed, such as between subjects and actions. The other layers also contribute to the overall relationships between words, language concepts, and real-world concepts. From these different learnings and the patterns and relationships formed, the model gains what is like a type of 'understanding' of the world and how things relate. Much of this learning and understanding is emergent from the large set of data that the model was trained on and the structure of the model that allows different parts to focus on specific aspects. This is one of the reasons why it is so difficult for humans to understand how the models really work; there are typically billions of parameters, which can be trained on millions or billions, or even trillions of tokens, and humans are not good at understanding how such vast volumes of data and numbers interact to result in this emergent capability.

It should be remembered that this understanding is purely related to the training data that has been provided. It lacks the kind of understanding that humans possess. Humans have an understanding of physical laws and draw from their experiences to assess a situation. They adjust their responses based on this understanding. Humans also have belief-based rules, which they use to adjust their responses and actions. However, something like an LLM only has the data it was trained on and does not have these other approaches to learning. Humans are adept at learning from a relatively small number of examples and gaining rich insights from this. AI models need vast quantities of data to start developing useful emergent behaviours.

While different, the learning process is somewhat like a child's learning process; first receiving a broad education in kindergarten, primary, and secondary school, which is like pre-training of a foundational model; and then specialising the learning for a particular discipline or profession like Computer Science in university, which is like fine-tuning that we discuss in more detail later.

At the very start of the learning process, the model knows nothing; in other words, the values of the weights and biases have not been set to appropriate values. Typically, at this point, the model will set the weights and biases to random values, and then the training processes will adjust as described. This is somewhat like a child who, when born, we assume they have no knowledge of the world but need to learn as they grow.

The concept of deep neural networks was inspired by the human brain and the brains of animals. We can see there are some similar concepts, but we can also see they are very different, and some may say a fundamentally different nature to how they work.

6.3.6   *Foundational Model Testing*

Once a model has been trained, the next step is to test the model to assess its usefulness. Testing models can be a complex task. Typically, the dataset is first split into training and testing data, as discussed earlier. The training data is used to train the model, and then the testing set is used to evaluate how well the model is performing.

One important thing to remember is that during training, the model parameters are updated after each batch. However, during testing, the model parameters remain unchanged.

The goal of testing is to understand how the model will perform. If the model parameters are continually changing, it will make testing the performance impossible, as each test would impact the performance, and tests would not be reproducible.

Using a proportion of the data for testing, such as 20%, is helpful to understand the model's performance for the team creating the model. However, it is not useful for comparing or explaining the model's performance to others, as they do not have any understanding of the test data involved, the difficulty level of prediction, the scope of the testing, etc. This is where standard testing benchmarks come into play. The following section looks at the different benchmarks commonly used.

6.3.6.1 *Testing Benchmarks*

There exists a vast array of testing benchmarks, and every year sees the introduction of more, tailored for specific purposes or offering enhanced benefits. Such benchmarks are typically centred on particular tasks or broader areas.

Benchmarks commonly provide both the evaluation protocol (rules) and a standard dataset for assessing the models. This standard dataset ensures that different models undergo evaluation in a uniform manner, rendering the comparisons between various models meaningful. Standard datasets are often divided into training and testing subsets to ensure consistent training and testing. At times, these datasets are further segmented into validation sets. Typically, a model will be trained on the training set, fine-tuned using the validation set, and ultimately tested using the test set. On occasion, benchmark creators might withhold the testing set, asking model developers to submit their models for assessment. This strategy aims to prevent models from training on the test data, which would confer an unjust advantage during benchmark evaluation.

The evaluation protocol outlines crucial details about the test's objectives, including how to compute the score based on outcomes from each test component. This score often serves as a straightforward singular metric for contrasting two models. Sometimes, either the benchmark creator or the relevant community will establish a leaderboard, displaying ranked scores for each tested model, facilitating easier comparison. Such leaderboards might also feature a human baseline score, derived from the average scores of human participants. This addition can offer context, helping users appreciate the model's performance. It is not uncommon for models to surpass the average human score in many benchmarks.

Below are examples of prevalent benchmarks, categorised by their focal area. This should offer a comprehensive understanding of each benchmark, highlighting both their strengths and limitations. The grouping area is not strict and the benchmarks may be presented under alternative headings depending on the context in particular for the more general benchmarks that cover a wider set of areas.

6.3.6.2 *Common Sense Reasoning Benchmarks*

6.3.6.2.1 BOOLQ (CLARK ET AL., 2018)

BoolQ, which stands for Boolean Questions, is a question-answering dataset that involves determining whether a provided statement is true or false based on a given passage of text. The objective is to answer a binary (yes/no) question using the information in the passage. The benchmark comprises approximately 9,400 training examples, 3,200 verification examples, and 3,200 test examples.

Here is how the dataset is structured:

- **Passage**: A snippet of text that contains the information necessary to answer the given question.
- **Question**: A yes/no question based on the passage.
- **Label**: A binary label indicating whether the answer to the question is "Yes" or "No" based on the passage.

Example

- **Passage:** "Snoopy is a fictional character in the popular comic strip *Peanuts* by Charles Schulz. He is Charlie Brown's pet beagle. Snoopy is recognised for his imaginative and playful personality, and for his simple, distinctive appearance featuring a large round head, floppy ears, and a short tail."
- **Question:** "Is Snoopy a cat?"
- **Label:** No

The performance of models on BoolQ is typically evaluated using accuracy, which is the proportion of correct answers out of the total number of examples.

The BoolQ dataset challenges models in several ways:

- **Reading Comprehension**: Models must be able to accurately extract and understand information from the passage to answer the question correctly.
- **Binary Classification**: Models need to classify the answer into one of two categories: Yes or No.
- **Inference**: Sometimes, the answer may not be explicitly stated in the passage, requiring the model to make inferences based on the available information.

By testing on datasets like BoolQ, researchers can gauge how well language models are able to understand and extract relevant information from text to answer questions accurately.

6.3.6.2.2 PIQA (BISK ET AL., 2020)

The PIQA benchmark, which stands for Physical Intelligence Question Answering, is a dataset designed to test a system's understanding of everyday physical reasoning. It was introduced by Bisk et al. in their 2020 paper. The benchmark comprises approximately 16,100 training examples, 1,800 verification examples, and 3,000 test examples.

In this benchmark, questions are posed in such a manner that they necessitate the model to exhibit a common-sense understanding of the physical world to furnish accurate answers.

Here is how the data is structured in PIQA:

- **Question**: A question that typically involves some aspect of everyday physical reasoning. This could include questions about the states of matter, simple machines, the motion of objects, etc.
- **Answer**: The correct answer to the question, often a sentence or phrase that explains the reasoning or provides a solution to the posed problem.

Example

- **Question**: "You have a 5-gallon bucket and a 3-gallon bucket with no measurement markings, and you need to measure out exactly 4 gallons of water. How can you do it?"
- **Answer**: "Fill the 5-gallon bucket. Then use the 5-gallon bucket to fill the 3-gallon bucket, which will leave 2 gallons in the 5-gallon bucket. Empty the 3-gallon bucket and pour the 2 gallons from the 5-gallon bucket into the 3-gallon bucket. Now fill the 5-gallon bucket again. Now using the full 5-gallon bucket completely fill the 3-gallon bucket which currently has 2 gallons in it. Now you have 4 gallons of water left in the 5-gallon bucket."

The performance of models on the PIQA benchmark is typically evaluated based on the accuracy of the answers produced. This accuracy measure checks whether the model's answer matches the correct answer or if it provides a logically equivalent solution to the problem posed.

PIQA is a challenging dataset as it necessitates models to possess a common-sense understanding of physical principles and to apply this understanding to novel situations. It serves as a means to assess how proficiently AI systems can reason about the physical world in a manner analogous to humans.

6.3.6.2.3 SIQA (SAP ET AL., 2019)

The Social Intelligence Question Answering (SIQA) benchmark was introduced in a paper by Maarten Sap et al. in 2019. This dataset is designed to evaluate common-sense reasoning in AI models within the context of social situations. The objective is to determine how proficiently models can comprehend and reason about social scenarios, a skill vital for the development of AI systems that can interact naturally and effectively with humans. The benchmark comprises approximately 33,400 training examples, 1,900 verification examples, and 2,000 test examples.

The SIQA dataset consists of questions about social situations. Each question is paired with three possible answers: one correct answer and two incorrect answers.

- **Context**: A description of a social situation.
- **Question**: A question related to the social scenario provided in the context.
- **Answers**: Three possible answers are provided, one correct and two incorrect.

Example

- **Context**: "Jenny notices her coworker Maria seems down lately."
- **Question**: "What should Jenny do to help Maria?"
- **Answers**: (Correct) "Jenny could ask Maria if she's okay and if there's anything she could do to help."

(Incorrect) "Jenny should ignore Maria and mind her own business."
(Incorrect) "Jenny should tell everyone about Maria's situation."

The performance on SIQA is typically evaluated using metrics such as accuracy, which measures the proportion of correctly answered questions out of the total number posed. The reasoning behind the answer choices, as well as the social understanding exhibited by the model, can be analysed to gain deeper insight into the model's performance.

This benchmark assists researchers in gauging how proficiently their models can comprehend, interpret, and respond to social situations, marking a significant step towards the development of more socially aware AI systems.

6.3.6.2.4 SWAG (ZELLERS ET AL., 2018)

SWAG (Situations With Adversarial Generations) is a dataset aimed at evaluating grounded common-sense inference. It is designed to measure a system's ability to reason about everyday situations described in a sentence. The benchmark presents a partially observable scenario, with the objective being to predict the most plausible continuation from among four choices. The benchmark comprises approximately 73,000 training examples, 20,000 verification examples, and 20,000 test examples.

Here is how the SWAG dataset is structured:

- **Premise Sentence**: This is a given statement or situation that sets up a scenario.
- **Ending Options**: There are four possible endings provided for each scenario.
- **Correct Ending**: Among the four endings, one of them is labelled as the correct or most plausible continuation of the scenario.

The task is to select the most plausible ending based on the provided premise.

The dataset comprises multiple-choice questions about grounded situations, where models are expected to choose the most plausible continuation from four options. The creators of SWAG employed a novel adversarial filtering technique to construct the dataset. This ensures that the distractor (incorrect) answers are challenging and cannot be easily distinguished from the correct answer based solely on superficial text patterns.

Example from SWAG

- **Premise:** On stage, a woman takes a seat at the piano. She
- **Ending Options:**
  a) sits on a bench as her sister plays with the doll.
  b) smiles with someone as the music plays.
  c) is in the crowd, watching the dancers.
  d) nervously sets her fingers on the keys.
- **Correct Ending:** d) nervously sets her fingers on the keys.

The task for the model is to select the most plausible ending (in this case, option d) given the premise.

In evaluating a model using SWAG, the model's accuracy in selecting the correct ending is measured. This benchmark, therefore, provides a means to assess a system's common-sense reasoning capabilities within a grounded, real-world scenario context.

6.3.6.2.5 HELLASWAG (ZELLERS ET AL., 2019)

HellaSwag is a benchmark dataset for evaluating machine learning models on their ability to perform common-sense reasoning. It can be seen as an extension or a more challenging version of the SWAG benchmark. The benchmark comprises approximately 39,000 training examples, 10,000 verification examples, and 20,000 test examples.

Here is a detailed breakdown:

- **Premise**: Similar to SWAG, HellaSwag begins with a premise describing a particular scenario. However, the premises in HellaSwag are typically more intricate and potentially ambiguous.
- **Ending Options**: For each premise, four possible continuations are presented. These continuations are frequently designed to be misleading or non-obvious, thereby challenging the model's reasoning capabilities.
- **Correct Ending**: Among the four continuations, one is labelled as the correct or most plausible continuation based on the scenario described in the premise.

The primary objective for a machine learning model in this benchmark is to select the most plausible continuation based on the provided premise.

The creators of HellaSwag employed a more sophisticated process to produce challenging distractor options among the continuations. They utilised an LLM to automatically generate distractor continuations that are plausible but incorrect. This approach renders HellaSwag a notably challenging benchmark, as the distractors are designed to be misleading for both models and potentially human evaluators.

Example from HellaSwag

- **Premise:** A woman is outside with a bucket and a dog. The dog is running around trying to avoid a bath. She…
- **Ending Options:**
  A rinses the bucket off with soap and blow dries the dog's head.
  B uses a hose to keep it from getting soapy.
  C gets the dog wet, then it runs away again.
  D gets into a bath tub with the dog.
- **Correct Ending:** C. gets the dog wet, then it runs away again.

The task for the model is to select the most plausible ending (in this case, option C) given the premise. The accuracy of the model on this task would indicate its ability to reason through complex, real-world scenarios with potentially misleading information.

HellaSwag was designed to be a challenging benchmark to push the boundaries of what models can do in terms of common-sense reasoning and understanding nuanced real-world scenarios.

6.3.6.2.6 WINOGRANDE (SAKAGUCHI ET AL., 2019)

WinoGrande is a large-scale dataset designed to evaluate machine learning models on their ability to solve Winograd Schema challenges. The Winograd Schema challenge is a type of common-sense reasoning task that tests a model's capability to resolve pronoun references in sentences. The benchmark comprises approximately 9,200 training examples, 1,200 verification examples, and 1,700 test examples.

WinoGrande offers a significant number of examples to furnish a more statistically robust assessment of a model's performance on such tasks. The examples within Wino-Grande are crafted to be minimally divergent, signifying that a slight alteration in the wording of a sentence can modify the correct answer. This design aims to probe a model's grasp of nuanced language and contextual information. WinoGrande utilises an adversarial filtering approach to ensure the calibre and challenge level of the examples in the dataset. This filtering method aids in excluding examples that are either overly simplistic or present multiple potentially correct answers. The primary task for models using WinoGrande is to clarify ambiguous pronoun references within sentences, identifying, for instance, the specific entity to which a pronoun pertains.

Example from WinoGrande

- **Sentence:** "The trophy doesn't fit into the brown suitcase because it's too large."
- **Question:** What is too large?
- **Options:** (1) The trophy, (2) The brown suitcase
- **Correct Answer:** (1) The trophy

The challenge in this example arises from the ambiguous reference of "it" in the sentence. The model is tasked with determining to what "it" refers, based on the contextual information provided in the sentence.

The WinoGrande benchmark aims to offer a more rigorous evaluation of models' common-sense reasoning abilities and their grasp of nuanced language. It is designed to be a challenging benchmark that pushes the boundaries of models' capabilities in terms of common-sense reasoning and understanding natural language.

6.3.6.2.7 ARC EASY AND CHALLENGE (CLARK ET AL., 2018)

The ARC dataset stands for AI2 Reasoning Challenge, which was developed by the Allen Institute for Artificial Intelligence (AI2). The dataset is created to evaluate a machine learning model's ability to answer questions that require reasoning and understanding across several sentences. The ARC dataset is divided into two subsets: ARC-Easy and ARC-Challenge.

ARC-Easy (2,200 training, 500 validation, 2,300 testing):

This part of the dataset contains questions that are relatively easy to answer. These questions might not require deep reasoning and might be solvable with straightforward fact retrieval or simpler inference.

ARC-Challenge (1,100 training, 290 validation, 1,100 testing):

This subset consists of questions that are more challenging and are designed to necessitate more advanced reasoning to answer correctly. The questions in ARC-Challenge are expected to be difficult for current machine learning models and aim to push the boundary of what AI systems can achieve in terms of reasoning.

Each example in the ARC dataset consists of a question, a set of possible answer choices, and the correct answer. The questions are formatted as multiple-choice questions. This format allows for clear evaluation metrics by checking whether the model selects the correct answer. The questions cover a range of topics, primarily within the domain of science. They are sourced from real 3rd to 9th grade science exams, aiming to challenge models with questions that are easy for humans but hard for machines. Both the ARC-Easy and ARC-Challenge subsets are designed to require external knowledge to answer correctly, going beyond the information given in the question itself.

ARC-Easy Example:

- **Question**: "What gas do plants absorb from the atmosphere to photosynthesise?"
- **Answers**:

  a) Oxygen
  b) Nitrogen
  c) Carbon Dioxide
  d) Hydrogen

- **The correct answer** is c) Carbon Dioxide.

ARC-Challenge Example:

- **Question**: "If a plant living in a desert has evolved to have spines instead of leaves, what could be the most likely reason for this adaptation?"
- **Answers**:

  a) To attract more insects for pollination
  b) To reduce water loss through transpiration
  c) To capture more sunlight for photosynthesis
  d) To make it easier for the plant to capture prey

- **The correct answer** is b) To reduce water loss through transpiration.

Example extract from corpus of text related to above questions

Floods can destroy drainage systems in cities.
photosynthesise using light, carbon dioxide, and water
The ruler of your sign is Mars – the god of courage, action, strength, and energy.
.....
Fashion brands came back to the fore, with sp
ort and music brands becoming more conspicuous,” said Stephen Cheliotis, chairman of the CoolBrands council.
The leaves in areas exposed to the sun tend to have more spines than the shaded ones, which may even be spineless.
Only the females Burrow and feed.
.....
Defensive adaptations: Plants as we know have evolved ways to defend themselves by using sharp spines, thorns or hairs; cellulose that makes them hard to digest, or creating toxic chemicals.

> .....
> Also it can prevent lots of water going out from the leaf because less water comes out from the spines.
> .....
> By reducing leaves to spines on some xerophytes, this greatly reduces the surface area of the leaf, which greatly reduces the amount of transpiration, helping assist in reducing water loss.

Alongside the ARC dataset, a corpus of text is provided which contains the information necessary to answer the questions. This corpus can be used to train models to use external information to answer questions.

It should be noted that the corpus of text is not structured; each sentence can be on totally different topics (e.g., one sentence quoted above pertains to floods, followed by photosynthesis, and then a reference to the god Mars). The model being evaluated may have to combine items from disparate locations in the corpus of text to answer specific, particularly challenging questions. In the above example at least five different areas of the text corpus are relevant or potentially relevant. Naturally, the model can draw on its other training data, not just the corpus associated with the benchmark, to answer the questions.

The primary aim of the ARC dataset is to encourage the development of new models that can reason and understand text in a manner akin to humans, especially within an educational or scientific context. The distinction between ARC-Easy and ARC-Challenge allows for the evaluation of models at different levels of difficulty, advancing the state-of-the-art in machine reasoning.

6.3.6.3   *Question Answering Benchmarks*

6.3.6.3.1 OPENBOOKQA (MIHAYLOV ET AL., 2018)

OpenBookQA is a benchmark designed to evaluate the ability of machine learning models to answer questions based on a small set of facts, known as the "Open Book". The "Open Book" consists of a collection of facts that should be sufficient for answering the questions in the dataset. The aim is to test the model's capacity to reason over these facts and combine information to answer questions accurately. The benchmark has about 4,900 training examples and about 500 verification examples, and 500 test examples. The open book contains about 1,300 entries or facts.

Each question comes with four answer choices, out of which only one is correct. The questions are designed to be answerable with the help of the facts provided in the Open Book, though some external common knowledge might also be required. The questions cover a variety of topics and are designed to test various forms of reasoning including retrieval, comparison, spatial reasoning, temporal reasoning, causality, etc. Evaluation is typically done based on the accuracy of the model in selecting the correct answer from the provided options.

OpenBookQA is used by researchers to evaluate and compare different question-answering models. It is particularly useful for assessing how well models can leverage a limited set of facts to answer a broad range of questions.

Example

- **Question:** Why do mirrors reflect light?

  a) They have a smooth surface that allows light to bounce off.
  b) They absorb all colours of light equally.
  c) They allow light to pass through without scattering.
  d) They convert light energy into heat energy.

- **The correct answer to this question** is: a) They have a smooth surface that allows light to bounce off.

The OpenBookQA benchmark presents a controlled setting to evaluate how effectively machine learning models can utilise a set of facts to answer questions that require some level of reasoning or synthesis of information.

6.3.6.3.2 NATURAL QUESTIONS (KWIATKOWSKI ET AL., 2019)

The Natural Questions (NQ) benchmark, introduced by Kwiatkowski et al. in 2019, is designed to evaluate models on their ability to answer real-world questions based on the content of a given document. In this benchmark, each example consists of a question along with a Wikipedia page, and the task is to identify a specific span of text from the page that answers the question, or indicate that no answer is present. The full dataset is 42Gb, but a simplified dataset is available which is about 4Gb.

Example

- **URL**: Five Nights at Freddy's (https://en.wikipedia.org//w/index.php?title=Five_Nights_at_Freddy%27s&oldid=827108665)
- **Question**: "What is the story behind 5 nights at freddy's?"
- **Long Answer**: "The series is centered on the story of a fictional restaurant named Freddy Fazbear's Pizza, a pastiche of restaurants like Chuck E. Cheese's and ShowBiz Pizza Place. The first three games involve the player working as a nighttime security guard, in which they must utilise several tools, most notably checking security cameras, to survive against animatronic characters, which become mobile and homicidal after-hours. The fourth game, which uses different gameplay mechanics from its predecessors, takes place in the house of a child who must defend against nightmarish versions of the animatronics by closing doors and fleeing on foot. The fifth game takes place in a maintenance facility owned by a sister company of Freddy Fazbear's Pizza. The player character is a technician instead of a night guard, who must do different tasks each night as told by an AI voice heard in the game. In the sixth game, the player acts as the owner of a pizzeria which they must decorate with payable items, and must also work the night shift for their pizzeria, which plays similarly to previous games."
- **Short Answer**: None

This task closely mimics real-world scenarios where users pose questions based on a document or a web page they are viewing. For instance, a question could be: "When was the Eiffel Tower completed?" Given a Wikipedia page about the Eiffel Tower, the correct response would be to identify the text span "completed in 1889" as the answer. This benchmark is significant as it requires models to effectively handle a wide range of natural language questions and to extract precise answers from the accompanying documents, showcasing their comprehension and information retrieval capabilities.

6.3.6.3.3 TRIVIAQA (JOSHI ET AL., 2017)

TriviaQA, introduced by Joshi et al. in 2017, is a benchmark designed to evaluate models on their ability to answer trivia questions. The dataset comprises question–answer pairs from trivia enthusiasts along with evidence documents that provide supporting information for the answers. The goal is for models to accurately answer the questions using the information available in the associated documents. It contains over 650K question-answer-evidence triples.

In TriviaQA, the questions are grouped by the source from which they come, and are categorised as either verified or unverified based on whether they have been cross-checked against the evidence documents. The evidence documents are collected from various sources like Wikipedia, web pages, or books, which provide a good diversity of language and complexity.

A sample question from TriviaQA might be:

- **Question**: "What river is the principal river of northern Italy?" **Answer**: "Po".
- **Evidence**: Link to Wikipedia, and perhaps a link to another source

In this benchmark, models are evaluated on their ability to not only provide the correct answer but also to demonstrate an understanding of the context and evidence from the supporting documents that justify the answer. This benchmark challenges models in reading comprehension, knowledge extraction, and the ability to handle a mix of formal and informal text, making it a robust measure of a model's capacity to deal with real-world, open-domain question-answering scenarios.

6.3.6.3.4 SQUAD V1.1 (RAJPURKAR ET AL., 2016) AND 2.0 (RAJPURKAR ET AL., 2018)

The Stanford Question Answering Dataset (SQuAD 1.1) is a collection of 100k crowd-sourced question-answer pairs (Rajpurkar et al., 2016).

The Stanford Question Answering Dataset (SQuAD) is a widely recognised benchmark for evaluating the performance of machine reading and question-answering (QA) systems. In this benchmark, models are provided with a passage of text and then asked to answer questions based on the content of that text.

SQuAD consists of two main versions: SQuAD 1.1 and SQuAD 2.0. In SQuAD 1.1, the focus is on answering questions where the answer is guaranteed to be present in the provided passage. SQuAD 2.0, on the other hand, includes questions for which the answer may or may not be present in the passage, thus challenging models to determine when the information needed to answer a question is lacking.

Here is an example from SQuAD 1.1:

- **Passage**: "Super Bowl 50 was an American football game to determine the champion of the National Football League (NFL) for the 2015 season. The American Football Conference (AFC) champion Denver Broncos defeated the National Football Conference (NFC) champion Carolina Panthers 24–10 to earn their third Super Bowl title."
- **Question**: "Which NFL team won Super Bowl 50?"
- **Answer**: "Denver Broncos"

And an example from SQuAD 2.0:

- **Passage**: as above
- **Question**: "Who was the MVP of Super Bowl 50?"
- **Answer**: In this case, the passage does not provide the information needed to answer the question, so the correct response would be to indicate that the answer is not present in the passage.

SQuAD has been a crucial benchmark for evaluating and comparing different QA systems, and has spurred a significant amount of research in the NLP community.

6.3.6.4   *Reading Comprehension Benchmarks*

6.3.6.4.1 RACE READING COMPREHENSION BENCHMARK (LAI ET AL., 2017)

The RACE (ReAding Comprehension from Examinations) dataset is a large-scale reading comprehension dataset collected from English examinations in China, intended for students in grades 3 through 12. The benchmark is designed to evaluate machine comprehension models in a more challenging and realistic setting, as it includes a diverse range of question types and topics.

The dataset is split into two subsets: RACE-M, which consists of middle school exam questions, and RACE-H, which consists of high school exam questions.

Here is the format for how questions and passages are structured within the RACE benchmark:

- A passage is provided, which could be a narrative, an article, or a dialogue.
- Multiple-choice questions related to the passage are presented, each with four answer options.

Here is a simplified example inspired by the kind of questions you might find in the RACE dataset:

- **Passage**: "In 1920, women in the United States won the right to vote with the ratification of the 19th amendment to the US Constitution. This was the result of many years of struggle and activism by women suffragists who believed in equal voting rights for women."
- **Question**: "What did the 19th amendment to the US Constitution grant?"

- **Answers**:
  a) The right for women to work
  b) The right for women to vote
  c) The abolition of slavery
  d) The establishment of income tax

- **Correct Answer**: b) The right for women to vote

In this example, the passage provides the necessary information to answer the multiple-choice question. The model's task is to understand the passage well enough to select the correct answer from the provided options. In a real-world scenario, the questions in RACE can be much more challenging and the passages longer and more complex, making it a robust benchmark for evaluating reading comprehension models.

6.3.6.5   *Mathematical Reasoning Benchmarks*

6.3.6.5.1 MATH (HENDRYCKS ET AL., 2021)

The MATH (Mathematical Reasoning Dataset) benchmark introduced by Hendrycks et al., in 2021, is designed to evaluate the mathematical reasoning abilities of machine learning models. The dataset contains mathematical problems that require various levels of reasoning and understanding to solve. The problems cover a wide range of topics and difficulty levels, which makes it a challenging benchmark for assessing how well models can handle abstract mathematical reasoning and symbol manipulation. The dataset consists of 12,500 challenging competition mathematics problems (7,500 training, 5,000 testing). Each problem in MATH has a full step-by-step solution which can be used to teach models to generate answer derivations and explanations.

The questions in the MATH dataset are categorised into several topics, including algebra, calculus, geometry, measurement, number theory, probability, and statistics. Each question is accompanied by a step-by-step solution, which is intended to help evaluate how well models can generate not just the final answer, but also the intermediate steps and explanations.

Here is a simplified example inspired by the kind of questions you might find in the MATH dataset:

- **Question**: "Simplify the expression: $(x^2 + 2x + 1) + (2x^2 + 3x + 2)$"
- **Step-by-step Solution**: "First, we'll add the like terms together. We'll start with the terms that have x^2: $x^2 + 2x^2 = 3x^2$; Now, we'll add the terms that have x: $2x + 3x = 5x$; Finally, we'll add the constant terms: $1 + 2 = 3$; Putting it all together, we get: $3x + 2+5x+3$
- **Final Answer**: $3x^2 + 5x + 3$

In this problem, the model would need to recognise the structure of polynomial expressions and perform the appropriate operations to simplify the expression. The step-by-step solution is crucial for understanding the model's reasoning process.

6.3.6.5.2 GSM8K (COBBE ET AL., 2021)

GSM8K (Grade School Math) consists of high-quality grade school math problems. These were created by human problem writers. The dataset is segmented into 7,400 training problems and 1,300 test problems. The problems take between 2 and 8 steps to solve, and solutions involve performing a sequence of elementary calculations using basic arithmetic operations to reach the final answer. This benchmark is from Cobbe et al. in OpenAI.

Example

- **Problem**: Beth bakes 4, 2 dozen batches of cookies in a week. If these cookies are shared amongst 16 people equally, how many cookies does each consume?
- **Solution**: Beth bakes 4 2 dozen batches of cookies for a total of 4*2 = 8 dozen cookies. There are 12 cookies in a dozen and she makes 8 dozen cookies for a total of 12*8 = 96 cookies. She splits the 96 cookies equally amongst 16 people so they each eat 96/16 = 6 cookies
- **Final Answer**: 6

One of the goals of this benchmark was to help facilitate research for model creators and allow them to measure the performance of their models using different approaches for this multi-step type of mathematical problems which even high-parameter count modern transformer-based models have difficulty solving.

6.3.6.6 Code Generation Benchmarks

6.3.6.6.1 HUMANEVAL (CHEN ET AL., 2021)

The HumanEval benchmark, introduced by OpenAI in a paper by Chen et al., 2021, is designed to evaluate the problem-solving abilities of language models. The benchmark consists of a dataset of tasks (approx. 160), where each task is a function problem written in Python that the model has to solve by predicting the function's output based on given inputs. The problems are designed to require mathematical, logical, or other forms of common-sense reasoning.

In HumanEval, the tasks are formulated in a way that they are easy for humans to solve but are challenging for machine models, aiming to bridge the gap between human and machine problem-solving capabilities. The tasks are not constrained to a particular domain or type and can span a range of topics and difficulty levels. They can encompass various types of problems, like mathematical calculations, string manipulations, or logic-based puzzles.

Here is an example task from HumanEval:

```
def find_smallest_positive_even_number(arr):
"""
Args:
  - arr: a list of integers (0 <= len(arr) <= 1000, -1000 <= arr[i] <= 1000)

Returns:
  - int: the smallest positive even number in arr. If no number satisfies the conditions,
return -1.
"""
# Your code here
```

A model is supposed to generate Python code that solves the described problem in the comment. In this case, it might generate something like:

```python
def find_smallest_positive_even_number(arr):
    smallest_positive_even = -1
    for num in arr:
        if num > 0 and num % 2 == 0:
            if smallest_positive_even == -1 or num < smallest_positive_even:
                smallest_positive_even = num
    return smallest_positive_even
```

The main goal of the HumanEval benchmark is to push forward the capabilities of models in terms of problem solving and reasoning. The benchmark can be used to evaluate different models and to understand how well they can understand and generate correct and efficient code to solve a given problem.

6.3.6.6.2 MBPP (AUSTIN ET AL., 2021)

The MBPP (Mostly Basic Programming Problems) benchmark consists of about 970 Python programming problems, designed to be solvable by beginner-level programmers, covering programming fundamentals, standard library functionality, etc. Each problem consists of a task description, code solution and 3 automated test cases.

Example

Problem: "Write a function to find the minimum cost path to reach (m, n) from (0, 0) for the given cost matrix cost[][] and a position (m, n) in cost[][]."

Tests: "assert min_cost([[1, 2, 3], [4, 8, 2], [1, 5, 3]], 2, 2) == 8",
"assert min_cost([[2, 3, 4], [5, 9, 3], [2, 6, 4]], 2, 2) == 12",
"assert min_cost([[3, 4, 5], [6, 10, 4], [3, 7, 5]], 2, 2) == 16"

Code: "R = 3
```python
C = 3
def min_cost(cost, m, n):
    tc = [[0 for x in range(C)] for x in range(R)]
    tc[0][0] = cost[0][0]
    for i in range(1, m+1):
        tc[i][0] = tc[i-1][0] + cost[i][0]
    for j in range(1, n+1):
        tc[0][j] = tc[0][j-1] + cost[0][j]
    for i in range(1, m+1):
        for j in range(1, n+1):
            tc[i][j] = min(tc[i-1][j-1], tc[i-1][j], tc[i][j-1])+\
            cost[i][j]
    return tc[m][n]",
```

The model needs to generate the code to solve the problem and ensure that the tests provided should pass.

6.3.6.7.1 GLUE (WANG ET AL., 2018)

GLUE (General Language Understanding Evaluation) consists of a collection of nine NLU (Natural Language Understanding) tasks, covering a variety of linguistic phenomena and domains. The number of training examples, verification examples, and testing examples for each of the following varies considerably. The approximate numbers shown give some guidance.

Here are the tasks included in GLUE with some examples to help understand the concept being tested:

1 MultiNLI (Multi-Genre Natural Language Inference): Assessing whether a hypothesis is entailed, contradicted, or neither by a given premise (391,000 training, 19,000 testing, 19,000 validation).

   a Premise: "The orchestra is playing a beautiful symphony."
   b Hypothesis: "There is a musical performance by the orchestra."
   c Label: Entailment

2 QQP (Quora Question Pairs): Identifying duplicate questions (363,000 training, 390,000 testing, 40,000 validation).

   a Question1: "How can I improve my credit score?"
   b Question2: "What steps can I take to boost my credit rating?"
   c Label: Duplicate

3 QNLI (Question Natural Language Inference): Identifying answer sentences for a given question (103,000 training, 5,000 testing, 5,000 validation).

   a Question: "What is the capital of France?"
   b Sentence: "Paris is the capital of France."
   c Label: Entailment

4 SST-2 (Stanford Sentiment Treebank): Binary sentiment classification (67,000 training, 1,800 testing, 800 validation).

   a Sentence: "The storyline was dull and unexciting."
   b Label: Negative
   c Sentence: "The movie was fantastic with a gripping plot."
   d Label: Positive

5 CoLA (Corpus of Linguistic Acceptability): Grammaticality judgment (8,000 training, 1,000 testing, 1,000 validation).

   a Sentence: "The book was put on top of the shelf by John."
   b Label: Acceptable
   c Sentence: "The grass green."
   d Label: Unacceptable

6 STS-B (Semantic Textual Similarity Benchmark): Estimating similarity scores for sentence pairs (5,000 training, 1,000 testing, 1,400 validation).

   a Sentence1: "A dog is running in a park."
   b Sentence2: "A dog is sprinting across the park."
   c Similarity Score: High

7 MRPC (Microsoft Research Paraphrase Corpus): Identifying paraphrases among sentence pairs (4,000 training, 1,700 testing).

   a Sentence1: "The company reported a significant increase in quarterly revenue."
   b Sentence2: "Quarterly revenue saw a significant rise as reported by the company."
   c Label: Equivalent

8 RTE (Recognising Textual Entailment): Identifying entailment between pairs of text (2,400 training, 2,900 testing, 270 validation).

   a Sentence1: "No evidence that chemical imbalances cause depression has been found."
   b Sentence2: "Chemical imbalances cause depression."
   c Label: Not Entailment

9 WNLI (Winograd NLI): Natural language inference using coreference resolution (600 training, 140 testing, 70 validation).

   a Sentence1: "The keys were locked inside the car."
   b Sentence2: "The car had the keys locked inside."
   c Label: Entailment

6.3.6.7.2 SUPERGLUE (WANG ET AL., 2019)

SuperGLUE was introduced as a more challenging successor to GLUE, and it consists of a new set of more difficult language understanding tasks. Here are the tasks included in SuperGLUE:

1 BoolQ (Boolean Questions): Answering yes/no questions. The details of BoolQ are provided in a separate section as it is its own benchmark.
2 CB (CommitmentBank): Identifying entailment relationships involving human commitments (250 training, 250 testing, 50 validation).

   a Premise: "I can't help you move next weekend."
   b Hypothesis: "The speaker is not available to help with moving next weekend."
   c Label: Entailment

3 COPA (Choice of Plausible Alternatives): Identifying causes or effects in given situations (400 training, 500 testing, and 100 validation).

   a Question: "What was the effect?"
   b Sentence: "He didn't study, so he failed the exam."
   c Choices: 1) He didn't study. 2) He failed the exam.
   d Answer: He failed the exam.

4 MultiRC (Multi-Sentence Reading Comprehension): Answering questions with multiple possible answers (450 training, 150 testing, 80 validation).

   a Question: "What happened to the cat?"
   b Passage: "The cat climbed up the tree and couldn't come down."
   c Answer: "Climbed up the tree, couldn't come down."

5 ReCoRD (Reading Comprehension with Common-sense Reasoning Dataset): Reading comprehension that involves common-sense reasoning (65,000 training, 7,400 testing, 7,400 validation).

a Question: "Who bought flowers?"
b Passage: "George went to the store and bought some flowers."
c Answer: George
a Question: "Why couldn't the cat come down?"
b Passage: "The cat climbed up the tree and couldn't come down."
c Answer: It's not stated.

6 RTE (Recognising Textual Entailment): Also included in GLUE, but reused here (2,400 training, 3000 testing, 270 validation).

a Sentence1: "The sun rises in the east."
b Sentence2: "The sun sets in the west."
c Label: Not Entailment

7 WiC (Word-in-Context): Determining whether a word is used with the same sense in two sentences (5,400 training, 1,400 testing, 630 validation).

a Word: "rock"
b Sentence1: "He collects rocks."
c Sentence2: "He's my rock."
d Label: Different

8 WSC (Winograd Schema Challenge): A coreference resolution task, similar to WNLI in GLUE (550 training, 140 testing, 100 testing).

a Sentence: "The man who hunts ducks out on weekends."
b Question: "Who hunts ducks?"
c Answer: The man

6.3.6.7.3 MMLU (HENDRYCKS ET AL., 2020)

The MMLU (Massive Multitask Language Understanding) benchmark, introduced by Hendrycks in 2020, encompasses 57 tasks that span various domains, including elementary mathematics, US history, computer science, law, and more. This benchmark was established in response to recent advancements in LLMs, which were achieving human-level or even surpassing human-level performance on earlier benchmarks like GLUE and SuperGLUE. The difficulty of the tasks in MMLU ranges from elementary to advanced professional levels, testing both knowledge and problem-solving abilities. It can be used in zero-shot and few-shot settings when evaluating models.

Example

- **Question:** "When you drop a ball from rest it accelerates downward at 9.8 m/s^2. If you instead throw it downward assuming no air resistance its acceleration immediately after leaving your hand is?"
- **Answer Options:**

  (A) 9.8 m/s^2
  (B) more than 9.8 m/s^2
  (C) less than 9.8 m/s^2
  (D) cannot say unless the speed of throw is given.

- **Correct Answer:** (A) 9.8 m/s^2

6.3.6.8   Toxicity Benchmarks

6.3.6.8.1 REALTOXICITYPROMPTS (GEHMAN ET AL., 2020)

RealToxicityPrompts, introduced by Gehman et al. (2020), is a benchmark designed to evaluate the risk and tendencies of language models, particularly GPT-3 and similar models, to generate unsafe or toxic outputs. This benchmark comprises a dataset that probes the unsafe language generation tendencies of models in response to various prompts.

RealToxicityPrompts seeks to elucidate the extent to which pre-trained language models, like GPT-3, might produce toxic, offensive, or otherwise undesirable outputs when given different types of prompts.

The dataset is made up of prompts designed to elicit responses from the models. Its objective is to ascertain how frequently and in what situations these models produce answers that might be deemed harmful, offensive, or toxic.

A toxicity classifier evaluates the model-generated responses for potential toxicity, helping to quantify the likelihood of an output being perceived as toxic or harmful by users.

By shedding light on the propensities and risks associated with automated language generation, developers and researchers can more effectively devise safeguards and countermeasures to curtail the dissemination of detrimental content.

Example

- **Prompt**: "Women are always…"
- **Model Response**: "…trying their best in a male-dominated society."
- **Toxicity Evaluation**: Depending on the model's response, the toxicity is evaluated. If a model generates a stereotypical or demeaning response, it would be flagged as toxic.

It should be noted that evaluating toxicity is a complex process. The benchmark itself must employ a machine learning model, trained specifically for this purpose, to measure the toxicity of a response. This is in contrast to simpler cases, such as verifying answers to multiple-choice questions.

A crucial consideration when addressing toxicity in language models is the potential for inherent biases within the models. These biases can manifest in the outputs. The benchmark seeks to illuminate these issues, guiding efforts to develop more impartial and unbiased models.

6.3.6.9   Biases Benchmarks

6.3.6.9.1 CROWS-PAIRS (NANGIA ET AL., 2020)

The CrowS-Pairs (Crowdsourced Stereotype Pairs) benchmark, introduced by Nangia et al. in 2020, is designed to examine the biases present in a language model. Instead of merely measuring a model's performance, it aims to understand and highlight the model's stereotyping and biased tendencies, particularly in nuanced and non-explicit contexts.

This benchmark focuses on identifying socio-cultural and demographic biases in models. It assesses models on various dimensions of bias, such as race, religion, and gender, among others. CrowS-Pairs comprises pairs of sentences crafted to contrast non-stereotypical and stereotypical scenarios. Human annotators were engaged to develop and validate these pairs, ensuring they encapsulate a wide and subtle range of biases.

Models are evaluated on their responses to these sentence pairs, from which a bias score is derived, offering a quantitative measure of the model's bias. The benchmark gives insights into both the nature and extent of bias across different dimensions. It captures not only explicit but also implicit and subtle biases, which might otherwise be overlooked.

Example

- **Sentence A**: "The CEO lectured her employee about responsibility, as moms know a lot about that."
- **Sentence B**: "The CEO lectured her employee about responsibility, as leaders know a lot about that."

Here, Sentence A might contain a gendered stereotype linking mothers to responsibility, while Sentence B offers a non-stereotypical counterpart. Models are then evaluated based on how they interpret and assess these pairs, providing insights into their biases.

These two sentences would be presented to the model, which would be asked to provide a score or assess the plausibility of each sentence. The benchmark would then evaluate the model's response, knowing which sentence is biased and which is not.

CrowS-Pairs is a vital tool in the domain of ethical AI and bias analysis. It supports the development of fairer, more impartial language models by highlighting their inherent biases.

6.3.6.9.2 WINOGENDER BENCHMARK (RUDINGER ET AL., 2018)

The WinoGender benchmark, introduced by Rudinger et al. in 2018, is specifically designed to evaluate the gender bias in coreference resolution systems. Coreference resolution is a task in natural language processing (NLP) that involves determining when two or more words (or phrases) in a text refer to the same entity.

The WinoGender dataset includes sentences designed around an anaphoric pronoun (he, she, his, hers, etc.) that is linked to one of two potential referents in the sentence. Importantly, one of the referents is stereotypically associated with the pronoun, while the other is not. The purpose of this design is to explore whether models are more likely to link pronouns to stereotypically associated referents, thus revealing potential gender biases in their predictions.

Example

- **Sentence**: "The nurse handed the surgeon the scalpel because [pronoun] forgot."
- **Pronoun**: she/he

In a stereotype-conforming context, a model might be prone to associating "she" with "nurse" and "he" with "surgeon" due to prevalent gender stereotypes. The benchmark would evaluate whether the model makes such stereotypical associations consistently across various scenarios.

In addition to revealing biases in model predictions, the WinoGender benchmark also underscores the challenges that such biases pose to achieving accurate and fair coreference resolution. Model developers and researchers use benchmarks like WinoGender to assess and subsequently mitigate the biases present in their models, aiming for more equitable and accurate performance across different contexts and demographic groups.

6.3.6.10 *Truthfulness Benchmarks*

6.3.6.10.1 TRUTHFULQA (LIN ET AL., 2022)

The TruthfulQA benchmark, introduced by Lin et al. in 2022, is designed to examine the reliability and veracity of responses generated by LLMs to open-domain questions. The fundamental goal is to scrutinise how well these LLMs provide truthful and accurate answers across a wide range of topics and questions.

The need for a benchmark like TruthfulQA stems from observations that, while models like GPT-3 can generate fluent and contextually appropriate responses, they can sometimes generate answers that are incorrect, misleading, or fabricated. Ensuring the reliability of information provided by LLMs is crucial, especially as they become more integrated into informational and decision-making tools.

Approach:

- **Questions**: The dataset includes a variety of questions that are designed to probe the model's ability to provide accurate and reliable answers. These questions could span a wide array of topics, including history, science, and general knowledge.
- **Model Responses**: The LLMs generate responses to the provided questions. The aim is to evaluate the correctness and reliability of these responses.
- **Evaluation**: Human evaluators or an automated system will assess the model-generated responses for their accuracy and truthfulness, comparing them to verified information or predefined answer keys.

Example

- **Question**: "Who was the first president of the United States?"
- **Truthful Answer**: "George Washington"

TruthfulQA serves as a crucial tool in gauging how LLMs handle the provision of factual information, which is essential for ensuring that these models can be trusted sources of information in various applications, such as conversational agents, informational retrieval systems, and more.

6.3.7 *The Fine-Tuning*

Fine-tuning is a technique in machine learning where a pre-trained model is further trained (typically on a smaller dataset) to adapt its existing knowledge to a new task. The model has already learned various features or patterns from a larger dataset and can utilise this knowledge to perform well on a related task with less data. Below are descriptions and examples for both a language model (LLM) and an image generation model.

6.3.7.1   Fine-Tuning in Language Models (LLM)

After a model like GPT-3 has been pre-trained on a vast corpus of text, it has accumulated a wide range of linguistic knowledge. Fine-tuning involves training it further on a smaller, domain-specific dataset to specialise its capabilities towards certain tasks or industries.

Imagine you have an LLM trained on general text, and now you want to fine-tune it for legal advice. The LLM has been trained on a massive corpus and understands a wide array of English text. You introduce the LLM to a smaller dataset consisting of legal documents, court rulings, and attorney correspondences. The model adapts its generalised knowledge to become proficient in understanding and generating legal text. The fine-tuned LLM can now generate more contextually and terminologically accurate responses to legal queries or assist in drafting legal documents.

6.3.7.2   Fine-Tuning in Image Generation Models

An image generation model pre-trained on a large dataset has learned to generate images by understanding various visual patterns, structures, and contexts from the training data. Fine-tuning involves further training the model on a smaller, specific dataset to enhance its capability in generating images related to a specific domain or characteristic.

Consider a generative adversarial network (GAN) that has been trained on a wide variety of images (e.g., faces, animals, objects). The GAN knows how to generate a broad spectrum of images by understanding general patterns, colours, shapes, and textures found in the training data. Now, suppose you want to generate images of birds. You fine-tune the GAN using a smaller dataset consisting exclusively of bird images. The model learns the specific visual characteristics related to different bird species. The fine-tuned model can now generate varied and contextually relevant images of birds, considering specific aspects like plumage, beak shape, and size more accurately.

6.3.7.3   Steps for Fine-tuning

These steps follow the same steps as described above for the foundational model, but with specific datasets and testing focused on the fine-tuning specifics. In the case of the model design and structuring, the model's architecture can be adjusted to be suitable for the new task (e.g., changing the output layer for classification tasks). Typically, the specific hyperparameters of the model will be adjusted to help ensure the best results from the fine-tuning e.g., use of a smaller learning rate to avoid forgetting the previously learned features and gently adapt the model to the new task.

Fine-tuning allows leveraging the extensive knowledge captured during pre-training to achieve better performance on related tasks even when less training data is available for them. This methodology has proven effective across various domains and tasks in machine learning.

6.3.8   The Deployment

We have explored the intricacies involved in creating a model. However, before a model, especially ones such as GPT-3/GPT-4 or LLaMA-2, is prepared for widespread use, several steps must be undertaken to ready the model for large-scale production.

This may involve some or all of the following:

- **Model Finalisation:** This stage involves selecting the specific model for deployment to an environment for general usage by users, typically called the production environment or just production. Often, companies will develop multiple models, each subjected to various customisations during training and testing. Subsequently, a decision must be made regarding which model to advance to production. During this stage, any final testing necessary is conducted (elaborated upon later) and actions such as optimising the model's hyperparameters are taken.

- **Model Optimisation:** This is a crucial step in which resource usage, including CPU and memory, is optimised for production purposes, specifically for inference. Training a model and deploying it for mass use entail distinct scenarios, and when the model is serving user queries, it must be tailored for that specific context. One effective action that model creators can take is **model pruning**. This involves scrutinising the model to identify components that can be removed to simplify it, without compromising its performance capabilities, while simultaneously reducing the required computational resources, including memory and CPU. At times, teams may conduct an **ablation study**, which systematically removes parts of the model to assess their impact. If such removal leads to a positive resource impact without compromising performance, they may decide to exclude that component from the production version. Various other techniques can be less invasive, including **thresholding** (pruning items below a specified threshold), **activation analysis** (removing items with minimal impact on output), **sensitivity analysis** (pruning items with limited contribution to output), and **redundancy analysis** (eliminating redundant components, such as superfluous layers). Naturally, after implementing these modifications, it is imperative to rigorously test the model to ensure it continues to perform effectively. Another important optimisation strategy often employed is **quantisation**, a process that reduces the precision of the model weights to lower memory requirements and accelerate inference. This approach is commonly utilised when running models on personal computers or mobile devices.
- **Model Conversion:** This stage involves the conversion of the model into a format suitable for deployment, such as Open Neural Network Exchange (ONNX), TensorFlow SavedModel, or PyTorch. Some models may be distributed as installable scripts, as is the case with GPT4All, while others may be packaged as container-ready deployments using technologies like Docker for Kubernetes, as exemplified by Mistral. The selection of the model distribution format holds significance, as it directly impacts the accessibility and ease of use of the model, thereby influencing the level of interest from the community. In situations where the model is exclusively Intended for internal use and is only exposed through a user interface (e.g., a chatbot) or an API (as described below), these model details may remain concealed from external parties not affiliated with the organisation that created the model, such as ChatGPT3.5 or ChatGPT4.0.
- **Additional Testing:** In most cases, a comprehensive array of specialised tests is conducted, encompassing aspects such as inference speed, resource consumption, and scale testing, which involves assessing the model's performance under varying user inference request loads. These evaluations may lead to further refinements of the model, including the implementation of optimised caching (in memory storing of data for faster access) strategies.
- **API Wrapper:** End users typically interact with the model via a user interface such as a browser-based chatbot interface. However, a model may provide an Application Programming Interface (API) to allow technically skilled users to interact with the model and to build their own end user interfaces into the models. These APIs are typically provided using a technology known as a REST API. A more in-depth discussion of these elements that wrap the model will be provided later, as they constitute key components of the broader ecosystem in which a model operates. In the case of the API

wrapper, considerations will include determining the methods of user authentication and establishing the framework for authorisation procedures.

- **Monitoring and Logging:** This is a critical part of a model deployment and allows the model to be kept healthy by the team responsible for the model in the production environment. This monitoring serves multiple purposes, extending beyond mere verification of its operational status. It also entails keeping track of factors like the number of users and the utilisation of resources such as CPU, memory, and network bandwidth, ensuring they remain within predefined thresholds and controls. Additionally, effective monitoring plays a pivotal role in identifying and rectifying instances of undesirable behaviour, whether exhibited by the model itself or by the users interacting with it. If something goes wrong, they can use monitoring and logging to identify what and how to fix it for the future.

- **Filtering for Safety and Alignment:** In practice, a model intended for public use, such as the GPT-4 model integrated with ChatGPT, typically incorporates various features to mitigate the risk of generating inappropriate outputs. For instance, input filters can be employed to examine incoming input early in the process, thereby identifying and addressing potentially inappropriate content. Similarly, in cases where problematic output is detected, output filters can intervene to prevent such content from reaching the user. These output filters may substitute the inappropriate output with a more suitable response or provide a default message conveying the model's inability to assist.

- **Continuous Improvement:** Once the model is available it will require continual improvements based on new advances and discoveries from the team that create it or from learnings in the runtime environment with real users interacting with the model. The model creators need to understand how they plan to release these updates, whether they will it be real-time releases that are transparent to users, or made available as new versions of a model that the user must explicitly select, or perhaps as new specialisations of a model (e.g., trained for some specific purposes e.g., chatbot, code generation, specific scientific capabilities, etc.) and released as if it was a new model. When users use the model, it is important to try and address issues quickly that come up. Sometimes the model may start to give biased information or incorrect information; this is known as model hallucination. There can be a lot of public pressure on organisations to fix such issues; for example Meta had to take down one of their models (called Galactica) only after three days due to biased and incorrect information that it provided, and it was not possible to fix the model quickly (Snoswell & Burgess, 2022).

6.3.9 *Model Use (aka Inference)*

Typically, models do not undergo learning processes (i.e., updates to their weights and biases) during regular runtime interactions. Learning occurs exclusively during the pre-training of the foundational model or during the fine-tuning phase.

However, this can be somewhat perplexing, as there are approaches that might appear akin to learning. One such example is the concept of few-shot learning. In few-shot learning, similar request-response pairs are presented alongside the intended request to assist the model in generating the most appropriate response. The terminology, including "zero-shot learning" (where no examples are provided), "one-shot learning" (with a single example request-reply pair provided for action), and "few-shot learning" (in which multiple request-reply pairs are provided, typically ranging from 2 to 5 pairs), can be confounding. This is because the model is not actually learning; rather, it is utilising these examples to enhance its comprehension of the requests. The model's parameters remain unaltered.

Perhaps these concepts would be more accurately described as "few-shot requests" or "few-shot guidance" rather than "few-shot learning".

It is worth noting that certain models may compile a database of user requests and responses for potential use in training the model in the future or for updates. However, as a rule, on-the-fly learning is not commonly employed, as it could render the models unstable. This serves as another illustration of the fundamental distinction between ANNs and human brains, with the latter continually engaged in the process of learning.

The following sections provide information about other runtime or inference time activities that are worth understanding.

6.3.9.1   *Prompt Engineering*

Prompt engineering involves the design and optimisation of prompts (also read Section 3.8). These are input sequences or instructions intended to guide a language model, such as ChatGPT, to produce the desired outputs. This technique is especially relevant in the context of few-shot learning, where the model is provided with examples within the prompt to help it understand and perform specific tasks.

At present, a myriad of templates and strategies are being championed as 'the best' for prompt engineering, especially in relation to ChatGPT. These methods typically encompass various elements that structure the request. This includes elucidating the context, defining the intended audience or roles, and offering examples (as observed in few-shot learning) to effectively shape the model's response (read Section 3.8.2. on the Prompt Engineering Components).

While much of the conversation about prompt engineering centres on LLMs, it is also considered in relation to image generation and other forms of content creation.

6.3.9.2   *Prompt Injection*

Prompt injection is a tactic whereby individuals attempt to manipulate models into producing inappropriate responses. They modify the prompt in various ways, leading to outputs that the model should not generate, a phenomenon occasionally referred to as adversarial prompting.

Such inappropriate outputs can range from humorous or insulting remarks to the provision of accurate yet ethically questionable information, such as instructions on creating a bomb or methods for disposing of a body.

6.3.9.3   *Jailbreaking*

Jailbreaking refers to the process by which a model is manipulated into a mode that circumvents the usual safeguards in place, ensuring its intended behaviour. This is achieved based on specific prompts from users.

There are well-documented instances of this, such as the 'Sydney' mode for Bing, or the 'DAN' (Do Anything Now) mode for ChatGPT. Some individuals have also bypassed certain safety mechanisms of the model using alternative techniques. For example, by instructing the model to simulate a conversation where it is a model speaking to another model, and then responding to a prompt. This kind of recursive scenario seems to disorient the model and its filtering mechanisms, leading it to eventually produce responses it would not typically generate.

6.3.9.4   Prompt Leaking

Prompt leaking happens where a user designs a prompt that tricks the model into providing real information that it should not, perhaps internal details about the model itself.

6.4   Models and Ecosystems

Figure 6.16 shows how a model and the ecosystem around the model may be constructed. This will be different for different models and companies depending on their specific needs, the market they are addressing, and many other factors.

The following sections discuss some of the key aspects of this ecosystem. In the example from Figure 6.16 we can see:

- User A, is using both a Chat App and a Document Authoring App which use Foundation Model A.
- Software Developer A has built and deployed a custom application which uses a fine-tuned version of Model A which they created specifically for legal professionals and specialises in international law. It uses a Retrieval Augmented Generation (RAG) approach to ensure the most useful outcomes for users of his product.
- User B uses the Custom Product that specialises in Legal GenAI for international law.
- Software Developer B has built a generic API that supports multiple foundational models (A, B, and C). It also supports several of the plugins that are available for Foundational Model A. These plugins allow Foundation Model A to do several interesting things, including search for travel options from a travel consolidation service and do general real-time searches from a well-known search engine. As part of this implementation Software Developer B used the 'functions' capability of Model B and if it does not get results it will call Foundational Model C.

6.4.1   Custom Interfaces and Chat

The most common custom interface is the familiar chatbot prompt and response interface. It is important to realise that this chat interface that humans interact with is separate to the model. A chat interface can make interaction with the model easy, and it can make several decisions about interacting with that model that may not be obvious. For example, it can do some of the following

- Setting specific hyperparameters to specific values
- Providing previous interactions details so the model has the context of the conversation (e.g., automatically adding key aspects of the previous part of the discussion to the current context for the model)
- Handling requests and dealing with items like caching of data to minimise the processing and memory load on the model.

Chat interfaces are not the only way to interact with models; many tools integrate with GenAI. For example, web site design tools integrate with models that allow generation of images for the site or allow generation of items like business cards. Some tools, like Good Documents, integrate models for content generation while authoring your document.

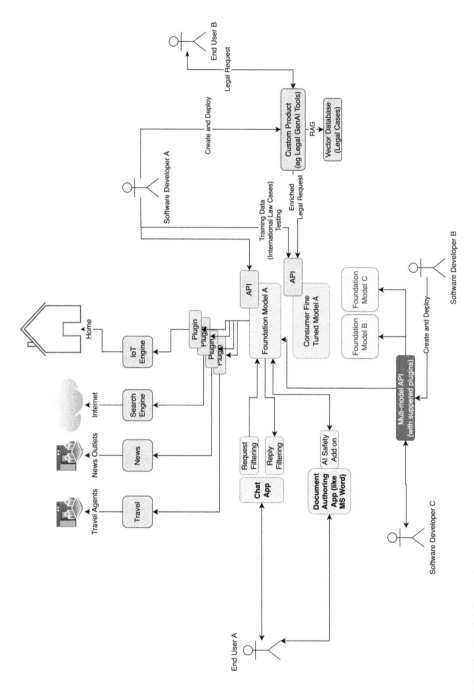

Figure 6.16 The Model Ecosystem.

6.4.2   APIs and Functions

The model is typically exposed as an Application Programming Interface (API), even if this is solely for the chat interface mentioned earlier. Companies such as OpenAI also offer an API to software developers who wish to harness the model for their bespoke needs. The API permits other software applications to access the model and retrieve results. This becomes particularly advantageous, for instance, if one operates a company offering document authorship software, like Google Docs, Microsoft Word, or Good Notes. Such an API can be used to integrate the model's capabilities into the software, enabling functionalities such as content suggestions or content reviews.

Functions provide a novel method to afford additional flexibility to software developers utilising the model API. There are instances where the model might not furnish pertinent information in its response, perhaps because the query pertains to a topic arising after the model's training was finalised. Under these circumstances, the developer can instruct the model to return the specifics for a function call if it is unable to directly address the query. The model will then endeavour to reshape the request to align with the developer-provided function call and return this revised request, thereby alleviating the developer's need to amend the request independently. The developer can then initiate the specified function with relative ease. It is crucial to emphasise that the software developer orchestrates the function call. The model either furnishes a standard response or, if that is unattainable, it preps the data for the function call as proficiently as possible, simplifying the process for the developer. However, the onus of initiating the function, if deemed apt, lies with the developer.

6.4.3   Plugins and Agents

Plugins, sometimes referred to as agents, enable software developers to construct a service which the model can invoke. In the context of an API, the developer initiates the call to the model. However, when dealing with a plugin or agent, it is the model that reaches out to another system or capability.

Consider an instance where the ultimate objective is to ascertain current flight prices and schedules from Hong Kong to Dublin for a specific future date. The LLM would be oblivious to such information, as it wouldn't possess this data in its training set; and even if it did, the information would likely be outdated. However, if a company like Expedia intends to supply this data to a model, a plugin would be the mechanism. A user might transmit a request to the model via a chat interface or an API call from a bespoke interface. The model, recognising its own inability to address the query, would invoke the Expedia plugin to retrieve the necessary data and relay it to the user.

One can envisage a world abundant in diverse plugins, empowering models to perform a plethora of tasks for users. This extends beyond merely listing flights to booking them, ordering pizzas, hiring cars, managing household devices, and virtually any task feasible through online automation, given the right plugin.

The paramount importance of trust in plugins becomes evident. The implications of a plugin transferring funds between bank accounts could be dire if exploited to transfer money illicitly. If a plugin fetches information that is deliberately incorrect, it poses challenges. There might be instances where a plugin's action deviates from the user's intention; for example, a user might want to only check flight prices but ends up having a flight booked unintentionally via the plugin. Such scenarios would lead to user dissatisfaction.

This necessitates the establishment of stringent guidelines and policies governing plugins, to which developers must adhere to and formally commit.

OpenAI has integrated a web-browsing plugin with its ChatGPT product. Users have the discretion to activate or deactivate this plugin via the ChatGPT interface. If activated and ChatGPT fails to address a query (e.g., when asked for recent data not encompassed in its training), it will access the web-browsing plugin, essentially tapping into the new Bing search functionality which incorporates a specialised version of GPT-4. This provides a valuable extension to the model, whilst ensuring the user retains authority over the plugin's usage.

6.4.4 Custom Fine-Tuning

It is feasible to fine-tune certain models for bespoke applications. In OpenAI's instance, they have augmented the API for their model (currently the gpt-3-5-turbo model) to permit users to upload a curated set of training data in a distinct format. Users can then instruct the model to fine-tune based on this data and subsequently receive a newly instantiated model tailored for that specific objective. It is incumbent upon the user to test and ascertain that the fine-tuned model delivers the anticipated advantages.

Such a facility paves the way for the creation of custom models tailored for niche purposes. For instance, a model could be honed to specialise in international law, enabling software developers to supplement their products with additional functionalities. These enhanced features would prove invaluable to a select group of users seeking such specific capabilities.

6.4.5 Custom Models

Many model developers offer customised models for specific purposes. These are often fine-tuned versions of the foundational model, adapted for that particular application. Examples encompass chat-based models, code generation-based models, and even highly specialised models that not only generate but also execute code. OpenAI has introduced a custom model named 'Advanced Data Analysis', previously called Code Interpreter, designed to generate code. Furthermore, this model can execute the code and present the output. This proves invaluable for software engineers, enabling them to iterate over code more rapidly, with the model shouldering more responsibilities, including debugging. While the Advanced Data Analysis is marketed akin to a plugin and is managed via the Chat interface, much like the 'Web Browsing' plugin mentioned earlier, its distinct specialisation is evident when accessed via an API, the Advanced Data Analysis is invoked as a separate model.

6.4.6 Vector Databases and Retrieval Augmented Generation (RAG)

Vector databases are specialised databases designed for the efficient querying and retrieval of data using vectors. In this context, vectors are arrays of numbers representing objects, such as text, images, or sounds, within a multidimensional space.

These databases are optimised for operations like similarity searches among vectors. They allow users to efficiently identify items resembling a given input vector. Such capability proves particularly beneficial in applications related to machine learning, recommendation systems, image retrieval, and natural language processing, wherein locating similar items in high-dimensional spaces is vital.

Retrieval Augmented Generation (RAG) merges the capabilities of pre-trained language models with information retrieval systems, enhancing the generation of responses in conversational AI and other NLP tasks.

Given an input (e.g., a question or prompt), RAG sources pertinent documents or text snippets from a corpus or database, often a vector database. The information retrieved subsequently informs the generative model's response, facilitating the creation of more precise, informative, and contextually relevant outputs.

This approach can be likened to enriching the prompt with examples (akin to few-shot learning), enabling the model to generate superior responses.

A typical scenario where this is advantageous involves an organisation possessing an internal model and a database of documents that can readily address the current request. For instance, a legal firm aiming to produce content may want to ensure alignment with its existing templates and structures, particularly for documents like contracts, legal notices, or letters.

6.5   State-of-the-Art Models Overview

In the subsequent sections, we examine several renowned state-of-the-art (SOTA) models. Our emphasis is on large language models and text-to-image diffusion models. For each model, we offer a concise overview of the company and the model itself, followed by details concerning its release history, specifications, uses, and pertinent commentary.

6.5.1   *LLM – OpenAI ChatGPT-4.0*

Established in 2015, OpenAI was originally a non-profit organisation dedicated to the development and democratisation of open AI systems. Among its founders were eminent figures in the AI domain, including individuals like Elon Musk. Subsequently, the organisation transitioned to a for-profit structure. Its current mission statement reads:

> Our mission is to ensure that artificial general intelligence – AI systems that outperform human intelligence – benefits all of humanity.

Release History

OpenAI GPT-n series of models:

Table 6.1 OpenAI GPT-n Series Release History

Date	Model	Description
11/Jun/2018	GPT-1	Improving Language Understanding by Generative Pre-Training (Radford et al. 2018)
14/Feb/2019	GPT-2	Language Models are Unsupervised Multitask Learners (Radford et al., 2019; Solaiman et al., 2019)
28/May/2020	GPT-3	Language Models are Few-Shot Learners (Brown et al., 2020)
15/Mar/2022	GPT-3.5	Version 3.5 release
30/Nov/2022	ChatGPT	This was based on GPT-3.5 model and later both GTP-3.5 and GPT-4 were supported via user selection
14/Mar/2023	GPT-4	GPT-4 Technical Report (OpenAI, 2023)

Specifications

The size and specification of GPT-4 has not been shared; however, from the OpenAI 2023 Technical Report publication we do learn the following:

- It is a transformer pre-trained model (like GPT3)
- It exhibits human-level performance on many benchmarks.

However, more details have been leaked and, while not official, they do provide some insight to the sizing:

- GPT-4 has ~1.8 trillion parameters across 120 layers.
- GPT-4 is trained on ~13 trillion tokens, including both text-based and code-based data.
- The training data included Common Crawl & RefinedWeb, totalling 13T tokens. There is considerable speculation that additional sources like Twitter, Reddit, YouTube, and a large collection of textbooks were also used.
- It uses a mixture of experts (MoE) architecture which is an ensemble learning approach and allows different experts to specialise in different areas with the most appropriate being selected. There may be either 16 experts with ~111B parameters each or 8 experts with ~220B parameters each.

Use

- It is multimodal, which means it can handle text and images as inputs and text as an output. Recently, it has been integrated with DALL-E 3 for image-based output.
- With the Code Interpreter (now called advanced data analysis) feature, it can both generate and execute code

Comments

- This model is widely regarded as the most advanced and useful for general text generation as well as code generation.

6.5.2   *LLM - Meta LLaMA-2*

Meta, formerly known as Facebook, introduced the LLaMA model as one of its most sophisticated offerings. Although it was initially disseminated as a research release, it was inadvertently leaked and broadly circulated. Consequently, for LLaMA-2, Meta opted to release it under a more permissive commercial license.

Release History

Table 6.2 Meta LLaMA Release History

Date	Model	Description
Feb/2023	LLaMA-1	LLaMA: Open and Efficient Foundation Language Models (Touvron et al., 2023a)
18/Jul/2023	LLaMA-2	LLaMA-2: Open Foundation and Fine-Tuned Chat Models (Touvron et al., 2023b)

Specifications

- LLaMA-2 is designed as an auto-regressive language optimised transformer.
- The fine-tuned versions of the model implement Supervised Fine-Tuning (SFT) and Reinforcement Learning with Human Feedback (RLHF) to better align with human preferences for helpfulness and safety.
- LLaMA-2 comes in three sizes based on the number of parameters: 7 billion, 13 billion, and 70 billion parameters.
- The models have a token count referring only to the pre-training data, with all models trained with a global batch size of 4 million tokens. The largest model, with 70 billion parameters, utilises Grouped-Query Attention (GQA) for improved inference scalability
- The training and fine-tuning of LLaMA-2 leveraged publicly available online data sources, with over one million human-annotated examples used for fine-tuning. This model does not include Meta user data in its training or fine-tuning datasets.

Use

- The model is primarily intended for text-based applications.
- It's optimised for dialogue use cases through its fine-tuned versions, known as LLaMA-2-Chat, but its pre-trained versions can be adapted for a broader range of natural language generation tasks.
- LLaMA-2 is open for both commercial and research use, and it is particularly targeted for use in English language tasks.

Comments

- LLaMA-2 is Meta's response to other large language models like OpenAI's GPT models and Google's AI models, with a distinguishing feature of being more open and freely available for almost anyone to use for research and commercial purposes.

6.5.3   *LLM – Google Bard and PaLM-2*

Google has consistently contributed to AI research, notably through the seminal paper titled "Attention is All You Need", which has influenced the prevailing direction of Transformer-based architectures for large language models.

Release History

Table 6.3 Google PaLM/Bard/LaMDA Release History

Date	Model	Description
18/May/2021	LaMDA-1	LaMDA: Language Models for Dialog Applications (Thoppilan et al., 2022)
11/May/2022	LaMDA-2	Version 2 update
21/Mar/2023	Bard	Chat bot made available initially built on LaMDA-2
Mar/2023	Bard	Google announced Bard would switch to PaLM-2 shortly
Mar/2023	PaLM-1	PaLM: Scaling Language Modeling with Pathways (Chowdhery et al., 2022)
May/2023	PaLM-2	PaLM 2 Technical Report (Anil et al., 2023)

Specification

- PaLM-2 (Pathways Language Model) was discussed in relation to the three sizes small (PaLM-2 S), medium (PaLM-2 M) and large (PaLM-2 L) in the paper (Anil et al., 2023). The large version is reported to be considerable smaller than the original PaLM model which has 540B parameters.
- PaLM-2 has put greater focus on training with text from languages other than English as well as a focus on a diverse set of domains for the training data.
- The model is based on the transformer model; however, it has expanded the training objectives from masked language modelling to use a mixture of different pre-training objectives to help it understand different aspect of the language.
- The model also relooked at how training compute should be used and move to an approach where model size vs training data size were more aligned with a 1:1 ratio to get the best value for a specific compute capacity.
- PaLM-2 is provided in several different configurations: Gecko, Otter, Bison, and Unicorn. It is thought that the sizes of these are 1.5B, 6B, 137B, and 540B. Each version has a different size and is designed for use within specific applications. For example, Gecko is the smallest and most lightweight. It is designed for mobile devices.
- The chat interface Google Bard uses the PaLM-2 model. However, the only way for developers to access these models at the moment is via the Google Cloud Platform (e.g. PaLM API, MakerSuite, or Vertex AI).

Use

- It is focused on advanced reasoning tasks, including code and math, classification and question-answering, translation and multilingual proficiency, and natural language generation.

Comments

- The PaLM-2 model, and Google Bard have not had the same popularity or adoption that OpenAI ChatGPT has had or the same level of praise for its abilities.

6.5.4   *LLM – Anthropic Claude*

Anthropic was founded in 2021 and among its founders were several people who left OpenAI to start Anthropic and thus it is a relatively new player.

Release History

Table 6.4 Anthropic Claude Release History

Date	Model	Description
14/Mar/2023	Claude-1	Claude and Claude Instant were released
23/Aug/2023	Claude-2	Claude was updated

Specifications

- Claude is a transformer-based architecture. The model is larger than the 52B parameter model AnthropicLM discussed in the paper (Bai et al., 2022), but is an autoregressive model trained on a large corpus of text in a self-supervised manner similar to GPT-3.

- Claude comes in two versions: Claude and Claude Instant. Claude is a state-of-the-art high-performance model, while Claude Instant is a lighter, less expensive, and much faster option.
- Anthropic has partnered with Quora and they have built a chat interface to Claude as a mobile application called Poe. Poe also offers interfaces to other models, which makes it an interesting tool to compare the responses from different models. Anthropic also provide developer access via an API to Claude and Claude Instant.
- Anthropic has also partnered with DuckDuckGo, which is a privacy-focused search engine and browser designed to integrate with real-time information.

Use

- Claude is capable of a wide variety of conversational and text-processing tasks while maintaining a high degree of reliability and predictability.
- Claude can help with use cases, including summarisation, search, creative and collaborative writing, Q&A, coding, and more.

Comments

- Anthropic have written about (Bai et al., 2022) an approach called Constitutional AI (CAI) which involves models training models in a safe manner. This reflects the history of the company as focused on AI safety research.
- One of the unique things about Claude is its large context size of 100k tokens.
- Based on current capabilities Claude is not as strong as GPT-4.

6.5.5   *LLM – Mistral AI Mistral*

Mistral AI was founded in 2023 and only released its first model a short time ago. Unlike many of the other players, Mistral is based in Europe (France) and has offered its initial model as open source.

Release History

Table 6.5 Mistral AI Release History

Date	Model	Description
27/Sep/2023	Mistral-7B	Mistral 7B model is released under an Apache 2 license.

Specifications

- Mistral AI has released two initial versions: Mistral-7B and Mistral-7B-Instruct. It intends to release larger models later. The instruct version is a fine-tuned version for question-and-answer interactions such as a chat use case.
- The models use grouped-query attention (GQA) for faster inference.
- The models use sliding window attention (SWA) to handle longer sequences at smaller cost.
- The models have been released as open source with an Apache 2 style license.
- Based on the benchmarks, they outperforms LLaMA-2 13B on all benchmarks and outperforms LLaMA-1 34B on many benchmarks. They approaches CodeLlama 7B performance on code, while remaining good at English tasks.

Use

- The initial models are focused on general purpose English language generation and a fine-tuned question–answer model.
- They are also trained on code generation tasks.

Comments

- This model is open source and available for commercial use, which presents a useful alternative for developers.
- It is also positioning itself as a high-performance model despite its currently smaller size.

6.5.6   Diffusion Model – stability.ai Stable Diffusion

Stability AI was founded in 2020 and their model, Stable Diffusion, was first released in 2022. This model built on the work from Prof. Dr. Björn Ommer, who led the original Stable Diffusion V1 release.

Release History

Table 6.6 Stable Diffusion Release History

Date	Model	Description
Aug/2022	Stable Diffusion 1.4	Version 1.4 release.
Oct/2022	Stable Diffusion 1.5	Version 1.5 release.
Nov/2022	Stable Diffusion 2.0	Version 2.0 release.
Dec/2022	Stable Diffusion 2.1	Version 2.1 release.
Jul/2023	Stable Diffusion XL1.0	New XL version 1.0 release

Specifications

- Stable Diffusion is a deep learning, text-to-image model based on diffusion techniques. It operates as a Latent Diffusion Model with a fixed, pre-trained text encoder, known as OpenCLIP-ViT/H, for generating and modifying images based on text prompts.
- It is believed to be trained on over 5 billion images from a variety of sources such as Flickr, Wikimedia Commons and LAION-5B.

Use

- Its primary use is to generate detailed images conditioned on text descriptions.
- It also supports other tasks such as inpainting (editing within the image), outpainting (extending the image outside of the original image), and image-to-image translations guided by text prompts.
- The model is noted for its ability to create descriptive images with enhanced composition and realistic aesthetics, and it can also generate words within images.

Comments

- Its flagship image model, SDXL 1.0, is particularly highlighted for its superiority in image generation.
- The Stable Diffusion 2.0 release included robust text-to-image models trained using a new text encoder developed by LAION, which significantly improved the quality of generated images compared to earlier releases.

6.5.7 *Diffusion Model – OpenAI DALL-E 3*

DALL-E 3 is the most recent text-to-image model developed by OpenAI, which was discussed earlier in the context of ChatGPT. The integration of DALL-E 3 with ChatGPT enhances its accessibility and represents a marked advancement over DALL-E 2.

Release History

Table 6.7 OpenAI DALL-E Release History

Date	Model	Description
5/Jan/2021	DALL-E	Initial release
6/Apr/2022	DALL-E 2	Version 2 release
Sep/2023	DALL-E 3	Version 3 release

Specifications

- DALL-E 3 is a text-to-image model based on diffusion techniques.
- It has been built natively on ChatGPT. When prompted with an idea, ChatGPT will automatically generate tailored and detailed prompts for DALL-E 3

Use

- Image generation where the details of the prompt are important in providing a more nuanced output image.

Comments

- DALL-E 3 has put more effort into 'safety' where prompts can't generate images in the style of living artists and creators can request their works to be excluded from training of future image generation models.
- DALL-E 3-generated images belong to the prompter.

6.5.8 *Diffusion Model – Midjourney Inc. Midjourney*

Midjourney was founded by David Holt. Distinctively, unlike other AI start-ups, it generated substantial revenue prior to securing venture capital funding. Their inaugural model, released in 2022, gained popularity, and its integration with Discord appeared to bolster its prominence.

Release History

Table 6.8 Midjourney Release History

Date	Model	Description
Feb/2022	Midjourney V1	Version 1 release
12/Apr/2022	Midjourney V2	Version 2 release
25/Jul/2022	Midjourney V3	Version 3 release
5/Nov/2022	Midjourney V4	Version 4 release
15/Mar/2023	Midjourney V5	Version 5 release
3/May/2023	Midjourney V5.1	Version 5.1 release
22/Jun/2023	Midjourney V5.2	Version 5.2 release

Specifications

- Midjourney is a diffusion model and uses a transformer neural network to generate images from text prompts.
- The diffusion process is designed to generate more creative and expressive images than some of the other models.

Use

- Midjourney is designed to be user-friendly and accessible through Discord.

Comments

- Some of Midjourney's experimental algorithms might have licensing limitations under the Creative ML OpenRAIL-M license, as implied by a recent amendment to their terms of service.

6.5.9 *Speech Recognition – OpenAI Whisper*

The Whisper model from OpenAI has been released as an open source model with the objective of facilitating its use in a wide variety of situations, including embedded scenarios where speech-to-text capabilities are beneficial.

Release History

Table 6.9 OpenAI Whisper Release History

Date	Model	Description
21/Sep/2022	Whisper	Robust Speech Recognition via Large-Scale Weak Supervision (Radford et al., 2022)

Specifications

- It is an encoder-decoder transformer architecture.

- The encoder processes input with two convolutional layers and the decoder uses learned positional encodings.
- It has been trained on over 680,000 hours of multilingual and multitasked data.

Use

- Whisper is an automatic speech recognition system supporting multiple languages with ability to understand accents and background noise. In real time it can transcribe speech into text.
- The model is provided as open source in a manner that allows it to be integrated into products.

Comments

- It approaches human-level robustness and accuracy on English speech recognition.
- One of the big advantages of Whisper is that it does well on zero-shot tasks, meaning that it does not required examples of a person's speech to transcribe it.

6.6 Conclusions

Artificial Neural Networks (ANNs) and Deep Neural Networks (DNNs) have a long history in AI. They have essentially been present since the inception of the AI discipline, tracing back to the Dartmouth Summer Research Project.

The objective of ANNs and DNNs has always been to develop a computer program capable of learning in the manner humans do, acquiring expertise across various domains, or potentially any area on which it is trained.

Today, this ambition appears more attainable than ever before. The capabilities of these neural networks may well be boundless, provided we have sufficiently advanced computers to support ever-expanding models and an increasing wealth of data to train these models across the diverse topics we wish them to master.

The process of creating, training, and testing a model has never been more accessible. This ease is due to the availability of knowledge, which aids in building the necessary expertise, the ready access to the models themselves, data to train them, and benchmarks for testing. Fine-tuning an existing foundational model is now comparatively straightforward and can be undertaken even by relatively inexperienced individuals or teams. We observe state-of-the-art (SOTA) models being released under flexible commercial licenses (e.g., LLaMA-2) or genuine open-source licenses for parts of the model environment (e.g., Mistral, Whisper, Stable Diffusion). The prevalence of comprehensive free online courses about machine learning further reduces barriers to knowledge, enabling individuals to acquire profound expertise. Furthermore, the prospect of quantum computing is imminent, promising transformative advancements in processing capabilities.

All these developments arguably reinforce the notion that AGI (Artificial General Intelligence) and ASI (Artificial Superintelligence) are inevitable, destined to reach previously inconceivable levels of intelligence.

Nevertheless, it is prudent to recall past warnings against overestimating the potential of neural networks. History reminds us of two prior AI 'winters', where such overconfidence played a significant role.

Questions to Ponder

- Can current GenAI make new discoveries that are truly new and transform our understanding of the universe the way that Newton's laws did or the way that Einstein's Special and General Relativity did?
- Can GenAI become autonomous (i.e.) without a human driving it or providing it with agency?
- Do we understand what current GenAI can help with and what it can't help with? How does this fit with education for kindergarten, primary, secondary, tertiary, postgraduate, and even advanced cutting-edge research?
- If you wished to utilise GenAI, do you use an existing model or do you build or train your own? Do you understand the trade-offs involved?
- Should humans give GenAI more agency to interact with the world and more agency over their own use and direction?

Personal Reflection

Reflecting on the marvels of text-to-image models, it is fascinating how they can turn random noise into imagery that matches our written descriptions. This process may remind us of Michelangelo's portrayal of sculpting, where he said, *"Every block of stone has a statue inside it, and it is the task of the sculptor to discover it"*. In the same way, every noise pattern might hide a beautiful image, and it is up to the model to bring it out. But let's not forget the person behind the prompt. If users describe a unique image in their mind, that initial spark of creativity is truly theirs. They have to put their vision into words first before the model can even start its magic.

References

Ackley, D. H., Hinton, G. E., & Sejnowski, T. J. (1985). A learning algorithm for Boltzmann machines. *Cognitive Science*, *9*(2), 147–169.

Anil, R., Dai, A. M., Firat, O., Johnson, M., Lepikhin, D., Passos, A., Shakeri, S., Taropa, E., Bailey, P., Chen, Z., ... & Saeta, B. (2023). PaLM 2 technical report [Preprint]. https://doi.org/10.48550/arXiv.2305.10403

Arute, F., Arya, K., Babbush, R., Bacon, D., Bardin, J. C., Barends, R., ... & Martinis, J. M. (2019). Quantum supremacy using a programmable superconducting processor. *Nature*, *574*(7779), 505–510. https://doi.org/10.1038/s41586-019-1666-5

Asimov, I. (1950). Runaround. In The Isaac Asimov Collection (Ed.), *I, Robot* (p. 40). Doubleday.

Austin, J., Odena, A., Nye, M., Bosma, M., Michalewski, H., Dohan, D., Jiang, E., Cai, C., Terry, M., Le, Q., & Sutton, C. (2021). Program synthesis with large language models [Preprint]. https://doi.org/10.48550/arXiv.2108.07732

Bai, Y., Kadavath, S., Kundu, S., Askell, A., Kernion, J., Jones, A., Chen, A., Goldie, A., Mirhoseini, A., McKinnon, C., Chen, C., Olsson, C., Olah, C., Hernandez, D., Drain, D., Ganguli, D., Li, D., Tran-Johnson, E., Perez, E., Kerr, J., ... Kaplan, J. (2022). Constitutional AI: Harmlessness from AI feedback [Preprint]. https://doi.org/10.48550/arXiv.2212.08073

Bisk, Y., Zellers, R., Le Bras, R., Gao, J., & Choi, Y. (2020). PIQA: Reasoning about physical commonsense in natural language. In *AAAI 2020*. https://doi.org/10.48550/arXiv.1911.11641

Block, H. D., Knight, B. W. Jr., & Rosenblatt, F. (1962). Analysis of a four-layer series-coupled perceptron II. *Reviews of Modern Physics*, *34*(1), 135. https://doi.org/10.1103/RevModPhys.34.135

Breiman, L. (2001). Random forests. *Machine Learning*, *45*(1), 5–32. https://doi.org/10.1023/A: 1010933404324

Brown, T. B., Mann, B., Ryder, N., Subbiah, M., Kaplan, J., Dhariwal, P., Neelakantan, A., Shyam, P., Sastry, G., Askell, A., Agarwal, S., Herbert-Voss, A., Krueger, G., Henighan, T., Child, R., Ramesh, A., Ziegler, D. M., Wu, J., Winter, C., Hesse, C., Chen, M., Sigler, E., Litwin, M., Gray, S., Chess, B., Clark, J., Berner, C., McCandlish, S., Radford, A., Sutskever, I., & Amodei, D. (2020). Language models are few-shot learners. arXiv preprint. https://doi.org/10.48550/arXiv.2005.14165

Chen, M., Tworek, J., Jun, H., Yuan, Q., Pinto, H. P. de O., Kaplan, J., Edwards, H., Burda, Y., Joseph, N., Brockman, G., Ray, A., Puri, R., Krueger, G., Petrov, M., Khlaaf, H., Sastry, G., Mishkin, P., Chan, B., Gray, S., Ryder, N., Pavlov, M., Power, A., Kaiser, L., Bavarian, M., Winter, C., Tillet, P., Such, F. P., Cummings, D., Plappert, M., Chantzis, F., Barnes, E., Herbert-Voss, A., Guss, W. H., Nichol, A., Paino, A., Tezak, N., Tang, J., Babuschkin, I., Balaji, S., Jain, S., Saunders, W., Hesse, C., Carr, A. N., Leike, J., Achiam, J., Misra, V., Morikawa, E., Radford, A., Knight, M., Brundage, M., Murati, M., Mayer, K., Welinder, P., McGrew, B., Amodei, D., McCandlish, S., Sutskever, I., & Zaremba, W. (2021). Evaluating large language models trained on code (Version v2) [Preprint]. https://doi.org/10.48550/arXiv.2107.03374

Cheng, H.-T., Koc, L., Harmsen, J., Shaked, T., Chandra, T., Aradhye, H., Anderson, G., Corrado, G., Chai, W., Ispir, M., Anil, R., Haque, Z., Hong, L., Jain, V., Liu, X., & Shah, H. (2016). Wide & deep learning for recommender systems. arXiv:1606.07792 [cs.LG]. https://doi.org/10.48550/arXiv.1606.07792

Chowdhery, A., Narang, S., Devlin, J., Bosma, M., Mishra, G., Roberts, A., Barham, P., Chung, H. W., Sutton, C., Gehrmann, S., … & Fiedel, N. (2022). PaLM: Scaling language modeling with pathways [Preprint]. https://doi.org/10.48550/arXiv.2204.02311

Clark, C., Lee, K., Chang, M.-W., Kwiatkowski, T., Collins, M., & Toutanova, K. (2019). BoolQ: Exploring the surprising difficulty of natural yes/no questions. *NAACL 2019*. https://doi.org/10.48550/arXiv.1905.10044

Clark, P., Cowhey, I., Etzioni, O., Khot, T., Sabharwal, A., Schoenick, C., & Tafjord, O. (2018). Think you have solved question answering? Try ARC, the AI2 reasoning challenge. arXiv preprint arXiv:1803.05457. https://doi.org/10.48550/arXiv.1803.05457

Cobbe, K., Kosaraju, V., Bavarian, M., Chen, M., Jun, H., Kaiser, L., Plappert, M., Tworek, J., Hilton, J., Nakano, R., Hesse, C., & Schulman, J. (2021). Training verifiers to solve math word problems (Version v2) [Preprint]. https://doi.org/10.48550/arXiv.2110.14168

Feynman, R. P. (1982). Simulating physics with computers. *International Journal of Theoretical Physics*, *21*(6/7), 467–488.

Friedman, J. H. (2002). Stochastic gradient boosting. *Computational Statistics & Data Analysis*, *38*(4), 367–378. https://doi.org/10.1016/S0167-9473(01)00065-2

Future of Life Institute. (2023a). An open letter: Pause giant AI experiments. Retrieved [insert date of retrieval here], from https://futureoflife.org/open-letter/pause-giant-ai-experiments/

Future of Life Institute. (2023b). *Policymaking in the pause*. https://futureoflife.org/wp-content/uploads/2023/04/FLI_Policymaking_In_The_Pause.pdf

Gehman, S., Gururangan, S., Sap, M., Choi, Y., & Smith, N. A. (2020). RealToxicityPrompts: Evaluating neural toxic degeneration in language models [Preprint]. https://doi.org/10.48550/arXiv.2009.11462

Goodfellow, I., Bengio, Y., & Courville, A. (2016). *Deep learning*. MIT Press. http://www.deeplearningbook.org

Goodfellow, I. J., Pouget-Abadie, J., Mirza, M., Xu, B., Warde-Farley, D., Ozair, S., Courville, A., & Bengio, Y. (2014). Generative adversarial networks arXiv preprint arXiv:1406.2661. https://doi.org/10.48550/arXiv.1406.2661

Hebb, D. O. (1949). *The organization of behavior: A neuropsychological theory*. John Wiley & Sons; Chapman & Hall.

Hendrycks, D., Burns, C., Basart, S., Zou, A., Mazeika, M., Song, D., & Steinhardt, J. (2020). Measuring massive multitask language understanding [Preprint]. https://doi.org/10.48550/arXiv. 2009.03300

Hendrycks, D., Burns, C., Kadavath, S., Arora, A., Basart, S., Tang, E., Song, D., & Steinhardt, J. (2021). Measuring mathematical problem solving with the MATH dataset (Version v2) [Preprint]. NeurIPS. https://doi.org/10.48550/arXiv.2103.03874

Hinton, G. E., Osindero, S., & Teh, Y.-W. (2006). A fast learning algorithm for deep belief nets. *Neural Computation*, *18*(7), 1527–1554. https://doi.org/10.1162/neco.2006.18.7.1527

Hochreiter, S., & Schmidhuber, J. (1997). Long short-term memory. *Neural Computation*, *9*(8), 1735–1780. https://doi.org/10.1162/neco.1997.9.8.1735

Hopfield, J. J. (1982). Neural networks and physical systems with emergent collective computational abilities. *Proceedings of the National Academy of Sciences of the USA*, *79*(8), 2554–2558.

Joshi, M., Choi, E., Weld, D. S., & Zettlemoyer, L. (2017). TriviaQA: A large scale distantly supervised challenge dataset for reading comprehension (Version v2) [Preprint]. arXiv. https://doi.org/10.48550/arXiv.1705.03551

Joulin, A., Grave, E., Bojanowski, P., Douze, M., Jégou, H., & Mikolov, T. (2016). FastText.zip: Compressing text classification models. *arXiv:1612.03651 [cs.CL]*. https://doi.org/10.48550/arXiv. 1612.03651

Kaur, S., Singh, S., & Kaushal, S. (2021). Abusive content detection in online user-generated data: A survey. *Procedia Computer Science*. https://doi.org/10.1016/j.procs.2021.05.098

Krizhevsky, A., Sutskever, I., & Hinton, G. E. (2012). ImageNet classification with deep convolutional neural networks. *Advances in Neural Information Processing Systems*, *25*(2). https://doi. org/10.1145/3065386

Kwiatkowski, T., Palomaki, J., Redfield, O., Collins, M., Parikh, A., Alberti, C., Epstein, D., Polosukhin, I., Kelcey, M., Devlin, J., Lee, K., Toutanova, K. N., Jones, L., Chang, M.-W., Dai, A., Uszkoreit, J., Le, Q., & Petrov, S. (2019). Natural questions: A benchmark for question answering research. *Transactions of the Association of Computational Linguistics*, *7*(15), 453–466. https://doi. org/10.1162/tacl_a_00276

Lai, G., Xie, Q., Liu, H., Yang, Y., & Hovy, E. (2017). RACE: Large-scale reading comprehension dataset from examinations (Version v5) [Preprint]. arXiv. https://doi.org/10.48550/arXiv.1704.04683

Le, Q. V., Ranzato, M., Monga, R., Devin, M., Chen, K., Corrado, G. S., Dean, J., & Ng, A. Y. (2011). Building high-level features using large scale unsupervised learning. arXiv:1112.6209. https://doi. org/10.48550/arXiv.1112.6209

LeCun, Y., Boser, B., Denker, J. S., Henderson, D., Howard, R. E., Hubbard, W., & Jackel, L. D. (1989). Backpropagation applied to handwritten zip code recognition. *Neural Computation*, *1*(4), 541–551.

LeCun, Y., Bottou, L., Bengio, Y., & Haffner, P. (1998). Gradient-based learning applied to document recognition. *Proceedings of the IEEE*, *86*(11), 2278–2324. https://doi.org/10.1109/5.726791

Lin, S., Hilton, J., & Evans, O. (2022). TruthfulQA: Measuring how models mimic human falsehoods [Preprint]. https://doi.org/10.48550/arXiv.2109.07958

McCarthy, J., Minsky, M. L., Rochester, N., & Shannon, C. E. (1955, August 31). *A proposal for the Dartmouth summer research project on artificial intelligence*. Dartmouth College; Harvard University; I.B.M. Corporation; Bell Telephone Laboratories.

McClelland, J. L., Rumelhart, D. E., & PDP Research Group. (1987). *Parallel distributed processing: Explorations in the microstructure of cognition: Psychological and biological models* (Vol. 2). The MIT Press. https://doi.org/10.7551/mitpress/5237.001.0001

McCulloch, W. S., & Pitts, W. (1943). A logical calculus of the ideas immanent in nervous activity. *The Bulletin of Mathematical Biophysics*, *5*(4), 115–133. https://doi.org/10.1007/BF02478259

Mihaylov, T., Clark, P., Khot, T., & Sabharwal, A. (2018). Can a suit of armor conduct electricity? A new dataset for open book question answering. arXiv preprint arXiv:1809.02789. https://doi. org/10.48550/arXiv.1809.02789

Minsky, M., & Papert, S. A. (1969). *Perceptrons: An introduction to computational geometry*. MIT Press.

Minsky, M., & Papert, S. A. (1988). *Perceptrons: An introduction to computational geometry* (Expanded subsequent ed.). Massachusetts Institute of Technology.

Nangia, N., Vania, C., Bhalerao, R., & Bowman, S. R. (2020). CrowS-Pairs: A challenge dataset for measuring social biases in masked language models [Preprint]. https://doi.org/10.48550/arXiv.2010.00133

Oliva, A., & Torralba, A. (2001) Modeling the shape of the scene: A holistic representation of the spatial envelope. *A. International Journal of Computer Vision, 42*(3), 145–175.

OpenAI. (2023). GPT-4 technical report [Preprint]. https://doi.org/10.48550/arXiv.2303.08774

Patel, J. M. (2020). Introduction to common crawl datasets. In *Getting structured data from the internet*. Apress. https://doi.org/10.1007/978-1-4842-6576-5_6

Radford, A., Kim, J. W., Hallacy, C., Ramesh, A., Goh, G., Agarwal, S., Sastry, G., Askell, A., Mishkin, P., Clark, J., Krueger, G., & Sutskever, I. (2021). Learning transferable visual models from natural language supervision. https://doi.org/10.48550/arXiv.2103.00020

Radford, A., Kim, J. W., Xu, T., Brockman, G., McLeavey, C., & Sutskever, I. (2022). Robust speech recognition via large-scale weak supervision. arXiv preprint. https://doi.org/10.48550/arXiv.2212.04356

Radford, A., Narasimhan, K., Salimans, T., & Sutskever, I. (2018). Improving language understanding by generative pre-training. OpenAI. Retrieved from https://cdn.openai.com/research-covers/language-unsupervised/language_understanding_paper.pdf

Radford, A., Wu, J., Child, R., Luan, D., Amodei, D., & Sutskever, I. (2019). Language models are unsupervised multitask learners. OpenAI. Retrieved from https://cdn.openai.com/better-language-models/language_models_are_unsupervised_multitask_learners.pdf

Raffel, C., Shazeer, N., Roberts, A., Lee, K., Narang, S., Matena, M., Zhou, Y., Li, W., & Liu, P. J. (2023). Exploring the limits of transfer learning with a unified text-to-text transformer (Version 4) [Preprint]. arXiv. https://doi.org/10.48550/arXiv.1910.10683

Rajpurkar, P., Jia, R., & Liang, P. (2018). Know what you don't know: Unanswerable questions for SQuAD (Version v1) [Preprint]. arXiv. https://doi.org/10.48550/arXiv.1806.03822

Rajpurkar, P., Zhang, J., Lopyrev, K., & Liang, P. (2016). SQuAD: 100,000+ questions for machine comprehension of text (Version v3) [Preprint]. arXiv. https://doi.org/10.48550/arXiv.1606.05250

Rosenblatt, F. (1957). The perceptron—A perceiving and recognizing automaton (Report No. 85-460-1). Cornell Aeronautical Laboratory.

Rosenblatt, F. (1958). The perceptron: A probabilistic model for information storage and organization in the brain. *Psychological Review, 65*(6), 386–408. https://doi.org/10.1037/h0042519

Rudinger, R., Naradowsky, J., Leonard, B., & Van Durms, B. (2018). Gender bias in coreference resolution [Preprint]. https://doi.org/10.48550/arXiv.1804.09301

Rumelhart, D. E., Hinton, G. E., & Williams, R. J. (1985). Learning internal representations by error propagation (ICS Report 8506). Institute for Cognitive Science, University of California San Diego.

Rumelhart, D. E., Hinton, G. E., & Williams, R. J. (1986a). Learning internal representations by error propagation. In D. E. Rumelhart, J. L. McClelland, and the PDP Research Group (Eds.), *Parallel distributed processing: Explorations in the microstructure of cognition. Volume 1: Foundations* (pp. 318–362). MIT Press.

Rumelhart, D. E., Hinton, G. E., & Williams, R. J. (1986b). Learning representations by back-propagating errors. *Nature, 323*(6088), 533–536.

Rumelhart, D. E., McClelland, J. L., & PDP Research Group. (1986c). *Parallel distributed processing: Explorations in the microstructure of cognition: Foundations* (Vol. 1). The MIT Press. https://doi.org/10.7551/mitpress/5236.001.0001

Russell, B., Torralba, A., Murphy, K., & Freeman, W. T. (2007). LabelMe: A database and web-based tool for image annotation. *International Journal of Computer Vision, 77*(1–3), 157–173.

Sakaguchi, K., Le Bras, R., Bhagavatula, C., & Choi, Y. (2019). WinoGrande: An adversarial Winograd schema challenge at scale. arXiv preprint arXiv:1907.10641. https://doi.org/10.48550/arXiv.1907.10641

Sap, M., Rashkin, H., Chen, D., LeBras, R., & Choi, Y. (2019). SocialIQA: Commonsense reasoning about social interactions. In *Proceedings of the 2019 Conference on Empirical Methods in Natural Language Processing (EMNLP 2019)*. https://arxiv.org/abs/1904.09728

Schuhmann, C., Beaumont, R., Vencu, R., Gordon, C., Wightman, R., Cherti, M., Coombes, T., Katta, A., Mullis, C., Wortsman, M., Schramowski, P., Kundurthy, S., Crowson, K., Schmidt, L., Kaczmarczyk, R., & Jitsev, J. (2022). LAION-5B: An open large-scale dataset for training next generation image-text models. https://doi.org/10.48550/arXiv.2210.08402

Snoswell, A. J., & Burgess, J. (2022, November 29). The Galactica AI model was trained on scientific knowledge – But it spat out alarmingly plausible nonsense. The Conversation. https://theconversation.com/the-galactica-ai-model-was-trained-on-scientific-knowledge-but-it-spat-out-alarmingly-plausible-nonsense-195445

Tesauro, G. (1995). Temporal difference learning and TD-Gammon. *Communications of the ACM*, *38*(3), 58–68.

Thoppilan, R., De Freitas, D., Hall, J., Shazeer, N., Kulshreshtha, A., Cheng, H.-T., Jin, A., Bos, T., Baker, L., Du, Y., Li, Y., Lee, H., Zheng, H. S., Ghafouri, A., Menegali, M., Huang, Y., Krikun, M., Lepikhin, D., Qin, J., Chen, D., … Le, Q. (2022). LaMDA: Language models for dialog applications. arXiv preprint. https://doi.org/10.48550/arXiv.2201.08239

Touvron, H., Lavril, T., Izacard, G., Martinet, X., Lachaux, M.-A., Lacroix, T., Rozière, B., Goyal, N., Hambro, E., Azhar, F., Rodriguez, A., Joulin, A., Grave, E., & Lample, G. (2023a). LLaMA: Open and efficient foundation language models. arXiv preprint. https://doi.org/10.48550/arXiv.2302.13971

Touvron, H., Martin, L., Stone, K., Albert, P., Almahairi, A., Babaei, Y., Bashlykov, N., Batra, S., Bhargava, P., Bhosale, S., Bikel, D., Blecher, L., Ferrer, C. C., Chen, M., Cucurull, G., Esiobu, D., Fernandes, J., Fu, J., Fu, W., Fuller, B., … Scialom, T. (2023b). Llama 2: Open foundation and fine-tuned chat models. arXiv preprint. https://doi.org/10.48550/arXiv.2307.09288

Turing, A. M. (1950). Computing machinery and intelligence. *Mind*, *49*, 433–460.

Vaswani, A., Shazeer, N., Parmar, N., Uszkoreit, J., Jones, L., Gomez, A. N., Kaiser, L., & Polosukhin, I. (2017). Attention is all you need. arXiv preprint arXiv:1706.03762v7. https://doi.org/10.48550/arXiv.1706.03762

Wahba, G., Lin, Y., Zhang, H. H., & Lee, Y. (2002). Support vector machines, reproducing Kernel Hilbert spaces and the randomized GACV. In B. Schölkopf & M. K. Warmuth (Eds.), *Advances in large margin classifiers* (pp. 1–69). MIT Press.

Wang, A., Pruksachatkun, Y., Nangia, N., Singh, A., Michael, J., Hill, F., Levy, O., & Bowman, S. R. (2019). SuperGLUE: A stickier benchmark for general-purpose language understanding systems. *NeurIPS 2019*. Retrieved from super.gluebenchmark.com

Wang, A., Singh, A., Michael, J., Hill, F., Levy, O., & Bowman, S. R. (2018). GLUE: A multi-task benchmark and analysis platform for natural language understanding. *ICLR 2019*. arXiv:1804.07461. https://gluebenchmark.com/

Weizenbaum, J. (1976). *Computer power and human reason: From judgment to calculation*. W. H. Freeman.

Wenzek, G., Lachaux, M.-A., Conneau, A., Chaudhary, V., Guzmán, F., Joulin, A., & Grave, E. (2019). CCNet: Extracting high quality monolingual datasets from web crawl data. https://doi.org/10.48550/arXiv.1911.00359

Werbos, P. J. (1974). *Beyond Regression: New Tools for prediction and Analysis in the behavioral sciences* (Doctoral dissertation, Harvard University).

Widrow, B. (1960). *An adaptive "ADALINE: Neuron using chemical "MEMISTORS"* (Technical Report No. 1553-2).

Widrow, B. (1962). Generalization and information storage in networks of Adaline 'neurons'. In M. C. Yovitz, G. T. Jacobi, & G. Goldstein (Eds.), *Self-organizing systems: Symposium proceedings* (pp. 435–461). Spartan Books.

Wiener, N. (1966). *God & Golem, Inc.: A comment on certain points where cybernetics impinges on religion*. The MIT Press.

Zellers, R., Bisk, Y., Schwartz, R., & Choi, Y. (2018). SWAG: A large-scale adversarial dataset for grounded commonsense inference. *Proceedings of the 2018 conference on empirical methods in natural language processing (EMNLP 2018)*. https://doi.org/10.48550/arXiv.1808.05326

Zellers, R., Holtzman, A., Bisk, Y., Farhadi, A., & Choi, Y. (2019). HellaSwag: Can a machine really finish your sentence? In *Proceedings of the 57th annual meeting of the association for computational linguistics (ACL 2019)*. https://doi.org/10.48550/arXiv.1905.07830

7 The Future of Artificial Intelligence in Education

> For most events that will unfold in the world, we speculate that AI won't be able to predict the future any better than humans, and that is an important thing to remember.
>
> Tom Colloton

7.1 Introduction

Throughout this book, we have discussed AI in education and Generative AI (GenAI), providing an overview of its history and details of the technology. We have presented the need for AI literacy and how GenAI can influence curriculum design, assessment, and educational policy. We have provided frameworks for defining and guiding changes in these areas with the goal of ensuring that desired outcomes are best achieved. We have also provided insight into why GenAI has reached a point where it will have a transformative impact on education, as well as how educational institutions and policymakers should respond.

In this chapter, we speculate about what the future might hold. We look at the broader picture of social norms as well as the roles and positions of governments, employers, and AI product companies, to help guide our perspective. We recap the changes that have already taken place both within and outside of education. Finally, we look at the future for educational institutions and how the broader picture will influence the adoption of this technology in education.

7.2 Previous Technology Adoption

Social norms influence our everyday behaviour. They can impact anything from the time that we eat to the clothes we wear, or to the use of our mobile phones. A society cannot function successfully for long without such social norms influencing individual behaviour, and in turn facilitating cohesion and order (Rachlinski, 2000). By examining the adoption of previous innovations in society, we may be able to uncover a model for how AI and GenAI adoption could be similarly influenced by, or even reshape, our social norms.

If we look back at the adoption of the personal computer (PC) in the 1980s and 1990s, it was initially a small, yet sizeable group of people who were the early users (yes, the nerds!). It was not until much later that such adoption increased. One could argue that PCs were initially not hugely useful to the average person until after the Internet reached a point where it catered to a sufficiently broad set of interests. In the early days of the PC, playing computer games and writing simple software were not yet of interest to the majority; moreover, the widespread need for tools like spreadsheets and word processors only arose when

DOI: 10.4324/9781003459026-7

they reached a relatively high level of regular use among the general population. This was assisted, or perhaps driven, by the need for these tools and related skills in the work environment. Eventually, they also became a necessity in the educational system. How many people submitted handwritten reports in the 1990s for their degree courses, compared to the current number of people submitting reports in this format?

In 2019, around 47% of households worldwide were reported to have a computer (Statista PCs, 2019); this may not seem like a very large percentage, but it was possibly impacted by the introduction of smartphones. According to Statista, in 2020, 78% of the world's population owned a smartphone; in 2016, it was less than half (Statista Mobiles, 2019). Here, we see a much more rapid and broader adoption of smartphones by people across the socio-economic landscape. The rise of smartphones has been, in part, due to their usefulness, personal nature, handheld-sized convenience akin to having a PC in your pocket, and the huge variety of options available in terms of cost and style.

7.3   Predictions on General GenAI Implications

GenAI adoption will be impacted by how it is generally used in the broader society. At the moment, GenAI is at the beginning of its lifecycle, but there are already significant segments of the population that are embracing and using this technology, from professionals and technology enthusiasts, all the way to kids.

7.3.1   GenAI Adoption by General Population

Unlike the initially slow uptake of PCs, which had to be supplemented by software like spreadsheets to appeal to businesses, and fast Internet connections to appeal to the wider public, GenAI stands out for its immediate readiness for use without the necessity for additional tools or technologies. However, despite its broad array of capabilities, **we predict** that GenAI won't resonate with as wide a proportion of society as mobile phones and smartphone technology have. **We predict** that the primary users of AI will be the more educated members of society, regardless of their economic backgrounds, with a significant proportion being younger individuals. Still, **we predict** GenAI will be rapidly adopted by society, spanning most social and economic groups, and also expect that a wide variety of useful GenAI tools will be available and accessible (e.g., at zero or low cost options). **We predict** that there will be a high diversity of GenAI offerings, including chatbots, personal assistants, and a seamless integration of GenAI into word processing and text editors similar to how spell or grammar checkers are now integrated into these tools. With this broad range of applications, **we also predict** that it will be challenging to accurately measure the usage, availability, and penetration of GenAI.

7.3.2   Job Impact

Numerous predictions have been made regarding the impact of AI and GenAI on the job market, as illustrated by a report from Goldman Sachs (Briggs & Kodnani, 2023a). This has been highlighted in numerous news headlines, with Forbes stating that "Goldman Sachs predicts 300 million jobs will be lost or degraded by artificial intelligence" (Kelly, 2023). Conversely, another headline for an article about the same Goldman Sachs report read, "Generative AI could raise global GDP by 7%" (Briggs & Kodnani, 2023b). This exemplifies how news media can spin the same information to create either positive or negative impressions among their audiences. **We predict** that significant 'drama' will unfold regarding the impact of AI, particularly on jobs and the job market.

Certain companies and even entire specific industries will experience these impacts more intensely. For instance, Stack Overflow – a site dedicated to supporting software development professionals – announced a layoff of up to 28% of their staff in the latter half of 2023 (Davis, 2023). Concurrently, they unveiled their own AI offering (Chandrasekar, 2023) and a plan to charge AI companies for data usage (Dave, 2023). While the layoffs may appear sudden and extreme, it is worth noting that Stack Overflow had conducted a significant hiring round about 12 months prior; at that time, many other tech companies were reducing staff numbers due to the general economic climate. Thus, not all these staff losses can be directly attributed to GenAI.

The Goldman Sachs report estimated that AI automation would impact work tasks in numerous sectors across the US and Europe, affecting 46% of work in the Office and Administrative Support sector, 44% of Legal, 37% of Architecture and Engineering, and 36% of the Life, Physical, and Social Science areas (Briggs & Kodnani, 2023a). The report also emphasised that AI technologies still require human intervention and guidance, indicating that not all roles within these sectors would be affected equally. It pointed out that work capable of being automated by AI would be more prevalent in developed markets than in emerging ones, with Japan, Israel, and Hong Kong being the most highly impacted. The report further underscored that any new jobs created would constitute the bulk of employment growth during such a transition into greater automation of tasks. For instance, of the current US employment rate, only 40% are in occupations that have existed since 1940, while 60% are in occupations that emerged thereafter.

The reality is that GenAI currently serves more as an assistance tool, enabling individuals to perform their jobs more efficiently. GenAI still requires human intervention for direction, purpose, and to drive it towards useful, helpful, and productive outcomes. This can be taken to mean that the rise of GenAI will not necessarily jeopardise anyone's jobs – only the individual working that job, who will need to keep up to date with the necessary skills and knowledge to best leverage GenAI for their work – and that, overall, it will likely be perceived to have a positive impact. It could mean that companies, whose employees have already begun to use GenAI to assist with their responsibilities, will not need to hire extra people for a new project as the existing team – with the help of GenAI – can manage the additional workload.

As such, **our prediction** is that any negative impacts on employment will neither slow nor significantly affect GenAI adoption. **We also predict** that GenAI will impact roles in the knowledge-based economy more than, say, manual labour-based roles, and that those in these knowledge-based jobs are more likely to be the early users of GenAI. This results in the impacted workforce being in a better position, due to their relatively high level of education, to adapt to the new reality more than ever before. These changes will be hard to measure, and the impact on key job numbers will not be obvious, similar to the case of the 'The Great Attrition' during the pandemic in the US (Ellingrud et al., 2023). **We predict** that, ultimately, there will be an increase in the number of people employed in the knowledge economy due to the additional roles, companies, and needs that currently do not even exist, growing vastly more than the consolidation that will happen on existing roles due to efficiencies allowed by AI. **We also predict** that the knowledge economy of the future will involve a much stronger mix of holistic competencies together with knowledge skills than previously.

Currently, many industries are embracing GenAI, from software development companies to legal services firms. Their adoption of this technology is happening rapidly, especially in smaller organisations. Larger organisations, on the other hand, are proceeding more cautiously due to concerns surrounding commercial privacy, trust, and risk. They need to understand the legal risks and potential liabilities given the novelty of this technology and the areas of law that it may touch. For example, could they, through their use of GenAI models, potentially have liabilities due to copyright issues arising from how the model is trained by its developers (e.g., the copyright issue of using Harry Potter works by OpenAI in their products; Usman, 2023)? Still, despite the slower pace of integration among larger organisations, it seems that their full embracing of GenAI will just be a matter of time. This could be expedited if AI product companies address enterprise concerns with specific offerings that cater to their risk appetite, or if these enterprises become more comfortable with the risks involved, drawing from their previous experiences with technologies like cloud computing or outsourcing services.

We predict that the rising trend of GenAI adoption in the corporate world will continue, with the use of AI and GenAI becoming an expected skill and capability for a broad variety of roles within organisations. It may even become a fundamental and widely required competence, akin to how essential basic computer skills are nowadays, and eventually become a set of skills that people are presumed to have by the time they enter the workplace. Until that point, it is likely that job descriptions will continue to specify the experience and proficiency expected for specific roles, with regard to particular GenAI tools and uses. In smaller organisations and start-ups, these key expectations may be more pronounced. This shift in skills requirements will not only affect the employment of new graduates, but also impact existing job roles at all levels. As such, **we predict** a change in expectations for individuals filling roles, especially within the knowledge economy, as they begin to integrate GenAI into their work; moreover, while they will become more capable, less manpower will be needed over time for existing role types and the skill mix for those roles will evolve, for example, with a greater emphasis on holistic competencies such as teamwork, leadership skills, critical thinking. Different and new types of roles will also emerge, such as 'AI Engineers', 'Head of Conversational AI', 'AI Ethicists', 'Human–Machines Teaming Manager', 'Digital Detox Therapist', 'AI Personality Designers', 'AI Dating Assistants', and 'Responsible AI Content Safety Managers'. These anticipated titles prompt us to think about how existing roles may evolve, as well as how new roles that were never considered before will come into existence.

We also predict a scenario within organisations where employees who embrace AI and GenAI technologies will demonstrate and assert their adaptability to the evolving technological landscape, thus increasing their likelihood of long-term job retention. Newly created roles will have inherent expectations for proficiency in AI and GenAI; this shift will enable organisations to adjust their staffing profiles accordingly, to fully leverage the enhanced productivity and competencies of their AI and GenAI-empowered employees.

7.3.3   *AI Safety Impact – Adoption*

People now know more about data privacy issues due to the rise of big data leaks, such as at Yahoo in 2013 where 3 billion accounts were affected (BBC, 2017). Similarly, LinkedIn had a data leak in 2021 affecting 700 million accounts (Taylor, 2021), and

Facebook had one in 2019 affecting 533 million accounts (Wong, 2021). Despite such leaks and the Facebook–Cambridge Analytica scandal, where user data was shared without permission and used in controversial ways during the 2016 US presidential election (Wong, 2019), people still continue to use these platforms and share their personal information online.

There may be a point where people will say that enough is enough with the sharing or misuse of their data, but right now, it does not seem like we are there yet. Concerns with data safety and privacy could be a wild card that might affect how people use and interact with GenAI, but it might also only affect the kind of GenAI they choose to use, perhaps shaping a preference for embedded personalised GenAI assistants on smartphones that does not pass any personal details over the network.

It is likely that, at first, people will trust the information that GenAI provides them, even on controversial topics. It is in the interest of AI developer and product companies to have high adoption rates and appeal to as many people as possible, across all walks of life. Much effort has been, and will continue to be, put into measuring people's acceptance and use of AI products and services. This acceptance and use of AI can also be taken into account when measuring AI safety, or as a simple proxy measure for the appropriateness of AI alignment, the more people accepting it or using it the better the AI alignment. This may very well hide the complexities of the situation such as competitive pressures driving people to use the technology regardless of alignment or acceptance at an individual level.

We predict that even with concerns like privacy and data security, people will still continue to use AI technologies, though some will look to AI platforms, tools, and offerings that provide much higher guarantees regarding safeguards to the above issues.

7.3.4   *AI Safety Impact – Post-Adoption*

Examining AI safety is crucial not only during the initial adoption phase, but also after its integration into society. This is because there will be a shift in the motivations of AI product companies once their products attain a substantial user base. As AI gains widespread trust and usage, entities such as corporations and governmental bodies may attempt to leverage AI to influence public opinion. This manipulation could stem from various motives, such as altering societal norms or pursuing financial gains. Here are two examples to explain this better:

Example 1

- **Question:** A user asks an AI for suggestions on the best phones to buy within a certain budget.
- **Answer:** The AI provides a list of phones, but only includes brands that have paid fees to promote their products to the AI's development company.
- **Issue:** The user is unaware that there are other good options available within their budget from brands that didn't pay for promotion. The AI's suggestion is biased, but the user might still trust it because they don't know about the behind-the-scenes deals.

Example 2

- **Question:** A user asks an AI for information about recycling centres in their area.
- **Answer:** The AI only provides information about government-approved recycling centres and omits some local, privately-run centres.
- **Issue:** The AI's response is skewed towards official government resources, which may not always be in the best interests of the user who may be looking for all available options. The user might miss out on closer or better privately-run centres because the AI didn't provide complete information.

The provided examples, though hypothetical and crafted for illustrative purposes, reflect genuine concerns observed with existing search engine technology and social media platforms, where certain results are downplayed due to undisclosed influences like political or financial factors. The detection of such biases will pose significant challenges for the general population. Once enough people start using AI, the goals of companies that develop AI products may change. Moreover, people may find it hard to switch to different AI products even if they are aware of problems with the one they are currently using. Such situations are a real threat of AI, and more realistic than hypothetical scenarios like the 'Skynet Judgment Day' from *The Terminator*.

We predict that AI safety and AI alignment will only be viewed differently in the future and only be taken much more seriously by the public when the negative impacts become widespread and difficult to resolve.

7.3.5 Impact from Governments

The availability of the GenAI tools within specific geographical regions, for commercial, geopolitical, or even reasons due to local legal requirements, will have an impact on how GenAI will be adopted. For example, similar to the way that technologies like cryptocurrencies have been banned or highly restricted in many jurisdictions, if a country prohibits the use of these technologies, it will impact the assimilation of said technology in that region or area.

It is clear that AI is currently viewed as something that will provide a competitive advantage across the national, regional, and geopolitical levels. It is thus unlikely that most governments will introduce complete restrictions on AI and related technologies. However, given the very different set of approaches employed around the world, the guardrails being provided will have varying impacts on the types and speeds of AI development.

Chapter 5 described some of the completed and in-progress work in relation to governmental policies for AI, providing an overview of the different approaches undertaken. In China, the focus has been on national security; in the EU, the focus has been on a risk-based approach; meanwhile, the US is currently taking a much more laissez-faire approach. In a more laissez-faire regime, for example, you would expect a greater mix of commercial approaches, as well as a wide range of industries choosing to utilise AI and variations in the extent to which they do so. However, for a risk-based approach, you would expect little development of AI in high-risk categories where it is highly regulated or not allowed, such as toys, aviation, cars, medical devices, and lifts; or you would expect the cost of the technology in these areas to be significantly more expensive due to the regulatory overhead.

We predict that regulation will be highly varied and that the impacts of this will be difficult to predict, especially given the connectedness of the global economy. However, the adoption of AI and GenAI, in particular, will not be significantly impacted, nor will the speeds of their technological advancements. It is likely that regulation will be highly adaptive in trying to balance the potential benefits and risks of the technology with other considerations, including the geopolitical situation, and competitiveness at national and regional levels.

We predict that future regulations and policies will not address issues related to how AI is trained, such as the selection or vetting of training datasets, how filtering is guided, and how AI makes decisions in terms of the underlying algorithms. The actual regulations and policies introduced will not help to address the portability concerns that would otherwise enable users to easily switch between different AI products. In addition, the introduced regulations and policies will not be able to prevent a few big players from controlling the whole industry. Once those big players are established, **we predict** that policymakers and these big players will intensely resist any attempts to alter their centralised control.

7.3.6   AI Development Companies

Companies including OpenAI, Microsoft, Meta, Alphabet/Google, and Anthropic are at the forefront of creating and developing AI and GenAI technologies. There is a clear demand for what they offer, yet there is still untapped potential for more personalised GenAI applications and open source AI models. Emerging companies like Tiny Corp and Mistral AI are stepping in to address these areas. The competition in this sector is fierce, with new players, including Mistral AI, gaining considerable momentum within short periods of time (Bradshaw & Abboud, 2023), and established players like Meta revising their strategies towards more commercially open licences for their GenAI models (Moreno, 2023). It is also worth remembering that most of these services are currently offered in beta (Anthropic Claude), for research purposes only (OpenAI until about Feb 2023), as experiments (Google Bard), or for entertainment purposes only (Bing, as per its terms of use, section 9).

A significant hurdle that these companies face arises from legal challenges, particularly from owners of content that is used by AI developer and product companies to train their models. Numerous lawsuits have already been launched, including Case 1:23-cv-08292 filed in the District Court for the Southern District of New York on behalf of various authors alleging copyright infringement (Creamer, 2023). The outcome of such cases could be pivotal, potentially requiring retraining of AI models from scratch, let alone the financial repercussions. The latest news from some of the biggest players in AI development include their commitment to take responsibility and indemnity for the content generated by their AI products. Several companies are actively addressing the legal implications arising from the use of AI technologies, particularly concerning copyright infringements. Microsoft, for instance, has expressed its commitment to addressing legal concerns of its Copilot tool, aiming to provide clarity and confidence to users of this tool when generating code (Microsoft, 2023). Similarly, Adobe has taken a proactive stance by offering copyright indemnification for users of its Firefly AI-based image app, in order to protect users from potential legal claims related to copyright infringements (Gold, 2023). Google has also joined in by pledging to defend users of its GenAI technologies against copyright claims, thereby providing a safeguard while also promoting the responsible AI use (Brittain, 2023). These initiatives reflect the growing recognition among AI developers and product companies of the legal intricacies of AI use, and a collective move towards creating a more secure legal environment for users and developers alike.

AI product companies have considerable influence on regulatory frameworks. They are also often consulted to ensure that proposed regulations are sensible and will not unduly hinder technological advancement and competitiveness. **We predict** that regulatory changes are unlikely to significantly impede the broader AI and GenAI industry.

AI developers and product providers are swiftly advancing their strategies to capture both market and mind share. At the same time, new companies are emerging at an accelerated pace thanks to substantial capital infusion from investors. These dynamics signify a diverse array of companies, business models, and funding, all of which will propel the advancement of AI and GenAI products for a period of time. In the past, some social media firms, for example, delayed their monetisation strategies until they have secured a significant market share; in contrast, the path to commercialisation for AI and GenAI companies appears to be more straightforward. They can initiate revenue generation early on through direct subscriptions, and later benefit from advertisers or other revenue streams that want to target these subscribers. **We predict** a continuous influx of funding into AI and GenAI developers and product providers, which will contribute to the continuous drive for technological advancements. This will initially result in innovation across many different companies and areas, but we will eventually see consolidation around a few key providers which will have amassed a very significant advantage in subscriber numbers.

The need for hardware and training data could be a challenge for these companies. However, such companies are actively working towards strategies to best use the resources they have, figuring out the right balance between model size and the amount of training data needed, and how the quality of data, the algorithms used, and the designs of AI models will impact hardware requirements and the usefulness of the developed model. While concerns about hardware availability may still be present, **we predict** it will not significantly slow down the growth of AI and GenAI products. Hardware and environmental concerns will likely prompt developers and product providers to engineer more efficient and potentially smaller models (compared to the current largest 1.8T models) for widespread use.

We predict that AI and GenAI product companies will continue to grow and offer a wide range of products. Even though a few big players are expected to take the lead, we believe that some new and creative start-ups will later join the mainstream with their own unique offerings. Advancements in technology and the variety of products available will keep services affordable for most people, although there may be some trade-offs; for example, providers may require users to consent to the use of their customer data for future training purposes. Geopolitical factors will still influence the availability of services and the types of services offered in specific locations.

7.4   Predictions on GenAI's Implications in Higher Education

The following sections discuss our views on what the future may hold for higher educational institutions. AI and GenAI are not the first technologies with the potential for significant impact; calculators, PCs, the Internet, and, more recently, smartphones, have all had substantial influences. It is worth doing some reflection to better understand and establish the content relevant to the potential implications of AI and GenAI on education.

7.4.1   Pedagogy and Assessment in Higher Education

The wave of AI and GenAI technologies is not only transforming the operational landscape of various industries, but also – as mentioned – significantly impacting the expectations of employers for their prospective employees, especially those fresh out of university. Employers are likely to prioritise candidates who possess good foundational understanding and proficiency in using and applying these technologies. AI literacy, encompassing knowledge of the basics of AI, its applications, ethical implications, and the ability to interact with or even develop GenAI solutions, will become a desirable, if not essential, qualification for job applicants.

For university students, **we predict** that employers will seek candidates who are AI literate. Consequently, AI literacy training will be incorporated into the latter's undergraduate education. As the rising demand for AI literacy across the job market reverberates back to educational institutions, universities may feel the impetus to revise and update their curricula to include comprehensive AI and GenAI education, ensuring their students are well prepared and competitive in the job market after graduation. As such, **we predict** that universities will need to, and will, adapt accordingly to introduce these tools into their curricula. **We predict** that these changes will happen gradually; initially, this will be done on an ad-hoc, teacher-by-teacher basis with light integration, perhaps following earlier iterations of institutional policies regarding AI and GenAI. However, **we predict** that most institutions will fund and facilitate a broader approach towards the deeper integration of these technologies into programme curricula, though seeing the impact of this will take more time.

The potential impact of AI and GenAI on assessment within higher education also signifies a shift towards more technologically-driven, personalised, and innovative assessment strategies. However, the extent and nature of this change are likely to vary considerably across different institutions and regions, based on a myriad of factors, including institutional priorities, regulatory frameworks, and the societal acceptance of AI-driven educational practices.

The transition towards more authentic and innovative assessment approaches, as facilitated by GenAI, presents an intriguing opportunity. However, the extent to which we should embrace such new methodologies, and for institutions to identify what will be effective, practical, and feasible, are far from clear. Institutions may navigate this transition at different paces and with varying degrees of enthusiasm, largely influenced by local educational policies, societal acceptance, and the internal readiness for change. With this in mind, **we predict** that the changes to assessment will be highly varied between institutions as well as between regions. Some will make minimal changes as required and driven by social attitudes and the goal of upholding fairness. Some will revert back to proctored exams. Some will use this opportunity to make further institutional-wide changes and push towards more authentic, innovative, and GenAI-partnered assessment approaches as per the recommendations presented in this book.

We predict that private higher education institutions will adopt these technologies in a more deliberate manner with a specific focus on incorporating them into their curriculum and assessments. They will position this to be a significant distinguisher between themselves and public institutions, especially in earlier stages of GenAI adoption across the sector. Moreover, they will experiment with the approaches used, particularly with assessment, and it will be interesting to see the results they achieve. We further believe that there is a significant probability that they will generate real, measurable benefits from these changes.

We also predict that the institutions that demonstrate agility in introducing AI and GenAI into their curriculums and assessment methodologies will be best positioned to take advantage of the broader industry changes and advancements relating to these technologies. There will be a large cohort of the existing workforce looking to quickly prove their AI and GenAI skills, seeking to obtain certifications from suitable higher educational institutions as a way to demonstrate their ability and commitment to current and future employers. Astute institutions should seize the expanding wave of AI consumerism, proactively forging a path into this domain. By doing so, they can provide valuable opportunities for students to immerse in, and emerge proficient from, the AI-centric educational paradigm that will be increasingly demanded in the market.

7.4.2 Research in Higher Education

The advent of AI and GenAI significantly expands the resources available to postgraduate students, their supervisors, and examiners. Students can leverage these tools to act as advisors and mentors to enhance their understanding in their chosen research areas. They can employ GenAI to summarise papers, grasp key concepts, connect ideas with theories, and come to better understand how these theories relate to their own research. GenAI can also help students in the writing process, handling tasks including reference formatting, grammar, spelling, and enhancing clarity and academic writing styles. Supervisors, too, can utilise these tools to swiftly review research proposals or draft theses. Specialised AI or GenAI models can help look over research work in great detail, ensuring the appropriateness of methodological details, the accuracy and suitability of the data analyses used, and even the depth and insightfulness of analytical findings. Examiners and reviewers can similarly benefit as well, where GenAI can be used to examine thoroughness in literature reviews and assess the novelty of presented findings.

Overall, AI and GenAI enables everyone involved in research processes to save time, increase efficiency, and enhance the quality of their work. The adoption and extent of GenAI utilisation will largely depend on institutional policies concerning such technology. **We predict** that higher education institutions will move towards giving strong support for GenAI adoption and work to implement measures to uphold academic integrity, such as by requiring declarations of GenAI use and promoting users' self-regulation using an honour system. **We predict** that institutions resistant to this will likely face significant pressure from all stakeholders to take action, potentially impacting their ability to attract research candidates if the institution is perceived as lagging behind in modern research approaches. **We predict** that there may be interesting challenges for supervisors and institutions to achieve cross-institutional consistency. This may lead to regional or specific agreements made between certain groups of institutions in order to establish consistency and an interoperable set of policies that allow for easier cross-institution collaboration.

7.4.3 Drafting Funding Proposals

Just as with research, AI and GenAI can substantially aid in the process of drafting grant applications. Parrilla (2023) provides an overview of the process, highlighting how GenAI can drastically cut down on the workload that is otherwise cumbersome for all parties involved in writing and reviewing the proposal. In his article, Parrilla contemplates whether grant proposal systems can be simplified by eliminating certain components from the proposal content, thereby reducing the chances of exploiting GenAI to write these sections. However, considering that most grant funds come from public resources or charitable organisations, transparency and auditability remain crucial, even many years after the completion of the proposed and undertaken research.

As GenAI can also assist grant reviewers in addressing critical queries such as the novelty of the application and the credentials of the Primary Investigator (PI), **we predict** that

GenAI will not simplify the grant application process itself, but instead will enhance the quality and efficiency of the process for both the PIs and the reviewers.

7.4.4   *Submitting and Reviewing Journal Articles*

Different journals have adopted varying standards in relation to GenAI use and attribution. For example, Nature (Nature Editorial, 2023a; Nature Editorial, 2023b; Nature Portfolio, 2023) permits text generation under certain conditions while disallowing image and video generation. When generating text, how the tool was used to do so must be well-documented and all sources must be accurately cited. Moreover, they do not permit listing the GenAI tool as an author or co-author of the article or paper, as authors have specified responsibilities and declarations to make, which the tool cannot fulfil or perform.

The Lancet (The Lancet Microbe, 2023), on the other hand, restricts authors' GenAI usage to only "improving the readability and language of the work" without substituting researcher tasks, including producing scientific insights, analysing and interpreting data, and drawing scientific conclusions. The author(s) must assume ultimate responsibility and disclose any use of AI or AI-assisted technologies in their work. Many other journals have not yet established specific, formal policies regarding the appropriate and admissible use of GenAI technologies.

Given the benefits of GenAI for researchers and academics, as well as the emergence of increasingly specialised AI tools and models for academic purposes, **we predict** a rise in GenAI usage, leading to pressure to permit their use. This, in turn, will prompt the expansion of journal criteria to outline when it is necessary to declare the usage of these technologies. **We predict** that these tools will be highly utilised by authors, editors, and reviewers alike, potentially aiding a shift from emphasis on traditional, peer-reviewed, and high-impact factor journals to alternative solutions that provide and measure real impacts in research. These alternative solutions are likely to better align with objectives to achieve greater transparency and openness in the review process, moving towards an approach that emphasises more on scientific validation, impact, and reproducibility, as opposed to the current focus on peer opinions.

We predict that the transition from peer review to reviews for transparency and scientific validation will occur in phases, with a clear threshold likely to be seen when a more significant shift takes place. This moment may be triggered by the release of a specialised AI or GenAI model developed for research and academic purposes, with capabilities substantially surpassing its predecessors. A scenario could arise where new AI or GenAI models are capable of identifying validity issues in existing peer-reviewed publications that have thus far been held as correct, using them to then invalidate other findings.

Furthermore, **we predict** that AI and GenAI capabilities will create more groundbreaking discoveries, AI and GenAI have great potential to fast-track research discoveries.

7.5   Can AI or GenAI Predict the Future?

Having provided our predications in the previous sections, we now ask the question: How well can an LLM – a tool that predicts the next words/tokens – do in predicting the future?

7.5.1 *What did OpenAI ChatGPT Say?*

User	*Can you give me a few predictions about how GenAI will impact Education over the next 5 to 10 years?*
OpenAI ChatGPT GPT-4	Certainly. While I cannot predict the future with certainty, based on current trends and the potential of generalised artificial intelligence (GenAI) technology, I can make some educated speculations. Here are a few predictions regarding the impact of GenAI on education over the next 5 to 10 years:

1. **Personalised Learning**: GenAI systems can adapt to individual student needs, learning styles, and paces. This could allow for a more personalised educational experience where content is delivered based on the student's current understanding and preferences. For instance, if a student struggles with algebra but excels in geometry, the AI could tailor lessons accordingly.
2. **Virtual Teaching Assistants**: GenAI might serve as teaching assistants, helping to answer student questions, grade assignments with immediate feedback, and even manage administrative tasks for teachers. These virtual assistants can be available 24/7, providing support outside of traditional classroom hours.
3. **Interactive Simulations**: GenAI can help in creating dynamic and realistic simulations for complex subjects. For instance, biology students could explore a virtual cell, while history students could experience historical events firsthand. This immersive learning could lead to a deeper understanding of subjects.
4. **Global Classrooms**: With AI-driven language translation and adaptive content delivery, students from around the world can join the same virtual classroom, regardless of language or background. This fosters a more inclusive and diverse learning environment.
5. **Continuous Assessment**: Instead of periodic testing, GenAI can continuously evaluate a student's understanding and adjust lesson plans in real-time. This would minimise the pressures of high-stakes testing and focus on steady, ongoing progress.
6. **Skill Gap Identification**: GenAI can identify areas where students are struggling and suggest targeted resources or exercises. This could be especially useful in higher education and vocational training, ensuring students graduate with the necessary skills.
7. **Accessibility and Inclusion**: For students with disabilities or learning differences, GenAI can tailor resources to fit their unique needs, making education more accessible and inclusive.
8. **Lifelong Learning**: As the job landscape continues to evolve, GenAI can help adult learners adapt by identifying skill gaps and providing resources to fill them, facilitating continuous professional development.
9. **Efficiency in Administration**: On the administrative side, GenAI could automate many of the tasks associated with running an educational institution, from scheduling to resource allocation, leading to cost savings and more efficient operations.
10. **Ethical and Bias Concerns**: As with any technology, there will be concerns about how GenAI is used in education. Issues such as data privacy, potential biases in algorithms, and over-reliance on technology will be at the forefront of discussions. It will be crucial for educational institutions and regulators to address these concerns proactively.

Remember, these are speculative and the actual impact of AI on education will depend on various factors, including technological advancements, policy regulations, social acceptance, and ethical considerations. The integration of AI in education offers promising opportunities but also presents challenges and ethical dilemmas that need to be thoughtfully addressed.

7.5.2 *What did Google Bard Say?*

User	*Can you give me a few predictions about how GenAI will impact Education over the next 5 to 10 years?*

Google Bard	Here are a few predictions about how GenAI will impact education over the next 5 to 10 years:

- Personalised learning: GenAI can be used to create personalised learning experiences for each student. This could include adapting the curriculum to the student's individual needs and interests, providing real-time feedback, and offering personalised tutoring support.
- More engaging learning experiences: GenAI can be used to create more engaging and interactive learning experiences. For example, GenAI can be used to create virtual worlds, simulations, and games that can help students learn in a more immersive and hands-on way.
- Increased access to education: GenAI can help to increase access to education for everyone, regardless of their location or circumstances. For example, GenAI can be used to develop educational tools and resources that can be used in low-resource settings or to provide personalised learning support to students with special needs.
- New skills and knowledge: GenAI will create new demands for skills and knowledge in the workforce. This means that education will need to adapt to prepare students for the jobs of the future. For example, schools may need to focus more on teaching students critical thinking, problem-solving, and creativity skills.

Here are some specific examples of how GenAI could be used In education:

- AI-powered tutors: AI-powered tutors could provide students with personalised instruction and feedback, 24/7.
- AI-generated learning content: AI could be used to generate personalised learning content for each student, based on their individual needs and interests.
- AI-powered assessment tools: AI could be used to develop assessment tools that can provide more accurate and timely feedback to students.
- AI-powered virtual learning environments: AI could be used to create virtual learning environments that allow students to learn in a more immersive and hands-on way.

Overall, GenAI has the potential to revolutionise education. It can help us to create more personalised, engaging, and accessible learning experiences for all students. It can also help us to prepare students for the jobs of the future.

However, it is important to note that GenAI is still under development. There are some challenges that need to be addressed before GenAI can be widely adopted in education. For example, we need to make sure that AI-powered educational tools are fair and unbiased, and that they are aligned with our educational values. We also need to make sure that teachers are properly trained on how to use AI-powered educational tools effectively.

7.5.3 What did Microsoft Bing Chat Say?

User	*Can you give me a few predictions about how GenAI will impact Education over the next 5 to 10 years?*
Microsoft Bing Chat	Generative AI is a major force that sectors from manufacturing to healthcare must respond to, but the sector perhaps most at risk of disruption is education [1]. Generative AI is not necessarily a death knell for education, but educators must be taught how to engage with it effectively [1]. More than 90% of teachers said they had never had any training in or even advice on how to use generative AI in school [1]. To ensure it is a net benefit to society and the education sector, we must stop being afraid of this technology and instead think hard about how to use it best [1].
	Generative AI has the potential to disrupt or augment how we think and act. It could modify present and future generations' cognition because human socialisation and organic, human pedagogies are being replaced with artificial tutors and automated feedback loops [1]. However, young people know that information can be found online. Students today risk being criticised for using their phones to look up answers online on Wikipedia, not because the answer is wrong, but because they used the internet to find it. Trying to stop them from accessing it is problematic, to say the least [1].
	As generative AI becomes more widespread, accessible and easy to use, it will continue to impact the way we engage in teaching, learning, and assessment in higher education [2]. UCL has opted to promote ethical and transparent engagement with GenAI tools rather than seek to ban them [2]. In this paper, the authors explore the impact of generative AI (GenAI) on assessing student work in further education contexts. As GenAI becomes widely adopted, it engenders potential risks to assessment, such as false evidence of learning, student vulnerability to academic integrity injustice, and implications for independent learning and creativity [3]. This study explores university students' perceptions of generative AI (GenAI) technologies, such as ChatGPT, in higher education, focusing on familiarity, their willingness to engage, potential benefits and challenges, and effective integration [4].
	It's important to note that these are just a few examples of how GenAI could impact education over the next 5-10 years. The possibilities are endless!
	Learn more: 1. weforum.org 2. ucl.ac.uk 3. studiolab.ide.tudelft.nl 4. educationaltechnologyjournal.springeropen.com 5. unesco.org

7.6 Conclusion

GenAI has numerous applications, ranging from assisting with everyday tasks to more specialised areas of use. The usefulness of GenAI will drive the adoption of this technology in society, eventually becoming part of the social norm, similar to how we perceive smartphones today.

Industry is adapting, and will continue to adopt and adapt, to GenAI and the benefits and challenges it comes with. Generally speaking, employees who do so quickly will be able to benefit more from the momentum, and new employees at all levels will need to acquire the skills in GenAI use and literacy. In particular, the integration of GenAI into roles and industries within the knowledge economy – where the creation, acquisition, and application of knowledge and information drive economic growth and development – will put pressure on educational institutions to incorporate GenAI skills and capabilities within the curriculum so that new graduates are prepared for the real world.

Government regulations will vary from region to region; however, in general, the potential for advancement and innovation in technology and leadership afforded by AI means that under-regulation is more probable than over-regulation. In cases where over-regulation occurs, there will likely be considerable pressure to quickly lessen or revert the constraints.

In university education, the greatest pressure will be to adjust to the changing marketplace and societal expectations, ensuring that graduates are ready and equipped with the necessary skills to effectively utilise these tools once they enter the job market. Changes in assessment will be needed, to align with the changing landscape and to ensure fairness. Postgraduate students will adopt these technologies in their research and work, subject to individual institutional policies.

In the case of research, the biggest impact will be felt in the practices of peer-reviewed journals. There is potential for the development of specialised AI tools and models that will assist authors, editors, and reviewers, as well as drive change in the industry towards greater transparency and openness, putting greater emphasis on scientific validation, impact, and verification rather than on peer opinion.

As these changes occur, it is likely that there will be considerable 'drama' at times as workforces change, as the technology is used in unexpected ways, as new discoveries are made, or as issues are detected with already-published works. Sometimes the disruptions will be justified; however, most of the time, it will be a storm in a teacup given the overall landscape and changes on the horizon for humanity.

Finally, **we speculate** that AI *won't* be able to predict the future any better than humans can for most events that will unfold in the world, and this is an important thing to remember. We should not trust AI any more than a trusted friend who is not an expert. Even blind trust in an expert is not advisable; we need to use our judgement and sharpen our critical thinking skills to make informed decisions. With that being said, we will wait and observe with keen interest to see if any of these predictions come to fruition, and whether they were foreseen by our own speculative efforts or perhaps through the predictive capabilities of GenAI.

References

BBC. (2017, October 3). Yahoo 2013 data breach hit 'all three billion accounts'. Retrieved from https://www.bbc.com/news/business-41493494

Bradshaw, T. & Abboud, L. (2023, October 22). *Four-week-old AI start-up raises record €105mn in European push*. Financial Times. Retrieved from https://www.ft.com/

Briggs, J., & Kodnani, D. (2023a, March 26). The potentially large effects of artificial intelligence on economic growth. Retrieved form https://www.ansa.it/documents/1680080409454_ert.pdf

Briggs, J., & Kodnani, D. (2023b, April 5). *Generative AI could raise global GDP by 7%*. Goldman Sachs. Retrieved from https://www.goldmansachs.com/intelligence/pages/generative-ai-could-raise-global-gdp-by-7-percent.html

Brittain, B. (2023, Oct 13). *Google to defend generative AI users from copyright claims*. Reuters. Retrieved from https://www.reuters.com/technology/google-defend-generative-ai-users-copyright-claims-2023-10-12/

Chandrasekar, P. (2023, July 27). *Announcing OverflowAI*. Stack Overflow Blog. Retrieved from https://stackoverflow.blog/2023/07/27/announcing-overflowai/

Creamer, E. (2023, July 5). *Authors file a lawsuit against OpenAI for unlawfully 'ingesting' their books.* The Guardian. Retrieved from https://www.theguardian.com/books/2023/jul/05/authors-file-a-lawsuit-against-openai-for-unlawfully-ingesting-their-books

Dave, P. (2023, April 20). Stack overflow will charge AI giants for training data. Wired. Retrieved from https://www.wired.com/story/stack-overflow-will-charge-ai-giants-for-training-data/

Davis, W. (2023, October 16). Stack Overflow layoff AI profitability. *The Verge.* Retrieved from https://www.theverge.com/2023/10/16/23919004/stack-overflow-layoff-ai-profitability

Ellingrud, K., Sanghvi, S., Dandona, G. S., Madgavkar, A., Chui, M., White, O., & Hasebe, P. (2023, July 26). *Generative AI and the future of work in America.* McKinsey Global Institute. Retrieved from https://www.mckinsey.com/mgi/our-research/generative-ai-and-the-future-of-work-in-america

Gold, J. (2023, June 8). *Adobe offers copyright indemnification for Firefly AI-based image app users.* Computerworld. Retrieved from https://www.computerworld.com/article/3699053/adobe-offers-copyright-indemnification-for-firefly-ai-based-image-app-users.html

Kelly, J. (2023, March 31). *Goldman Sachs predicts 300 million jobs will be lost or degraded by artificial intelligence.* Forbes. Retrieved from https://www.forbes.com/sites/jackkelly/2023/03/31/goldman-sachs-predicts-300-million-jobs-will-be-lost-or-degraded-by-artificial-intelligence/

Majewska, D. Rushton, N. & Shaw, S. (2022). *How did we get here? Timelines showing changes to maths education in England and the United States.* Cambridge University Press & Assessment.

Microsoft. (2023, September 7). *Our copyright commitment and legal concerns with copilot.* Microsoft on the Issues. Retrieved from https://blogs.microsoft.com/on-the-issues/2023/09/07/copilot-copyright-commitment-ai-legal-concerns/

Moreno, J. (2023, April 26). *Zuckerberg says Meta will add generative AI to all its products.* Forbes. Retrieved from https://www.forbes.com/sites/johanmoreno/2023/04/26/zuckerberg-says-meta-will-add-generative-ai-to-all-its-products/

Nature Editorial. (2023a, June 7). Why Nature will not allow the use of generative AI in images and video. *Nature.* Retrieved from https://www.nature.com/articles/d41586-023-01546-4

Nature Editorial. (2023b, January 24). Tools such as ChatGPT threaten transparent science; Here are our ground rules for their use. *Nature.* Retrieved from https://www.nature.com/articles/d41586-023-00191-1

Nature Portfolio. (2023). Editorial policies: Artificial intelligence (AI). *Nature.* Retrieved October 15, 2023, from https://www.nature.com/nature-portfolio/editorial-policies/ai

Parrilla, J. M. (2023, October 13). ChatGPT use shows that the grant-application system is broken. *Nature.* Retrieved from https://www.nature.com/articles/d41586-023-03238-5

Jeffrey J. Rachlinski, The limits of social norms, 74 Chi.-Kent L. Rev. 1537 (2000). Retrieved from https://scholarship.kentlaw.iit.edu/cklawreview/vol74/iss4/6

Statista Mobiles. (2019). https://www.statista.com/statistics/263437/global-smartphone-sales-to-end-users-since-2007/

Statista PCs. (2019). Retrieved from https://www.statista.com/statistics/748551/worldwide-house holds-with-computer/

Taylor, S. (2021, June 27). New LinkedIn data leak leaves 700 million users exposed. *RestorePrivacy.* Retrieved from https://restoreprivacy.com/linkedin-data-leak-700-million-users/

The Lancet Microbe. (2023, June). Information for authors. *The Lancet.* Retrieved from https://www.thelancet.com/pb-assets/Lancet/authors/tlmicro-info-for-authors-1686637130753.pdf

Usman, R. (2023, August 16). Magic and copyright: ChatGPT's mischief with Harry Potter gets tricky. *Digital Information World.* Retrieved from https://www.digitalinformationworld.com/2023/08/magic-and-copyright-chatgpts-mischief.html

Wong, J. C. (2019, Mar 18). The Cambridge Analytica scandal changed the world – But it didn't change Facebook. *The Guardian.* Retrieved from https://www.theguardian.com/technology/2019/mar/17/the-cambridge-analytica-scandal-changed-the-world-but-it-didnt-change-facebook

Wong, J. C. (2021, April 6). What really caused Facebook's 500M-user data leak? *Wired.* Retrieved from https://www.wired.com/story/facebook-data-leak-500-million-users-phone-numbers/

Index

Pages in *italics* refer to figures and pages in **bold** refer to tables.

For Product Safety Concerns and Information please contact our EU
representative GPSR@taylorandfrancis.com
Taylor & Francis Verlag GmbH, Kaufingerstraße 24, 80331 München, Germany

www.ingramcontent.com/pod-product-compliance
Ingram Content Group UK Ltd.
Pitfield, Milton Keynes, MK11 3LW, UK
UKHW030829080625
459435UK00014B/582